The Experiential Educator

The Experiential Educator

Principles and Practices of Experiential Learning

ALICE Y. KOLB AND DAVID A. KOLB

Experience Based Learning Systems Inc.

Kaunakakai, HI 96748

© 2017 Alice Y. Kolb & David A. Kolb

Printed in the United States of America
First Printing May 2017
ISBN-10: 0998599905

ISBN-13: 9780998599908
Library of Congress Control Number: 2017903139
Experience Based Learning Systems,Kaunakakai,HAWAII

To: Tokue and Shunzo Oku
Ethel and Jack Kolb
Our Primal Experiential Educators

Contents

Introduction

The Experiential Educator and Experiential Learning

*The future of the world is in my classroom today, a future
with the potential for good or bad...Several future presidents
are learning from me today; so are the great writers of the
next decades, and so are all the so-called ordinary people who
will make the decisions in a democracy. I must never forget
these same young people could be the thieves and murderers
of the future. Only a teacher? Thank God I have a calling
to the greatest profession of all! I must be vigilant every day,
lest I lose one fragile opportunity to improve tomorrow.*

—Ivan Welton Fitzwater

This book has been many years in the making. It represents the coming
to fruition of hundreds, even thousands, of conversations we have had
with educators in all arenas of life who come to us through their interest in experiential learning and the promise it might hold for increasing
their effectiveness and fulfillment as educators. Many are professors and
administrators in higher education, others are in public and private K–12
education. In the business and in the public sector we have encountered

human-resource and organization-development practitioners, coaches and consultants. We have also talked with many leaders in profit and not-for-profit organizations who have recognized that a substantial portion of their work is to help their coworkers to learn how to respond to the challenges they and their organization face. A number have been concerned with their role as educators in their personal lives, raising their children and helping their friends and neighbors. The questions they raise are about learning and particularly about how they can help others learn.

A Focus on Learning

For education, today it is "the best of times and the worst of times." We have been awakened from our complacency to a true crisis that permeates the educational establishment everywhere. The dimensions of this crisis are multifaceted—political, economic, educational, and cultural; it is beyond the scope of this book to enumerate. It is, however, the best of times as there is a renewed dedication to facing the issues and a realization that fundamental changes are needed. New e-learning technologies such as MOOC's (Pappano, 2012; Passarelli, 2014), and online degrees, new organizational arrangements, and educational structures such as the flipped classroom are springing up.

Chief among these changes is a focus on learners and learning. Recent efforts to improve higher education, including reports from the National Research Council (Bransford, Brown, & Cocking, 2000), the American Psychological Association (1997), and a number of other scholars (Baxter Magolda, 1999; Boyatzis, Cowen, & Kolb, 1995; Keeton, Sheckley, & Griggs, 2002; King, 2003; Light, 2001; Mentkowski & Associates, 2000; Zull, 2002, 2011) have focused on improving the learning process in education through the application of research from what has been called "the new science of learning."

One stream of this research is focused on the concept of experiential learning. Experiential learning is often misunderstood as a set of tools and techniques to provide learners with experiences from which they can learn. Some have used the term to describe learning that is a mindless recording of experience. In fact, experiential learning is actually a philosophy of education based on what Dewey (1938) called a "theory of experience." He argued that while traditional education had little need for theory since practice was determined by tradition, the new experiential approach to education needed a sound theory of experience to guide its conduct.

Since their emergence in the early 1970s, the principles and practices of experiential learning have been used to create curricula and conduct educational courses and programs. Many of the nontraditional educational innovations that have flowered during this period, such as college programs for adult learners and prior learning assessment, have used experiential learning as their educational platform. As experiential, learner-centered education has gained widespread acceptance in the twenty-first century (Prince & Felder, 2006; Slavich & Zimbardo, 2012), more and more educators are considering or experimenting with experiential learning practices such as service learning (Bielefeldt, Dewoolkar, Caves, Berdanier, & Paterson, 2011; Brower, 2011), problem-based learning (Bethell & Morgan, 2011; Gurpinar, Bati, & Tetik, 2011), action learning (Foy, 1977; Keys, 1994; Revans, 1980), adventure education (Fuller, 2012; Timken, & McNamee, 2012) and simulation and gaming (Schaefer, Vanderbilt, Cason, Bauman, Glavin, Lee, & Navedo, 2011; Shields, Zawadzki, & Johnson, 2011; Taylor, Backlund, & Niklasson, 2012).

Since its first statement in 1971 (Kolb, 1971; Kolb, Rubin, & McIntyre, 1971), there have been many studies using Experiential Learning Theory (ELT) to advance the theory and practice of experiential learning. Since 2000, ELT research in many fields around the world has more than quadrupled. The current ELT bibliographies include over four thousand entries from 1971–2017 (Kolb & Kolb, 2017). A 2013 review of management-education research (Arbaugh, Dearmond, & Rau) showed that 27 percent of the top-cited articles in management-education journals were about experiential learning and learning styles.

Alice Y. Kolb and David A. Kolb

Since ELT is a holistic theory of learning that identifies learning-style differences among different academic specialties, it is not surprising to see that ELT research is highly interdisciplinary, addressing learning and educational issues in many fields. ELT is being used extensively by experiential educators as a guide for practice in at least thirty fields and academic disciplines (Kolb & Kolb, 2013a, chapter 7). Included are research studies from every region of the world with many contributions coming from the United States, Canada, Brazil, the United Kingdom, China, India, Australia, Japan, Norway, Finland, Sweden, the Netherlands, and Thailand. These studies support the cross-cultural validity of ELT and the Kolb Learning Style Inventory (KLSI) and also support practical applicability across cultures. The KLSI has been translated into many languages including English, Spanish, French, Portuguese, Arabic, Russian, Dutch, German, Swedish, Chinese, Romanian, Persian, Thai, and Japanese. The value of the holistic ELT framework for understanding cultural differences has been shown in a number of studies on cross-cultural management (Kayes, Kayes, & Yamazaki, 2005, 2006; Yamazaki & Kayes, 2004, 2007).

The studies cover a broad range of applications using ELT and the KLSI. Some studies have used the KLSI and the experiential learning cycle to understand and manage differences between students' and faculty's learning styles. Some educators have used an experimental design to compare the effectiveness of an experiential learning method with a more traditional course format, whereas others have developed and implemented instructional methods using the experiential learning model as a framework. The principles and concepts of ELT have been used widely to develop and deliver programs in K–12 education (McCarthy, 1996, 2000), undergraduate education (Mentkowski, 2000), and professional education (Boyatzis, Cowan, & Kolb, 1995; Reese, 1998). In human-resource development, many training and development activities and executive coaching practices have been developed based on experiential learning concepts (Chapman, 2006; Matsuo, 2014).

A Journey of Becoming

The journey to become an experiential educator can be challenging, surprising, frustrating, and, ultimately, rewarding, as the following examples illustrate:

- One teacher said, "Actually, teaching was easier before I learned about experiential learning. My main focus was to collect and organize my course material and present it clearly. I had never thought much about how the students were reacting and their thoughts about the material."

- A gaming educator stressed, "The courage to let the simulation flow, whether the students are making a mess of it or not, or making wrong or unwise decisions. He or she must learn not to interfere…It should be said from experience that this role, which combines that of manager/organizer, facilitator, and learner, is a very difficult one to assume. It can, in the early stages…be very threatening but it is, in the end, very effective and fulfilling (Thatcher, 1990, p. 271).

- An experienced teacher reported, "I was beginning to get really bored presenting the same material year after year. Experiential learning has opened up conversations with the students about their experience and ideas and now I am actually learning new things along with them."

- An executive coach described how her coaching practice was transformed by the adoption of the ELT concepts of the learning cycle and learning style. "Becoming an experiential coach has increased my understanding of myself as a learner and a coach. This insight allows me to recognize the parts in the coaching process that I might overemphasize and to be deliberate about completing the steps in the process I might underemphasize. The learning cycle provides a process map for any coaching session and, over the longer term, any coaching engagement. During a session, I use the learning cycle to help the client connect with her own experience, to reflect on that experience, to analyze and plan, and to take some action to experiment with new behaviors or approaches. I also use the KLSI 4.0 to identify the client's learning style so that I will know how best to communicate and structure the session and to understand how the client will approach personal change. By framing the change in an approach that resonates with the client, I am more successful in facilitating this desired change."

- A professor at a university in the Middle East contacted us on our website, saying that he had read the papers on experiential learning there and sought advice about how to apply these ideas in his university. He described how students and faculty alike followed the traditional lecture, memorize, and test process with little participation, questioning, or independent inquiry. "I worked up the courage to experiment with Dewey's ideas about participation in my class but to my dismay after 20 minutes I found myself drifting back into the lecture mode where students seemed more comfortable."

- An organizational-behavior professor at an undergraduate college adopted a textbook based on experiential learning (Osland, Kolb, Rubin, & Turner, 2007) using the experiential exercises in it to experiment with teaching experientially. Initially students were hesitant with the new format that involved them working in learning groups, discussing preclass work in preparation for in-class exercises. However, as the semester progressed, the professor noticed that the students' outlook dramatically improved. They became more engaged in the exercises. The professor noted, "I was able to act as their guide to learning the material, which they then took ownership of." She describes students' involvement in the experiential exercises as enabling them to more fully understand key concepts, such that sometime later the students would recall the experiences and their learning with ease.

Our conversations and our own experiences have led us to the conclusion that becoming an experiential educator is about more than acquiring tips, techniques, and methods for teaching. In fact, many of our K–12 educator colleagues feel inundated by a parade of one new educational program and technique after another. We have sometimes felt a palpable sense of resistance to our programs on experiential learning with teachers thinking "Here comes another one!" The current focus on educational programs, systems, technologies, and techniques may have caused us to lose sight of the fact the educator relationship is above all a human relationship, where what the educator shows is as important as what he or she says. We can easily forget that we are role models for learners. We display our values, character, integrity, and authenticity for all to see.

We become educators by learning from our experience and it is this hard-won wisdom that is the foundation for our work. As in the title of David Hunt's profound work, we start by *Beginning with Ourselves*. Hunt put it this way:

> Working as a practical theorist, I became dissatisfied with the conventional view that if a logical theory were developed and verified through research, then it could be directly applied to classroom practice…but it did not offer a satisfactory account of how we were actually working together. Describing our work together in this abstract way cut us off from our direct experience, thereby removing us from the realities of the practice we were trying to improve. (1987, pp. 1–2)

Hunt proposes an "inside-out" approach rooted in our own experience as the starting point for becoming an experiential educator. Here the "outside-in" knowledge of the expert is not rejected but tested against the realities of the educator's experience-in-context. The experiential educator is a unique person in relationship with equally unique students, influenced by a wide variety of contexts. The findings of scientific research must be implemented by educators integrating scientific knowledge and practical experience. Edelbring (2012) describes this process with a quotation from John Dewey. Dewey argues against educational science providing recipes to educators, and, furthermore, reinforces the artistry responsibility of the teacher to use available science in conjunction with situational knowledge:

It is very easy for science to be regarded as a guarantee that goes with the sale of goods rather than as a light to the eyes and a lamp to the feet. (Dewey 1929, p. 15)…knowledge is therefore not aimed at being *directly* applied in practice but interpreted and enriched by the person taking part of it. The richness is produced when readers (such as educators and other researchers) understand the results from both the perspective they were created in and from their own culture of practice. The perspective of the researcher and readers coincide towards a pragmatic end in an enriching process similar to the fusion of experiences of the author and reader in interpreting cultural understanding of texts. (Gadamer, 1989) (Edelbring 2012, p. 18)

Teachers, coaches, consultants, managers, parents, or others who have jobs and responsibilities to help others learn can benefit by adopting the larger identity of educator in the process of becoming through learning from experience. In our view, the experiential educator is one who embraces this process of becoming through learning, no matter how accomplished and successful he or she might be. To become an experiential educator involves raising our sights from the preoccupations, demands, and institutional constraints of our daily work to embrace a larger vision of what it is to be an educator. A great number of those we have worked with had already discovered through their own practice some of the concepts of experiential learning, such as the value of connecting with and beginning from the learner's experience and individual differences in how learners learn best. They were looking for a guiding framework, theory, or personal philosophy to give a vision and direction to their careers as educators.

Some of our most unsettling conversations have been with educators who are overwhelmed and overstressed by their positions and institutions, often feeling "burned out" in their jobs. Many felt frustrated and trapped by the systems and contexts they worked in, struggling to find ways to focus on learning in spite of system constraints that often are preoccupied with everything but learning—performance, certification, discipline, research productivity, the list goes on and on. They found it hard not to be cynical about their institutions and their apparent lack of a genuine focus on learners and learning. We could certainly empathize with their cynicism, but we were also aware that even in the most anguished cases there was still a glimmer of hope, a vision of the possibility for fostering learning and development and a desire to overcome the obstacles they faced. They had, after all, come to ask about experiential learning and its promise for educators.

Educating Is a Profoundly Human Activity

We believe that their hope, vision, and desire are deeply rooted in who we are as human beings. As humans we share a capacity for learning with almost all living beings; but we are far more unique in our capacity for educating. The great psychoanalyst Erik Erikson called us the "teaching species" that passes on, through generations, the accumulated wisdom of our collective experience:

> For we are a teaching species…Only man can and must extend his solicitude over the long parallel and overlapping childhoods of numerous offspring united in households and communities. As he transmits the rudiments of hope, will, purpose and skill, he imparts meaning to the child's bodily experiences; he conveys a logic much beyond the literal meaning of the words he teaches; and he gradually outlines a particular world image and style of citizenship. I have, therefore, postulated an instinctual and psychosocial stage of generativity. Parenthood is, for most, the first, and for many, the prime generative encounter; yet the continuation of mankind challenges the generative ingenuity of workers and thinkers of many kinds. (Erikson, 1961, pp. 159–160)

The relationship between parent and child is the primal educational relationship and forms the model from which other forms of educating have evolved. As educators we carry with us to some degree the spirit of unconditional love and selfless giving that characterizes that primal relationship. So it is no surprise that two of the central foundational scholars of experiential learning, Jean Piaget and Lev Vygotsky, should have devoted their lives to the study of child development.

The newborn infant is a center of pure experiencing, and in the learning space created by loving parents he or she embarks on a lifelong journey of learning from experience. The pristine nature of this educator relationship gradually becomes more complicated and complex as the child becomes more conscious and independent and the challenges of an expanding life space pose greater learning challenges. The parent as educator is challenged at each successive life stage to convey his or her wisdom while encouraging independent growth and self-direction. For the professional educator the work becomes even more challenging. The loving intimacy of the family is no longer appropriate; it is replaced in the best of cases by authenticity and genuine respect for the learner. The learning agenda for learners becomes larger, more symbolic and abstract than concrete and behavioral. The relationship is no longer private and therefore the educator must contend with the many public contractual, managerial, cultural, and community stakeholders that seek to influence it.

But for most of us, the satisfactions and achievements of our work as educators still retain the vestiges of the primal-educator role. Herb Shepard in his classic article, "A path with heart," argued that to have such a "path of knowledge, a path with a heart, made for a joyful journey and was the only conceivable way to live"(1984, p. 149).

Learning through Shared Experience

The primal parental educator role, with its emphasis on learning through shared direct experience, has particular relevance for the experiential educator. For educators, the magic of experiential learning lies in the unique relationship that is created between teacher, learner, and the subject matter under study. Traditional approaches to education have relied on an information-transmission model of learning where knowledge about the subject is communicated, often by lecture, through the teacher's discourse about the subject. Learners, having no direct contact with the subject, are unable to investigate, explore, and judge for themselves. They are left one-down in a power relationship with only the choice of "taking the teacher's word for it." Teachers for their part are left in a one-way "conversation" that is ultimately deadening and boring. Often responses from learners have to be demanded and rewarded by points for participation.

The experiential approach places the subject to be learned in the center, to be experienced by both the educator and learner. This has a leveling effect on their relationship, to the extent that both can directly experience the subject. Everyone has a perspective on the subject. Those with different learning styles, for example, will view the subject experience through their own lens for processing experience. Questioning differences that arise from these multiple perspectives is the fuel for learning and new insights. Challenging the expert's viewpoint even becomes possible. This can be quite unsettling to novice experiential educators; but also it becomes a source of unpredictable new insight and learning for them. In becoming an experiential educator with this approach, the teacher also becomes an experiential learner. Parker Palmer, a strong advocate for the subject-centered approach, put it this way:

> The subject-centered classroom is characterized by the fact that the third thing (the subject) has a presence so real, so vivid, so vocal, that it can hold teacher and students alike accountable for what they say and do. In such a classroom there are no inert facts. The great thing is so alive that teacher can turn to student or student to teacher, and either can make a claim on the other in the name of that great thing. Here teacher and students have a power beyond themselves to contend with—the power of a subject that transcends our self-absorption and refuses to be reduced to our claims about it. (Palmer, 1998, p. 117)

These contrasting models of learning are shown in figure 0.1. The discourse model of teaching is based on an information-transfer model of learning whereby concepts are communicated to learners through lecture and texts. Learning is evaluated by how well the learner is able to record the concepts in declarative memory and recall them when asked questions about them. The experiential learning model is more focused on episodic memory. In addition to the "what" of declarative memory it is also concerned with the "how"—how the learner has come to this understanding through the process of inquiry about direct experience. Episodic memory includes, in addition to "the facts," recall of how the self-in-context achieved understanding about the subject. This self-in- context learning becomes the basis for future actions by the learner in other contexts.

Figure 0.1

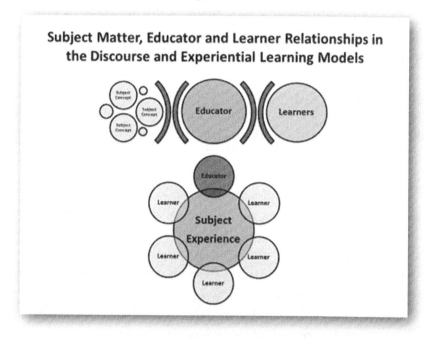

The experiential educator in the subject-centered approach is challenged to invent ways to bring experiences of the subject matter that have "a presence so real, so vivid and so vocal" into the center of the conversation. Many experiential learning techniques, such as service learning, problem-based learning, and internships have been developed for this purpose. Equally important is the creation of learning spaces that stimulate inquiry and open minds and create good learning conversations, enabling participants to move from the experience to deep reflection, conceptualization, and action. This book reports the many ways that the experiential educator can accomplish these objectives.

Overview of the Book

Our goal in writing this book is to share with educators the current state of the art of ELT research and practice. In addition to bringing our latest research and thinking about experiential learning, we also aim to distill the wisdom of those educators who have shared their experiences and research on experiential learning with us; enriching, expanding, and applying ELT. The book is divided into three parts.

Part I describes the basic principles of ELT with an emphasis on how educators can use these ideas to enhance their practice. The first chapter emphasizes the importance for the educator of a personal educational philosophy. It brings the experience and insights of the foundational scholars of experiential learning to this task. Chapter 2 describes the two central concepts of ELT, the learning cycle and learning style, describing how recent research has clarified the inextricable relationship between these concepts. Chapter 3 describes how research on the brain deepens our understanding of the process of experiential learning. Chapter 4 is focused on the relationship between learning and development, describing how the learning cycle is really a spiral of lifelong development. Chapter 5 examines the concept of learning identity and its role in learners' willingness to engage in learning. Chapter 6 focuses on the concept of deliberate, intentional learning and how educators can assist learners in directing and controlling their own learning process by developing metacognitive skills in the use of mindfulness, learning identity, learning relationships, learning times and spaces, and deliberate practice. Chapter 7 describes how these ELT concepts apply at the level of the team and organization.

Part II focuses on how educators can create effective spaces for learning. Chapter 8 describes the concept of learning space in ELT, examining the contextual and situated nature of experiential learning where learning is, in Lewin's famous phrase, a function of the person and the environment. Chapter 9 is about how to create a hospitable, safe space for learning that achieves an optimal mix of challenge and support. Chapter 10 describes the principles for the creation of good conversation and dialogue in the learning space. Chapter 11 is focused on the creation of learner-centered learning spaces. Chapter 12 is about the construction of learning spaces for reflective thinking. Chapter 13, the ludic learning space, is about creating play spaces for creative learning. Chapter 14 explores learning spaces that deepen and sustain learning.

Part III concentrates on the practice of experiential education. It begins in chapter 15 with a case study of curriculum change through the application of experiential learning principles and learning space concepts showing how experiencing, reflecting, thinking, and acting are integrated, making room for learners to complete the whole learning cycle. Chapter 16 focuses on an important principle of ELT—teaching around the learning cycle. It describes how educators can assist learners in traversing the cycle by adopting educator roles appropriate to the stages of the learning cycle. Chapter 17 describes in detail the best practices for each of the educator roles—coach, facilitator, subject expert, and evaluator.

Finally, we would be remiss if we did not share a confession with you. We both, Alice and David, began our work on this book with the feeling that we were pretty good educators—not great teachers with lots of teaching awards, but workmanlike educators with many successful courses, training programs, and consulting experiences that we felt good about. As we reach the conclusion of this project, we now see that in many cases we could have done so much better with the benefit of what we have learned in writing this book. Through our studies of these many great scholars and practitioners of learning and education, we have been humbled by the recognition that we have much to learn; that we, too, are continuing in our own process of becoming experiential educators.

Part I

PRINCIPLES OF EXPERIENTIAL LEARNING THEORY

One

THE PHILOSOPHY OF EXPERIENTIAL EDUCATION— FOUNDATIONAL EL SCHOLARS AS GUIDES FOR THE EXPERIENTIAL EDUCATOR

I think that only slight acquaintance with the history of education is needed to prove that educational reformers and innovators alone have felt the need for a philosophy of education. Those who adhered to the established system needed merely a few fine-sounding words to justify existing practices. The real work was done by habits which were so fixed as to be institutional. The lesson for progressive education is that it requires in an urgent degree, a degree more pressing than was incumbent upon former innovators, a philosophy of education based on a philosophy of experience.

—JOHN DEWEY, *EXPERIENCE AND EDUCATION*

A defining characteristic of the teacher, coach, consultant, manager, or parent, who begins to think of himself or herself as an educator, is the process of thinking about his or her practice more systematically and broadly—the development of a personal philosophy of education. Such a philosophy can bring many benefits. It can increase self-confidence that the potentially life-changing decisions we make as educators have a secure foundation. It provides a theoretical base from which to evaluate the ever-changing parade of "new" technologies and techniques that promise to revolutionize education. It provides a foundation for innovation and creativity by expanding possibilities and alternatives for practice. It increases awareness of those conditions that are mis-educative and dysfunctional for learners. It enables consideration of the wider and long-term consequences of approaches that may seem expedient in immediate circumstances. It can help explain to others why one is deviating from conventional tradition and practice.

We both began experimenting with experiential learning methods early in our teaching careers. Or maybe we should say playing. In her teaching of Japanese language and business practices to English-speaking engineers and business executives, Alice literally had them play with toy models of cars, buildings, and cities while telling stories about them in Japanese. This concretizing of words seemed to help with recall and the play, while initially uncomfortable for grown-ups, soon provided a fun, safe space for spontaneity and reduced self-consciousness about mistakes. David had a rather dismal beginning to his teaching career while lecturing to MIT business students and engineers about the psychology he had learned at Harvard. He taught the way he was taught, even though he never liked being taught that way himself. Not surprisingly, his students responded the same way. He introduced games, role plays, and other experiential exercises out of desperation to spark student engagement and interest.

We found great success with these methods and doubled down on our use of experiential learning approaches. It wasn't long, however, before we began bumping into the boundaries of the traditional university institution. "What are you doing?" was a question that was raised, often with a disapproving nonverbal expression. Teaching, in any event, can be a solitary and even lonely profession, locked as we often are in a classroom, left to our own devices with our students. Our major preparation is often only the recollection of how we were taught.

It was here that the discovery of those great thinkers we have come to call the "foundational scholars of experiential learning" gave us such comfort, confidence, and guidance. For David, John Dewey's *Experience and Education* gave solace that he was not alone and provided him with ammunition to engage skeptical colleagues. For Alice, it was Paulo Freire's *Pedagogy of the Oppressed* that provided inspiration and guidance. Our list of scholars whose work described the principles and practices of experiential learning soon expanded, adding William James, Kurt Lewin, Jean Piaget, Lev Vygotsky, Carl Jung, Mary Parker Follett, and Carl Rogers.

It soon became clear that our play with experiential learning techniques had opened the door to a broader and more fundamental definition of experiential learning. For the foundational scholars, experiential learning was not techniques or methods but a general theory of learning that emphasized the role of conscious experience in the learning process. Some have even suggested that the term experiential learning is redundant, since learning itself is generally conceived to be the result of experience as opposed to genetics, biological development, or instinct (e.g. Fenwick, 2003).

This is in contrast to a common usage of the term "experiential learning," defined as a particular form of learning from life experience; often contrasted with lecture and classroom learning. Keeton and Tate offered this definition: "Learning in which the learner is directly in touch with the realities being studied. It is contrasted with the learner who only reads about, hears about, talks about, or writes about these realities but never comes into contact with them as part of the learning process" (1978, p. 2). In this view of experiential learning, the emphasis is often on direct-sense experience and in-context action as the primary source of learning, often downplaying a role for thinking, analysis, and academic knowledge. Many educational institutions think of experiential learning as an educational technique offering experiential education programs such as internships, field projects, and classroom experiential learning exercises to add a direct experience component to their traditional academic studies.

Our philosophy of experiential learning and education has continued to develop throughout our careers by continued study of the works of the foundational scholars and integration of their perspectives with contemporary research. Our practice as experiential educators continues to evolve as theoretical insights suggest new ideas and approaches; and our theoretical perspective has been shaped by the results of our practical experience. Kurt Lewin's famous statement, "There is nothing so practical as good theory" was enhanced when our colleague and friend David Hunt reversed it, "There is nothing so theoretical as good practice" (Hunt, 1987). The first systematic statement of our philosophy that we called Experiential Learning Theory (ELT) was *Experiential Learning*, first published in 1984 and updated in a second edition in 2015. In this current work we continue the evolution of ELT with an emphasis on its application by experiential educators.

The Foundational Scholars and Their Contributions to ELT

Figure 1.1 depicts the nine foundational scholars of ELT and a summary of their contributions to experiential learning. Their contributions span over a hundred years, beginning at the end of the nineteenth century with William James, John Dewey, and Mary Parker Follett, and ending at the end of the twentieth century with the deaths of Carl Rogers and Paulo Freire. In spite of the Western origins of their work, their influence today is global; East and West, North and South. Their approaches were in many respects similar to East Asian Confucian and Taoist spiritual traditions that were shaped by the five-thousand-year-old Chinese text *The Book of Changes* (Trinh & Kolb, 2011). Jung in particular was influenced in his later years by Hinduism, Buddhism, and Taoism, concluding that development toward integration and individuation is central to all religions. James also studied Eastern thought and his radical empiricism became a central focus for the great Japanese Zen philosopher, Kitaro Nishida (1911).

Figure 1.1

A remarkable similarity among these nine scholars, in addition to their emphasis on the role of experience in learning, is that they all were what might be called liminal scholars. Like the reformers and innovators that Dewey noted in the introductory quotation to this chapter, they stood at the boundaries of the mainstream establishment of their fields and worked from theoretical and methodical perspectives that ran counter to the prevailing scientific norms of their time. As a result, it is only in recent years that their ideas have reemerged to influence learning, education, and development in profound ways.

The scholars not only studied experiential learning; they lived it. They approached their scientific inquiry as learning from experience, examining their own personal experience, using careful observation, building sophisticated and creative theoretical systems, bringing a passionate advocacy for their ideas for the betterment of humanity. I suspect they would all subscribe to Carl Rogers's description of his approach to research:

I have come to see both research and theory as being aimed toward the inward ordering of significant experience. Thus research is not something esoteric, nor an activity in which one engages to gain professional kudos. It is the persistent, disciplined effort to make sense and order out of the phenomena of subjective experience. Such effort is justified because it is satisfying to perceive the world as having order and because rewarding results often ensue when one understands the orderly relationships which appear to exist in nature. One of these rewarding results is that the ordering of one segment of experience in a theory immediately opens up new vistas of inquiry, research, and thought, thus leading one continually forward. (I have, at times, carried on research for purposes other than the above to satisfy others, to convince opponents and sceptics, to gain prestige, and for other unsavory reasons. These errors in judgment and activity have only deepened the above positive conviction). (1959, p. 188)

We are inspired by the passionate advocacy of many of the scholars for the betterment of the world through learning. The leadership provided by John Dewey and Mary Parker Follett to the Progressive Movement of the 1920s focused the profound insights of their thinking on democracy, social justice, education, and advocacy for the needy. Paulo Freire was first a social activist where he developed his theories based on this work. His work on literacy campaigns in Brazil, later extended to other countries in South America and Africa, became powerful instruments of democratic social change.

William James (1841–1910)—Radical Empiricism and Dual-Knowledge Theory. William James, with examination of conscious experience in his two-volume magnum opus, *The Principles of Psychology*, is a prime example of a liminal scholar who found himself outside of the mainstream of the behaviorist psychology that dominated the early twentieth century. He devoted the last two-thirds of the work to what he called the "study of the mind from within" (James, 1890, p. 225). But today, his ideas about consciousness have been resurrected by modern neuroscientists such as Karl Pribram and Roger Sperry who drew on James' work for their own formulations. The geneticist Francis Crick, reviewing the philosophical implications of biological advances in our understanding of consciousness has invoked James as a guiding philosopher who had said it all a hundred years ago. (Taylor & Wozniak 1996, p. xxxii)

His examination of the role of attention in conscious experience and his ideomotor theory of action, addressing how consciousness of one's learning process can be used to intentionally improve learning, were foundational for the later work on metacognition and deliberate experiential learning described in chapter 6. He is also recognized as the founder of the contemporary dual-processing theories (Evans, 2008) derived from his dual-knowledge concepts of apprehension and comprehension.

William James proposed radical empiricism as a new philosophy of reality and mind that resolved the conflicts between nineteenth-century rationalism and empiricism and integrated both sensation and thought in experience. For James, everything begins and ends in the continuous flux and flow of experience. In short, experience is all there is—"We start with the supposition that there is only one primal stuff or material in the world, a stuff of which everything is composed...we call that stuff 'pure experience'" (1977, p. 4). In this formulation, the duality between the mind (thought) and physical world (thing) is resolved since both are experienced but with different characteristics—thought is the concrete here-and-now experience "redoubled" in reflection:

> If it be the self-same piece of pure experience taken twice over that serves now as thought and now as thing...how comes it that its attributes should differ so fundamentally in the two takings? As thing, the experience is extended; as thought, it occupies no space or place. As thing, it is red, hard, and heavy; but who ever heard of a red, hard or heavy thought." (1977, pp. 27–28)

Speaking of "tangles" created by philosophical and psychological inquiry in his time, he succinctly describes the central principles of both philosophies:

> It seems to me that if radical empiricism be good for anything, it ought, with its pragmatic method and principle of pure experience, be able to avoid such tangles, or at least simplify them somewhat. The pragmatic method starts from the postulate that there is no difference of truth that doesn't make a difference of fact somewhere; and it seeks to determine the meaning of all differences of opinion by making the discussion as soon as possible hinge on some practical or particular issue. The principle of pure experience is also a methodological postulate...Everything real must be experienceable somewhere, and every kind of thing experienced must be somewhere real." (1943, pp. 159–160)

As described in the above quotation, James is the originator of ELT in his philosophy of dual-knowledge theory, knowing by apprehension (concrete experience) and comprehension (abstract conceptualization). According to this theory, humans acquire knowledge through two independent but connected modes of knowing, one dealing with subjective sense experience and the other with abstract thoughts and concepts. The following quotation describes James's view of these two kinds of knowledge:

> There are two kinds of knowledge broadly and practically distinguishable: We may call them respectively knowledge of acquaintance and knowledge-about. I am acquainted with many people and things, which I know very little about, except their presence in the places where I have met them. I know the color blue when I see it, and the flavor of pear when I taste it; I know an inch when I move my finger through it; a second time when I feel it pass;...but about the inner nature of these facts or what makes them what they are, I can say nothing at all. All the elementary

natures of the world, its highest genera, the simple qualities of matter and mind, together with the kinds of relation that subsist between them, must either not be known at all, or known in this dumb way of acquaintance without knowledge-about...We can relapse at will into a mere condition of acquaintance with an object by scattering our attention and staring at it in a vacuous trance-like way. We can ascend to knowledge about it by rallying our wits and proceeding to notice and analyze and think. What we are only acquainted with is only present to our minds; we have it, or the idea of it. But when we know about it, we do more than merely have it; we seem, as we think over its relations, to subject it to a sort of treatment and to operate upon it with our thought. The words feeling and thought give voice to the antithesis. Through feelings we become acquainted with things, but only by our thoughts do we know about them. Feelings are the germ and starting point of cognition, thoughts the developed tree.(James, 1890, Vol. I, pp. 221–222).

Learning occurs through the dynamic relation between knowledge of acquaintance and knowledge about. According to James, what we subjectively experience is empty and meaningless unless it is grounded in concepts. Through concepts we introduce order into what would otherwise be a seamless, unpredictable flow of sense experiences. Conversely, immediate sense experiences serve as the checks and balances of the validity of a particular concept in both fact and value. A particular concept acquires meaning and value only through connection with our direct, subjective experiences.

James's dual-knowledge process is critical for educators to understand the nature and meaning of learning. Schools and universities often favor the abstract and logical pole of the knowledge dialect and not enough attention and emphasis are placed on the students' subjective experiences. Without a doubt, many students enter classrooms with a narrow and dogmatic worldview with tenacious reliance on their subjective feelings. Our role is to free them from their dogmatic stance toward life, but not at the expense of undermining their personal experience. If we are to succeed in changing their attitudes and beliefs, it is not through the dogmatic embrace of abstract concepts and generalizable knowledge; it is through understanding of their unique experiences that generated their worldviews in the first place.

As we will see in chapter 11, James's dual-knowledge theory offers a profound insight into how we deal with our students' values and beliefs, regardless of the disciplines or subjects we teach. More importantly, as educators we need to be aware of our own assumptions and belief systems that guide our teaching and the way we come to know our students. We are free to learn precisely because we are capable of subjecting our experience as well as concepts and theories to the rigor of our own inquiry. As educators, we want our students to know that they are free to learn and to choose and chart the course of their own destiny.

John Dewey (1859–1952)—Experiential Education. Without a doubt, it is John Dewey, the most influential educational theorist of the twentieth century, who best articulates the guiding principles of experiential learning. Dewey's contribution to experiential education began in the progressive-education movement he founded by establishing the Laboratory School at the University of Chicago in 1896. Dewey rejected the nineteenth-century-psychology conception of mind as a blank slate and put forth a radically different vision of humans as active creators of meaning through their interactions with the world. As Jackson (1998) observed, Dewey rejected the individualistic conception of humans as inhabitants of their own subjective world of feelings and thoughts, unable to share their experiences with others; humans were intrinsically social beings, whose lives were shaped and influenced as much by their contacts with others as by their interaction with their natural environment.

Dewey's innovative philosophy embodied his vision of experiential education in both its content and methodology. In *My Pedagogic Creed* (1897), the propositions he articulates give direction to the educational practices he envisioned for his schools. The following excerpts in particular represent the key propositions of experiential learning:

1. Education must be conceived as a continuing reconstruction of experience…the process and goal of education are one and the same thing. (p. 13)
2. I believe that education is a process of living and not a preparation for future living.(p. 7)
3. I believe that education which does not occur through forms of life that are worth living for their own sake is always a poor substitute for genuine reality and tends to cramp and to deaden. (p. 7)
4. I believe that interests are the signs and symptoms of growing power. I believe they represent dawning capacities. I believe that only through the continual and sympathetic observation of childhood's interests can the adult enter into the child's life and see what it is ready for. (p. 15)

In line with his espoused principles, the school activities in progressive schools were carefully designed to bring children's experiences closer to their social world. Dewey's concept of "active occupations" represented by woodworking, cooking, sewing, weaving, and spinning introduced children to both intellectual and practical undertakings in a holistic and balanced manner. In Dewey's view,

> the fundamental point in the psychology of an occupation is that it maintains a balance between the intellectual and the practical phases of experience. As an occupation it is active or motor; it finds expression through the physical organs—the eyes, hands, etc. But it also involves continual observation of materials, and continual planning and reflection, in order that the practical or executive side may be successfully carried on. Occupation as thus conceived must, therefore, be carefully distinguished from work which educates primarily for a trade. It differs because its end is in itself; in the growth

that comes from the continual interplay of ideas and their embodiment in action, not in external utility. (Dewey, 1933, p. 92)

The continual interplay of ideas and their embodiment in action echoes James's dual-knowledge theory in that all matters of learning require the interplay of both; the direct experience guides reflection and planning, which in turn drive execution and completion of any learning activity. Dewey was also keenly aware of the intrinsic nature of any learning pursuit and therefore education was never a "preparation for life" but the "process of living itself." In the progressive school, children learned together, actively engaged in diverse learning activities with freedom to discover and pursue their deep interests.

While Dewey's vision of the progressive school curriculum held promise for a lively education connected to the real world, it was received with skepticism particularly by parents who expressed concern whether "active occupation" approach would in fact help their children master necessary skill sets to earn a living in the future.

The scope of Dewey's vision for experiential education and the resistance he met from various stakeholders at that time continues today as the pressure and need for development of specialized skills in an increasingly specialized society puts pressure on educators to focus on preparing the students for "future living" and to forgo the kind of education that grows out of interplay of experiences and their embodiment in action.

Mary Parker Follett (1868–1933)—Learning Relationships. Mary Parker Follett was awarded a Lifetime Achievement Award by the International Leadership Association only in 2011. She graduated "summa cum laude" from Radcliff College but was not allowed to pursue a PhD because she was a woman. She was a broad thinker who spanned disciplines and schools of thought, challenging her academic colleagues to think outside their disciplinary boxes. True to her theory of relations, she refused to identify with any particular school of thought but stood in "the space between" drawing insights from both perspectives. For example, while many see her as a Gestalt theorist along with Lewin, she drew from both Gestalt theory and the opposing school of behaviorism in creating her approach. While she was a popular lecturer and writer in her day, Peter Drucker observed that "she gradually became a 'non-person'" after her death in 1933. Her radical circular theory of power that emphasized cooperation and humanistic ideas about management and organizations was foreign to the culture of management in the 1930s and 40s. Today she has gained new recognition as a foundational figure. According to Warren Bennis, "Just about everything written today about leadership and organizations comes from Mary Parker Follett's writings and lectures" (Smith, 2012).

A truly interdisciplinary and radical thinker, Mary Parker Follett placed experience and human interaction at the center of her theory of human development. For Follett, experience was the primary source of creativity, thoughts, and purpose. She believed:

> All that I am, all that life has made me, every past experience that I have had—woven into the tissue of my life—I must give to the new experience…We integrate our experience, and then the richer human being that we are goes into the new experience; again we give our self and always by giving rise above the old self. (Follett, 1924, pp. 136–137).

Mary Parker Follett along with Carl Rogers, Lev Vygotsky, and Paulo Freire gave a central place to the relationship between educator and learner in their theories. True to her Gestalt influence she saw everything in relation. Anticipating Norbert Weiner's discovery of cybernetics by many years she describes how we cocreate one another in relationship by circular response. Through circular-response transactions we create each other. In this cocreation, she describes how we can meet together in experience to evoke learning and development in one another:

> The essence of experience, the law of relation, is reciprocal freeing: here is the "rock and the substance of the human spirit. This is the truth of stimulus and response: evocation. We are all rooted in that

great unknown in which are the infinite latents of humanity. And these latents are evoked, called forth into visibility, summoned, by the action and reaction of one on the other. All human interaction should be the evocation by each from the other of new forms undreamed of before, and all intercourse that is not evocation should be eschewed. Release, evocation—evocation by release, release by evocation—this is the fundamental law of the universe...To free the energies of the human spirit is the high potentiality of all human association." (Follett, 1924, p. 303)

Kurt Lewin (1890–1947)—Field Theory. Often described as the founder of social psychology, Kurt Lewin's work has been vast in its scope of influence, ranging from leadership and management style to mathematical contribution to social-science field theory. Lewin's influence in the field is so pervasive that it is hard to define. Warren Bennis said simply, "We are all Lewinians." John Thibaut, one of Lewin's research assistants at MIT, said:

It is not so difficult to understand why he was influential. He had an uncanny intuition about what problems were important and what kinds of concepts and research situations were necessary to study them. And though he was obsessed with theory he was not satisfied with the attainment of theoretical closure but demanded of the theory that its implications for human life be pursued with equal patience and zeal. (Cited in Marrow, 1969, p. 189)

Yet, paradoxically, he too was a liminal scholar, working for the most part outside the psychological establishment. "No prestigious university offered him an appointment. (His significant work was done in odd settings, such as the Cornell School of Home Economics and the Iowa Child Welfare Research Station.) The American Psychological Association never selected him for any assignment or appointed him to any important committee" (Marrow, 1969, p. 227).

As a true practical theorist, Lewin approached his research methods and theory building with inventiveness and creativity. His best known quotation: "There is nothing so practical as a good theory" symbolizes his commitment to the integration of theory and practice. His development of the action-research methodology has had a great continuing influence. His commitment to solving social problems and conflicts was born out of his marginalization growing up as a Jew in the strongly anti-Semitic culture of East Prussia, and continued throughout his life, culminating in his creation of the Center for Group Dynamics at MIT and his leadership in the Commission on Community Interrelations (CCI) that conducted many action-research projects. Chief among these was his group dynamics work with The Connecticut State Interracial Commission to combat racial and religious prejudice, which led to the creation of the T-Group, one of the most influential educational innovations in the twentieth century.

Lewin's T-group laboratory method and action-research inspired the creation of the concept of experiential learning cycle, an integrated learning process that best facilitates learning, change, and growth. The cycle begins with here-and-now experience followed by collection of data and observation of that experience. The analysis of that data and the conclusions drawn from the analysis becomes the starting point of new experiences. It is worth noting that T-group experiment and action-research techniques uncovered the importance of a dialectic tension between learners' concrete experience and the expert's conceptual knowledge of a subject matter in any given learning situation. When learners' immediate experiences and the expert's knowledge were brought together in an open dialogue, learning was far more creative, lively, and transformative.

Perhaps the most systematic framework for describing experience comes from another of Lewin's seminal works (1951) based on his field theory and the concept of life space, which was inspirational for the ELT concept of learning spaces described in chapter 8. For Lewin, the person and the environment are interdependent, a concept that Lewin translated into a mathematical formula, $b=f(p, e)$, where behavior is a function of person and environment. In Lewin's terms, to understand an individual learner's behavior, we need to grasp the life space of the learner in its totality including his or her personal needs, goals, visions, as well as subjective experiences of the immediate environment. Lewin believed only the factors present in the here-and-now influence the learner's behavior in any significant way. What we can learn from Lewin is the importance for education of defining the learning space in terms of the learner's experience:

> One of the basic characteristics of field theory in psychology, as I see it, is the demand that the field which influences an individual should be described not in "objective physicalistic" terms, but in the way that it exists for that person at that time...A teacher will never succeed in giving proper guidance to a child if he does not learn to understand the psychological world in which that child lives...To substitute for that world of the individual the world of the teacher, of the physicist, or anybody else is to be, not objective, but wrong." (Cartwright, 1951, p. 62)

We deeply admire Lewin for the many students and colleagues he nurtured and developed to become outstanding scholars in their own right. His influence in the field came not so much from his published works, which are hard to find, but from those who worked with him. He consistently put their names forward in publications. Jerome Frank, a graduate student of Lewin, describes how he accomplished this:

> Each new idea or problem seemed to arouse him, and he was able to share his feelings with colleagues and juniors...Seminars were held in his home, and it was hard to distinguish the influence of his ideas from the influence of his personality. Because Lewin could be critical without hurting, he stimulated creativity in all those around him...He seemed to enjoy all kinds of human beings and, open and free as he was, shared his ideas immediately—even if they were

half-formed—eager for comments and reactions while the original idea was still being developed. (Cited in Marrow, 1969, p. 54)

Jean Piaget (1896–1980)—Constructivism. Piaget's legacy is enormous and far reaching. His work on the stages of development of cognitive processes in childhood not only became one of the cornerstones of theory of experiential learning, but it uncovered the nature of human intelligence itself. Simply stated, Piaget's theory describes how intelligence is shaped by experience. Contrary to the commonly accepted view of children as passive recipients of information from the outside world, Piaget contended that children were actively constructing their cognitive world by interacting with the environment.

As radical as he was in his thinking, so was the method he chose for his research. Piaget refused to conduct traditional laboratory experiments with children and chose to observe his own children in their natural environment where they were growing up. His initial research relied upon the extensive and meticulous observations he made of his three children at their various stages of development. He presented them with cleverly designed puzzles and problems to understand the process of how they solved them. Unlike Binet, his mentor and creator of the IQ test, and other intelligence researchers, he was less interested in correct answers than how children arrived at these answers.

Not surprisingly, his research method came under harsh attack and criticism from various academic fronts at the time. His successive case-study technique was not well received in American psychology when it was introduced in 1926. He ignored sample sizes, statistical tests, experimental and control groups in the creation of his theories. His case studies with small samples were questioned for their applicability to a larger population. However, by the 1950s, with the rise of cognitive psychology and, particularly, Jerome Bruner's generous advocacy for his approach, his ideas and methods gained widespread acceptance and influence in education. To his critics' amazement, researchers conducted studies with larger populations of children exactly replicating Piaget's stage observations, and discovered the same pattern of cognitive development in their samples (Ginsburg & Opper, 1969).

Piaget observed that children constructed their cognitive world through two distinct, but inseparable, processes of adaptation: accommodation and assimilation. Assimilation occurs when a new experience is incorporated into the preexisting knowledge, whereas accommodation occurs when an individual structurally adjusts to newly acquired information. Although conceptually described as two distinct phenomena, they occur simultaneously in any given developmental stage. The relationship between the two varies dramatically, both within and between stages, in that some cognitive acts may be heavily inclined toward one over the other. Therefore, the relationship between accommodation and assimilation is a crucial determinant of the nature of the cognitive process of individuals at different stages of development. The relationship of assimilation-accommodation is dialectic one, in which both are pulled in opposite directions to achieve balance. However, this balance is not a permanent one since any cognitive process is a dynamic one, characterized by continual change.

Throughout his life he continued to be strong advocate for the child's capacity to create knowledge. Later in his life, Piaget contended:

> What interests me is the creation of new things that are not performed nor predetermined by the nature of the encounter with the environment, but are constructed within the individual himself… the essential thing is that in order for a child to understand something, he must construct it himself, he must re-invent it. Every time we teach a child something, we keep him from inventing it himself. On the other hand, that which we allow him to discover by himself will remain with him visibly. (Cited by Piers, 1972, pp. 25–27)

The implication of constructivism for education was profound at all levels all over the world. From a constructivist viewpoint, learning is best facilitated by a process that draws out the students' beliefs and ideas about a topic so that they can be examined, tested, and integrated with new, more refined ideas. In addition, his stage theory has formed the foundation of nearly all theories of adult development.

Lev Vygotsky (1896–1834)—Zone of Proximal Development. Lev Vygotsky whose prodigious brilliantly creative career was ended prematurely by his death from tuberculosis at age thirty-eight was called the Mozart of psychology by Stephen Toulmin. This is in spite of the fact that he never had any formal training in psychology, being interested in literature, poetry, and philosophy when he was young. The Soviet authorities of his time kept him under pressure to toe the ideological Marxist line in his theories, and after his death the government repudiated his ideas. Today, however, his work is hugely influential in education around the world (Tharpe & Gallimore, 1988) and his ideas about the role of culture in the development of thought are widely cited as foundational for liberation ideologies, social constructionism, and activity theory (Bruner, 1986; Holman, Pavlica, & Thorpe, 1997).

While much attention has been given to the origins of experiential learning in the constructivism of Piaget, less attention has been given to its basis in the social constructivism of Vygotsky (Kayes, 2002). Piaget focused on the process of internal cognitive development in the individual, while Vygotsky's attention was directed to the historical, cultural, and social context of individuals in relationship, emphasizing the "tools of culture" and mentoring by more knowledgeable community members. He is best known for his theory of the development of the higher psychological process, the Zone of Proximal Development (ZPD). In the course of joint activity between the adult and the child, Vygotsky saw that the adult teaches the child tools such as language, signs, and symbols, which will enable the child to reach a more advanced level. The central idea of the ZPD is that through adult mediation, a child learns to self-regulate his behaviors. A good example is offered by Luria:

For example, when a mother says no to a child to prevent the child from doing something dangerous and undesirable, she is both regulating the child's behavior and supplying the child with a tool of self-regulation. The child starts to say no aloud to himself or herself to overcome a temptation to do something inappropriate (so-called egocentric or private speech), sometimes even imitating the mother's voice. (Karpov & Haywood, 1998, p. 27).

A key technique for accomplishing the transition to a higher-level psychological order is called "scaffolding." In scaffolding the educator tailors the learning process to the individual needs and developmental level of the learner. Scaffolding provides the structure and support necessary for learners to progressively master new knowledge and skills.

Carl Jung (1875–1961)—Integrative Development. Carl Jung was arguably the most radical scientific experiential learner, deriving most of his theory from deep engagement with his intense personal experiences, dreams, and unconscious symbols. This is particularly true of his concept of individuation and the course of development from specialization to integration that he developed as a result of what has been called his own midlife crisis (Staude, 1981). Carl Jung is arguably the most important scholar to influence the ELT concepts of holistic adaptation to the world with his theory of psychological types and the concept of individuation. In his theory of psychological types, Jung developed a holistic framework for describing individual differences in human adaptive processes. For Jung, humans fell into two distinct categories in their ways of relating to the world: the extroverts who were oriented toward the external world; and the introverts, who were oriented toward the internal world. He further identified four basic functions of human adaptation: two describing alternative ways of perceiving—sensation and intuition; and two that describe alternative ways of making judgment about the world—thinking and feeling.

In his view, human individuality develops through transactions with the social environment that reward and develop one function over the other. Jung saw a conflicting relationship between specialized psychological orientation required for individuals to adapt to societal demands and their need to express their full range of psychological functions for their own individual fulfillment. Through the process of individuation, Jung believed people would achieve holistic growth by integrating the dominant and non-dominant modes of adaptation to the world in a harmonious way.

Carl Rogers (1902–1987)—Deep Experiencing. Rogers's work has had four major influences on ELT. The first is the focus on experiencing as central to the fully functioning person and its importance for learning and change. A fully functioning person is open to experience, living each moment fully, accepting the fluidity and complexity of the experiencing process with spontaneity and trust. Because their locus of evaluation is centered within themselves, they trust their own judgment to act and behave appropriately at each moment, unencumbered by the external norms and rules.

The second influence is his identification of unconditional positive regard, respect, and psychological safety as essential conditions for a therapeutic or educational environment to promote learning and development. Under these conditions, an individual develops a sense of self-worth "through a relationship in which he is prized as a separate person, in which the experiencing going on within him is empathically understood and valued and in which he is given the freedom to experience his own feelings and those of others without being threatened in doing so" (Rogers, 1964, p. 165).

The third is his theory of development toward self-actualization based on the individual's capacity for deep experiencing. In youth, an individual tends to introject the values of loved ones in order to gain their respect and approval:

> He learns to have a basic distrust for his own experiencing as a guide to his behavior. He learns from others a large number of conceived values and adopts them as his own, even though they may be widely discrepant from what he is experiencing. (1964, p. 162)

Development toward genuine experiencing occurs when, in the growth-producing climate described above, he can slowly begin to value the different aspects of himself. Most importantly, he can begin, with much difficulty at first, to sense and feel what is going on within him, what he is feeling, what he is experiencing, how he is reacting. He uses his experiencing as a direct referent to which he can turn in forming accurate conceptualizations and as a guide to his behavior. (1964, p. 163).

The last and perhaps less known Rogers's contribution to experiential learning is the application of his central ideas into the realm of teaching and learning. In his book *Freedom to Learn* (1969), Rogers articulated his vision of an "experiential and meaningful type of learning" addressed to teachers, educators, and educational institutions at large. The following key propositions summarize his learning-centered approach to education:

1. *It has a quality of personal involvement*—a learner must be involved in a learning situation as a whole person, with feeling and thinking fully engaged.
2. *It is self-initiated*—learnings that change behaviors and attitudes in significant ways can only be self-discovered.
3. *It is evaluated by the learner*—the locus of evaluation resides always within the learner; only she will know what she must learn and when her learning needs were met. (Rogers, 1969, p. 5)

Paulo Freire (1921–1997)—Dialogue among Equals. The radical and revolutionary educator Paulo Freire's great contribution to experiential learning is his concept of "critical consciousness," the active exploration of the personal, experiential meaning of abstract concepts through dialogue among equals. He contrasted this educational approach to the "banking concept of education" where ideas are deposited in learners' heads. His view of education and learning can be seen as the revolutionary extension of the Dewey's liberal, progressive, humanistic education and Lewin's laboratory-training approach to social change.

The literacy campaigns he created in Brazil, and later extended to other countries in South America and Africa used what he called culture circles based on his theory of conscientiziation, the ability to problematize and take transformative action on the social, political, economic, and cultural realities that shape us. Culture circles in their process were much like Lewin's T-groups where group participants were active participants in creating the topics to be explored through dialogue with the help of a coordinator. They differed from the T-group, however, in that the focus was on actively shaping the reality of the participants' lives—exploring topics such as the vote for illiterates, nationalism, the political revolution in Brazil, and democracy and freedom:

> The first experiments with the method began in 1962 involving 300 rural farmers who were taught how to read and write in 45 days. In 1964 20,000 culture circles were planned to be set up. However, the military coup in that year interrupted Freire's work. He was jailed for seventy days and later went into exile in Chile. (Nyirenda, 1996, p. 4)

Principles for a Philosophy of Experiential Education

From the works of the foundational scholars of experiential learning we have distilled six principles that are central to their work. Taken together, they form the foundation of ELT.

Learning Is Best Conceived as a Process, not in Terms of Outcomes. Although punctuated by knowledge milestones, learning does not end at an outcome, nor is it always evidenced in performance. Rather, learning occurs through the process of ongoing experience; ideas and thoughts never remain the same but are formed and re-formed through experience. No two thoughts are ever the same, since experience always intervenes. If ideas are seen as fixed and immutable, then it seems possible to measure how much someone has learned by the amount of these fixed ideas that the person has accumulated. Such fixed and constant view of thoughts and ideas has had a profound impact on prevailing approaches to learning and education, resulting in a tendency to define learning only in terms of outcomes. Approaches to learning and education focused on fixed outcomes can become a definition of nonlearning, in the sense that the failure to modify ideas and habits as a result of experience is maladaptive.

Learning Is a Continuous Process Grounded in Experience. Knowledge is continuously derived from and tested out in the experience of the learner. Put simply, it implies that all learning is relearning. How easy and tempting it is in designing a course to think of the learner's mind as being a blank slate. Yet this is not the case. Everyone enters every learning situation with more or less articulate ideas about the topic at hand. We are all psychologists, historians, and atomic physicists. It is just that some of our theories are more crude and incorrect than others. But to focus solely on the refinement and validation of these theories misses the point. The important point is that the people we teach have held these beliefs, whatever their quality, and that until now they have used them whenever the situation called for them to be atomic physicists, historians, or whatever.

One's job as an educator is not only to implant new ideas but also to dispose of or modify old ones. In many cases, resistance to new ideas stems from their conflict with old beliefs that are inconsistent with them. Learning will be enhanced if the educational process begins by bringing out the learner's beliefs and theories, examining and testing them, and then integrating the new, more refined ideas into the person's belief systems.

Learning Requires the Resolution of Conflicts between Dialectically Opposed Modes of Adaptation to the World. Conflict, differences, and disagreement are what drive the learning process. These tensions are resolved in iterations of movement back and forth between opposing modes of reflection and action and feeling and thinking. Learning is by its very nature filled with tension and conflict. Effective learners need four different kinds of abilities—concrete experience abilities, reflective observation abilities, abstract conceptualization abilities, and active experimentation abilities. That is, they must be able to involve themselves fully, openly, without bias in new experiences. They must be able to reflect on and observe their experiences from many perspectives. They must be able to create concepts that integrate their observations into logically sound theories, and they must be able to use these theories to make decisions and solve problems. Yet, in the real life situation this is difficult to achieve. How can one act and reflect at the same time? How can one be concrete and immediate and still be theoretical? Learning requires abilities that are polar opposites, and learners must continually choose which set of learning abilities they will bring to bear in any specific learning situation.

When we consider the higher forms of adaptation—the process of creativity and personal development—conflict among adaptive modes needs to be confronted and integrated into a creative synthesis. At the highest stages of development, the adaptive commitment to learning and creativity produces a strong need for integration of the four adaptive modes. Development in one mode precipitates development in the others. Increases in symbolic complexity, for example, refine and sharpen both perceptual and behavioral possibilities. Thus, complexity and the integration of dialectic conflicts among the adaptive modes are the hallmarks of true creativity and growth.

Learning is a Holistic Process of Adaptation to the World. Experiential learning involves the integrated functioning of the total organism—thinking, feeling, perceiving, and behaving. To learn is not the special province of a single specialized realm of human functioning such as cognition or perception. In addition to knowing how we think and how we feel, we must also know when behavior is governed by thought and when by feeling. In addition to addressing the nature of human specialized functions, ELT is also concerned with how these functions are integrated by the person into a holistic adaptive stance toward the world.

Learning is *the* major process of human adaptation. It encompasses other, more limited adaptive concepts such as the scientific method, creativity, problem-solving, decision-making, and attitude change that focus heavily on one or another of the basic aspects of adaptation. This concept of learning is considerably broader than that commonly associated with the school classroom. It occurs in all human settings, from schools to the workplace, from the research laboratory to the management board room, in personal relationships and in the aisles of the local grocery. It encompasses all life stages, from childhood to adolescence, to middle and old age. When learning is conceived as the major adaptive process, it provides conceptual bridges across life situations such as school and work, portraying learning as a continuous, lifelong process.

Learning Involves Transactions between the Person and the Environment. Knowledge is the result of the transaction between social knowledge and personal knowledge. The former, as Dewey noted, is the accumulation of human cultural experience, whereas the latter is the accumulation of the individual person's subjective experiences. Knowledge results from the transaction between these objective and subjective experiences in a process called learning. The concept of transaction implies more fluid, interpenetrating relationships between objective conditions and subjective experience, such that once they become related, both are essentially changed. As learners, we do not simply respond to a fixed environment but we actively create situations that meet our learning objectives.

Learning Is the Process of Creating Knowledge. There is an intimate relationship between learning and knowledge. To understand learning, we must understand the nature of knowledge, and vice versa. Knowledge is structured differently in each field of inquiry as their inquiry is guided by unique assumptions about the nature of knowledge and truth. In this sense, the content and the learning process is unique to each knowledge system. It is essential for educators to take into account the nature of the subject matter to be taught in deciding how to help the student learn the material at hand. Helping learners develop skills in empathic listening is a different educational task, requiring a different teaching approach from that of teaching statistics.

Two

The Learning Cycle and Learning Style

If a child can't learn the way we teach,
Maybe we should teach the way they learn.

—Ignacio "Nacho" Estrada

The cycle of learning from experience and learning style are perhaps the two best known and widely used concepts of ELT. The learning cycle has been used to develop and deliver programs in K–12 education (McCarthy, 1996), undergraduate education (Mentkowski, 2000), professional education (Boyatzis, Cowan, & Kolb, 1995; Reese, 1998) and training programs (Brooks Harris & Stock-Ward, 1999); as well as a framework for the assessment of prior learning (Willingham, Valley, & Keeton, 1977) and as a guide for the coaching process (de Haan. E., Culpin, V., & Curd, J., 2011; Kolb & Peterson, 2013; Turesky & Gallagher, 2011). A Google image search of "learning cycle" produces a seemingly endless array of reproductions and variations of the cycle from around the world. The concept of learning style and the KLSI have been used to describe the learning preferences of learners in different disciplines, cultures, and careers as well as used as a tool for developing learners' metacognitive learning skills and study of the decision-making process.

The two concepts, as we will see below, have tended to be treated separately in the literature; in ELT they are in fact inextricably related in the holistic ongoing process of learning. Learning styles are different ways that individuals use the learning cycle to learn. For the learning cycle this means that there is not just one way to go through the learning modes of experiencing, reflecting, thinking, and acting but many different ways that vary for different individuals and their learning tasks. An individual's style of learning is not an independent personality trait but a habitual process of learning that emphasizes some learning modes over others. It is not a fixed trait but a dynamic state that can be changed and developed.

Origins of the Learning Cycle and Learning Style Concepts

The ELT concepts of the learning cycle and learning style were developed in the late 1960s as part of a curriculum-development project to use experiential learning methods in a required organizational psychology course for MBAs at the Sloan School of Management at MIT. The original course, a lecture format with 150 students, was initially broken down into ten small groups of fifteen persons each that used a sensitivity training T-group format led by faculty and graduate student facilitators. These efforts met with mixed results in spite of our persistent attempts. While some students "got it," for many it was confusing because of the lack of structure and deviation from the traditional classroom learning process they were accustomed to. These difficulties spurred us to reflect more deeply in a search for a way to extract the "active experiential learning ingredient" that made these groups so powerful, and harness it to produce a more effective learning process.

The Learning Cycle. What we extracted was the experiential learning cycle based on Lewin's laboratory method. T-groups were typically introduced by saying "We are going to share *experiences* together, *reflect* and share their meaning for us and together *think* about the implications for our group. From this understanding we can *act* to create the kind of group we want." We ask ourselves if the learning cycle described to introduce the groups might be a way to structure learning experiences that would bring the fifteen topics covered in the lecture syllabus into the room. Concrete experiences generated by exercises, business games, role plays, and cases provided a common experiential starting point for participants and faculty to explore the relevance of behavioral concepts for their work. Topics like motivation, perception, and group decision-making were organized around the learning cycle providing the experience, structured reflection and conversation exercises, conceptual material, and a personal application assignment. The teachers' role was to manage a learning process that was basically learner-directed. They helped students to experience in a personal and immediate way the phenomena in their field of specialization. They stood ready with alternative theories and concepts as students attempted to assimilate their observations into their own conception of the topic. They helped students to deduce the implications of their conclusions for their own life and work and to test these implications through practical, real-world experience. The new approach proved quite successful and resulted in the first management textbook based on experiential learning (Kolb, Rubin, & McIntyre, 1971) which is now in its eighth edition (Osland, Kolb, Rubin, & Turner, 2007).

Experiential Learning (Kolb, 1984, 2015) described the theoretical origins of the learning cycle concept in the works of James, Dewey, and Lewin. It further suggested that Piaget's more linear model of development is made consistent with the learning cycle by adding his two dialectical dimensions of concrete phenomenalism/abstract constructionism (concrete vs. abstract) and active ego-centrism/internalized reflection (active vs. reflective). The resulting ELT learning cycle is a dynamic view of learning driven by the resolution of the dual dialectics of action/reflection and concrete experience/ abstraction. Learning is defined as "the process whereby knowledge is created through the transformation of experience. Knowledge results from the combination of grasping and transforming experience" (Kolb, 2015, p. 41). Grasping experience refers to the process of taking in information, and transforming experience is how individuals interpret and act on that information.

The ELT model portrays two dialectically related modes of grasping experience—Concrete Experience (CE) and Abstract Conceptualization (AC)—and two dialectically related modes of transforming experience—Reflective Observation (RO) and Active Experimentation (AE). Learning arises from the resolution of creative tension among these four learning modes. This process is portrayed as an idealized learning cycle or spiral where the learner "touches all the bases"—experiencing (CE), reflecting (RO), thinking (AC), and acting (AE)—in a recursive process that is sensitive to the learning situation and to what is being learned. Immediate or concrete experiences are the basis for observations and reflections. These reflections are assimilated and distilled into abstract concepts from which new implications for action can be drawn. These implications can be actively tested and serve as guides in creating new experiences (figure 2.1).

Figure 2.1
The Experiential Learning Cycle

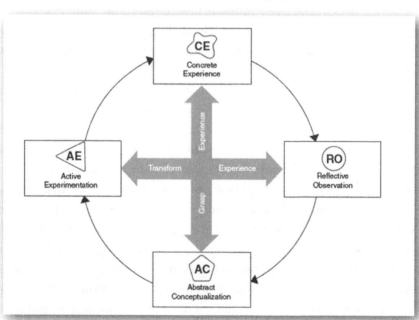

The most important aspect of the learning cycle is that it describes the learning process as a recursive circle or spiral as opposed to the linear, traditional information-transmission model of learning used in most education where information transferred from the teacher to the learner is stored in declarative memory for later recall. In the linear model the learner is a passive recipient of information, whereas in the cycle of learning learners receive information through concrete experiences and transform it through reflection and conceptualization and then transform it again by acting to change the world including what information is attended to in the new experience. They are both receivers and creators of information.

Learning Style. The concept of learning style also emerged from the MIT experiential learning curriculum-development project. In the course of implementing the experiential curriculum based on the learning cycle, we noticed changes in student reactions to the course. While there was a general, resigned passive acceptance of the lecture format course, the new experiential format provoked a range of different reactions. Some complained that the professor wasn't lecturing, that is, giving the overview and correct answers about the topic. Others were visibly anxious and uncertain, while a number of students were highly involved and enjoyed the experiential format. We hypothesized that students were used to the traditional lecture format and confused about how to navigate the experiential format. We also noted that greater individual differences appeared in the experiential format. The Kolb Learning Style Inventory (KLSI—Kolb, 1971, 1976a) was invented to help students understand the experiential learning cycle and to identify their preferred way of learning. A session on learning was added to the syllabus with the objective of helping students learn how to learn in the experiential format. This involved taking the KLSI and talking in small groups with students of the same style to examine similarities, and then reporting the group results across groups to identify differences. The KLSI proved to be very popular with the students who felt the inventory gave them greater understanding of themselves and also insight into their relationships with others whose style was different from theirs. The fact that this simple self-assessment exercise helped learners gained some insights about themselves and others as learners inspired further development and systematic research with the instrument to define its theoretical foundation and to explore its reliability and validity.

Learning style describes the unique ways individuals spiral through the learning cycle based on their preference for the four different learning modes—CE, RO, AC, and AE. Since the primary purpose of the KLSI is to provide learners with information about their preferred approach to learning, the most relevant information for the learner is about intra-individual differences—his or her relative preference for the four learning modes—not inter-individual comparisons. In the KLSI, a person's learning style is defined by their unique combination of preferences for the four learning modes defining a "kite" shaped profile of their relative preference for the four phases of the learning cycle. Because each person's learning style is unique, everyone's kite shape is a little different (Kolb, 2015; Kolb & Kolb, 2013a—see Appendix 2).

Research with KLSI has shown that learning styles are influenced by culture, personality type, educational specialization, career choice, and current job role and tasks (Kolb & Kolb, 2013a; Kolb, 2015). These patterns of behavior associated with the four basic learning styles are shaped by transactions between persons and their environment at five different levels—personality, educational specialization, professional career, current job role, and adaptive competencies. While some have interpreted learning style as a personality variable (Furnam, Jackson & Miller, 1999; Garner, 2000), ELT defines learning style as a social psychological concept that is only partially determined by personality. Personality exerts a small but pervasive influence in nearly all situations; but at the other levels learning style is influenced by increasingly specific environmental demands of educational specialization, career, job, and tasks skills (see figure 2.2).

Figure 2.2 Factors That Influence Learning Style

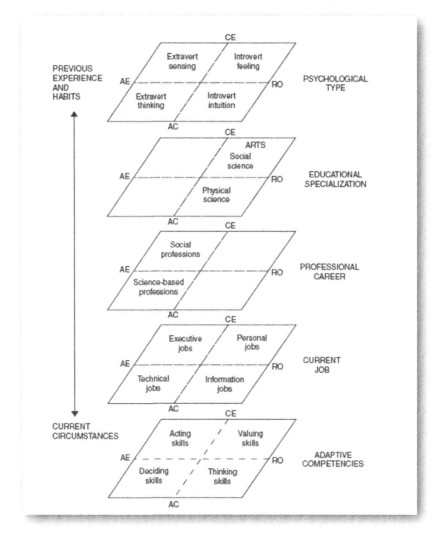

Personality Type. Although the learning styles of and learning modes proposed by ELT are derived from the works of Dewey, Lewin, and Piaget, many have noted the similarity of these concepts to Carl Jung's descriptions of individuals' preferred ways for adapting in the world. Several research studies relating the KLSI with the Myers-Briggs Type Indicator (MBTI) indicate that Jung's Extraversion/Introversion dialectical dimension correlates with the Active/Reflective dialectic of ELT and the MBTI Feeling/Thinking dimension correlates with the KLSI Concrete Experience/Abstract Conceptualization dimension. The MBTI Sensing type is associated with the concrete (CE) and active (AE) dimensions and the MBTI Intuitive type with the abstract (AC) and reflective (RO) dimensions. MBTI Feeling types have scores that are concrete and reflective on the KLSI and Thinking types score high on abstraction and active experimentation. (Kolb, 2015, pp. 119–120).

Educational Specialization. Early educational experiences shape people's individual learning styles by instilling positive attitudes toward specific sets of learning skills and by teaching students how to learn. Although elementary education is generalized, there is an increasing process of specialization that begins in high school and becomes sharper during the college years. This specialization in the realms of social knowledge influences individuals' orientations toward learning, resulting in particular relations between learning styles and early training in an educational specialty or discipline. For example, people specializing in the arts, history, political science, English, and psychology tend to have concrete and reflective learning styles, while those majoring in more abstract and applied areas like medicine and engineering have abstract and active learning styles. Individuals with active and concrete styles often have educational backgrounds in education, communication, and nursing, and those with abstract and reflective learning styles specialize in mathematics and physical sciences.

Professional Career. A third set of factors that shape learning styles stems from professional careers. One's professional career choice not only exposes one to a specialized learning environment, but it also involves a commitment to a generic professional problem, such as social service, that requires a specialized adaptive orientation. In addition, one becomes a member of a reference group of peers who share a professional mentality, and a common set of values and beliefs about how one should behave professionally. This professional orientation shapes learning style through habits acquired in professional training and through the more immediate normative pressures involved in being a competent professional. Research over the years has shown that social service and arts careers attract people with concrete and active learning styles. Professions in the sciences and information or research have people with abstract and reflective learning styles. The abstract and active learning style tends to be dominant among professionals in technology-intensive fields like medicine and engineering. Finally, the active and concrete learning style characterizes people with careers in fields such as sales, social service, and education.

Current Job Role. The fourth level of factors influencing learning style is the person's current job role. The task demands and pressures of a job shape a person's adaptive orientation. Executive jobs, such as general management, that require a strong orientation to task accomplishment and decision-making in uncertain emergent circumstances require an active and concrete learning style. Personnel jobs, such as counseling and human resources, that require the establishment of personal relationships and effective communication with other people demand a concrete and reflective learning style. Information jobs, such as planning and research, that require data gathering and analysis, as well as conceptual modeling, require an abstract and reflective learning style. Technical jobs, such as bench engineering and production that require technical and problem-solving skills require an abstract and active learning orientation.

Adaptive competencies. The fifth and most immediate level of forces that shape learning style is the specific task or problem the person is currently working on. Each task we face requires a corresponding set of skills for effective performance. The effective matching of task demands and personal skills results in an adaptive competence. Active and concrete learning styles encompass a set of competencies that can best be termed "acting skills": leadership, initiative, and action. The concrete and reflective learning style is associated with valuing skills: relationship, helping others, and sense-making. The abstract and reflective learning style is related to thinking skills: information-gathering, information-analysis, and theory building. Finally, the abstract and active learning style is associated with decision skills like quantitative analysis, use of technology, and goal-setting (Kolb, 2015).

Alice Y. Kolb and David A. Kolb

Some Misinterpretations of the ELT Cycle and Style Concepts

There has been some confusion and misunderstanding of the learning cycle and learning style concepts, often resulting from their being taken out of the context of the wider ELT framework. While the scholarly literature on both concepts is extensive (Kolb & Kolb, 2017, scholarship about research and practice on the two topics often has proceeded in two separate directions with learning style research following psychometric conventions and the learning cycle studies focused more on process aspects of educational design and individual development. This division has resulted in some misunderstandings of both concepts, since, as we have noted, the two are significantly intertwined. The simple step-by-step interpretation of the learning cycle has created misunderstanding about the nature of experience and experiencing and a failure to recognize the dual dialectics that are the foundations of the learning style typology. Learning style, on the other hand has been mischaracterized as a trait and not a dynamic state in the learning cycle process. While styles in ELT are conceived as relative habitual preferences for interdependent poles of the dialectics of action and reflection and experiencing and thinking, learning style is mistakenly seen as an independent trait variable, for example, saying "She is an abstract person."

The Learning Cycle. While we and many others have found considerable heuristic value in the learning cycle as a guide to the design of learning experiences and curricula, others have seen the cycle as an oversimplified description of the learning process (Garner, 2000; Holman, Palvicia & Thorpe 1997; Jarvis, 1987, 1995; Miettinen, 2000). Seaman, who called for an end to the "Learning Cycles Era," suggests that "the definition of experiential learning as an orderly series of steps is either false…or represents only a narrow type of experiential learning…The intent of this article is not to suggest that the routine patterns used in different experiential practices…should be abandoned. This approach has unquestionably served many practitioners throughout the years. Rather, this article has argued against the claim that experiential learning can be fundamentally understood as *equivalent* to these patterns" (2008, p. 15).

One oversimplification is the description of the cycle as a rigid four-stage process. Bergsteiner, Avery, and Neumann say, for example, "Learning stages refer to sequential steps in a learning cycle" (2010, p. 31). De Ciantis and Kirton (1996) in a much-cited critique of ELT see the cycle as similar to cycles in the information-processing literature "that represents an idealized schema, showing the underlying structure of an exact number of progressive events in learning from a start to a finish in the order in which they appear." (1996, p. 812). While this may be true of information processing models, it does not apply to the ELT learning cycle because of the dialectic dynamics of opposing learning modes and learning style differences in the way individuals apply the learning modes. DeCiantis and Kirton recognize this aspect of ELT, since the main thrust of their critique is to reject it, arguing that *level*, *learning style*, and *process* "answer different questions or meet different needs and are not to be conflated into a single concept or measure" (1996, p. 812).

Another aspect of this simplification is the idea that learning must always begin with concrete experience and proceed through the other stages around the cycle. A number of our experiential educator friends are strong advocates of beginning learning experiences with a direct concrete experience, and they have strong arguments for the practice. They argue, as we did in the introduction, that beginning with a shared direct experience "brings the subject into the room," democratizing the learning process between educator and learners. In addition, the puzzles or problems presented by direct experience involve learners and motivate inquiry and reflection, initiating the learning cycle.

These pragmatic benefits, however, can overshadow the fact that learners with different styles may begin with their preferred style and engage the learning modes in their own way regardless of the educator's plan. While there may be pragmatic utility in organizing education around an idealized cycle that begins with concrete experience, followed by reflection alone or with others, introducing concepts and theory to organize and conclude the meaning of the experience and then action to test the conclusions in new experience, as learners our experiences are seldom so orderly. One moment we may be lost in thought only to be jolted to awareness of a dramatic event, sparking immediate action or cautious observation depending on our habit of learning. Our learning style may dictate where we begin a process of learning and/or the context may shape it. Learning usually does not happen in one big cycle but takes place in numerous small cycles or partial cycles. Thinking and reflection can continue for some time before acting and experiencing. Experiencing and reflecting can also continue through much iteration before concluding in action. Sometimes it may be wiser to begin where the learner is. Learners with strong thinking styles, for example, may be overwhelmed by the experiential and prefer to begin learning with theory.

In addition to learning style considerations, confusion stems from the ambiguous meaning of experience in the learning cycle. The revised edition of *Experiential Learning* (Kolb, 2015) attempts to clarify the role of experience in learning by outlining the foundations of experiential learning in James's radical empiricism. As described in the previous chapter, radical empiricism argues that experience is an inclusive concept that includes the direct sensations of British empiricism along with the cognitive relationships of French rationalism. James's radical empiricism helps us to understand that all modes of the learning cycle are experiences—"If we take conceptual manifolds, or memories, or fancies, they also are in their first intention mere bits of pure experience" (1904, p. 483). "Pure" Concrete Experience is but one special form of experience—moment-to-moment here-and-now consciousness, "The immediate flux of life which furnishes the material to our later reflection with its conceptual categories." Dewey called this "immediate empiricism" and agreed with James's radical empiricism that "it is in the concrete thing *as experienced* that all the grounds and clues to its own intellectual and logical rectification are contained" (1905, p. 397).

James distinguishes between direct concrete experience that he calls "pure experience" and abstract thought, the "doubling" of a pure experience "in retrospection into a state of mind." His description of the primacy of the direct perception of CE and how it is altered by transformation through the other learning modes may be the first description of the experiential learning cycle:

The instant field of the present is at all times what I call "pure experience." It is only virtually or potentially either object or subject as yet. For the time being it is plain, unqualified actuality, or existence, a simple *that* (CE). In this *naïf* immediacy it is of course valid; it is *there*, we *act* upon it (AE); and the doubling of it in retrospection into a state of mind and a reality intended thereby (RO), is just one of the acts. The "state of mind" first treated explicitly as such in retrospection will stand corrected or confirmed (AC), and the retrospective experience in its turn will get a similar treatment; but the immediate experience in its passing is always "truth," practical truth, something *to act on*, at its own moment. If the world were then and there to go out like a candle, it would remain truth absolute and objective, for it would be the "last word," would have no critic, and no one would ever oppose the thought in it to the reality intended. (1912, pp. 23–24)

Likewise, Dewey saw that much experience was conservative, habitual "empirical experience" and required being "stuck" or "struck" to provoke critical reflection and learning. In this he presaged contemporary research on automaticity that suggests that conscious acts of self-regulation are rare and as much as 95 percent of behavior occurs automatically without them (Bargh & Chartrand, 1999; Baumeister et al., 1998; Baumeister and Sommer, 1997). This insight is of profound importance for experiential learning. While many have stressed that critical reflection is of primary importance for learning from experience, we see here that a concrete "pure" experience that violates the expectations of previous convictions and habits of thought is necessary to activate such reflection in the first place, suggesting that experience shorn of habit and cultural interpretation is necessary for learning anything new. While some learning probably occurs from empirical experience, it is probably the kind that reinforces previous conclusions or refines thought or behavior in small ways. For bigger changes such as overcoming addiction, we see that a "shock" that disrupts life is necessary.

Yet, it is not only the CE mode of learning that is experiential; all modes of the learning cycle (see figure 2.1) are included in experience. Both modes of grasping experience—CE and AC and both modes of transforming experience—RO and AE—are part of the experiential learning process. Many use the term experiential learning to refer to exercises and games used to involve students in the learning process. However, a classroom lecture may be an abstract experience but it is also a concrete one, when, for example, a learner admires and imitates the lecturer. Likewise a learner may work hard to create an abstract model in order to make sense of an internship experience or experiential exercise. From the learner's perspective, solitary reflection can be an intensely emotional concrete experience and the action of programming a computer can be a highly abstract experience.

Learning Style. Just as the learning cycle, stripped of the dialectic dynamics that drive it and the influence of individual differences in learning style, is oversimplified, so too the concept of learning style is distorted by the failure to connect it to ELT and the learning cycle. This failure to recognize these unique characteristics of the ELT learning style concept is in part due to the tendency to lump the ELT learning style concept with the many other learning style approaches, a tendency that Scott decries. "To speak of 'learning styles' is thus an attempt to shoehorn an eclectic mix of theories into one category in which they patently do not fit" (Scott, 2010, p. 6). Since the term "learning style" was coined in the late 1960s to distinguish styles of learning from experience from cognitive styles (Kolb, 1971; Kolb, Rubin, & McIntyre, 1971), over a hundred other learning style frameworks and assessments have been created. They assess a wide spectrum of human individuality—cognitive styles, preferences for sense modalities, Jungian personality types, study strategies, instructional preferences, preferences for learning alone in groups, and so on. The theory base and research evidence for these different learning style frameworks vary widely. Consistent with the prevailing psychometric tradition, they see learning styles as fixed traits or personality characteristics. Scott, citing Dweck (2008), argues that this trait approach is an entity approach to ability that promotes stereotyping and labeling rather than a process approach that emphasizes developmental potential and contextual adaptation.

Also, surprisingly, none of the learning style instruments other than the KLSI are based on a comprehensive theory of learning (Vanhear,

2013). The dimensions of individuality that they assess are hypothesized to influence learning, but how the dimensions are connected to the learning process is not made explicit. An individual may prefer to work alone or in a group, for example; but how is this preference related to learning?

ELT posits that learning style is not a fixed psychological trait but a dynamic state resulting from synergistic transactions between the person and the environment. This dynamic state arises from an individual's preferential resolution of the dual dialectics of experiencing/conceptualizing and acting/reflecting.

> The stability and endurance of these states in individuals comes not solely from fixed genetic qualities or characteristics of human beings: nor, for that matter, does it come from the stable fixed demands of environmental circumstances. Rather, stable and enduring patterns of human individuality arise from consistent patterns of transaction between the individual and his or her environment… The way we process the possibilities of each new emerging event determines the range of choices and decisions we see. The choices and decisions we make to some extent determine the events we live through, and these events influence our future choices. Thus, people create themselves through the choice of the actual occasions that they live through. (Kolb, 2015, pp. 99–100).

In ELT, different styles of learning are different ways of engaging the learning cycle. Because ELT is a holistic, dynamic, and dialectic theory of learning, the four modes that comprise the experiential learning cycle, CE, RO, AC, and AE are conceived as interdependent. Learning involves resolving the creative tension among these learning modes in response to the specific learning situation. Since the two learning dimensions, AC-CE and AE-RO are related dialectically, the choice of one pole involves not choosing the opposite pole. Therefore, because ELT postulates that learning in life situations requires the resolution of conflicts among interdependent learning modes, to be ecologically valid the learning style assessment process should require a similar process of conflict resolution in the choice of one's preferred learning approach. The format of the KLSI is a forced choice format that ranks an individual's relative choice preferences among the four modes of the learning cycle. This is in contrast to the common psychometric-normative or free-choice format, such as the widely used Likert scale, that rates absolute preferences on independent dimensions (see Appendix 1).

Conventional psychometric assumptions proceed from a linear, dualistic logic of formal reasoning that assumes independence and stable reliability, while ELT dynamics are based on dialectic thinking. Dialectic thinking is based on holism, change, and contradiction (Basseches, 1984, 2005; Tong, Yao, Liu, & Wang, 2013). The dialectic approach integrates experiencing and conceptualizing ways of knowing (Alexander & Langer, 1990) where opposites are seen as poles of one concept that contains contradiction and paradox in movement and process, while thought based on formal reason is dualistic, choosing one pole over another. The conflicts between opposing dialectics help explain the dynamic, constantly changing nature of experience (Basseches, 1984, 2005), as in Piaget's ongoing to-and-fro between assimilating experiences into existing concepts and accommodation of concepts to new experiences, or in Dewey's recursive uniting of desire and idea to form purpose. The dialectic opposites open a space for experiencing that embraces the multidimensional aspects of experience and all modes of the learning cycle as described in James's radical empiricism and in phenomenology. Experiencing, reflecting, thinking, and acting are not separate independent entities but are inextricably related to one another in their dialectic opposition. They are mutually determined and in dynamic flux. The dialectic dimensions are the basis of the concept of learning style; a habit of learning that is formed when one or more of the learning modes are preferred over others to shape experience, resulting in a constriction and limiting of the experiencing space around those mode(s).

When learning style is seen as a habitual way of resolving the dialectic polarities of the learning cycle, the concept loses its static stereotype prone character. Instead, the recognition of a style preference as emphasizing strengths in some learning modes as well as some weakness in opposite modes opens development potentialities and the challenge of full-cycle learning—to develop the ability to engage all modes of the learning cycle in a holistic and fluid manner. The latest version of the KLSI (Version 4.0—Kolb & Kolb, 2011, 2013a) was designed to clarify the interrelation between the learning cycle and learning style through a refined definition of the different kite shapes that portray typical interdependent preferences for the four modes of the learning cycle. In addition, the concept of learning flexibility is introduced, allowing learners to assess their ability to engage all modes of the learning cycle as the situation dictates.

The KLSI 4.0 and the New Nine Learning Style Typology

Recent research and the development of the Kolb Learning Style Inventory 4.0 has enhanced our understanding of the relationship between the learning cycle and learning style giving a new perspective on the learning cycle and a more precise understanding of different learning styles and how they are dynamically flexible. Data from empirical and clinical studies over the years has shown that these original four learning style types—Accommodating, Assimilating, Converging and Diverging—can be refined further into a nine-style typology that better defines the unique patterns of individual learning styles and reduces the confusions introduced by borderline cases in the old four-style typology (Boyatzis & Mainemelis, 2000; Eickmann, Kolb, & Kolb, 2004; Kolb & Kolb, 2005a, 2005b). With feedback from users we first began noticing a fifth "balancing" style describing users who scored at the center of the Learning Style grid. Later we discovered that individuals who scored near the grid boundary lines also had distinctive styles. For example an "Experiencing" style was identified between the Accommodating and Diverging styles. Four of these style types emphasize one of the four learning modes—Experiencing (CE), Reflecting (RO), Thinking (AC), and Acting (AE) (Abbey, Hunt, & Weiser, 1985; Hunt, 1987). Four others represent style types that emphasize two learning modes, one from the grasping dimension and one from the transforming dimension of the ELT model—Imagining (CE & RO), Analyzing (AC & RO), Deciding (AC &AE), and Initiating (CE & AE). The final style type balances all four modes of the learning cycle—Balancing (CE, RO, AC, & AE; Mainemelis, Boyatzis, & Kolb, 2002).

The new KLSI 4.0 introduces these nine style types by moving from a four-pixel to nine-pixel resolution of learning style types as described below. The learning style types can be systematically arranged on a two-dimensional learning space defined by Abstract Conceptualization-Concrete Experience and Active Experimentation-Reflective Observation. This space, including a description of the distinguishing kite shape of each style, is depicted in figure 2.3. See Appendix 2 for detailed descriptions and case studies of the nine types.

Figure 2.3
The Nine Learning Styles in the KLSI 4.0

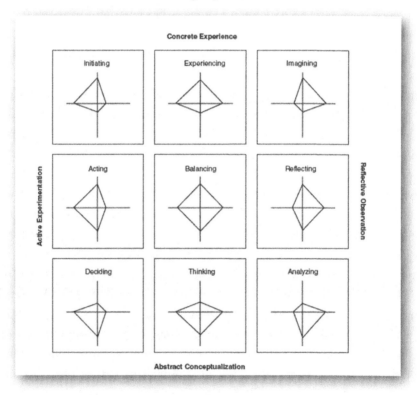

The Initiating style—initiating action to deal with experiences and situations. The Initiating style is characterized by the ability to initiate action in order to deal with experiences and situations. It involves active experimentation (AE) and concrete experience (CE).

The Experiencing style—finding meaning from deep involvement in experience. The Experiencing style is characterized by the ability to find meaning from deep involvement in experience. It draws on concrete experience (CE) while balancing active experimentation (AE) and reflective observation (RO).

The Imagining style—imagining possibilities by observing and reflecting on experiences. The Imagining style is characterized by the ability to imagine possibilities by observing and reflecting on experiences. It combines the learning modes of concrete experience (CE) and reflective observation (RO).

The Reflecting style—connecting experience and ideas through sustained reflection. The Reflecting style is characterized by the ability to connect experience and ideas through sustained reflection. It draws on reflective observation (RO) while balancing concrete experience (CE) and abstract conceptualization (AC).

The Analyzing style—integrating ideas into concise models and systems through reflection. The Analyzing style is characterized by the ability to integrate and systematize ideas through reflection. It combines reflective observation (RO) and abstract conceptualization (AC).

The Thinking style—disciplined involvement in abstract reasoning and logical reasoning. The Thinking style is characterized by the capacity for disciplined involvement in abstract and logical reasoning. It draws on abstract conceptualization (AC) while balancing active experimentation (AE) and reflective observation (RO).

The Deciding style—using theories and models to decide on problem solutions and courses of action. The Deciding style is characterized by the ability to use theories and models to decide on problem solutions and courses of action. It combines abstract conceptualization (AC) and active experimentation (AE).

The Acting style—a strong motivation for goal-directed action that integrates people and tasks. The Acting style is characterized by a strong motivation for goal-directed action that integrates people and tasks. It draws on active experimentation (AE) while balancing concrete experience (CE) and abstract conceptualization (AC).

The Balancing style—adapting by weighing the pros and cons of acting vs. reflecting and experiencing vs. thinking. The Balancing style is characterized by the ability to adapt; weighing the pros and cons of acting versus reflecting and experiencing vs. thinking. It balances the four learning modes.

The Nine-Style Learning Cycle and Dialectic Polarities. These nine KLSI 4.0 learning styles further define the experiential learning cycle by emphasizing four dialectic tensions in the learning process. In addition to the primary dialectics of Abstract Conceptualization/Concrete Experience and Active Experimentation/Reflective Observation, the combination dialectics of Assimilation/Accommodation and Converging/Diverging are also represented in an eight-stage learning cycle, with Balancing in the center. The formulas for calculating the continuous scores on these combination dialectics are reported in the KLSI 4 Guidebook (Kolb & Kolb, 2013a).

Thus, the Initiating style has a strong preference for active learning in context (Accommodation) while the Analyzing style has a strong preference for reflective conceptual learning (Assimilation). The concepts of assimilation and accommodation are central to Piaget's (1952) definition of intelligence as the balance of adapting concepts to fit the external world (Accommodation) and the process of fitting observations of the external world into existing concepts (Assimilation). This measure was used in the validation of the Learning Flexibility Index (Sharma & Kolb, 2010—see Chapter 6) and has been used by other researchers in previous studies (Allison & Hayes 1996; Wierstra & de Jong, 2002).

The Imagining style has a strong preference for opening alternatives and perspectives on experience (Diverging) while the Deciding style has a strong preference for closing on the single best option for action (Converging). The concepts of converging and diverging originated in Guilford's (1988) structure of intellect model as the central dialectic of the creative process.

This dialectic concept has been used in research on ELT by Gemmell (2012) and Kolb (1984).

Some studies have used continuous balance scores for ACCE and AERO to assess balanced learning style scores (Mainemelis, Boyatzis, & Kolb, 2002, Sharma & Kolb, 2010). These variables compute the absolute values of the ACCE and AERO scores adjusted to center on the fiftieth percentile of the normative comparison group. figure 2.4 depicts this expanded learning cycle and illustrates how an individual's particular style represents his or her preferred space in the cycle.

Figure 2.4
The Nine Learning Styles and the Four Dialectics of the Learning Cycle

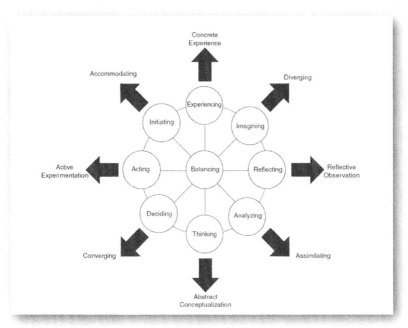

Learning Flexibility. Another important aspect of learning style is learning flexibility, the extent to which an individual adapts his or her learning style to the demands of the learning situation. As we have seen above, learning style is not a fixed personality trait but more like a habit of learning shaped by experience and choices—it can be an automatic, unconscious mode of adapting or it can be consciously modified and changed. The stability of learning style arises from consistent patterns of transaction between individuals and learning situations in their life. This process is called accentuation—the way we learn about a new situation determines the range of choices and decisions we see; the choices and decisions we make influence the next situation we live through and this situation further influences future choices. Learning styles are thus specialized modes of adaptation that are reinforced by the continuing choice of situations where a style is successful (Kolb, 2015, pp. 164–166).

Since a specialized learning style represents an individual preference for only one or two of the four modes of the learning cycle, its effectiveness is limited to those learning situations that require these strengths. Learning flexibility indicates the development of a more holistic and sophisticated learning process. The learning style types described above portray how one prefers to learn in general. Many individuals feel that their learning style type accurately describes how they learn most of the time. They are consistent in their approach to learning. Others, however, report that they tend to change their learning approach depending on what they are learning or the situation they are in. They may say, for example, that they use one style in the classroom and another at home with their friends and family. These are flexible learners.

The KLSI 4.0 also includes an assessment of learning flexibility by integrating the Adaptive Style Inventory (ASI) into the instrument. Chapter 8 of *Experiential Learning* (Kolb, 2015) describes the creation of the ASI, which was designed to assess the individual's level of integrative complexity as he or she progressed from the specialized to integrated stage of the ELT developmental model (EL figure 6.3). The instrument assessed adaptive flexibility by measuring how individuals change their learning style in response to different situational demands. It was based on the theory that if people show systematic variability in their response to different contextual learning demands, one could infer a higher level of integrative development because systematic variation would imply higher-order decision rules or metacognitive processes (Kolb & Kolb, 2009) for guiding behavior. A number of researchers have found evidence to support the link between learning flexibility and integrative development. Early studies (Kolb, 2015) found that ASI adaptive flexibility is positively related to higher levels of ego development on Loevinger's sentence-completion instrument (Kolb & Wolfe, 1981). Individuals with higher levels of adaptive flexibility perceived themselves to be more self-directed in their current life situation and to have greater flexibility. They had higher levels of differentiation in their personal relationships, and used more constructs to describe their life structure. In addition, they experienced less conflict and stress in their life despite experiencing their life to be more complex. Subsequent research on learning flexibility has replicated some of these findings. Perlmutter (1990) studied fifty-one medical professionals and found significant relationships between Loevinger's ego-development instrument and adaptive flexibility. Thompson (1999), in a sample of fifty professionals from various fields, found that self-directed learners had higher levels of adaptive flexibility than those who were not self-directed.

Another study by Mainemelis, Boyatzis, and Kolb (2002) examined the relationship between learning style as measured by the KLSI (KLSI—Kolb, 1999, 2005) and ASI adaptive flexibility. They tested the hypothesis that learners with equal preferences for dialectically opposed learning modes would be better able to integrate them into a flexible learning process. They proposed that a balanced learning style (as given by the absolute value for the dialectics of experiencing/conceptualizing and acting/reflecting adjusted for population mean) would be related to learning flexibility. In other words, the more an individual is balanced on the conceptualizing/experiencing and acting/reflecting dialectics, the more will he or she exhibit learning flexibility. This was supported for the dialectic of conceptualizing/experiencing. No significant result was found for the dialectic of acting/reflecting. However, they also found an equally strong relationship between learning flexibility and a preference for concreteness over abstraction, the KLSI AC-CE score.

Akrivou (2009) found a relationship between learning flexibility and integrative development as measured by her Integrative Development Scale (IDS).

She created this scale by identifying items that describe the integrative stage of adult development as defined in the works of Kegan (1982, 1994), Kolb (1984, 1988, 1991), Loevinger (1966, 1976, 1993), Perry (1970), and Rogers (1961). In her comprehensive review of ASI research, Bell (2005) reported other construct validity evidence but suggested a need for revision of the original instrument and the creation of new measures of adaptive flexibility.

Sharma and Kolb (2010) modified the ASI to fit the format of the KLSI and created a Learning Flexibility Index (LFI) based on the Kendall's W statistic. They showed construct validity for the LFI measure by testing six hypotheses about the place of the LFI in a nomological net. The LFI was negatively related to age and educational level. Women and those in concrete professions tended to be more flexible. Individuals with an assimilating learning style tended to be less flexible. The LFI was positively related to Akrivou's IDS, replicating her earlier findings. Individuals who are men, older, highly educated, and specialists in abstract, paradigmatic fields were more assimilative in learning style and had less learning flexibility. The results suggest that it is the orientation toward abstraction and reflection characteristic of the assimilative learning style that leads to inflexibility. Since it is the assimilative style that is the most favored and most developed in formal education systems, one might ask if this abstract approach is producing the unintended negative consequence of learning inflexibility. Emphasis on conceptual learning at the expense of contextual learning may lead to dogmatic adherence to ideas without testing them in experience, what Whitehead called "the fallacy of misplaced concreteness" (1978, p. 7). Contextual learning approaches like experiential learning (Kolb, 1984), and situated learning (Lave & Wenger, 1991) may help education to nurture integrated learners who are as sensitive to context as they are to abstract concepts. A related issue concerns the priority placed on specialized over integrative learning in education. Specialization in subject matter and the learning style most suited to learning it may well produce higher levels of specialized mastery. Mainemelis et al. (2002) found that specialized learning styles led to greater development of learning skills related to the specialization than did balanced learning styles.

A study by Moon (2008) using the new KLSI 4.0 Learning Flexibility Index examined sales performance in financial services, finding that learning flexibility influenced sales success as measured by monthly volume of sales. Gemmell (2012) studied 172 technology entrepreneurs who were founders/CEOs of their current company. He examined the relationship between their KLSI and LFI 4.0 scores and their company's innovation and performance. Results showed a positive relationship between Active Experimentation (AE-RO) and experimentation, which in turn influenced innovation and performance. Entrepreneurs with a high learning flexibility were more likely to take longer to make key strategic decisions. However, in the process of doing so, they were more innovative. "Technology entrepreneurs who are flexible learners—in spite of the enormous environmental pressures—appear to achieve greater innovation by taking slightly longer to consider more alternatives, to reflect upon those alternatives and to ultimately converge to a solution and take action" (p. 90).

Learning flexibility indicates the development of a more holistic and sophisticated learning process. Following Jung's theory that adult development moves from a specialized way of adapting toward a holistic integrated way, development in learning flexibility is seen as a move from specialization to integration. Integrated learning is a process involving a creative tension among the four learning modes that is responsive to contextual demands. Learning flexibility is the ability to use each of the four learning modes to move freely around the learning cycle and to modify one's approach to learning based on the learning situation. Experiencing, reflecting, thinking, and acting each provide valuable perspectives on the learning task in a way that deepens and enriches knowledge.

This can be seen as traveling through each of the regions of the learning space in the process of learning. The flexibility to move from one learning style to another in the learning cycle is important for effective learning. When one can engage all learning styles in their learning process, they are using the most powerful form of learning that we call full-cycle learning. Learning flexibility can help us move in and out of the learning space regions, capitalizing on the strengths of each learning style. Learning flexibility broadens the learning comfort zone and allows us to operate comfortably and effectively in more regions of the learning space, promoting deep learning and development. In addition to providing a measure of how flexible one is in their approach to learning, the KLSI 4.0 also provides an indication of which learning space they move to in different learning contexts—their backup learning styles. Figure 2.5 shows the backup styles of Initiating and Balancing for an Experiencing type with a low flexibility score and the backup styles of Experiencing, Imagining, Balancing, Reflecting, and Thinking for an Initiating learning style with a high flexibility score. High flexibility individuals tend to show more backup styles and hence a greater ability to move around the learning cycle.

Figure 2.5
Backup Styles for High- and Low-Learning Flexibility Learners

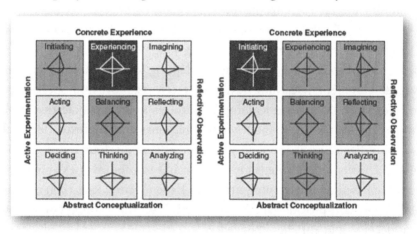

Knowing one's primary learning style and where one flexes to use other learning styles can be a starting point to develop underused styles and engage in full-cycle learning. Educators can empower learners toward full-cycle learning by designing their courses with attention to which of the nine styles they intend to develop in each of their educational activities. Appendix 3 shows how styles can be used as learning objectives in two sample educational activities.

Three

*I have proposed that each of the four elements of the
learning cycle heavily, but not exclusively engage different
regions of the neocortex. Each is associated with different
functions, so that the cycle engages four different broad
functions of cognition and learning... The four brain
functions engaged are: sensing, remembering, theorizing,
and acting. I have called these the four pillars of learning.*

—JAMES ZULL

The ELT concepts of learning style and the learning cycle are an integrated perspective on the process of learning from experience and the unique way that individuals engage this process. The model, however, raises a number of important questions about just how learning happens. What role does memory play in learning from experience? Is conscious awareness necessary for learning or is unconscious learning possible? Are the different ways that individuals with different learning styles go through the learning cycle related to brain functioning? What is the role of emotion and action in learning? Current neuroscience research on learning and the brain provides a window to insight about these and other questions about learning from experience.

Research in neuroscience has made great advances since the 1990s when John Bruer (1997) argued that the educational application of neuroscience was "a bridge too far." The decade of the 1990s was designated the "decade of the brain" by President G. W. H. Bush and today cognitive neuroscience research on brain processes and structures and their role in learning is expanding dramatically, as methods for directly examining brain engagement in cognition such as the fMRI became available. In 2008 alone, more than 26,500 refereed articles were published in over four hundred neuroscience journals. The Society for Neuroscience's first conference in 1979 had thirteen hundred attendees; by 2000, twenty-four thousand people attended. Today the brain has entered popular culture everywhere and disciplines from education to law to marketing to economics to ethics have developed specialties called neuro-education, neuro-law, and so on (Rose & Abi-Rached, 2013).

We would argue that the bridge between this research and education is progressing, but it still is not complete. The promise of an evidence-based practice of neuroscience education currently offers more provocative possibilities than proven practices. The immense complexity, plasticity, and adaptability of the human brain with its one hundred billion neurons and one thousand trillion synaptic connections (Shermer, 2011) makes even the most amazing research findings only a tiny piece of a very large puzzle. There is a tendency to overgeneralize the implications of research as we saw with the "Mozart effect" and earlier interpretations of left- and right-brain differences. More recently, the discovery of mirror neurons and their functions has generated similar grand speculation. Mirror neuron areas of the brain are where action and perception converge for high-level sensory association and motor planning, a process that is central to the exploration/mimicry learning cycle described below. They are called mirror neurons because they are also activated by the sight of movement by others. It has been claimed that these cells are the source of empathy, they are what shaped human civilization, and their malfunction causes autism. But Jarrett sounds a note of caution:

No doubt about it—mirror neurons are an exciting, intriguing discovery—but when you see them mentioned in the media, remember that most of the research on these cells has been conducted in monkeys...mirror neurons are not merely activated by incoming sensory information, but also by formulations developed elsewhere in the brain about the meaning of what is being observed...they are embedded in a complex network of brain activity. (2013, p. 3)

Immordino-Yang (2008) calls the involvement of other brain functions and the sociocultural environment "the smoke around the mirrors" emphasizing, for example, how shared culture aids in the interpretation of the intentions of others.

While we need to recognize the limits of our current state of knowledge about the brain and its role in learning, there are still many powerful educational implications to be drawn from neuroscience. Brain-based learning, founded on the basis of principles articulated by Caine & Caine (1990, 1995) is one popular approach:

Using the latest neural research, educational techniques that are brain friendly provide a biologically driven framework for creating effective instruction. This theory also helps explain recurring learning behaviors, and is a meta-concept that includes an eclectic mix of techniques. Currently, related techniques stress allowing teachers to connect learning to students' real lives and emotional experiences, as well as their personal histories and experiences. This form of learning also encompasses such newer educational concepts like: mastery learning, experiential learning, learning styles, multiple intelligences, cooperative learning, practical simulations, problem-based learning, movement education, also known as embodied learning. (Wilson, 2013, p. 1)

In this chapter we examine the contributions of the neuroscience research to our understanding of experiential learning. We begin with an examination of how the learning cycle is manifested in brain functioning and an exploration of two variations of the full learning cycle that involve different regions of the neocortex—the exploration/mimicry cycle and the instruction/recall cycle. We then suggest how these different variations of the learning cycle are related to three different types of memory—procedural, semantic, and episodic. Experiential full-cycle learning is shown to be particularly effective in producing the highest and most complex form of memory, episodic memory.

Learning Cycles and the Brain

When combined with work in cognitive and developmental psychology, education, and other disciplines, neuroscience provides a powerful theoretical foundation for the experiential educator to follow. In this spirit, our colleague and friend James Zull, a biologist and founding director of CWRU's University Center for Innovation in Teaching and Education (UCITE), began an inquiry into the neuroscience basis of experiential learning in his 2002 book, *The art of changing the brain: Enriching teaching by exploring the biology of learning.* His basic idea was that knowledge resides in networks of neurons in the neocortex constructed through learning from experience. In constructivist terms, learning is a process that is built on the foundation of each individual's neuronal structure and thus every learner is unique and will interpret experience uniquely. Learning from experience results in modification, growth, and pruning of neurons, synapses, and neuronal networks. Learning physically changes the brain and, thus, educating is the art of changing the brain.

Zull saw a link between ELT and a macro-level view of the brain, suggesting that understanding of the brain's structure and processes can enrich our understanding of the process of experiential learning. This relationship between the ELT learning cycle and the process of brain functioning is shown in figure 3.1.

> Put into words, the figure illustrates that concrete experiences come through the sensory cortex, reflective observation involves the integrative cortex at the back, creating new abstract concepts occurs in the frontal integrative cortex, and active testing involves the motor brain. In other words, the learning cycle arises from the structure of the brain." (Zull, 2002, pp. 18–19)

While pointing out the greater complexity of brain functioning, he proposed that these regions of the brain were heavily, but not exclusively involved in the modes of the learning cycle. He describes a cognitive neuroscience experiment showing that monkeys can distinguish cats from dogs and, more importantly, in doing so they followed the sequence of the learning cycle in the brain regions that his theory predicted:

> *sensory* (perceiving major aspects of images of cats and dogs), *memory* (comparing the perceived image to remembered ones), *theorizing* (deciding the nature of the perceived image as cat or dog) and testing the judgment by a specific *action* (pressing a red button if dog and a green button if cat).

> These results come as close to a direct physical test of our theory as possible. They allow us to peer directly into a process of thought, and in so doing see the cycle of learning. (2012, p. 171)

Figure 3.1
The Experiential Learning Cycle and Regions of the Cerebral Cortex

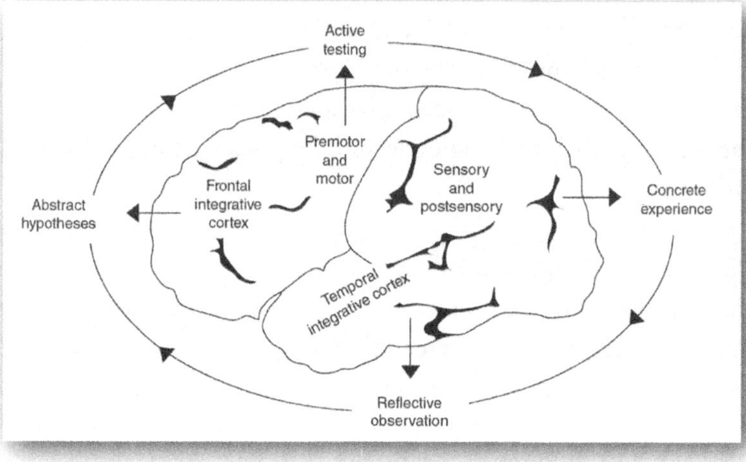

Reprinted with permission of the author (Zull, 2002)

In *The art of changing the brain* and his 2011 book *From brain to mind* he describes in great detail the brain structures and processes that influence learning and the complexities of the learning cycle model. One particularly important discovery is his identification of what he calls "the great transformation," the process of changing perception to action and the beginning of mind:

> The most striking line of functional division in the cortex is the boundary between the somatosensory and the primary motor. It divides the cortex into a front half and a back half. (2002, p. 175)

For Zull, action is the most important part of the learning cycle:

> First, since we always end up with action when we try to trace brain activities back to their origins; our main thesis regarding the central-ity of action is growing stronger. Second, the primary function of eye movements is exploration, not mimicry. Everything begins with explo-ration...The third suggestion has to do with mastery. The biological

pathway to mastery requires us to repeatedly use and recycle the action-perception transformations. We see, we do, we see what we do, we do something new et cetera, et cetera, et cetera! (2011, p. 40)

Zull argues that acting and "sense-luscious" real experiences that flood all the senses are the best for learning:

We are more likely to trust sensory input from the experience itself. I suspect that this confidence and trust in our sensory experience of the "real thing" has a calming effect on our amygdala. And a calmer amygdala means clearer thinking. (2002, p. 145)

Action closes the learning cycle and reconnects the processing inside the brain with the world. It generates consequences there that create new experiences that begin the cycle anew. This happens in two ways, one directly from the sensory cortex to the motor cortex and the other around the learning cycle through the back (reflecting) integrative cortex and the front (thinking) integrative cortex.

The Exploration/Mimicry Learning Cycle. In a young child, this transformation takes place through the first way, a direct route across this boundary illustrated by the simple reflex—stimulus and response with no intervening cognitive activity. More complex activities are exploration and mimicry. Exploration is the continuing interaction between sensing and acting as in the way the eyes continuously move to explore something. Sensory exploration increases the density and complexity of synaptic connections. Mimicry is copying sensory information and repeating it in action as when a child repeats her mother's words to learn language. Here, "pruning" takes place with neuron connections becoming more focused and less complex as skill increases. The neurons involved in mimicry are the mirror neurons described earlier. Mirror neurons match observations with actions and are located in Broca's area that is, with other brain regions, involved in language. This exploration/mimicry learning cycle is true embodied mind that is embedded in the immediate specific context through ongoing feedback cycles of perception and response that largely occur outside of conscious awareness (see figure 3.2).

Figure 3.2
The Exploration/Mimicry Learning Cycle

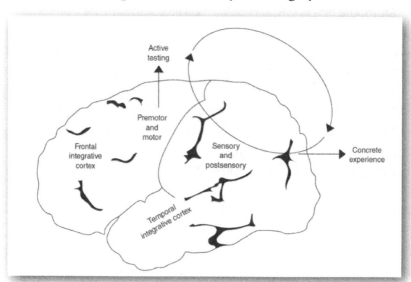

This, of course, is the stage of sensory-motor development that Piaget described as the first stage of cognitive development, followed later by stages that develop reflection and abstract thought. With those developments comes the full learning cycle shown in figure 3.1, involving conscious critical reflection, analysis, generalization, and hypothesis formation to control action. Full-cycle learning engages previous memories that generate goal-directed action, coming to the motor cortex where coordinated voluntary muscle contractions that produce movement are triggered. These carry out plans and goals originating in the front integrative cortex, including the actions of producing language through speech and writing.

As adults, we retain both the exploration/mimicry learning cycle along with the mature capacity for full-cycle learning. Immordino-Yang (2008) describes the two cycles this way:

A learner interacts with the social and physical environment either by mentally conjuring it or by directly experiencing it, she engages dynamic feedback loops between what she perceives and how she acts, thinks, and feels. As she moves through dynamic cycles of perception and action, actual, recalled or imagined, she creates skills that reflect three general dimensions, one that is perceptual, one that is motoric and one that is goal-directed and results from the convergence of the other two. Because she is acting and perceiving in a social and physical world, the goals she constructs will reflect the social, cultural, and physical constraints of the environment. (2015, p. 69)

The Instruction/Recall Learning Cycle. Another variation of the learning cycle places relatively little emphasis on the phases of the learning that are so important in the exploration/mimicry cycle—acting and concrete experiencing through the senses. This cycle might be called the "instruction/recall" learning cycle since it is strongly shaped by traditional formal education. It is based on an information-transfer model of learning, emphasizing reflective absorption of abstract information to be thought about with working memory and stored in declarative memory (see figure 3.3). The formal learning space in which it occurs usually has little room for action and testing of ideas in the world. Instead, the emphasis is on mental action through recursive iteration between thinking and reflecting about the meaning of ideas.

The instruction/recall cycle is a mirror image of the exploration/mimicry cycle that is seen by some as a superior way of knowing and a corrective to experiential learning. When they contrast experiential learning, defined as a naturalistic ongoing process of direct learning from life experiences through trial and error (contrary to the ELT definition that includes all four learning modes; see Chapter 2), with the systematic learning of formal science and education; the picture that emerges is that experiential learning is haphazard, unreliable, and misleading and must be corrected by academic knowledge. Buchmann and Schwille (1983) argue against education based on this definition of experiential learning, and further propose that the purpose of formal education is to overcome the biases inherent in the process of learning from ongoing life experience. They cite numerous sources of error in judgments based on experience, such as Tversky and Kahneman's availability heuristic where the availability of objects and events in memory such as those experienced firsthand tend to be overused. Similarly, vivid experiences tend to be weighted more highly than objective data. One's experience is necessarily in-fluenced by one's political and social context and thus is biased in judging social and political issues from other perspectives in the social order. They ar-gue that reading is in some ways superior to reflection on personal experience because it broadens possibilities and perspectives. Secondhand knowledge is more generalizable and can go beyond what is known from experience. They conclude, "The measure of education is the degree to which it allows all peo-ple to access the objective contents of thought, to theoretical systems, prob-lems and ideas with a range of implications not yet known."(Buchmann and Schwille 1983, p. 46; see Brehmer, 1980; Eisenstein & Hutchinson, 2006; March, 2010 for similar views.)

Figure 3.3
Instruction/Recall Learning Cycle

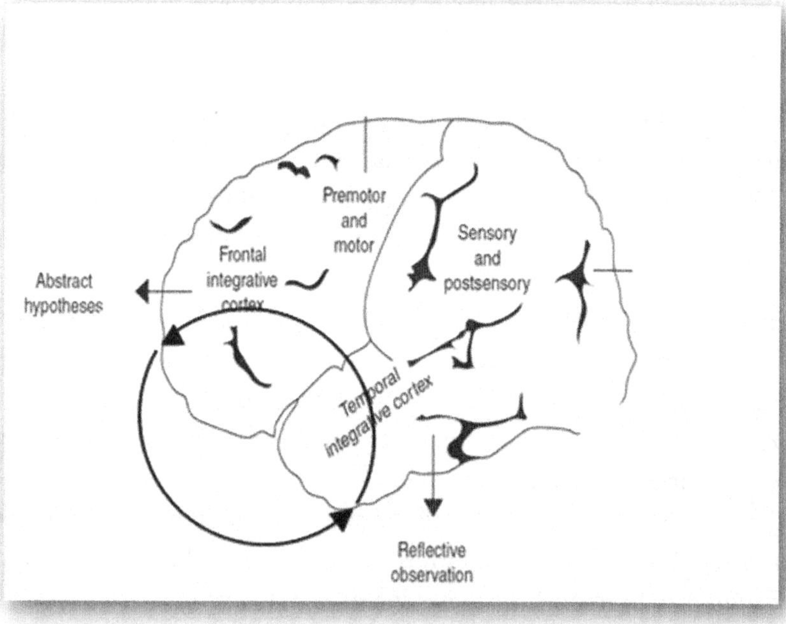

The focus on learning generalizable "secondhand knowledge" empha-sizes cycling between the temporal integrative cortex and the frontal in-tegrative cortex. Information in the form of abstract symbols, language, and images is received usually by auditory or visual senses and decoded in the back integrative cortex that integrates sensory information to create images and meaning. It is involved in memory formation and recall, enabling object recognition. It is also involved in language comprehension and spatial relationships. Memory is extended by neuronal networks distributed throughout the cortex that are dynamically growing, connecting, and decaying with other memories and our feelings about them. This plasticity results in the constant revision of memories over time. Supporting James's radical empiricism view that all modes of the learning cycle are experiences with reflection and thought as the "doubling" of a pure experience "in retrospection into a state of mind" is the intimate link between the back integrative cortex and emotional centers of the brain. The most important part of forming a memory is its link with emotion. To endure, the memories must have neuronal pathways to emotion structures such as the amygdala, nucleus accumbens, and hypothalamus.

The frontal integrative cortex uses short-term working memory to choose, plan, problem-solve, and make decisions. It makes judgments and evaluations directing the rest of the brain and actions of the body. It does this through abstract conceptualization, manipulating concepts and images to go beyond present knowledge to invent and choose new actions. These functions are most associated with intelligence, though Zull stresses that the frontal cortex is driven by emotion through the dopamine reward system of the nucleus accumbens. The emotional aspects of learning and problem-solving are as important as the mechanistic ones. They are driven by our desires and needs. He particularly emphasizes the feeling of ownership as essential for voluntary purposeful action.

Working memory is limited. With some help from long-term memory, about seven elements can be activated in working memory with only two or three under voluntary attention and control (Cowan, 1988). In working memory, we select memories and facts from the back integrative cortex and organize them into a sequence of actions that will solve a problem. This is accomplished by a unique network of neurons in the cortex that fire when stimulated but continue firing for a while after the stimulus ends, "remembering" the stimulus. But if another stimulus occurs, the firing is interrupted, making short-term memory unstable and limited in how much it can hold. Working memory literally requires work and paying attention to avoid being distracted.

Working-memory limitations have caused many brain and learning scholars to be concerned about cognitive load as a limiting factor in learning. For example, one important tip for educators about cognitive load is to keep lectures short and focused (with estimates ranging from ten to twenty minutes, covering four or five main points) and providing breaks to give learners time for mental rehearsal either alone or in pairs. Hoover, Giambatista, and Belkin (2012) have suggested that vicarious observational experiential learning lightens the cognitive load of full-cycle experiential learning. Similarly Kirschner, Sweller, and Clark (2006) argues that minimal guidance techniques—discovery learning, problem-based learning, inquiry learning, constructivist learning, and experiential learning—are not effective educational strategies for novices, arguing that these unguided learning techniques force learners to focus on both the what and the how of learning, producing cognitive overload of working memory.

Multiple Cycles of Learning in the Brain. In *Thinking fast and slow*, Daniel Kahneman (2011) identifies a fast-thinking experiencing self and a slow-thinking remembered/thinking self that is described by the two learning cycles described above. The fast-thinking experiencing self is based on direct, present-oriented concrete experience. This is the exploration/mimicry cycle of sensing and acting in the moment without intervening cognitive interpretation. The remembered/thinking self is constructed through remembered memories of concrete experiences that have been given meaning through cognitive interpretation through the instruction/recall learning cycle. While the remembered/thinking self is inevitably a biased representation of the directly experienced self, it is nonetheless the basis on which we make most life choices and decisions.

The experiencing self that lives each moment barely has time to exist…Unlike the experiencing self, the remembering self is relatively stable and permanent. It is a basic fact of the human condition that memories are what we get to keep from our experience, and the only perspective we can adopt as we think about our lives is that of the remembering self. (Kahneman & Riis, 2005, pp. 285–286)

Thus, the two learning cycles can operate in true dialectic fashion producing conflicting behavioral "advice." The intuitive sensing/acting cycle can respond immediately to a complex and rapidly changing context while the instruction/recall analytic cycle produces generalizations that only partially grasp the contextual terrain. Direct recursive cycling between experience and action or "trial-and-error" learning can actually produce skill mastery with little cognitive help. On the other hand, the instruction/recall analytic cycle draws conclusions that can direct attention to the proven aspects of a situation or problem that are particularly relevant and important, as well as to aspects of the situation that are absent when theory says they should be there (recall the Sherlock Holmes case of "The Dog that Didn't Bark," a clue that told him that the murderer was known to the victim).

A theory of hitting is too slow to direct the batter's eye movements that track the incoming curve ball and the swing of the bat; but it can help the batter prepare for the moment with training in proper body mehanics and pitch recognition based on analysis of the "book" on the pitcher. The conflict between the two cycles is most evident in clutch situations where a batter can "choke," performing poorly because of conscious attention to proceduralized skills (Beilock & Carr, 2001). Here the batter may override unconscious muscle-memory skills with self-conscious monitoring of their hitting skill and/or awareness of the critical implications of the situation, making what is typically an unconscious and automatic procedural response slower and ineffective.

An interesting experiment by Decker, Lourenco, Doll, and Hartley (2015) investigated the influence of the two cycles placed in conflict, comparing children and adolescents with adults on a probabilistic learning task. They predicted that, for adults, instruction would influence the processing of experiential feedback, while children and adolescents, because of their less-mature cognitive functions, would be less influenced by instruction. In the experiment, children, adolescents, and adults were all first given a learning phase where they chose between color-coded mouse holes, one with a high probability of reward for the hungry mouse and one with a lower probability. They received feedback after each choice by a picture of a happy or sad mouse and could thus learn from their choice experiences. They received inaccurate instruction that one of the mouse holes had a high probability of reward when it was in fact low, setting up a conflict between experiential reward and instruction advice. In a subsequent test phase with no feedback, children and adolescents showed less influence of the false instruction on their choices than did adults, while the instruction altered the processing of experiential feedback in adults. Children and adolescents remained attuned to reward feedback in the experiment, enabling experience to prevail in directing their actions. The authors explain their results in terms of maturation of brain function from childhood to adulthood:

> Previous research has demonstrated that providing adults with instruction or advice induces a behavioral confirmation bias in which recommended actions are valued more highly than those learned solely through experience, even when those recommendations turn out to be inaccurate...Many aspects of cognition e.g., working memory, attentional control and executive function improve as individuals mature from childhood through adulthood, typically conferring advantages for adults in learning and decision-making. Similarly, the effective recruitment of instruction to guide one's actions may generally be advantageous, allowing an individual to benefit from the knowledge and prior experience of others. However, our results suggest that this ability may also come at the cost of introducing pronounced bias in the processing of experiential feedback...The absence of confirmation biases in the children and adolescents observed in this study represents a paradoxical developmental advantage of youth over adults in the unbiased evaluation of actions through positive and negative experience. (2015, p. 10)...

Experiential learning is thought to depend critically on dopaminergic prediction errors, through which the striatum can learn the value of an action. Explicit instruction is proposed to bias this striatal learning process through the top-down influence of the prefrontal cortex that amplifies the effect of instruction-consistent outcomes and diminishes the influence of instruction-inconsistent outcomes on the striatal learned values. (2015, pp. 1–2)

Recalling the kite-shaped learning-mode preferences of the nine learning styles described in the previous chapter, we can see an association between the exploration/mimicry learning cycle pattern of brain organization with the Initiating learning style and between the instruction/recall cycle with the Analyzing style. One can imagine other learning cycle patterns of brain organization associated with the other learning styles. For example, the Imagining style would cycle between the sensory and postsensory region and the temporal integrative cortex with sensory experiencing, sparking recall of ideas, feelings, and emotions that further deepen experiencing and so on. The Deciding style would cycle between the frontal integrative cortex and the premotor and motor regions, generating hypotheses to be tested in action and goals to be achieved in performance. The complexity and plasticity of the brain suggest that numerous other learning cycle patterns are possible.

Memory, Learning, and the Brain

Research in neuroscience and cognitive psychology has increased our understanding of the role of memory in the experiential learning process. Most educators would agree with Semb and Ellis when they say, "Enhancing memory for what is taught in school should be a primary goal for any educator" (1994, p. 279). More strongly, Kirshner, Sweller, and Clark (2006) argue:

The aim of all instruction is to alter long-term memory. If nothing has changed in long-term memory, nothing has been learned. Any instructional recommendation that does not or cannot specify what has been changed in long-term memory, or that does not increase the efficiency with which relevant information is stored or retrieved from long-term memory is likely to be ineffective. (2006, p. 77)

Their exclusive emphasis on storing and recalling declarative knowledge from long-term memory is, as we will see, debatable; particularly by embodied cognition advocates and critics of constructivism.

Memory is not a unitary process; there are many kinds of memory that function in different way and are located in different areas of the brain. Some are localized in specific areas, while others are distributed throughout the brain. We have already discussed working memory. Information-processing models of memory suggest that information is received in the sensory receptors, lasting only a few seconds unless attention passes it to working memory. Sensory experiences that are not attended to are lost, giving a neurological basis for James statement, "My experience is what I agree to attend to." In working memory, the information is processed or "thought about." Mental rehearsal is necessary to maintain it in working memory. Working memory transfers knowledge to long-term memory semantically by meaning and association, connecting the new information with prior knowledge. Knowledge stored in long-term memory is permanent, with a seemingly unlimited capacity; however recall can be problematic and depends on how a specific idea is interconnected with "tags" to facilitate recall.

There are different typologies of the types of long-term memory systems (Tulving, 1985a). One distinguishes between explicit declarative memory and implicit procedural memory. Procedural memory is memory for how things are done; the acquisition, retention, and use of perceptual, cognitive, and motor skills. It is called implicit because the performance of a skill like riding a bicycle happens with little conscious awareness and does not need conscious control. It operates outside of working memory and is relatively closed to introspection.

A further distinction in declarative memory is between semantic and episodic memory. Semantic declarative memory is memory for symbolic words and symbols that represent abstract concepts, facts, names, ideas, theories, and other knowledge about the world. These memories are generalized in the sense that they are independent from personal experience and context. Episodic memory is memory for autobiographical experiences occurring in a time and space context, including the emotions associated with the experience. Particularly vivid episodic memories are called "flash-bulb" memories, such as where you were on 9/11.

These types of long-term memory all operate together, though they are located in different areas of the brain. In learning to play golf, for example, one may recall declarative semantic memories from reading "how to" books, episodic memories of playing rounds, and procedural memories from repetitive practice. The process of learning is different in these three different memory systems, and can be related to the three different learning cycles we have described above—the exploration/mimicry learning cycle, the instruction/recall learning cycle, and full-cycle learning (see figure 3.4).

Figure 3.4
Learning Cycles and Long-Term Memory Types

Experiential Learning Cycles	Exploration/Mimicry 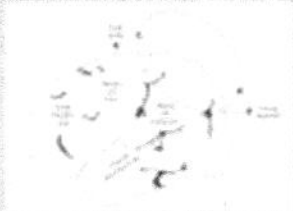	Instruction/Recall 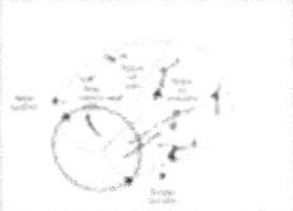	Full Cycle Learning 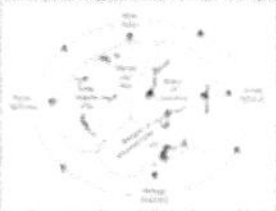
Long Term Memory Type	Implicit Procedural Memory	Explicit Semantic Memory	Explicit Episodic Memory
Brain Region	Pre-motor and Motor cortex	Frontal and Temporal Cortex	Distributed in Neocortex and Integrated in Hippocampus
Tulving's Type of Consciousness	Anoetic Non-knowing	Noetic Knowing	Auto-noetic Self-knowing
Time/Space Relationship	Present-oriented in Time and Space	Independent of Time and Space	Self Remembering Past to Imagine Future

Procedural memory retains learned connections between stimulus and response, including complex stimulus patterns and response chains such as those involved in learning to speak a language. It is created through the procedural learning process of the exploration/mimicry cycle repeating cycles of perception and action until all of the relevant neural systems work together to automatically produce the activity. Procedural learning occurs in the sensory and motor areas of the brain and does not involve the cognitive activity of working memory. In Tulving's framework, procedural knowledge is *anoetic*, unconscious knowing that operates only in the "now" of the present time/space context.

Semantic memory development is the primary focus of the instruction/ recall learning cycle of reflection and abstraction. Semantic learning and memory mainly activates the frontal integrative cortex and the temporal integrative cortex. In Tulving's framework, semantic knowledge is *noetic*, consciously known symbolic knowledge of the world that is internalized and detached from the context and conditions in which it originated. It is organized in terms of meaning, retaining conceptual representations including the meanings of words, numbers, rules, and social constructs. Such knowledge is capable of creative reorganization. It has the capacity to represent states of the world that are not perceptually present and to create mental models of the world that can be transformed through reflection and analysis.

Episodic memory is associated with the full learning cycle, integrating sensing, reflection, abstraction, and action. The hippocampus is the center for the integration of episodic memories, the different aspects of which are stored throughout the neocortex in visual, olfactory, and auditory areas of the brain. In Tulving's framework, episodic knowledge is *autonoetic*, including the self that remembers an experience in its fully lived quality. Remembering means having an experience of recollecting where images, feelings, and context-specific details come to mind, with the self mentally reliving the past experience. Episodic memory is organized and accessed in tems of spatio-temporal information. He argues that *autonoetic* consciousness encompasses extended subjective time and an individual's ability to use past episodes as a way of planning future action. He cites research (Tulving,

2005) showing that the same parts of the brain are used when remembering the past as when imagining a similar event in the future. He calls this *proscopic chronesthesia* or "mental time travel," allowing us to project ourselves either backward or forward in time in our personal lives.

Experiential Learning, Episodic Memory, and Long-Term Retention of Knowledge

Semb and Ellis (1994) conducted a meta-analysis of studies that provided quantitative information about the retention of knowledge learned in school. The sixty-two studies that they reviewed were focused primarily on learning and retention of semantic content, as one might expect given the focus of education on the instruction/recall learning cycle and semantic knowledge. The majority of the studies showed no differences between different instruction approaches in the degree of forgetting by students, though four studies described below did show differential forgetting effects:

> The common thread in these studies is that there were qualitative differences…in the way the content was taught. The instructional strategies investigated in these studies involved more that just giving students more practice or different feedback or a different delivery medium or display… *The four exceptions investigated strategies that more actively involved students in the learning process. We hypothesize that these strategies produced qualitatively different memories that are more resistant to forgetting.* (pp. 275–277; emphasis added)

Specht and Sandlin (1991) introduced experiential role plays of a lending decision to an undergraduate accounting course and compared retention with the traditional lecture method after the course and later after six-weeks, in a retest. While there was no difference between the two groups immediately after the course, six weeks later the scores of the control group declined significantly, showing an 18 percent decline in concept recognition and a 54 percent decline in problem-solving. The experiential role play group scores remained the same in concept recognition and declined only 13 percent in problem-solving. MacKenzie and White (1982) found that rich episodic experiences in school learning increased the long-term retention of knowledge. They found that high-school geography students who completed a program of study that included a fieldwork "processing" excursion that involved observing, sketching, thinking, and testing activities showed significantly greater long-term retention of knowledge than students who completed traditional classroom and excursion programs. Their interpretation of the results suggested that the processing excursion with active engagement produced easily recalled episodic memories that gave greater meaning to course content. Conway, Cohen, and Stanhope (1991, 1992) found that memory for facts, concepts, and particularly names declined over a very long recall period of 125 months while memory for research methods remained at high levels. They suggested that the high level of retention of research methods was the result of designing and creating their own research projects and analyzing the results, producing more stable long-term memory structures. Even small changes can make a differrence in long-term recall. Sturges, Ellis, and Wulfeck (1981) found that when text material was oriented to the job situation it resulted in greater retention after six months than text that was topic oriented.

The "qualitative difference" in the educational interventions in these four studies was the addition of an experiential component whereby students were involved in acting in a concrete contextual experience of the subject matter taught. This expanded the typical instruction/recall learning cycle of the traditional lecture approach to teaching semantic knowledge to full-cycle learning, producing richer episodic memories that made for increased long-term retention of learning. Herbert and Burt (2004) argue, " The greater the amount of remembering experienced early in learning, the more likely it is that the shift to knowing will occur in students." (p. 77) Similar to the above studies reported by Semb and Ellis, they found that students who studied material that was rich in cues to stimulate expisodic memory were more able to retain knowledge after a two-day interval and a five-week interval than students whose material lacked these cues.

Rich experiences that activate vivid sensory experiences, attention, and emotions, and require involved action are more likely to produce strong episodic memories that facilitate long-term knowledge retention.

The Tulving (1985b) remember-to-know theory of knowledge retention that Herbert and Burt tested suggests that a gradual transition from episodic to semantic memory can take place in learning. This occurs when episodic memory reduces its association to particular events and becomes generalized in semantic memory making it easier to be schematized in different theories and frameworks. In Tulving's (1985b) memory paradigm, the learner moves from "remembering" to just "knowing"; from contextual experiences to generalized knowledge. According to Herbert and Burt (2001, 2003):

> Two processes are suggested to be responsible for the remember-to-know shift, a loss of access to episodic details, and the development of conceptual organization. These processes occur from repeated experiences with the same information in different contexts, such as students encountering the same concepts and facts multiple times... resulting in a strengthening of the knowledge that is common to the varying episodic representations in memory. (2001, p. 618).

Hence knowledge becomes more abstract and generalized as it is decontextualized, enabling it to be schematized. When schematic representation of knowledge is formed and retained, the organization of knowledge in long-term memory becomes more stable and enduring.

> During early learning of a new domain, the individual usually encounters a large number of facts. Such pieces of information are often isolated conceptually for the student because while an expert or teacher may see this information within a schematic structure, it is most likely that the learner will not automatically see such inter-relationships...the information acquired early in learning is concrete rather than abstract and is bound to the specific context in which it occurs...to "fill" a developing schema with the details of

new concepts it is important for the individual to experience the concepts in concrete situations. (Herbert & Burt, 2004, p. 79)

Conway, Gardiner, Perfect, Anderson, and Cohen (1997) argue that this loss of episodic representation is necessary for schematization to occur and is facilitated by decontextualization through repetition of concepts in different episodic contexts allowing abstract generalization to occur across contexts. They suggest that this is an active process similar to that described by the learning cycle modes of experiencing, reflecting, and analyzing.

A further transition takes place in the development of expertise where declarative knowledge is integrated into procedural skills, becoming automatic and unconscious. This can result in a phenomenon known as "expert amnesia," where experts are unable to remember the steps and details of a procedure they performed (Beilock and Carr, 2001). Top performing athletes, for example, when interviewed after a game about a key play, often have no recollection of what they were thinking (see chapter 14).

The Mind: Embodied Cognition or Cognitive Construction

Finally, our analysis of the neural substrates of learning cycles and their relation to memory may provide some insight into the critique of cognitive constructivism by advocates of the theory of embodied cognition. Embodied cognition theorists view the mind as distributed throughout the body in constant interaction with the environmental context through sensation and action. In this view the mind is an embodied dynamic system in the world rather than a neural network in the head (Varela, Thompson & Rosch 1991). Hannaford argues that learning is holistic involving the whole body:

But we have missed a most fundamental and mysterious aspect of the mind: learning, thought, creativity and intelligence are not processes of the brain alone but of the whole body. Sensations, movements, emotions and brain integrative functions are grounded in the body. The human qualities we associate with the mind can never exist separate from the body. (1995, p. 11)

Embodied cognition theorists (see also Michelson, 1997, 1998, 1999; Seaman, 2008) see cognitive approaches to neuroscience as based on assumptions of Cartesian mind-body dualism, viewing the mind as residing solely in the brain. Fenwick defines constructivism as a process where:

The learner reflects on lived experience and then interprets and generalizes the experience to form mental structures. These structures are knowledge, stored in memory as concepts that can be represented, expressed and transferred to new situations...context is considered important but separate, as if it were a space in which an autonomous learner moves rather that a web of activity, subjectivities and language constituting categories such as learner. A particular context of learning presents possibilities from which learners select objects of knowing; thus the context influences both the content of experience and the ways people respond and process it. However, in the constructivist view the learner is still viewed as fundamentally autonomous from his or her surroundings. The learner moves through context, is in it and affected by it, but the learner's meanings still exist in the learner's head and move with the learner from one context to the next. Knowledge is thus a substance, a third thing created from the learner's interaction with other actors and objects and bounded in the learner's head. (2000,pp. 248-250)

This is certainly an accurate description of the instruction/recall learning cycle of traditional education and its aim to convert episodic memories into abstract schemas to be retained in long-term memory. Excessive reliance on this approach to learning, in the minds of embodied cognition theorists, has a negative impact on the effectiveness of educational systems:

The dominant approach to learning as a purely mental activity shapes expectations of student behavior held by parents, teachers, administrators and policy makers. Conventionally, students, or more specifically their brains, have been view as "empty vessels" or depositories into whom static knowledge can be poured. Adherence to this transfer model of education appears to have intensified since the enactment of the No Child Left Behind Act in 2001...As a result, most school children sit still hour after hour, day after day, week after week, year after year, expected to receive visual and auditory information through passive observation. In the meanwhile childhood obesity rates and school dropout rates skyrocket against this backdrop of sedentary education. (Osgood-Campbell, 2015, pp. 3–4).

Barbara Rogoff (2003) has pointed out the peculiar uniqueness of this approach to educating the young in Western societies by comparing educational practices in indigenous communities of the Americas with those of Western European heritage societies. In the Western societies, children are organized by tight age grades and segregated from the mature activities of the community, spending their time in institutions such as schools where they are taught generalized abstract knowledge to prepare them for their later life in the society. This system is supported and justified by models of development based on reason and abstract universal knowledge from the Enlightenment to Piaget. In the indigenous communities, children of all ages have wide access to community activities they will be expected to engage in. They engage in direct learning from ongoing experience, through observation, collaboration, and ongoing support from others. Her ethnographic studies of these communities suggest that children of these communities are more attentive and collaborative than Western middle-class children.

The above critique does not apply to the exploration/mimicry learning cycle that produces learning that involves the senses and whole body in a way that is deeply embedded in the environment through repetitive cycles of perception and action. This is more consistent with embodied cognition theories that "posit that bodily action and perception play central role in cognitive development. Some researchers in the field of Mind, Brain and Education explore this theory by researching the impact of sensorimotor activity on academic competencies such as language comprehension, mathematics and scientific thinking." (Osgood-Campbell, 2015, p. 3).

The full-cycle learning process proposed by ELT integrates the constructivist and embodied cognition perspectives into one that balances exploration/mimicry and instruction/recall learning much as Piaget proposed in his definition of intelligence as an integration of accommodation through the exploration/mimicry cycle and assimilation through the instruction/recall cycle. Full-cycle learning can integrate the sophisticated semantic memory concepts and schema and the contextual patterns of episodic memory with procedural learning to produce creative expert performance.

Four

THE SPIRAL OF LEARNING AND DEVELOPMENT

Throughout our investigations this idea of energy and growth under resistance seems consistently to be connected with the spiral, and we have found that idea recognized in the use of the spiral as a conventional decoration not only by the philosophers of ancient China but even by peoples as old as the Aurignacian civilization of 20,000 years ago... One of the chief beauties of the spiral as an imaginative conception is that it is always growing, yet never covering the same ground, so that it is not merely an explanation of the past, but is also a prophesy of the future; and while it defines and illuminates what has already happened, it is also leading constantly to new discoveries.

—SIR THEODORE COOK, *THE CURVES OF LIFE* (1914, P. 423)

In ELT, development occurs through learning from experience. This is based on the idea that the experiential learning cycle is actually a learning *spiral*. When a concrete experience is enriched by reflection, given meaning by thinking, and transformed by action, the new experience created becomes richer, broader, and deeper. Further iterations of the cycle continue the exploration and transfer to experiences in other contexts. In this process, learning is integrated with other knowledge and generalized to other contexts leading to higher levels of development.

In chapter 3 we described a link between ELT and neuroscience research, suggesting that the spiraling process of experiential learning is related to the process of brain functioning. The organization of the mind can be viewed as networks of learning spirals that are embodied in the neuronal networks that cover the surface layer of the neocortex. These neuronal networks are strengthened and enlarged by spirals of learning recursively cycling through these major regions of the neocortex—experiencing in the sensory cortex, reflecting in the integrative cortex, creating new abstract concepts in the frontal integrative cortex, and acting in the motor brain. Progress toward development is seen as increases in the complexity and sophistication of the dimensions associated with the four modes of the learning cycle—affective, perceptual, symbolic, and behavioral complexity—and the integration of these modes in a flexible full cycle of learning.

Life and Learning

The experiential learning spiral represents the highest culmination of a learning process that can be traced to the organization of life itself; the beginnings of which can be seen even in nonliving physical systems. Humberto Maturana (1970) discovered the learning spiral in his search for the answer to his question "What is the organization of the living?" What is the pattern of organization that characterizes all living systems and distinguishes them from nonliving physical systems? His answer was that the organization of the nervous system of all living things was basically circular; that living systems are, "organized in a closed circular process that allows for evolutionary change in a way that the circularity is maintained but not for the loss of the circularity itself," that is, a spiral. He called this process *autopoiesis*, which means "self-making"; emphasizing the self-referential and self-organizing nature of the network of production processes that produce and transform one another in a continual process of self-making through learning from experience.

With his colleague Francisco Varela, Maturana proceeded to develop the systems theory of cognition arguing that cognition, the process of knowing, was identical with *autopoiesis*, the process of life (Maturana & Varela, 1980). Their definition of cognition, however, was more akin to the holistic concept of experiential learning than the popular definition of cognition as thinking:

> The new concept of cognition, the process of knowing, is thus much broader than the concept of thinking. It involves perception, emotion, and action—the entire process of life. In the human realm cognition also includes language, conceptual thinking and all the other attributes of human consciousness. The general concept, however, does not necessarily involve thinking. (Capra, 1996, p. 175)

In fact Maturana and Varela argue that cognition is present in all living organisms, even those without brains or nervous systems.

The way in which *autopoietic* cognition is a learning process is further elaborated in the concept of structural coupling. Structural coupling defines the way a system interacts with its environment, recurrently renewing and recreating itself. The environment does not specify or direct structural changes in the organism because the system is self-referential and self-maintaining; but it triggers these structural changes that in turn produce changes in the future behavior of the system and its environment. Structural coupling describes the continuing path of the organism's structural changes over time and thus describes the course of the organism's learning and development.

The order-creating and self-maintaining characteristics of life can be seen to emerge in nonliving physical systems. The Belgian physicist and chemist Ira Prigogine won the Nobel Prize in Chemistry for his discovery of dissipative structures in physical systems. Dissipative structures arise in physical systems that are far from equilibrium, introducing unique higher-order structures that create "order out of chaos," to quote the title of his famous book. His research caused a revision in the then-prevailing view based on the second law of thermodynamics that says that the universe was "winding down," moving toward an ever-increasing entropy. Dissipative structures are created in this disorder and maintain and increase their order and complexity at the expense of the disorder around them just as living systems do. Prigogine believed that the discovery of these parallels between living and nonliving systems could help overcome the separation of man from nature that was fostered by Newtonian physics.

From Learning to Development: Constructivism in ELT

ELT is generally considered to be a constructivist theory of learning and development due to its heavy indebtedness to the constructivist approaches of Piaget and Vygotsky. These developmental theories emphasize that people construct new knowledge and understanding from what they already know and believe, based on their previous experience. While embracing this basic concept, ELT departs in some significant ways from these two foundational theorists.

Spiraling through the Learning Cycle: Linear versus Cyclical Development Piaget's constructivism describes the child's development from concrete and simple cognition to more complex and abstract stages of thinking driven by the dialectic tension between previous information acquired through the process of assimilation and the accommodation of these existing cognitive structures to new experience and information. While his account portrays a linear developmental progression toward internalized abstract thought independent of context, ELT depicts a cyclical return to experience in a learning spiral indicating that development is a continuous process of the integration of abstract cognitive frameworks with experience. Turner (1973) called this recentered thinking, in which the relationship of social knowledge to the specific knowing individual must be established in order for people to particularize general cognitive principles. This particularization requires the synthesis of affective and cognitive components. Although Piaget's developmental theory specifies how concepts gain independence from concrete experience, it does not specify the processes by which concepts are reintegrated with ongoing personal experience.

In Piaget's terms, assimilation ultimately takes priority over accommodation in his theory of development. O'Laughlin (1992) cites Broughton who argues that Piaget's assimilation/accommodation dialectic only applies in the infant's sensorimotor period of development and "the balance of the two tendencies breaks down in Piaget's accounts of post infant development, leading to an involuntary eclipse of the accommodation pole" (Broughton, 1981, p. 273). This served the purpose of Piaget's structural genetic epistemology whose aim was to describe the child's development toward the internalized logic of scientific rationality solely as an internal developmental process independent of culture and contextual experience. The implication for Piagetian constructivist education, however, was to promote disembodied thought and to distance the learner from "the world of everyday experience and concrete reality" (O'Laughlin, 1992, p. 800). Even Jerome Bruner, who was credited with introducing Piaget's work in America, notes that there is much his structural approach does not explain,

> Even from within the Piagetian fold, the research of Kohlberg, Colby and others point to the raggedness and irregularity of the so-called stages of moral development. Particularly, localness, context, historical opportunity, all play so large a role that it is embarrassing to have them outside Piaget's system rather than within. But they cannot fit within...the system failed to capture the particularity

of Everyman's knowledge, the role of negotiations in establishing meaning, the tinkerer's way of encapsulating knowledge rather than generalizing it, the muddle of ordinary moral judgment. As a system it...failed to yield a picture of self and of individuality. (1986, p. 147)

The ELT of development differs significantly from Piaget's theory and from most Piaget-inspired theories of adult development in its emphasis on development as a multilinear process that recognizes individual differences in the developmental process. In Piagetian schemes, individuality is manifest only in differential progression along the single yardstick of development—progression toward the internalized logic of scientific rationality. For Piaget, all development is *cognitive* development. Individuals are different only insofar as they are at different stages of development. In ELT, however, individuality is manifest not only in the stage of development but also in the course of development—in the particular learning style the person develops. ELT describes four developmental dimensions—affective complexity, perceptual complexity, symbolic complexity, and behavioral complexity—all interrelated in the spiraling process of learning. In this respect, the theory follows the Gestalt development approach of Heinz Werner:

> The orthogenetic law, by its very nature, is an expression of uni-linearity of development. But, as is true of the other polarities discussed here, the ideal uni-linear sequence signified by the universal developmental law does not conflict with the multiplicity of actual developmental forms...coexistence of uni-linearity and multiplicity of individual developments must be recognized for psychological just as it is for biological evolution. In regard to human behavior in particular, this polarity opens the way for a developmental study of behavior not only in terms of universal sequence, but also in terms of individual variations, that is, in terms of growth viewed as a branching-out process of specialization. (Werner, 1948, p. 137)

Alice Y. Kolb and David A. Kolb

Development as Transaction between Person and Environment.
Unlike the context-independent psychological process of cognitive development described by Piaget, the cognitive development focus for Vygotsky was on the historical, cultural, and social context of individuals in relationship, emphasizing the "tools of culture" and mentoring by more knowledgeable community members. Though still on a unilinear cognitive track, Vygotsky's social constructivism provided a strong counterpoint to Piaget, focusing as he did on the cultural tools, particularly language, and contexts that influence development. For Vygotsky, language influenced thought giving new meanings and ideas, whereas for Piaget language was the medium for the expression of thought developed through its own internal logic in a way that is not determined by language.

For both men, the relationship between thought and language is interactional, not transactional. Vygotsky's famous example of how Marxist ideas improve the conceptual development of the mind seems one-way and unilateral. Compare this with the transactional emergence of Gadamer's (1989) conversation, which is larger than the consciousness of any player, or with Freire's (1992) dialogue among equals (see chapter 10). In ELT, development is not an individual internal process of maturation but results from transactions between the person and environment. This is an important proposition, for it argues that the paths of development can be as varied as the many cultural contexts and systems of social knowledge, leading to many individualized and specialized paths of development.

The Gestalt foundational scholars, Kurt Lewin and Mary Parker Follett, as well as William James's radical empiricism, and Dewey's depiction of the difference between interaction and transaction, all portray an embedded and integrated view of learning as a transaction between the person and environment. The word transaction is more appropriate than interaction to describe the relationship between the person and the environment in ELT because the connotation of interaction is somehow too mechanical, involving unchanging separate identities that become intertwined but retain their separate identities. The concept of transaction implies a more fluid interpenetrating relationship between objective conditions and subjective experience, such that once they become related, both are essentially changed. Mary Parker Follett describes this process that she calls "circular response" in human relationships:

> Through circular response we are creating each other all the time… Accurately speaking the matter cannot be expressed by the phrase…I-plus-you meeting you-plus-me. It is I plus the-interweaving-between-you-and-me meeting you plus the-interweaving-between-you-and-me, etc., etc. 'I' can never influence 'you' because you have already influenced me; that is, in the very process of meeting, by the very process of meeting, we both become something different. (1924, pp. 62–63)

The ELT Theory of Development

The ELT developmental model (Kolb, 2015) follows Jung's theory that adult development moves from a specialized way of adapting toward a holistic integrated stage that he calls individuation; and Werner's orthogenetic principle that describes development as proceeding from an embedded lack of differentiation to a state of increasing differentiation and articulation to hierarchic integration. The model defines three stages: (1) *acquisition*, from birth to adolescence where basic abilities and cognitive structures develop; (2) *specialization*, from formal schooling through the early work and personal experiences of adulthood where social, educational, and organizational socialization forces shape the development of a particular, specialized learning style; and (3) *integration*, in midcareer and later life where nondominant modes of learning are expressed in work and personal life (see chapter 14).

The integrative phase highlights the importance of integrating the multiple dimensions of development. The transition from specialization to integration is a move from identification with a specialized approach to learning shaped by socialization into a particular career path that defines the self as its content, the abilities, knowledge, and values that it "has." Integration, following Jung, brings the emergence of nondominant approaches to learning into a holistic self-fulfillment that identifies with the process of learning, not *what* is learned.

Ya-hui Su suggests that the epistemological approach to lifelong learning is focused on "having," which is based on acquisition, storing, abstracting, and deferring rather than an ontological "being" approach of constructing, substantiating, and responding:

> Lifelong learning as authentic being is not simply based on thought and action but must also concern willingness or affect…Through the affective dimension…learners experience themselves as a willing cause of their own learning. When intuitive feeling is placed at the core of learning, a deeper, more primordial understanding is attained, where the learner and his or her world meet at the preconceptual level. (2011, p. 65)

The ELT developmental model portrays both ontological and epistemological directions of development. Through being with direct concrete experiences, intuitive affective knowing occurs, while through abstract conceptualization generalized knowledge is created.

Development through these stages is characterized by increased integration of the dialectic conflicts between the four primary learning modes (AC-CE and AE-RO) and by increasing complexity and relativism in adapting to the world. Each of the learning modes is associated with a form of complexity that is used in conscious experience to transform sensory data into knowledge such that development of CE increases affective complexity, of RO increases perceptual complexity, of AC increases symbolic complexity, and of AE increases behavioral complexity (figure 4.1). These learning modes and complexities create a multidimensional developmental process that is guided by an individual's particular learning style and life path.

Figure 4.1
The Experiential Learning Theory of Development

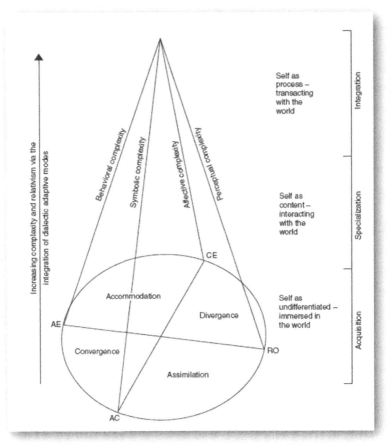

A study by Clarke (1977) of the accounting and marketing professions illustrates the ELT developmental model. The study compared the learning styles of cross-sectional samples of accounting and marketing students and professionals in school and at lower-, middle-, and senior-level career stages. The learning styles of marketing and accounting students were similar, being fairly balanced among the four learning modes. Lower-level accountants had convergent, abstract, and active learning styles, and this convergent emphasis was even more pronounced in middle-level accountants, reflecting a highly technical specialization. The senior-level accountants, however, became more accommodative in learning style, integrating their nondominant concrete learning style. Gypen (1980) found the same move from specialization to integration in his study of the learning styles of a cross-sectional sample of social work and engineering university alumni from early to late career. "As engineers move up from the bench to management positions, they complement their initial strengths in abstraction and action with the previously non-dominant orientations of experience and reflection. As social workers move from direct service into administrative positions they move in the opposite direction of the engineers" (1981, p. ii).

Notice that in both studies the transitions to nondominant learning modes in later life stages are associated with changes in the work environment. Development appears not to be solely a function of individual factors alone, but of the transaction between the person and his or her environment. For example, engineers who move from the "bench" into management may become more integrated because of the demands of the interpersonal and unstructured management role. However, choosing to move into the management position required individual development in interest and talent to do so.

The ELT developmental stages of acquisition, specialization, and integration by this analysis are not the hard stages of holistic cognitive organization defined by Flavell (1971) where there must be an abrupt jump to proficiency in the higher stage for all aspects of the total system. Rather they are soft or functional stages determined by one's individual life course where development occurs, not as an independent, internal, individual process; but through the spiraling of the learning cycle in a coevolution of mutually transforming transactions between ourselves and the world around us.

Kohlberg and Ryncarz (1990) argue that soft stages are optional, not necessary tracks of development. "Movement in these stages is an option for individuals who are induced by their own personalities and a life circumstance into those forms of reflection on life's meaning that soft stages represent." (p. 204). While hard stages only involve an abstract cognition, soft-stage theories also involve a concept of the self and self-awareness. Functional stages are environmentally influenced, referring to stages that emerge to perform new tasks or functions.

Is Up the Only Way? Stages models are unidirectional, indicating hierarchical integration of increasing complexity; requiring an explicit logic of what makes one position higher and more mature than another (Noam, 1993, p. 45). This unilinear and unidirectional assumption must be questioned for its upward orientation. Developmental advances are seen as higher, more all-encompassing abstractions that release us from our embeddedness in the ground and grind of daily existence. On the other hand, Mother Theresa in *Total Surrender* (1983) offers an alternative moral-development ideal of downward development, surrendering to committed engagement in the world and the struggles of others.

Carol Gilligan's refinement of Kohlberg's abstract justice-oriented model introduces an ethic of care and compassion that more appropriately seems like a downward embracing of caring and the concerns of others. She studied twenty-nine women considering abortions (1982). Her findings challenged Kohlberg's detached rational moral development theory by showing that women emphasize caring to deal with moral dilemmas in contrast to men's focus on justice. In *Women's Ways of Knowing*, Belenky, Clinchy, Goldberger, and Tarule (1986) challenged Perry's (1970) model of intellectual development in the same way. Their research identified two different dimensions of development—connected knowing and separate knowing. Women tended to use connected knowing, an empathetic approach that takes other's perspective to understand their ideas. Men, on the other hand, tend to detach themselves from others in an attempt to objectively challenge and doubt their ideas. Similarly, Baxter-Magolda (1992) in a replication of Perry's model found overlap between men and women in their positions in Perry's system but also found receptivity and interpersonal patterns of reasoning in women and impersonal mastery-oriented reasoning in men.

Knight and colleagues (1995, 1997) developed a measure of separate and connected knowing and related it to scores on the KLSI, predicting that separate knowing would be related to abstract conceptualization and connected knowing would be related to concrete experience. Concrete experience was significantly related to connected knowing, but primarily for men. However, men who scored lower on concrete experience had lower scores than female low scorers on connected knowing. In other words, high concrete experience men had connected scores equal to women who scored higher on connected knowing regardless of learning style. The interaction of gender and concrete experience was a strong predictor of connected knowing; but only gender predicted separate knowing.

Suzanne Cook-Greuter (2000) has recently suggest a modification in Loevinger's adult ego-development model suggesting that it is a curvilinear, not an upward and linear progression. Early development from the preconventional through the conventional stage of conscientiousness (specialization in ELT) is an upward separation from the ground of being; while postcoventional development (ELT integration) is a return to the ground with higher awareness or conscious unity. This is similar to Roger's curvilinear model of development in experiencing. His model describes a process whereby the infant child's pure experiencing process is blocked by the cultural introjections of significant others in the specialization phase of development only to emerge later as the person matures. For the adults he sees in therapy, the process is about recapturing the child's capacity to experience directly. He describes this as a process of:

> Letting oneself down into the immediacy of what one is experiencing, endeavoring to sense and to clarify all its complex meanings...the process is much more complex than it is in the infant...

For there is involved in the present moment of experiencing the memory traces of all the relevant learnings from the past...Likewise the moment of experiencing contains, for the mature adult, hypotheses about consequences...Past and future are both in this moment. (Rogers, 1964, p. 164)

Stages or States? For these reasons, in our recent work we have considered development in a way that is more context-specific, less age-related, and nonhierarchical. We have begun to depart from stage models of development to a view that recognizes the states described by the stage models; but sees these states as *modes of adaptation* that are not necessarily hierarchical. Differentiation and integration are not primarily broad life stages but continuous processes of development occurring throughout life. Working with many hundreds of individuals over the years, we have received pushback on the hierarchical stages of development, particularly from younger students who ask why they can't be at the integrative stage at their age. In some cases, when we talked with them in depth, it seemed that their primary concerns were developmental and holistic rather than specialized. Recently some millennials have suggested that their generation in general frequently operated at a more integrative developmental level.

We have redefined the three stages of development as states of adaptation that differ in their framing of time and space (Boyatzis & Kolb, 1999; Kolb, 2015—see figure 4.2). *Performance* is an adaptive state of learning confined to immediate time/space situations while the *learning* state extends the time/space frame to include similar specialized environments. The *development* state extends to the total life span and all life situations. Being in these different states of mind determines one's conscious experience. In the performance state consciousness is registrative, simply sensing the results of goal-directed action. In the learning state, consciousness takes on an interpretative role. Interpretative consciousness is primarily analytic where experiences can be treated singly and in isolation. In the development state, integrative consciousness adds a holistic perspective. Integrative consciousness is primarily synthetic, placing isolated experiences in a context that serves to redefine them by the resulting figure/ground contrasts. Another feature of integrative consciousness is its scope. Its concern is more strategic than tactical, and as a result, issues in integrative consciousness are defined broadly in time and space. Finally, integrative consciousness creates integrity by centering and carrying forward the flow of experience. The embrace of the dialectic nature of experience leads to a self-identification with the *process* of learning.

As one's state of consciousness changes, the same behavioral action is imbued with broader significance, representing an adaptation that takes account of factors beyond the immediate time and space situation. The infant will instinctively grasp the shiny toy before it; the young child may hesitate before picking up her brother's toy gun, knowing it will make him angry; an adult may ponder the purchase of that same toy gun, considering the moral implications of letting her child play with guns. Thus, what is considered the correct or appropriate response will vary depending on the conscious perspective used to judge it. When we judge performance, our concern is usually limited to relatively current and immediate circumstances. When we judge learning, the time frame is extended to evaluate successful adaptation in the future, and the situational circumstance is enlarged to include generically similar situations.

Figure 4.2
Performance, Learning, and Development Modes of Adaption

Developmental stage of maturation	Acquisition			Specialization			Integration		
Level of adaptation	Performance			Learning			Development		
Structure of consciousness:	Registrative			Interpretative			Integrative		
Extension in time	seconds	minutes	hours	days	weeks	months	years	decades	lifetimes
Extension in life space	responses	acts	tasks	projects	jobs	occupations	careers	lives	generations
Feedback structure	Goal-directed first-order feedback to achieve goals			Learning how to learn; second-order feedback to change goals and strategies			Consciousness/Integrity; third-order feedback to link goals to life purpose		
Hierarchic integration of learning modes	Many differentiated structures with low integration between them			Fewer but larger specialized structures; high integration within structures; low integration between structures			Development of complementary specialized structures; high integration between structures		
Concrete experience—affective complexity via apprehension	Direct sensing and feeling		Continuity of sensation and feeling emergence of enduring sentiments	Self-aware system of sentiments and values		Differentiating selfs and others' sentiments and values	Relativistic appreciation of value systems		Value commitment within relativism
Reflective observation—Perceptual complexity via intention	Attention		Watching—development of continuous images	Reflection; giving observations personal meaning		Creating alternative meaning and observation schemes	Relativistic appreciation of different meaning schemes and points of view		Intuition; choosing meaningful perspectives
Abstract conceptualization—Symbolic complexity via comprehension	Recognizing; enactive thought		Object constancy; "iconic" thought	Concrete symbolic operations		Formal hypothetico-deductive reasoning	Attaching concrete meanings to symbol systems		Finding and solving meaningful problems
Active experimentation—Behavioral complexity via extension	Responding to circumstance		Doing; short range intentional acts toward goals	Achieving; development of clear goals and longer-range		Risk taking; making goal and strategy tradeoffs	Experimental hypothesis testing; change goals and strategies based on results		Responsible action; accepting unknown emergent reality

When we evaluate development, the adaptive achievement is presumed to apply in all life situations throughout one's lifetime; and if the achievement is recorded as a cultural "tool," the developmental scope may extend even beyond one's lifetime.

Adaptive states of consciousness can be self-regulated and subject to deliberate development and flexible adaptation to meet different situational challenges (see chapter 6 on Deliberate Learning). Langer and colleagues suggest that adult development models have too conservative a view of change:

> There is too easy an understanding of what the next stage is going to be. "Development" is perceived as a time dependent continuity where the articulation of later stages "follows through" from participation in earlier stages. And there is all too definite an idea of what stages and possibilities lie ahead as persons make their way through development. (Alexander & Langer, 1990 pp. 135–136)

Individuals may be in any one of these states at varying times and situations in their life driven by personal choice or the challenges of their life circumstances. While these states may be typical of the acquisition, specialization, and development ELT developmental stages, there may be many exceptions in individual cases. Thus, a young person who has been primarily in a performance state may transition into a period in the development state "to figure out what to do with his life" or an older person in the development mode may return to the performance state to work on a project of importance to them.

Five

LEARNING IDENTITY

Our deepest fear is not that we are inadequate. Our deepest fear is that we are powerful beyond measure. It is our light, not our darkness, that most frightens us. We ask ourselves, "Who am I to be brilliant, gorgeous, talented and fabulous?" Actually, who are you not to be? You are a child of God. Your playing small doesn't serve the world. There's nothing enlightened about shrinking so that other people won't feel insecure around you. We were born to make manifest the glory of God that is within us. It's not in some of us; it's in everyone. As we are liberated from our own fear, our presence automatically liberates others.

—NELSON MANDELA, INAUGURAL SPEECH, 1994

Learning style, one's view of how they learn, is but one part of a larger aspect of self that we call learning identity. In our many years of sharing results from the KLSI with thousands of people, we have discovered to our surprise that not only do most people not understand their unique way of learning; many have not thought about what learning is or about themselves as learners. Yet, further conversation reveals that they do have ideas about themselves as learners and their ability to learn; ideas that are for the most part unexamined but accepted as "true." Our most gratifying experiences in interpreting the results of their KLSI scores with people have been when they come up and say, "My whole life I thought I was stupid because I didn't do well in school. Now I realize that it is just because I learn in a different way than schools teach." Understanding of one's unique learning preferences and capabilities and the match between these and the demands of learning tasks can increase learning effectiveness. It can suggest why performance is not optimal and suggest strategies for improvement, as well as help explain why some topics and courses are interesting and others are painful.

More people than we imagined do not think of themselves as learners at all and have what psychologist Carol Dweck (2000) calls a "fixed" view of themselves in varying degrees, believing that they are incapable of learning. If there is a starting point for learning from experience it must be in the belief that I *can* learn and develop from my life experiences. At the extreme, those who do not believe that they can learn, won't. Most learning requires conscious attention, effort and "time on task." These activities are a waste of time to someone who does not believe that he or she has the ability to learn.

A story from our recent work with an experiential learning-focused high school provides an example. A colleague at the school teaches remedial mathematics to freshmen and sophomore students. He was lamenting the fact that students were failing repeatedly to grasp the most elementary of mathematics concepts, and was frustrated that most never did any homework. He had just given a quiz that was an exact copy of the homework he had given the week before with the "heads-up" that the homework questions would be on the upcoming quiz. Still the majority of students failed. In desperation he asked the students what was going on. Why did they think that some students got better grades than others? Didn't they understand that if they just did the homework they would get better grades? To his surprise he found that students didn't believe that they could learn by studying and that the reason that some students got good grades was because they were "smart."

People with a learning identity see themselves as learners, seek and engage life experiences with a learning attitude, and believe in their ability to learn.

Having a learning identity is not an either-or proposition. A learning identity develops over time from tentatively adopting a learning stance toward life experience, to a more confident learning self that is specific to certain contexts and ultimately to a learning self-identity that permeates deeply into all aspects of the way one lives his or her life. This progression is sustained and nurtured through growth-producing relationships in one's life.

In ELT the concept of learning identity is based on the works of Carl Rogers and Paulo Freire. For both of these foundational scholars of experiential learning, people who see themselves as learners are those who trust their direct personal experiences and their ability to learn from them. Their primary focus is not on immediate performance or goal achievement but on the ongoing process of learning from these experiences. Instead of desiring some fixed goal they prefer the excitement of being in the process of potentialities being born.

In his classic paper on how values are learned, Carl Rogers emphasizes the central role of experiencing in the learning process of the mature person:

> He uses his experiencing as a direct referent to which he can turn in forming accurate conceptualizations and as a guide to his behavior. [The process of learning values is] fluid and flexible…highly differentiated…the locus of evaluation is within the person…There is also involved in this valuing process a letting oneself down into the immediacy of what one is experiencing, endeavoring to sense and to clarify all its complex meanings. (1964, pp. 163–164)

Echoing William James's radical empiricism, he emphasizes that experiencing includes not only direct sensations and emotions but also prior concepts:

> For there is involved in the present moment of experiencing the memory traces of all the relevant learnings from the past. This moment has not only its immediate sensory impact, but it has meaning growing out of similar experiences in the past.(p. 164)

He contrasts this approach of a mature learning person with fixed values formed through introjections acquired in youth in order to please loved ones:

These conceived preferences are either not related at all, or not clearly related, to his own process of experiencing. Often there is a wide discrepancy between the evidence supplied by his own experience and these conceived values. Because these conceptions are not open to testing in experience, he must hold them in a rigid and unchanging fashion. (p. 162)

In a very different context, Paulo Freire has also emphasized the critical role that learning centered on one's own personal experience plays in forming a learning identity. In *Pedagogy of the Oppressed*, he describes his literacy work with Brazilian peasant farmers, helping to liberate them from a self-identity formed through internalized oppression, the incorporation and acceptance by individuals within an oppressed group of the prejudices against them— "So often do (the oppressed) hear that they are good for nothing, know nothing and are incapable of learning anything—that they are sick, lazy and unproductive—that in the end they become convinced of their own unfitness" (19920, p. 49). His method for achieving the personal and social transformations necessary to escape this negative, fixed self-identity was to facilitate the creation of critical consciousness in these farmers through his version of the experiential-learning cycle that he called *praxis*, "Reflection and action on the world in order to transform it." In a definition echoing metacognition, Leistyna (2004) defines critical consciousness as presence of mind in the process of learning and knowing—the ability to analyze, pose problems, and change the political and cultural realities that affect our lives.

Freire argues that traditional education also promotes a form of internalized oppression and a nonlearning identity. It is based on a "banking concept" where all-knowing teachers deposit ideas in students' minds to be received uncritically, mechanically memorized, and repeated. He offers the alternative of "problem-posing education" that empowers a learning self-identity. This is based on a democratic relationship between student and teacher that begins with the here-and-now experience of students' lives and encourages the praxis of critical reflection and action to improve their lives.

Fixed versus Learning Identities

Carol Dweck (Molden & Dweck, 2006) has studied the "lay theories" that people have about themselves and others. In particular she and her colleagues have examined the differences between those who see their abilities and attributes as fixed and static and those who believe that they can incrementally learn and change themselves. Those individuals who believe that they can learn and develop have a positive learning identity. The learner approaches a difficult challenge with a "mastery response," while the person with a fixed identity is more likely to withdraw or quit. Learners embrace challenge, persist in the face of obstacles, learn from criticism, and are inspired by and learn from the success of others. The fixed-identity person avoids challenge, gives up easily, avoids criticism, and feels threatened by the success of others. Not surprisingly, students with a learning identity, regardless of their tested intelligence, are more successful in school than those with a fixed identity.

She studied these "lay theories" of school children, specifically their common-sense understanding of the brain and intelligence. With her research team, she found that teaching neuroscience findings about the neuro-plasticity of the brain improves their academic performance. Eight twenty-five minute classes for seventh graders focused on the message that "learning changes the brain by forming new connections and that students are in charge of this process" (Blackwell, Trzesniewski, & Dweck, 2007 p. 254) led to increased classroom motivation and reversed a decline in grades experienced by the control group. Similarly, Good, Aronson, and Inzlicht (2003) found that a similar incremental learning intervention led to significant improvements in adolescents' achievement test scores and Aronson, Fried, and Good (2002) found that such teaching led to higher grades among college students. The lesson of neuro-plasticity is that the mind can shape the brain as much as the brain shapes the mind.

Learning Identity and Math Anxiety in a Community College Developmental Mathematics Course. It is estimated that over 60 percent of the general population suffers from performance-inhibiting anxiety related to math. Students in postsecondary education are failing college developmental-math courses at an alarming rate, often exceeding 50 percent, leading to a shortage of people with the requisite level of math credits to complete a two-year college degree. The degree completion rate among the twenty thousand plus students in one community college was reported as low as 9 percent over a six-year period.

Samuel DeVries, while he was the Associate Dean of mathematics and technology at Cuyahoga Community College, created an experiential "learning to learn" course focused on transforming students' math-learning identity from one of anxious inferiority ("I don't do math") to one of confident self-efficacy ("I can totally do math"), as well as improving students' math-learning performance in developmental mathematics courses. The course, designed to be taken concurrently with a developmental-math course, provided for conversational group learning with active participation and self-reflection on students' learning practices and beliefs. He created a trusting learning space that was safe and inviting enough for people to take risks and abandon habitual behaviors, feelings, and perceptions. The teachers modeled transformation leadership behavior, involving others in the learning space by being authentically present themselves. Through self-directed learning into areas such as Learning Style and Psychological Type preferences, students begin to use inquiry, self-disclosure, conversation, and reflection to discover the interior world of self-directed learning. Further self-directed inquiry through journaling, and examination of affective information such as math anxiety helped students to learn to manage the motivation necessary for persistence through difficult courses. Self-directed learning behaviors (such as follow-through) or self-defeating behaviors (such as procrastination or struggles with authority) were examined in conversations together.

His research (Hutt, 2007) showed that the experiential course content and the teachers' attention to unconscious processes in the learning space, combined with the students' reflections on their learning experiences and negative self-talk, had a positive impact on learning. Students' mathematics anxiety was reduced, with students in the course feeling safer, more confident and efficacious about themselves as learners. Students in this "learning to learn" course performed a letter grade better than controls in their developmental-math course. Students' learning style preferences played an interesting role in the findings. Typically, in mathematics courses, students with an abstract learning style preference, which tends to match that of their instructor's teaching style, perform better than students with other learning styles. This learning style difference was erased for students in the experiential course where students of all learning style preferences earned better grades than controls. DeVries maintained that change from a fixed to learning self-identity requires a safe learning space characterized by unconditional positive regard (Rogers, 1951) from the teacher. This space reduces defensive behavior and allows persons to experience themselves as learners in a new way.

Learning Relationships and Learning Identity

Like other aspects of self-identity, learning identity is strongly influenced by one's important relationships. Learning identity is determined not by past learning successes and failures alone but by the self-attributions about these successes and failures that a person makes. These attributions are strongly influenced by important relationships. We have already seen Rogers's description of the lasting power that introjected evaluations from loved ones can have. Evaluations from others can also influence learning identity, sometimes in unexpected and subtle ways. Dweck (2000) has shown that teachers who reward students for successful learning by praising them for being "smart" actually promote a fixed identity and less expenditure of study effort ("I don't need to study because I am smart.") Peers also play a role in shaping learning identity. One of our colleagues shared this story of one of her undergraduate students who was struggling to preserve her learning identity in the face of stigmatizing messages from her team members:

> This student was working on a team project in my class that involved research and a team paper and presentation. She expressed frustration that once the other students in the team found out that she was taking developmental English (the course that students have to take if they score below a certain cut score on the SAT), the team members micro-managed her writing. Prior to discovering

this, each team member was "equal" and after she brought it up, they spent more time scrutinizing her writing than other team members. Her learning identity was challenged in this team interaction. Her frustration was that she was trying to change the stigma of being one of "those developmental English people." "I want people to think I am a good student, a good team member, a good writer…" Her conclusion was that she would hide this fact from future classmates, so that she could change.

Angela Passarelli conducted interviews with adult learners about their learning relationships and learning identity (Passarelli & Kolb, 2011), revealing two interesting patterns. First, learning relationships that create a hospitable space for learning seem to promote learning identity. This learning space provides an optimal balance of support and challenge, reminding us of Vygotsky's concept of the proximal zone of development (1978) where the learner is supported in incremental learning by models that set challenging but achievable goals.

Another intriguing finding is that learning identity may be contagious in the sense that those who have a learning identity tend to create relationships that stimulate it in others and those with fixed identities also act in ways that pass on fixed views of others. For example, those with a fixed vs. learning identity view of themselves show greater stereotype endorsement, perceive greater out-group homogeneity, and show greater intergroup bias and more biased behavior toward out-group members. They are more susceptible to the fundamental attribution error—believing that others' actions indicate the "kind" of person they are; underestimating the influence of situational factors on their behavior (Levy et al., 2001). One of our respondents describes how this contagion may be passed on through generations:

In the introduction I mentioned my Father and the impact that his upbringing has had on my Learning Style. I can recall stories of my Father describing a childhood in which he was shown very little love and was repeatedly told he was stupid. He was told that he wouldn't understand things. To this day, my Grandmother still says to him that she will tell him [confidential things] when he is old enough to understand. He is 63 years old. As a child, I remember my Father's dislike for any kind of game. On the rare occasion when he would play, he got angry and frustrated if he didn't do well and often quit. I now know that my father developed a "fixed" self-concept around learning. He was told he was stupid and wouldn't understand and therefore, in his mind, he was and didn't. He also criticizes educated people, which I can now link to the fixed self-identity. This fixed self-concept has implications beyond his attitude towards games—it impacted my learning development. As a child, I often heard my father ask me "What were you thinking?" when I did something wrong. I believe that contributed to the lack of confidence I have with my decision-making.

The Learning Identity Scale

Mai Trinh (2016) developed the Learning Identity Scale to help learners assess the extent to which they embraced a concept of themselves as learners. The original twenty-eight-item scale had five factors, the first and largest of which is Love of Learning. The other four factors were Learning Relationships, Learning Strategies, Resilience and Intentional Learning. The scale was further reduced to six items by eliminating redundant items in the first factor and picking the remaining items with the highest factor loading.

Her construct validity study of the instrument revealed a pattern of relationships with established constructs that increases our understanding of how a positive learning identity influences a person's self-image, attitudes, and behavior. Figure 5.1 shows the constructs that significantly relate to learning identity. Individuals with a strong positive learning identity showed greater openness to experience as measured by the so-called Big Five personality inventory (McCrae & Costa, 1987; McCrae, Costa, & Martin, 2005) and are less resistant to change (Oreg, 2003). They reported a wider range of interests (Berdie, 1945) and greater epistemic curiosity, "a desire for acquiring new knowledge and new sensory experience that motivates exploratory behavior" (Litman & Spielberger, 2003). They had greater self-esteem (Button et al., 1996; Dweck, Hong, & Chiu, 1993) and self-efficacy (Chen, Gully, & Eden, 2001). They were motivated by a learning goal orientation (Dweck, 1986; Dweck & Leggett, 1988), seeking to increase their understanding and mastery of something new rather than proving their performance competence. Their world-view was based on an organic paradigm (Johnson, Howey, Reedy, Gribble, & Ortiz, 1989) indicating a view of reality in terms of changing, holistic patterns. Persons with the organic view are imaginative, aesthetic, complex, and changeable. They tend to be fluid, changing and creative, nonconforming, participative, and imaginative in their cognitive style. They are interpersonally active, autonomous, and individualistic.

Figure 5.1
Construct Validity of the Learning Identity Scale

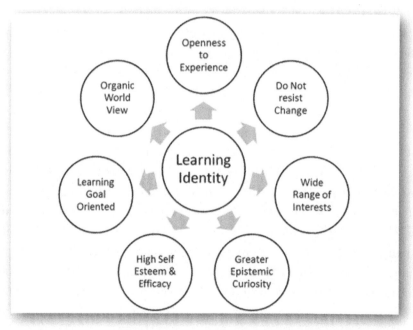

Strategies for Developing a Learning Identity

Becoming a learner, someone who can say with confidence, "I am a learner," is not accomplished overnight. Self-identity is deeply held and defended against experiences that contradict it. For the vast majority of us, our self-identity is a mix of fixed and learning beliefs. We may feel that we are good at learning some things like sports and not good at others like mathematics. Dweck and her colleagues argue that lay theories are domain specific, for example, one can believe that intelligence is fixed and morality is learned (Levy, Plaks, Hong, Chiu, & Dweck, 2001). Every success or failure can trigger a reassessment of one's learning ability.

Figure 5.2
Becoming a Learner

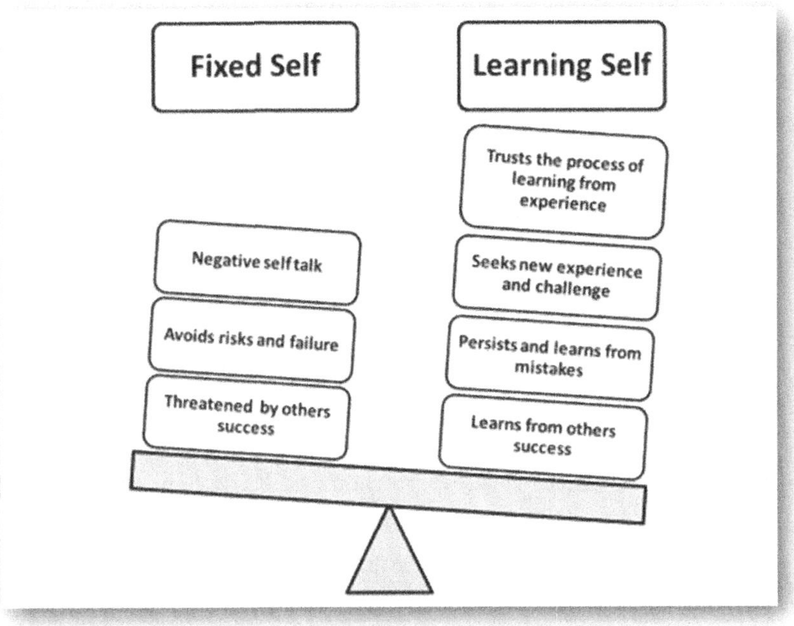

Figure 5.2 depicts self-identity as balancing characteristics that reinforce a fixed self—negative self-talk, avoidance of risk and failure, and being

threatened by the successes of others—and those that build a learning self—trusting one's ability to learn from experience, seeking new experiences and challenges, persistence, learning from mistakes, and using other's success as a source of learning. To develop your learning identity we suggest below some ways to overcome your fixed-self characteristics and improve your learning-identity characteristics, thus tipping the balance toward becoming a learner. **Trust the Process of Learning from Experience.** For both Paulo Freire and Carl Rogers, it is embracing the process of learning from experience that tips the balance from a fixed to a learning self-identity.

Trust your experience—Place experience at the center of your learning process, making it the focal point of your choices and decisions. This does not mean that you shouldn't learn from experts or the experience of others since this advice is also part of your experience. The key is to own your choice of what you learn and validate it in your experience. When you do this, you take charge of your learning and your life. A female student shares how she learned to own her experience by proactively creating a learning space of her own: "The first principle that would maximize my learning effectiveness is the ability and encouragement to make the learning space my own. By taking ownership of my own learning, I can incorporate the aspects that make me feel more participatory in my learning experience."

Trust the learning process—Avoid an excessive focus on the outcomes of immediate performance and focus instead on the longer-term recursive process of learning by tracking your performance progress over time. Rarely is a single performance test a matter of life and death, and to treat it as such only reinforces a fixed identity. Every performance is an occasion for learning and improvement in future performances. Karla Sahl, the Council for Adult and Experiential Learning 2008 Learner of the Year Award recipient, exemplifies a learner who is deeply committed to her learning process. She is described as the "*kind of woman who does not take 'No' for an answer.*" For us, what makes her a remarkable learner is her courage to say "No" to short-term gains and achievements and continue to create her own unique learning path toward achieving her long-term learning goal. Her five-year journey from waste technician to nuclear plant operator is a clear testimony of her strong self-identity as a learner.

Redefine Your Relationship to Failure. No one likes to fail, but failure is an inevitable part of doing something new. Thomas Edison provided a role model for the learning response to failure when he said "Failure is the most important ingredient for success." James Dyson, the inventor of the Dyson vacuum cleaner and founder of Dyson, Inc., sees Edison as a role model saying he, "achieved great success through repeated failure. His 10,000 failures pale in comparison to his 1,093 US patents. Each one of Edison's inventions, from the Dictaphone to the light bulb came from his inability to give up" (Yang, 2008, p. 28). Failures can also help focus your priorities and life path on your talents and strengths. In her commencement address to the 2008 graduates of Harvard University, J. K. Rowling described the low period in her life after graduation, which was marked by failure on every front, and talked about its benefits:

> Failure meant a stripping away of the inessential. I stopped pretending to myself that I was anything other than what I was, and began to direct my energy into finishing the only work that mattered to me. Had I succeeded at anything else, I might never have found the determination to succeed in the one arena where I believed I truly belonged. I was set free because my greatest fear had been realized and I was still alive, and I still had a daughter whom I adored, and I had an old typewriter and a big idea. (Rowling, 2008, p. 56)

Control emotional responses to learn from failure. Failures, losses, and mistakes provoke inevitable emotional responses. Yet it is important to learn to control emotional reactions that block learning and feed into a fixed identity. Golfers who slam their club and curse themselves and the game after a bad shot lose the opportunity to coolly analyze their mistake and plan for corrections on the next one. Another of our respondents, Carol, was a high-level executive who attended our master's program. She recounted in her paper her visceral experience during a team-building simulation exercise where she felt she had contributed to her team's disastrous performance. The Brushfire simulation required high-stakes decision-making in a very limited time period, where failure to make right calls would result in death of some or all team members. Because she felt that she let the team down, the experience provoked much reflection and she decided to turn it into a learning opportunity and apply the acquired knowledge into a real high-stake meeting few days later at work:

> The Bushfire simulation stirred two primary reactions: a basic hunger for understanding and recognition that my current position… occasionally requires analogous high-stakes decision-making in brief time period. How could I learn from this simulation and so be more effective in "real" ones? As chance would have it, the days immediately following the residency involved a high-pressure, rapidly developing situation at the office where organization leaders needed to consult and reach conclusions quickly. With the Bushfire simulation fresh in mind, I consciously waited and listened to the situations described and others' recommendations for action. In several instances my initial response was that we needed to gather more information before reaching a conclusion—even *if* time was short. In other moments during this situation I actually took the time to recognize my own emotional reactions (for example, to the need for quick responses) and then tamp them down. My goal was to consider options from a more analytical perspective. I wasn't always successful, but fortunately, one of the other participants in the discussion is overwhelmingly quantitative in orientation. I watched and tried to absorb as much as possible from the way he approached the issues at hand. Because of the complexity of the variables and individuals involved, we neither "burned" nor "escaped" this situation. But I felt my own contribution was enhanced by virtue of the lessons of the Bushfire simulation.

Risk Losing. Winning is not everything and too great a focus on it can block learning. Joel Waitzkin in *The art of learning* provides a handbook of his metacognitive learning based on his process of becoming first a chess master and then a martial-arts champion. He emphasizes the importance of losing in order to learn how to win:

> If a big strong guy comes into a martial arts studio and someone pushes him, he wants to resist and push the guy back to prove that he is a big strong guy. The problem is that he isn't learning anything by doing this. In order to grow, he needs to give up his current mindset. He needs to lose to win. The bruiser will need to get pushed around by little guys for a while, until he learns to use more than brawn. William Chen calls this *investment in loss.* Investment in loss is giving yourself to the learning process. (Waitzkin, 2007, p. 107)

Reassess Your Beliefs about How You Learn and What You Are Good at. It is important to consciously reflect on and choose how you define yourself as a learner. Often people are unaware of the way in which they characterize themselves and their abilities. Jim, one of respondents, retells how he successfully freed himself from a fixed perception of self and embraced his new identity as a learner. Being primarily an active learner, he was hesitant about accepting a new position that required competency in abstract skills:

> This was a dream job for any true Assimilator, but not for a forty-year-old Accommodator who started early in this new career with "negative self-talk." Fortunately for me though, I am able to positively embrace change and learned that I do have intellectual flexibility. So I was able to take this opportunity and instead of generating pain, I was able to generate a bounty of knowledge for myself.

Monitor the Messages You Send Yourself. Pay attention to your self-talk. Saying to yourself, "I am stupid," or "I am no good at..." matters and reinforces a negative fixed identity; just as saying, "I can do this" reinforces a positive learning identity. Beware of internalized oppression. Some of these messages are introjections from others that you have swallowed without careful examination. A male respondent who realized that his lack of self-confidence was a result of growing up internalizing opinions and views of others, decided to turn his learning identity around:

> I need a learning space where I can feel safe to express my opinions and I don't have to worry if they are not perfect enough. More specifically, I will accomplish this task by monitoring my self-talk while accessing the validity of the negative statements imposed by the circumstances or others thus limiting my internalized oppression. In addition, I will control my emotional reaction to perceived negative results to risk. Having accepted the ideology that failure is unappreciated success within results, I intend to let go of my toxic mindset.

Balance Your Success/Failure Accounts. Most of us remember our failures more vividly than our successes. For example, as teachers both of us tend to focus on the one or two negative remarks in our course ratings and ignore the praise and positive reactions. "Negative experiences have lasting negative effects *primarily* when they affect an individual's beliefs." (Blackwell, Trzesniewski, & Dweck, 2007, pp. 259–260). Sometimes it is useful to make an inventory of learning strengths and successes to balance your accounts.

Seek Positive Learning Relationships. Develop relationships that support the development of a positive learning identity and avoid those people and situations that make you feel bad about yourself and incapable of learning. One of the adult students we interviewed, Jennifer, describes how doing so can create positive learning identity contagion:

> What is important to me at this point in my life is I really try to align myself with people who will keep that dialogue going, expansive, limitless. If I start chatting with someone and everything is the worst-case scenario, I choose not to incorporate that person into my life. I'm just deliberate about that.

She gave the example of a recent job interview where she lost out to another candidate and chose who to share it with:

> It's funny because I was very careful about who I told I was going through this interview process…But she was one of the people I did tell because I knew that she would always keep it in a very positive frame of mind…It was funny, then when I called her and told her I didn't get the posting, there was no drama. It was like "I wonder what that was about?" And "I don't know, what do you think that was about?" So then we kind of dissected that. And it made sense.

> It was cool because with Rebecca when we dissected it, it was just OK, this is prepping. This is life. Is this what you really wanted? Helping you to get clear, versus some people would have been like "Oh my god, I'm so sorry. You must be so depressed." And it just takes you down and stops your learning process and stops your forward advancement.

> By sharing that with her and talking about it, keeping it in an optimistic frame of mind and laughing, it's like it started opening up all these other doors. Then two weeks later, this person sits next to me on the plane and gives me all that information that that job wasn't what it looked like on paper. And then when I get off the plane she taps me on the shoulder, and asks if I have a business card. You know "I might know of people at WHO or at FOA in Rome," or whatever. She said, "Keep in touch, you just never know." And that would have never happened. The conversation with Rebecca left it in a very positive frame. If I had gone the other route, then when I sat down next to that woman, I might have had a very different conversation. And she wouldn't have asked me for my business card and then in turn given me hers. I mean, I didn't ask. So that's for me the learning.

Six

Deliberate Experiential Learning

I believe that we learn by practice. Whether it means to learn to dance by practicing dancing or to learn to live by practicing living, the principles are the same. In each, it is the performance of a dedicated precise set of acts, physical or intellectual, from which comes shape of achievement, a sense of one's being, a satisfaction of spirit. One becomes, in some area, an athlete of God. Practice means to perform, over and over again in the face of all obstacles, some act of vision, of faith, of desire. Practice is a means of inviting the perfection desired.

—Martha Graham

I am a woman in process. I'm just trying like everybody else. I try to take every conflict, every experience, and learn from it. Life is never dull.

—Oprah Winfrey

A primary purpose of the KLSI 4.0 is empower learners to understand and intentionally improve their learning capability. By using the experiential-learning model, learners can better understand the learning process, themselves as learners, and the appropriate use of learning strategies based on the learning task and environment. This process of experiencing with awareness to create meaning and make choices is what we call deliberate experiential learning. Deliberate learning requires mastery of experiential learning, or more particularly, it requires a personal understanding of one's unique way of learning from experience and the ability to intentionally direct and control one's learning. When individuals engage in the process of learning by reflective monitoring of the learning process they are going through, they can begin to understand the important aspects of learning: how they move through each stage of the learning cycle, the way their unique learning style fits with how they are being taught, and the learning demands of what is being taught. This comparison results in strategies for action that can be applied in their ongoing learning process.

This ability to deliberately learn from experience is perhaps the most powerful source of adult learning. In leadership development for example, Ashford and DeRue point out:

> Consider the fact that leadership development programs customarily teach leadership concepts and skills, but rarely do development programs teach individuals how to learn leadership—which is ironic considering that over 70 percent of leadership development occurs as people go through the ups and downs of challenging, developmental experiences on the job. We contend that the return on investment in leadership development would be much greater if organizations invested in developing individuals' skills related to the learning of leadership from lived experiences, as opposed to simply teaching leadership concepts, frameworks, and skills. (2012, p. 147).

To assist learners in the application of experiential-learning principles in their own lives, deliberate experiential learning draws on theories in three areas: metacognition (Kolb & Kolb, 2009), mindfulness (Yeganeh, 2006; Yeganeh & Kolb, 2009), and studies of expert learning called deliberate practice (Ericsson, Krampe, & Tesch-Römer, 1993).

The central focus of deliberate experiential learning is individuals' conscious metacognitive control of their learning process. Metacognition enables them to monitor and select learning approaches that work best for them in different learning situations. We have identified six areas of metacognitive practice that are important for effective deliberate experiential learning. The six areas are deep experiencing, learning style, learning identity, learning spaces, learning relationships, and deliberate practice (see figure 6.1). These practices encompass skills that enable learners to become aware of how they learn and to evaluate and adapt these skills to become increasingly effective at learning.

Figure 6.1
The Practices of Deliberate Learning

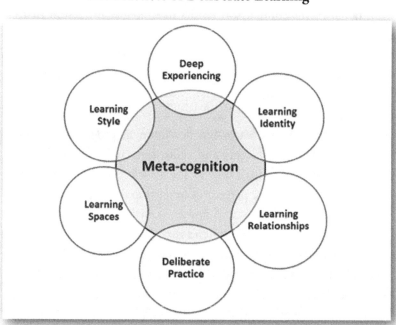

Metacognition—the Key to Deliberate Learning

Deliberate experiential learning requires individual conscious metacognitive control of oneself, one's goals, and of one's learning process by self-monitoring and selection of learning approaches that work best in different learning situations. James Zull described metacognition as the culmination of the journey from brain to mind—the mind's ability to reflect on itself and control its own process:

> In many ways, a learner's awareness and insight about development of her own mind is the ultimate and most powerful objective of education; not just thinking, but thinking about thinking. It is when we begin to comprehend our own thought that we can sense progress in our journey toward mind. This comprehension may be our highest and most complex mental capability. It is the thread that weaves back and forth through the cloth of the mind...Gaining a metacognitive state of mind offers greater possibilities for experiencing the joy of learning than, perhaps, any of the other objectives or goals discussed so far. (2011, p. 259)

The concept of metacognition originated in the work of William James in his examination of the role of attention in experience and his ideomotor theory of action described in his two-volume magnum opus, *The Principles of Psychology* (1890). For James, attention plays its focus "like a spotlight" across the field of consciousness in a way that is sometimes involuntary, as when a bright light or loud noise "captures" our attention; but often attention is voluntary. Voluntary attention is determined by one's interest in the object of attention. James defines a spiral of interest-attention-selection that creates a continuous ongoing flow of experience summarized in the pithy statement—"My experience is what I agree to attend to." (1890, p. 403). He defines interest as an "intelligible perspective" that directs attention and ultimately the selection of some experiences over others. Selection feeds back to refine and integrate a person's intelligible perspective serving as "the very keel on which our mental ship is built" (James, cited in Leary, 1992, p. 157). In his chapter on will, James developed a theory of intentional action, which is essential for any metacognitive knowledge to be useful in improving one's learning ability. His ideomotor action theory states that an idea firmly focused in consciousness will automatically issue forth into behavior—"Every representation of a movement awakens in some degree the actual movement which is the object; and awakens it in a maximum degree whenever it is not kept from so doing by an antagonistic representation present simultaneously to the mind" (James, 1890, p. 526).

Flavell (1979) reintroduced the concept of metacognition in contemporary psychology, dividing metacognitive knowledge into three subcategories: (1) Knowledge of person variables referring to general knowledge about how human beings learn and process information, as well as individual knowledge of one's own learning processes, (2) Task variables including knowledge about the nature of the task and what it will require of the individual, (3) Knowledge about strategy variables including knowledge about ways to improve learning as well as conditional knowledge about when and where it is appropriate to use such strategies. Until recently research on metacognitive learning has explored the influence of only relatively simple models of learning. For example, a study of fifth-grader self-paced learning of stories found that the best students spent more time studying difficult rather than easy stories, while there was no difference in study times for the poorer students. The findings suggest that the poorer students lacked a metacognitive model that dictated a strategy of spending more time on difficult learning tasks (Owings, Peterson, Bransford, Morris, and Stein, 1980).

More recently, Nelson (1996) and his colleagues have developed a model that emphasizes processes of monitoring and control in metacognition. An individual monitors their learning process at the level of their experience and relates the observations to a model of their learning process at the meta-level. The results of the conscious observation are used to modify the metacognitive model, which in turn controls actual learning at the experience level. We (Kolb & Kolb, 2009) have suggested a modification of Nelson's metacognitive model based on ELT that can help learners gain a better understanding of the learning process, themselves as learners, and the appropriate use of learning strategies based on the learning task and environment (see figure 6.2). Here an individual is engaged in the process of learning something at the level of direct concrete experience. His reflective monitoring of the learning process he is going through is compared at the abstract meta-level with his idealized experiential learning model that includes concepts such as: whether he is spiraling through each stage of the learning cycle, the way his unique learning style fits with how he is being taught, and the learning demands of what he is learning. This comparison results in strategies for action that return him to the concrete learning situation through the control arrow.

Figure 6.2
**Nelson's Metacognitive Model Modified to Include the
ELT Learning Cycle**

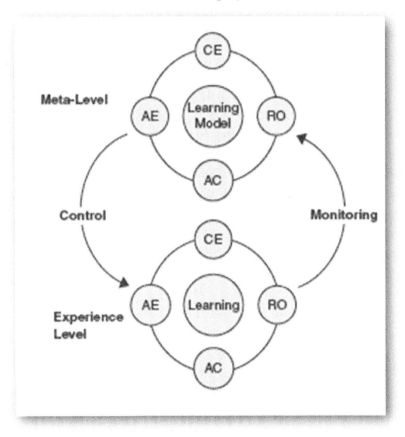

Deep Experiencing

It is not experience, but experiencing that is the source of learning. As educators we can make the mistake of assuming when we create learning experiences like field projects, role plays, and other experiential exercises that learners are experiencing and "getting out" of the exercise the lessons we intend. However, everyone's normal everyday experience is notoriously conservative. Dewey came to the realization that most experience is culturally mediated by many previous trips around the learning cycle:

> Experience is already overlaid and saturated with the products of the reflection of past generations and by-gone ages. It is filled with interpretations, classifications, due to sophisticated thought, which have become incorporated into what seems to be fresh naïve empirical material. It would take more wisdom than is possessed by the wisest historical scholar to track all off these absorbed borrowings to their original sources. (Dewey, 1933, p. 40)

He called this "empirical experience," which was conservative, tradition bound, and prone to conformity and dogmatism. To initiate reflection and learning he emphasized that this normal flow of experience must be interrupted by deep experiencing, such as when we are "stuck" with a problem or difficulty or "struck" by the strangeness of something outside of our usual experience (Dewey, 1933). Paulo Freire made a similar point arguing that *espanto* or shock, an intense direct experience such as a majestic sunrise, was necessary for deep learning.

Mary Parker Follett in *Creative Experience* (1924) emphasized the importance of surrendering past conceptions to the ongoing immediate experiencing of the learning cycle:

> The people who "learn by experience" often make great messes of their lives, that is, if they apply what they have learned from a past incident to the present, deciding from certain appearances that the circumstances are the same, forgetting that no two situations can

ever be the same…All that I am, all that life has made me, every past experience that I have had—woven into the tissue of my life—I must give to the new experience. That past experience has indeed not been useless, but its use is not in guiding present conduct by past situations. We must put everything we can into each fresh experience, but we shall not get the same things out which we put in if it is a fruitful experience, if it is part of our progressing life…We integrate our experience, and then the richer human being that we are goes into the new experience; again we give our self and always by giving rise above the old self. (Follett, 1924, pp. 136–137)

We refer to the process of stripping present-moment experiencing from habitual biases and interpretations as deep experiencing. The goal of deep experiencing is what James called "pure experience." Taylor and Wozniak (1996) note that James's radical empiricism, while foreign to Western thinking, was highly compatible with Eastern metaphysics and psychology, giving the example of the Theraveda Buddhist image of moment consciousness as a string of pearls. The great Japanese Zen philosopher Kitaro Nishida (1911, 1990), who sought to integrate Eastern and Western thought, embraced James's radical empiricism, making pure experience the center of his life's work. While for James pure experience was a philosophical concept rarely experienced fully, for Nishida it was an experience to be lived fully and cultivated as a path to realization of an authentic, integrated humanity,

To experience means to know facts just as they are; to know in accordance with fact by completely relinquishing one's own fabrications. What we usually refer to as experience is adulterated with some sort of thought, so by pure I am referring to the state of experience just as it is, without the least addition of deliberative discrimination. The moment of seeing a color or hearing a sound, for example, is prior not only to the thought that the color or sound is the activity of an external object or that one is sensing it, but also to the judgment of what the color or sound might be. In this regard, pure experience is identical with direct experience. When one directly experiences one's own state of consciousness, there is not yet a subject or an object, and knowing and its object are completely united. This is the most refined type of experience. (1990, p. 3)

Perhaps inspired by the Theraveda image of moment consciousness as a string of pearls, Daniel Kahneman has argued that our lives are made up of a succession of moments of pure experience:

An individual's life could be described—at impractical length—as a string of moments. A common estimate is that each of these moments of psychological present may last up to 3 seconds, suggesting that people experience some 20,000 moments in a waking day, and upwards of 500 million moments in a 70 year life. Each moment can be given a rich multidimensional description...What happens to these moments? The answer is straightforward: with very few exceptions, they simply disappear. (Kahneman & Riis, 2005, p. 285)

Kahneman says we have two selves, an experiencing self that lives briefly in each of these moments, and a remembering/thinking self constructed through remembered memories of concrete experiences that have been given meaning through cognitive interpretation. His identification of the experiencing and the remembered thinking self are consistent with James's dual-knowledge theory—knowledge of acquaintance and knowledge about, which formed the foundation for contemporary work on dual-processing (Evans, 2008) made popular by Kahneman's recent book *Thinking, Fast and Slow* (2011).

Unlike the experiencing self, the remembering/thinking self is relatively stable and permanent. "It is a basic fact of the human condition that memories are what we get to keep from our experience, and the only perspective we can adopt as we think about our lives is that of the remembering/thinking self." (2005, p. 286) The authors go on to say that these memories of experience are flawed by a number of cognitive illusions and are often wrong.

For example, a study of vacations found substantial difference between recalled enjoyment and actual experienced enjoyment. It was recalled enjoyment that predicted a desire to repeat the vacation. In another study, people predict that they are happier on their birthday, but actual experience of happiness is the same as other days. While the remembered self is inevitably a biased representation of the directly experienced self, it is nonetheless the basis on which we make most life choices and decisions. Practices of deep experiencing facilitate deliberate learning by empowering the experiencing self. Focusing on here-and-now experiencing and mindful cycling through the learning cycle can increase the congruence between the thinking and experiencing self.

Deep-Experiencing Practices. There are other ways besides "shock and awe" to strip a momentary concrete experience from its judgmental habitual biases. Two major deep-experiencing practices are: one derived from Carl Rogers's client-centered therapy and the other from concepts of mindfulness.

Mindfulness. The practice of mindfulness aims to overcome automaticity and to reach direct, pure experience through mindful awareness and attention. Meditative mindfulness is the core of Buddhist meditation; advocating the development of mindfulness through a discipline of anchoring the mind in the present moment. This is often accompanied with a practice of awareness and acceptance through breathing. Kabat-Zinn (1994, 2003) defines mindfulness as "paying attention in a particular way—on purpose, in the present moment, and non-judgmentally" (1994, p. 4). Nonjudgment, in mindfulness theory, is accepting the current state as part of a constant flow of changing experiences. This paradigm suggests that letting go of judgment strengthens the mind, and it challenges the illusion that overthinking something gives one control over it. Brown and Ryan (2003a) quote William James who stated that "Compared to what we ought to be, we are only half awake." They go on to say, "Mindfulness captures a quality of consciousness that is characterized by clarity and vividness of current experience and functioning that stands in contrast to the mindless less 'awake' states of habitual or automatic functioning that may be chronic for many individuals" (2003a, p. 823).

Our research on mindfulness and experiential learning (Yeganeh, 2006; Yeganeh & Kolb, 2009) suggests that the practice of mindfulness can help individuals learn from experience by enhancing presence and intentional attention. Yeganeh (2006) studied two predominant streams of mindfulness research and practice, meditative mindfulness and socio-cognitive mindfulness. Socio-cognitive mindfulness emphasizes cognitive categorization, context, and situational awareness. Ellen Langer relates this form of mindfulness to learning:

> When we are mindful, we implicitly or explicitly (1) view a situation from several perspectives, (2) see information presented in the situation as novel, (3) attend to the context in which we perceive the information, and eventually (4) create new categories through which this information may be understood." (Langer,1997, p. 111)

Mindfulness from the socio-cognitive perspective requires broadening of one's repertoire of cognitive categories. The idea of creating new categories was influenced by Langer's earlier studies in bias and prejudice. Explaining the practical benefits, she illustrates that "If we describe someone we dislike intensely, a single statement usually does it. But if, instead, we are forced to describe the person in great detail, eventually there will be some quality we appreciate" (Langer, 1989, p. 66). One of the reasons Langer's work is so compelling is that it thoroughly supports the notion that simple labels (e.g. good and evil) do not accurately reflect the complexity of the world. Instead they allow for mindless rationalizations that justify a broad range of dysfunctional behaviors, from ineffective to criminal.

Supporting the links between learning from experience and mindfulness, Yeganeh's research found that individuals who scored high on Langer's mindfulness scale emphasized direct concrete experience in their learning style while also scoring lower on reflective observation, suggesting that they were not "lost in thought" or rumination but were attentive to their immediate experiences. The results suggest two mindful-experiencing practices to help individuals learn from experience:

Focus on here-and-now experience uncluttered by preconceptions and bias. To be present and engaged in direct experience, one must anchor in present-centered awareness by attending to the five senses. One of the strongest ways to attend to the present moment is through calm and aware breathing. Attending to the present moment serves to quiet the mind; reducing automatic, habitual patterns of thinking and responding. This presence enhances Concrete Experience and allows the learning cycle to begin. In a sense, we cannot learn from experience if we do not first *have* an experience, and often automatic routines make it difficult for direct experiencing in the moment to occur.

Intentional attention. Being aware and choiceful about what we are attending to is, as James says, the process that creates our experience. Mindfulness practice can help us consider *how* we choose to process and learn from the events in our lives. By intentionally guiding the learning process and paying attention to how we are going through the phases of the learning cycle, we make ourselves through learning. We are in a real sense what we learn. How and what we learn determines the way we process the possibilities of each new emerging experience, which in turn determines the range of choices and decisions we see. The choices and decisions we make to some extent determine the events we live through, and these events influence our future choices. Thus, we create ourselves through the choices of the actual occasions we live through. For many, this learning choice is relatively unconscious, an autopilot program for learning. Mindfulness can put the control of our learning and our life back in our hands.

Focusing. Rogers's nondirective therapy method brings awareness and trust of one's inner experience through the creation of a psychologically safe environment of unconditional positive regard where clients feel that they are valued as persons and as a result can slowly begin to value the different aspects of themselves, opening the possibility for deep experiencing. Rogers describes this process of deep experiencing in this way:

> There is a growing and continuing sense of acceptant owner-ship of these changing feelings, a basic trust in his own process...

Experiencing has lost almost completely its structure bound aspects and becomes process experiencing—that is, the situation is experienced and interpreted in its newness, not as the past...The self becomes increasingly simply the subjective and reflexive awareness of experiencing. The self is much less frequently a perceived object, and much more frequently something confidently felt in process...Personal constructs are tentatively reformulated, to be validated against further experience, but even then to be held loosely... Internal communication is clear, with feelings and symbols well matched, and fresh terms for new feelings. There is the experiencing of effective choice of new ways of doing. (Rogers, 1961, pp. 151–152)

Eugene Gendlin, a phenomenological philosopher who developed a philosophy of implicit knowing, worked with Carl Rogers at the University of Chicago in the 1950s isolating the client's process of experiencing as the key transformative aspect of therapy. When he studied this kind of experiencing among clients of Rogerian and other forms of psychotherapy (1961, 1962), he discovered that assessments of a client's experiencing ability in the first two therapy sessions predicted the success or failure of the therapy. Experiencing ability was more important than anything the therapist did in predicting outcomes. Since then, many studies have been conducted reporting the correlation of higher experiencing levels with positive therapeutic outcomes (Hendricks, 2001).

Gendlin calls this "focusing," an embodied way of experiencing that is beneath thought, language, and emotion. When this bodily sense comes to awareness there is a physical change in the body, a felt shift that then can be analyzed and conceptualized:

According to Gendlin we know a lot more than we think we do. Everything we have ever thought, said or done is within us right now in an implicit complexity that both frames our possible choices and actions and is itself changed by them. In Gendlin speak, "Whatever

126

occurs happens into an implying and carries living forward." This complexity is *bodily* and can be *felt*. Through Focusing, we can learn to tap this vast storehouse of bodily knowledge, and to think, speak and act—more wisely—from this wider field. (Heuman, 2011, p. 43)

Like mindfulness practices, focusing emphasizes awareness in the present moment. Some Buddhist practitioners use the focusing technique to complement their meditative practices (Heuman, 2011). A key difference between mindfulness practice and focusing is that mindfulness is primarily a solitary individual process whereas focusing is greatly aided by having an empathic listener who creates a safe space and helps the focuser through the steps of the focusing process. Like Rogers's nondirective therapy, focusing and listening both engage the person's experiencing process and help it move forward.

In *Focusing* (Gendlin, 1978) he developed a basic six-step technique to guide individuals in learning how to engage in this kind of direct body experiencing. The first step involves making time for the activity in a *safe and quiet space* and then focusing attention inward on your body sensations. Wait until a sensation comes to the fore. This is called a *felt sense*. Pay attention to your sense of what all of the unclear problem feels like. Then find a "*handle*" for the felt sense, a word or phrase that feels right, trying different ideas until one fits. Next is *resonate*—going back and forth between the felt sense and phrase searching for a fit. Next *ask* of the felt sense "What is the whole problem that makes this felt sense, again sensing the felt sense?" Try out answers until one fits and creates a "felt shift" a kind of release. Finally *receive* the release and stay with it, reflecting for a few moments.

Learning Style

In chapter 2 we described how different styles of learning are different ways of engaging the learning cycle. The four modes that comprise the experiential learning cycle, Experiencing (CE), Reflecting (RO), Thinking

(AC), and Acting (AE) are interdependent. Learning involves resolving the creative tension among these learning modes in response to the specific learning situation. An individual's learning style is a way of describing the unique way he or she habitually navigates the learning cycle, with preferences for one or more of the learning modes over the others. Any learning style can be both a strength and weakness. A preference for Reflection and Thinking, for example, can facilitate learning mathematics, or a preference for Acting and Experiencing can aid the entrepreneur in initiative-taking and opportunity-seeking. On the other hand, the reverse combinations may be ineffective. Metacognitive awareness of one's unique learning preferences and capabilities, and the match between these and the demands of learning tasks, can increase learning effectiveness. It can suggest why performance is not optimal and suggest strategies for improvement, as well as help explain why some topics and courses are interesting and others are painful.

Many examples of the use of metacognitive knowledge about learning style come from our work with doctoral students on their dissertation research. Working with us they gain an understanding of ELT and, in many cases, a deep understanding of their learning style and its consequences for their learning. The PhD dissertation is a big, unstructured research project with the goal to produce an original contribution to the field. As such, successful completion requires navigating all phases of the learning cycle, presenting different challenges for individuals with different learning styles. One woman with strong reflecting and thinking preferences realized that her abstract writing style needed to include examples to communicate better. Another with similar analytic learning mode preferences realized that his great respect for the published literature was blocking him from expressing his own ideas. A woman with strong experiencing and reflecting preferences spent years discovering one new creative idea after another before finally accepting that in order to finish she needed to converge on one and complete it. Recognition of a learning style preference as emphasizing strengths in some learning modes as well as some weakness in opposite modes opens deliberate learning- development potentialities and the challenge of full-cycle learning—to develop the ability to engage all modes of the learning cycle in a holistic and fluid manner.

Those who use the KLSI to assess their learning style often decide that they wish to develop their capacity to engage in one or more of the four learning modes, Experiencing (CE), Reflecting (RO), Thinking (AC), and Acting (AE). In some cases this is based on a desire to develop a weak mode in their learning style. In others it may be to increase capability in a mode that is particularly important for their learning tasks. Because of the dialectic relationships among the learning modes, containing the inhibiting effects of an opposing learning mode can be as effective in getting into a mode as actively trying to express it. Overall learning effectiveness is improved when individuals are highly skilled in engaging all four modes of the learning cycle. One way to develop in the learning modes is to develop the skills associated with them. The Learning Skills Profile (Boyatzis & Kolb, 1991, 1995) was created to help learners assess the learning skills associated with the four modes of the learning cycle—interpersonal skills for CE, information skills for RO, analytic skills for AC, and action skills for AE.

Developing the Capacity for Experiencing. Experiencing requires fully opening oneself to direct experience as we just described in the deep-experiencing section. Concrete experience exists only in the here and now, a present moment of endless depth and extension that can never be fully comprehended. In fact, the thinking mode, being too much "in your head," can inhibit the ability to directly sense and feel the immediate moment. Engagement in concrete experience can be enhanced by being present in the moment and attending to direct sensations and feelings. This presence and attention are particularly important for interpersonal relationships. Interpersonal skills of leadership, relationship, and giving and receiving help in the development and expression of the experiencing mode of learning.

Developing the Capacity for Reflecting. Reflection requires space and time for it to take place. It can be inhibited by impulsive desires and/or pressures to take action. It can be enhanced by the practices of deliberately viewing things from a different perspective, and empathy. Stillness and quieting the mind foster deep reflection. Information skills of sense-making, information-gathering, and information analysis can aid in the development and expression of the reflecting mode of learning.

Developing the Capacity for Thinking. Thinking requires the ability to represent and manipulate ideas in your head. It can be distracted by intense direct emotion and sensations as well as pressure to act quickly. Engagement in thinking can be enhanced by practicing theoretical model-building and the creation of scenarios for action. Analytical skills of theory-building, quantitative data analysis, and technology management can aid in the development and expression of the thinking mode of learning.

Developing the Capacity for Action. Acting requires commitment and involvement in the practical world of real consequences. In a sense it is the "bottom line" of the learning cycle, the place where internal experiencing, reflecting, and thinking are tested in reality. Acting can be inhibited by too much internal processing in any of these three modes. Acting can be enhanced by courageous initiative-taking and the creation of cycles of goal-setting and feedback to monitor performance. Action skills of initiative, goal-setting, and action-taking can aid in the development and expression of the acting mode of learning.

Developing Learning Flexibility. A match between one's learning style and the demands of a particular learning task may well facilitate learning of the specialized material. The concept of learning flexibility, however, shifts the focus from specialized style-matching to the process of movement through all modes of the learning cycle. Learning effectiveness is increased when one can move from one learning mode to the other in the learning cycle in response to different learning tasks and context demands. A holistic process-oriented approach that combines a matching strategy with a corresponding emphasis on increasing learning skills in nondominant learning styles may well prove to be the most effective overall educational strategy.

Teachers can respond to the diversity of learning styles present in nearly every classroom by teaching around the cycle, using approaches that fit with all four learning modes. Even the most specialized educational program has a curriculum that requires learning subject matter with different learning style demands. When we consider liberal education and multidisciplinary programs, there are even greater demands for learning flexibility. In the contemporary management and leadership literature, there are consistent calls for adaptability and flexibility in coping with the continually changing dynamics of the global community. Similarly, individuals throughout their lives face a multitude of learning and problem-solving tasks that require a flexible approach in learning how to deal with them.

Fazey and Martin (2002) have argued that learning leads to understanding with greater retention and transfer when an "experiential space of variation" is created through repeated practice from different perspectives and under different conditions. This space of variation can be portrayed as the different learning modes that a person engages in during the learning process. Experiencing, reflecting, thinking, and acting each provide valuable perspectives on what you are learning in a way that deepens and enriches your knowledge. Another popular way of representing this idea is a learning pyramid, where learning retention is increased from 20 percent when one learning mode is engaged to 90 percent when all four modes are engaged (Dale, 1969; Reese, 1998).

The Application of Learning Style Metacognitive Practices. In every learning situation we face there is a dilemma whether to approach the situation with our comfortable learning style or to try another learning style approach. There is no absolute answer about when to "flex" and when to go with your strengths. Over time, developing your strengths in all of the learning modes is a desirable approach that would resolve the dilemma. Most of us, however, are in the process of reaching that goal and thus approach life with some combination of using our favored style or flexing to other learning approaches.

The following example shows how learning style and flexibility can combine in mastering situational challenges. Jason is a minister in his late thirties who recently became the head of a small congregation. His learning style shows preferences on the KLSI for reflecting, experiencing, and thinking, a style that is well suited to his spiritual calling:

I have both a strong inter-personal orientation and a deep interest in increasing my understanding of the world by way of exposure to models and theories, the more abstract the better. Another striking feature of my LSI report is the absolute absence of any preference for the Acting side of the transforming experience spectrum…when I am confronted with a challenge, my instinctive response remains to attend to lines of relationship and to gather information long before I feel ready to set a goal or take action. It also occurs to me that the more I feel grounded in an understanding on the level of theory or idea, the greater my comfort level with moving into active experimentation.

Throughout his career, Jason has experienced challenge and stress in dealing with the action demands of his work. His reflective style requires more time for reflection than these situations allow:

The challenge here feels like more than mere lack of preference for or experience with the particular skill set involved. It feels like a deeper psycho-emotional discomfort with the experience of being at the center of things and of seeing myself as a leader, or the driving force for an event or an organization. In meetings, I tend to sit back and listen and often even wait for someone to ask me a question before I open my mouth, but I have repeatedly received feedback from others that they would like to hear more from me.

Rather than moving into the acting region of the learning space to deal with the action demands of his job, Jason plans to use his learning style strengths of reflection and abstraction to plan and set priorities in order to reduce the stress he feels in action and leadership positions.

I will begin to incorporate a weekly template of tasks and ap-pointments into my planning process. Having this template will help to keep me from over scheduling myself, and it will also help to mitigate my tendency to allow meetings to last until the person I'm meeting with decides that it's time for them to go. Additionally, this template will contain built-in time for stress reduction instead of going straight from one thing to the next and it will have time clearly set aside for preparation processes so that I do not find myself preparing for so many things at the last minute. Even though I actually fly fairly well by the seat of my pants, I usually feel less good about the job I do compared to when I give myself adequate time to prepare beforehand.

Learning Identity

Metacognitive knowledge of learning style, one's understanding, and deliberate regulation of how one learns is but one aspect of the larger concept of learning identity. In addition to learning style, learning identity includes motivation to learn, belief in one's learning ability, and interest in learning about different things. In chapter 5 we have described the learning identity concept and outlined specific metacognitive practices to enhance a positive learning identity.

Learning Times and Spaces

In Part II of the book, Creating Learning Spaces, Chapters 8–14 describe the concept of learning space, emphasizing that learning needs a space to happen and that the nature of that space can either facilitate or hinder learning. It is a foundational truism of social psychology that we humans are greatly influenced by the situations we are in. Studies show powerful tendencies to conform to social norms and the influence of others (Janis, 1972) while evidence for the influence of individual characteristics shows only modest effects on behavior (Mischel, 1984). Time is an important factor in setting the boundaries of a learning space. In many situations, pressure to perform can drive out the time necessary for learning.

It is for this reason that metacognitive monitoring and control of one's learning time and space is so important. With this perspective one can exercise some choice in the learning spaces and times one makes, and create the kind of learning space that best facilitates one's learning. When embarking on a course of learning, it is useful to consider the learning spaces where this learning will happen and customize these spaces for yourself based on your learning style and the particular subject matter of your learning. When teachers plan their courses, they may or may not explicitly consider the kind of learning spaces they are creating and the appropriateness of these spaces for the students in their course and/or for the material being taught. For example, John and Tanya Reese (Reese 1998) created "Connecting with the Professor" workshops to help law students bridge the differences between the learning spaces created by law school professors and their own learning space preferences resulting from their individual learning style. Recognizing that law school professors were unlikely to change their course and learning style, they worked with students to develop the learning skills needed to succeed in the learning spaces created by their professors. Another strategy is to supplement the learning space that is given with other spaces that suit your style. For example, a person who learns best by imagining may want to form a group of classmates to talk about the material in the course, or a thinking style person may want to prepare in advance by reading about material to be covered in the course.

The principles for the creation of an effective space for experiential learning described in Part II can serve as a metacognitive guide to assess one's current learning space or to create a new one. For a learner to engage fully in the learning cycle, a space must be provided to engage fully in the four modes of the cycle—feeling, reflection, thinking, and action. It needs to be a hospitable, welcoming space that is characterized by respect for all. It needs to provide an optimal balance of support and challenge, reminding us of Vygotsky's concept of the proximal zone of development (1978) where the learner is supported in incremental learning by models that set challenging but achievable goals. It must allow learners to be in charge of their own learning, and allow time for the repetitive practice that develops expertise.

Learning Relationships

Another important area for the metacognitive monitoring and control of learning is learning relationships. Most learning involves others in some way. ELT defines learning relationships as connections between one or more individuals that promote growth and movement through the learning spiral, ultimately inspiring future learning and relationship building. Hunt (1987) suggests that parallel learning spirals are shared between individuals in human interaction. People relate to one another in a pattern of alternating "reading" and "flexing" that mirrors the experiential learning process. When one person is *reading*—receiving feedback (CE) and formulating perceptions (RO)—the other person is *flexing*—creating intentions based on those perceptions (AC) and acting on them (AE). As the exchange continues, their modes of experiencing shift back and forth. However, many interactions take place without mindful awareness of perception and intention, creating a sequence of feedback and action that bypasses key steps in the learning process. Those who seek to support the learning process in others can activate modes of experiencing in others by asking key questions that draw out different learning responses (Abbey et al., 1985).

Teachers, mentors, advisors, family, and friends all can influence learning for better or worse. The key metacognitive strategy for managing learning relationships is to focus on and develop those that are growth producing and to minimize and contain encounters with those "toxic" relationships that undermine learning and one's learning identity. Our research (Passarelli & Kolb, 2011) suggests that there is no minimum number of interactions for a learning relationship to take form. When asked who has recently impacted their learning growth and development, some learners told stories of a recent acquaintance making a positive impact on their learning journey. Others, however, were impacted by long-standing, close relationships with individuals such as a spouse, sibling, or mentor. What was common to all of the stories is that learners expressed a baseline level of positive feelings or perceptions of the other, even when the content of the interaction was not positive. Miller and Stiver (1997) suggest that relationships that foster growth are formed through interactions that are characterized by mutual empathy and empowerment. These interactions, or connections, need not always be positive, but they must include reciprocal engagement of both thought and emotion. The tone that arises from mutual empathy and empowerment creates the conditions for mutual growth where individuals experience an increase in their vitality, ability to take action, clarity about themselves and their relationship, sense of self-worth, and desire to form more connections. A connection is constituted by an interaction or series of interactions that build toward a deeper relationship. Learning relationships evolve as learning interactions increase in quality and frequency. Each interaction carries with it a sentiment, or emotional charge, that sets the tone for learning. Interactions characterized by compassion, respect, and support build the trust and positive emotional resources necessary to create space for learning—even when learning is challenging.

As we described in chapter 4 on Learning Identity, learning relationships can have a powerful impact on learning identity for better or worse. Some relationships can reinforce a fixed identity or create a codependency that does not allow for learning flexibility and growth. Learning identity may be contagious in the sense that those who have a learning identity tend to create relationships that stimulate it in others and those with fixed identities also act in ways that pass on fixed views of others.

Deliberate Practice

We all know that learning involves repeated practice. However, time spent practicing does not necessarily lead to learning and improved performance. Practice is not just the amount of time doing something, so experience with something alone is not a good predictor of performance. Going to the golf practice range and hitting bucket after bucket of balls doesn't necessarily improve your game and in fact may make it worse by ingraining bad habits. Expert performance research initiated in the early 1990s by K. Anders Ericsson (Baron & Henry, 2010; Ericsson, 2006; Ericsson & Charness,

1994; Ericsson, Krampe, & Tesch-Römer, 1993) teaches a great deal about learning from practice. The good news from this work is that greatness, for the most part, is not a function of innate talent; it is learned from experience. The not-so-good news is that it involves long-term commitment and hard work. To become a highly skilled expert can take an estimated ten thousand hours of a particular kind of practice, called deliberate practice. This, for example, works out to be twenty hours a week for fifty weeks a year for ten years. The basic techniques of deliberate practice are useful for improving our ability to deliberately learn from experience. In this sense, deliberate practice can be seen as mindful experiencing with the addition of focused reflection on a concrete performance. This experience is analyzed against a metacognitive ideal model to improve future action in a recurring cycle of learning.

Deliberate practice is a discipline requiring motivation fueled by deep interest and a long-time frame commitment. It involves intense, concentrated, repeated performance that is compared against an ideal or "correct" model of the performance. It requires feedback that compares the actual performance against the ideal to identify "errors" that are corrected in subsequent performance attempts. Feedback and positive reinforcement for improvement are essential. Preparation for practice with study of ideal models and goal setting is also important. Metacognitive skills in self-observation and reflection are critical for detecting and correcting errors. Deliberate practice is difficult and hard to maintain, mainly because it requires full concentration, a lot of effort, and is often not enjoyable. Daniel Coyle (2009) emphasizes that this kind of practice is difficult work requiring focused attention and thoughtful analysis and continuous repetition to eliminate mistakes and reach goals. He argues that most can only engage in this deep-learning activity for a couple of hours at a time.

For this reason a learning relationship where one acts as a coach can be of great help in deliberate practice by providing expert models, feedback, and support for the focused effort required. Coyle describes the great UCLA basketball coach John Wooden as a model;

What made Wooden a great coach wasn't praise, wasn't denunciation and certainly wasn't pep talks. His skill resided in the Gatling-gun rattle of targeted information he fired at his players. *This, not that. Here, not there.* His words and gestures served as short, sharp impulses that showed his players the correct way to do something. He was seeing and fixing errors. "The importance of repetition until automaticity cannot be overstated," he said. (Coyle, 2009, p. 170)

Ongoing deliberate practice can be seen as a learning spiral of recursive progression through the learning cycle over time. A key to learning success is the establishment of the appropriate time-frame expectation for its achievement. The most common time-framing error is the expectation of a "quick fix" and instant mastery. When it doesn't happen, the learning effort is abandoned. Learning to control one's weight is perhaps the best example. To embark on a "Lose 10 pounds in 10 days" diet is to limit oneself to one turn through the learning cycle; while weight control is a long-term process with spirals of learning around many issues (calorie intake, exercise, etc.) and many contexts. The inertia of old habits takes time to change and setbacks and failures are inevitable. By framing the learning process correctly as one that will happen with slow progress over time, quitting and negative fixed self-attributions can be avoided.

In *Mastery*, George Leonard describes the master's journey as a path that follows a recurring cycle of brief spurts of progress followed by dips of performance and a plateau of performance that is slightly higher than before where nothing seems to be happening until the next spurt. For many, this path, particularly the long plateaus, proves frustrating and efforts to learn and develop are abandoned. Leonard advises:

> To put it simply, you practice diligently, but you practice primarily *for the sake of practice itself.* Rather than being frustrated while on the plateau, you learn to appreciate and enjoy it as much as you do the upward surges. (1991, p. 17)

Learning How to Become a Deliberate Learner

The lesson from our work on deliberate experiential learning is that learning to learn is a lifelong process that never ends. Ten thousand hours may be a mythical, number but the number of learning cycles we go through in our lifetime is countless. Deliberate learning can improve the achievements we make as we go through them. Let us, in conclusion, examine how the meta-cognitive skills of deliberate learning can be developed to increase the ability to learn how to learn. Returning to figure 6.2, we have emphasized thus far two cycles of learning shown in the illustration. The cycle of learning at the experience level represents the learner's actual concrete learning experience. The cycle at the meta-level describes the learner's normative model of how his learning should be. A closer look at figure 6.2 reveals that the monitoring and control arrows between one's metacognitive model of experiential learning and his/her learning experience complete another cycle of experiential learning. This third learning cycle describes how individuals can monitor and develop their meta-level model of learning, that is, how they learn about their learning process.

Current metacognitive research suggests that these three cycles do not operate simultaneously; they operate sequentially. For example, judgments of how well one has learned something are less accurate when they are made immediately than when they are delayed for some time (Nelson, 1996). When people are immersed in a learning task like solving math problems, they may not be thinking much about their meta-model of how they should be going about the task and not at all about perfecting that meta-model. The meta-model of learning may be most useful prior to engagement in learning and for "after-action review." It can be used to plan strategies for engaging and mastering the immediate learning task. In this sense the concept of flow, where one is totally unconsciously immersed in his or her work, is the opposite of deliberate practice with its emphasis on conscious evaluation of feedback and corrective action.

The learning about learning cycle requires a longer time perspective and reflection on previous learning experiences and their fit with one's metacognitive normative learning model. We have already seen that educational interventions can facilitate this process and improve learning effectiveness (Blackwell, Trzesniewski, & Dweck 2007; Good, Aronson, and Inzlicht, 2003; Hutt, 2007; Reese, 1998). Supportive learning relationships and learning spaces are often essential to explore and change a deeply held learning identity and unconscious learning habits. Ultimately, however, it is the learners who manage their learning about deliberate learning and take control of their learning process through metacognitive monitoring and control. Learners can chart their path on the learning way by developing their metacognitive learning capacities and educators can pave the way by placing learning about learning on the agenda of their educational programs.

Try an Exercise in Deliberate Learning for Yourself. By taking a few minutes to experience deliberate learning for yourself you can see how it works for you in transforming experience into learning. Just follow the steps below. First read through the six steps. Then read each step and take time to complete it; then move on to the next.

1. *Create a learning space.* First you need to make a quiet space for yourself to focus on the exercise without distraction. Get physically comfortable and relaxed. Be aware of all that your mind is preoccupied with—and now, consciously set all of this stuff aside for a few minutes. You can come back to it when you are done.

2. *Focus on an immediate experience.* Let something emerge in the space you have made. Focus on it and tune in to your sensations and feelings about it. Resist the temptation to put words on it. Try to experience the sensations and feelings as vividly as possible. Take enough time for this so that distractions don't interfere with what you are feeling now.

3. *Move to reflection.* Sit back and review what you experienced in the last few moments. Become detached and think of yourself as an observer looking and listening to what you just went through. Don't try to explain the experience at this point. The goal is just to take it in and replay it in your mind as vividly as possible.

4. ***Conceptualize the experience.*** Now replay your reflections again and try to make sense of them. What is your interpretation of what you were feeling and experiencing? Try to create a concept, word, or idea that summarizes the various aspects of your experience.

5. ***Move to action.*** Think about what your explanation means for action. Do you want to do something about it? Actions can be big or small. You may want to tell someone about what you just went through and get their perspective. Or just write a note about this for later. It may suggest a decision to be made. **Do something.**

6. ***The cycle begins again.*** Your action will create new experience and feelings. These may be a little more focused than in the first cycle. You may want to repeat the above steps again. Or put it aside for later.

Seven

TEAM AND ORGANIZATIONAL LEARNING

*Individual experience...sets the stage for learning across the
organization, including the individual, team and system
levels of interaction...When individuals in organizations
are open to new experiences, reflect on successes and
failures, update their perspective and take calculated risks
and experiment, they learn. Organizations that cultivate
learning from experience build organizational resilience.*

—D. C. KAYES, *ORGANIZATIONAL RESILIENCE*

Experiential educators, in addition to their work with individual learners, also work to enhance learning in teams and organizations. ELT
offers a way to study the learning process at the level of the individual, the
team, and the organization. In ELT these three levels of human systems are
nested in the sense that teams promote and capitalize on the learning of
individual team members and integrate it into a collective process of team
learning, while at the organization level, networks of teams, differentiated by
function, tasks, and style, are hierarchically integrated into an organizational
learning process. At the team level, additional group factors such as norms,
decision processes, and roles must be considered to promote learning, while

at the organizational level still other factors such as leadership, organizational climate, and structure are involved. Teams are in the middle, playing a central role in enhancing learning for the individual, the organization, and the team itself.

In today's world, the focus on work in teams has becomes more prevalent in education and the workplace. Organizations increasingly rely on teams to get work done. Teamwork in organizations takes many forms, "from the shop floor to the executive suite"—ongoing work teams of various types, parallel teams for advice and employee involvement, temporary project teams, and management teams (Cohen & Bailey, 1997). In organizations with more than one hundred employees, over 80 percent use some form of teams (Guzzo & Shea, 1992). A survey of 1,000 Fortune 1000 companies in 1993 by the University of Southern California found that 68 percent of these organizations used self-managing work teams and 91 percent used some type of team to solve problems (Lawler, Mohrman, & Ledford, 1992, 1995).

The use of teams to promote student learning in education also has become more prevalent (Michaelsen, Bauman Knight, & Fink, 2004). For example, in his study of student learning at Harvard, Richard Light found student learning teams to be highly effective. "Specifically, those students who study outside of class in small groups of four to six, even just once a week, benefit enormously. Their meetings are organized around discussions of the homework. And as a result of their study group discussion they are far more engaged and far better prepared, and they learn significantly more" (2001, p. 52). Learning teams such as this have sometimes been referred to as collaborative learning (Davidson, 1990; Johnson & Johnson, 1994; Parker, 1984).

Team Learning

Teamwork, however, is not natural or easy, particularly in individualistic cultures like the United States. As a result more emphasis is being placed on team learning—the ability of individual team members to learn teamwork skills (Stevens & Campion, 1994) and the capability of the team as a whole to develop the "executive consciousness" necessary to self-organize and manage its work process (Mills, 1967).

Many who work in teams are not happy about it. Work-team members often complain about wasting time in meetings that did not result in any action. Students complain about being forced to work in teams with other students who do not pull their weight when their grade is dependent on their team's performance (Chen, Donahue, & Klimoski, 2004; Hall, 1996). Small-group research has identified a number of factors that negatively impact team performance and member satisfaction. These include phenomena such as overdependence on a dominant leader (Bion, 1959; Edmondson, Bohmer, & Pisano, 2001), the tendency to conform known as "groupthink" (Janis, 1972), overcommitment to goals (Staw, 1982), destructive goal pursuit where overcommitment to a narrowly defined goal leads to a failure to adapt to changing conditions due to face saving and thinking that things will work out (Kayes 2004, 2006), diffusion of responsibility (Wallach, Kogan, & Bem, 1964), a tendency to make risky or more conservative decisions than individuals acting alone (Clarke, 1971), social loafing (Latané, Williams, & Harkins, 1979) and the Abilene paradox (Harvey, 2001), in which groups take action that most members disagree with because they fail to express their true feelings.

These and other negative factors associated with teamwork can be overcome when teams become able to learn from their experience together. Teams can increase their effectiveness and team members can develop team skills when a team intentionally focuses on learning. To learn from its experience, a team must have members who can be involved and committed to the team and its purpose (concrete experience), who can engage in reflection and conversation about the team's experiences (reflective observation), who can engage in critical thinking about the team's work (abstract conceptualization), and who can make decisions and take action (active experimentation). Team development is thus a process in which a team creates itself by learning from its experience.

The Experiential Approach to Team Learning. The experiential approach to learning in teams has a long and rich history dating back to the

1940s and Kurt Lewin's research on group dynamics. Lewin's discovery of the T-group is worth examining. From this work emerged three key insights that have framed research on the experiential approach to team learning as it has evolved over the years: (1) the pivotal role of reflective conversation; (2) the theory of functional role leadership; and (3) the experiential learning process as the key to team development.

To learn from their experience, teams must create a conversational space where members can reflect on and talk about their experience together (see chapter 10). In the summer of 1946, Lewin and his colleagues designed a new approach to leadership and group dynamics training for the Connecticut State Interracial Commission. The two-week training program began with an experiential emphasis encouraging group discussion and decision-making in an atmosphere where staff and participants were peers. The research and training staff gathered extensive notes and recordings of the group's activities. They met each evening to analyze the data collected during the day's meetings. Although it was the scientific norm to analyze research objectively without the subjective involvement of the participants; Lewin was receptive when a small group of participants asked to join these discussions. One of the staff members in attendance was Ronald Lippitt, who described what happened in a discussion attended by three trainees:

> Sometime during the evening, an observer made some remarks about the behavior of one of the three persons who were sitting in—a woman trainee. She broke in to disagree with the observation and described it from her point of view. For a while there was quite an active dialogue between the research observer, the trainer, and the trainee about the interpretation of the event, with Kurt an active questioner, obviously enjoying this different source of data that had to be coped with and integrated…

> The evening session from then on became the significant learning experience of the day, with the focus on actual behavioral events and with active dialogue about differences of interpretation and

observation of the events by those who had participated in them (Lippett in Kolb, 2015, p. 9–10).

By creating a conversational space where staff in analytic, objective roles could integrate their ideas with the experiences and observations of active group participants, Lewin and his colleagues discovered the self-analytic group and with it a powerful force for team learning and development. A team can develop a composite image of itself by developing the capacity to reflect on its experience through conversations that examine and integrate differences in members' experiences on the team. To develop this shared self-image that Mills (1967) calls "executive consciousness" a team needs to create a hospitable conversational space. Members need to respect and be receptive to differing points of view, to take time to reflect on consequences of action and the big picture, and to desire growth and development (Baker, Jensen, & Kolb, 2002).

As a team develops from a group of individuals into an effective learning system, members share the functional roles necessary for team effectiveness. In 1948, Kenneth Benne and Paul Sheats described a new concept of team roles and team leadership based on the first National Training Laboratory in Group Development. In contrast to the then-prevailing idea that leadership was a characteristic of the person and that teams should be led by a single leader, Benne and Sheats discovered that mature groups shared leadership. While initially group members were oriented to individual roles focused on satisfying their personal needs, they later came to share responsibility for team leadership by organizing themselves into team roles. Some roles focused on task accomplishment, such as initiator-contributor, information seeker, co-ordinator, and evaluator-critic; other roles focused on group-building and maintenance, such as encourager, compromiser, standard-setter, and group-observer. While members tended to choose roles based on their personality dispositions, they also were able to adopt more unfamiliar roles for the good of the group (Benne & Sheats, 1948).

Teams develop by following the experiential learning cycle. The laboratories in group development, or T-groups as they came to be known, were based on a model of learning from experience known as the laboratory method.

This model was typically introduced by the group trainer as follows: "Our goal here is to learn from our experience as a group and thereby create the group we want to be. We will do this by sharing experiences together and reflecting on the meaning of these experiences for each of us. We will use these observations and reflections to create a collective understanding of our group, which will serve to guide us in acting to create the kind of group experience that we desire." The reader will recognize this laboratory training model as a form of the experiential learning cycle described in chapter 2. Experiential learning and engagement in the learning cycle provide the mechanisms by which teams can transition from lower to higher developmental stages.

Theodore Mills (1967) describes team development as successive stages in the sophistication of a team's ability to learn from experience. He described team learning as a reconfiguring of a group's purpose to achieve a continually greater and more complex purpose. Developmental progression occurs as the group learns to deal with the increasingly complex demands of achieving its purpose. He described five levels of team development:

1. Immediate gratification. In the first stage, members of the group seek to fulfill individual needs or desires. They come together simply to meet some immediate individual need without sustained effort at gratification.

2. Sustained conditions for gratification. In the second stage, individuals come together for gratification but develop ways to sustain the gratification. Effort to sustain gratification requires individual learning that involves developing informal strategies and implementing mechanisms to maintain the gratification over time.

3. Pursuit of a collective goal. The third-order purpose focuses on developing a collective goal. In this stage, a group becomes a team. This stage requires development of more formal strategies and structures to meet the group purpose. Here the members of the group must transform from individual learning to group learning, develop methods of coordination, develop adaptation mechanisms, and respond to changing external demands.

4. Self-determination. In the fourth order, the group no longer simply adapts to changes in the environment but makes self-directed changes directed by its stated desires. While external constraints are not completely eliminated, the group develops the freedom to set and pursue its own goals.
5. Growth. A group working at the fifth level can follow multiple goals, create high levels of innovation, manage diverse and conflicting types of innovation, and influence a number of different domains.

Mills described the role of intentional experiential learning in team development in the following way:

> Although accomplishment of a given order of purpose tends to increase the group's *potential* for advancing to the next higher order, that advance is not automatic or predetermined, but instead depends on the initiative of a member, or members, in conceiving the new purpose, formulating it, conveying it, acting according to it and having it generally accepted by others in the group...*Seeing* the new possibility and then *acting* on it are relevant, important and indeed critical to group growth. (1967, p. 114)

At the higher stages of development, a team develops a system of executive consciousness: "Consciousness is gained through adding to the function of acting the functions of observing and comprehending the system that is acting" (p. 19). At this level, team members take on an executive role following the experiential learning cycle: "They experience, observe, and assess the realities of the momentary situation. They act and assess the consequences of their actions upon the group's capability of coping with immediate demands and future exigencies" (p. 90).

All team members can take the executive role, forming what Mills calls the executive system:

The group's center for assessment of itself and its situations, for arrangement and rearrangement of its internal and external relations, for decision making and for learning, and for "learning how to learn" through acting and assessing the consequences of action. (p. 93)

Executive consciousness becomes a guiding light that enables the team to learn and shape itself to respond effectively to the challenges of its mission and environment. A team that cannot see itself accurately is ultimately flying blind. Executive consciousness can be likened to the individual metacognitive process described in chapter 6 on deliberate learning; the main difference being that this metacognitive awareness is intersubjective among team members, a shared mental model of how the team works together (see figure 7.1).

Figure 7.1
Team Executive Consciousness Monitors and Controls Learning

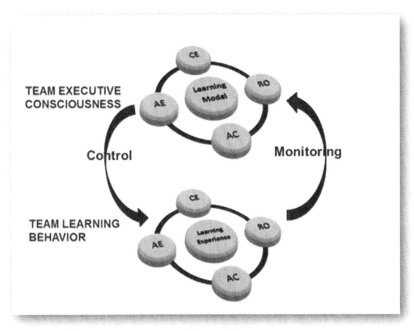

Alice Y. Kolb and David A. Kolb

Research on Experiential Learning in Teams. A wide body of research, involving different methodologies and different educational and workplace populations, has shown that ELT is useful in understanding team learning and performance. Studies support the proposition that a team is more effective if it follows the learning cycle in its work process and emphasizes all four learning modes. Of particular interest are studies that examine the role of team-member learning style, team roles, and team norms on the team-learning process.

Team-member learning style. There have been numerous studies that have investigated the impact of team-member learning style diversity on team effectiveness. Most find that teams whose members have different learning styles are more effective than homogenous learning style teams (Hall 1996; Halstead & Martin 2002; Jackson 2002; Kayes, 2001; Sandmire & Boyce, 2004; Sandmire, Vroman, & Sanders, 2000; Sharp, 2001; Wolfe, 1977). In the first experimental study of the effect of learning styles on team performance, Wolfe (1977) examined how homogeneous three-person teams of similar learning styles performed on a complex computer business simulation compared with heterogeneous teams. The four groups of homogeneous teams had similar performance results. However, the teams that had members with diverse learning styles performed significantly better, earning nearly twice the amount of money of the homogeneous learning style teams. Similarly, Kayes (2001) found that teams made up of members whose learning styles were balanced among the four learning modes performed at a higher level on a critical thinking task than teams whose members had specialized learning styles.

Sandmire and Boyce (2004) investigated the performance of two-person collaborative problem-solving teams in an allied health-education anatomy, physiology, and pathology course. They compared a group of high-abstract/high-concrete student pairs with a group of abstract pairs and a group of concrete pairs. The abstract/concrete pairs performed significantly better on a simulated clinical case than the abstract pairs and slightly better than the concrete pairs, indicating the value of integrating the abstract and concrete dialectics of the learning cycle. However, a similar study by Sandmire, Vroman, and Sanders (2000) investigating pairs formed on the action/reflection dialectic showed no significant performance differences.

Halstead and Martin (2002) found that engineering student teams that were formed randomly to include all learning styles performed better than self-selected teams. Furthermore, in her studies of engineering students, Sharp stated, "Classroom experience shows that students can improve teamwork skills with Kolb theory by recognizing and capitalizing on their strengths, respecting all styles, sending messages in various ways, and analyzing style differences to resolve conflict and communicate effectively with team members" (2001). In his study of a six-week teambuilding program, Hall (1996) reported difficulty with self-selected teams that tended to group on the basis of friendship. He advocated random team assignment, concluding, "If we had taken this approach there would have been more disagreement to work through, personality clashes to cope with and conflict to resolve. The stress would have been greater, but the *learning* probably more profound" (1996, p. 30).

Using another approach, Jackson studied the learning styles of ongoing workgroup team members who participated in a paired team competition. The exercise was designed to require teamwork skills. Results showed that teams with balanced learning styles performed better. In seventeen of the eighteen team pairs, the winning-team average score was higher than that of the losing team. Jackson concluded, "Designing teams that reflect the dynamic nature of team activities has great appeal in that it gives all team members a more equal opportunity to contribute and a more equal opportunity to be valued…The process model advocates that different team members lead in different team activities or learning situations (2002, p. 11).

Team roles. A number of studies have examined the theory of functional-role leadership using the ELT framework (Fernandez, 1986, 1988; McMurray, 1998; Gardner & Korth, 1999). Park and Bang (2002) studied the performance of fifty-two Korean industrial work teams using the Belbin team role model, which is conceptually linked to ELT (Jackson, 2002). They found that the best-performing teams were those whose members adopted at a high level in all nine of Belbin's roles covering all stages of the learning cycle. They also found that teams with roles that matched the particular stage of a team's work/learning process performed best.

McMurray (1998) organized his English-as-a-foreign-language classroom using ELT principles. He divided his Japanese students into four-person teams with maximally diverse learning styles. Students were assigned to one of four roles that matched their strongest learning mode: leader (concrete experience), artist (reflective observation), writer (abstract conceptualization), and speaker (active experimentation). The leader's role was to direct classmates in completing assignments; the artist's, to create ideas for presentations; and the writer's, to compose messages for speakers to read. Class lessons were organized to include all four stages of the learning cycle. Classroom observations supported the idea that students benefited from the team role assignment and from accounting for learning style in the course design.

Gardner and Korth used ELT, learning styles, and the learning cycle to develop a course for human-resource development graduate students that focused on learning to work in teams. They found strong relationships between learning styles and preference for learning methods—reflective/abstract styles preferred lectures, reading, writing, and individual work, while other styles preferred partner and group work. They advocated providing different student roles during team-learning activities to develop appreciation for, and skill in, all learning styles. "Part of the class could actively participate in a role play (active/concrete styles), while a second group observes and provides feedback to the participants (reflective/concrete styles), a third group develops a model/theory from what they have seen and shares it with the class (reflective/abstract styles) and the fourth group develops a plan for applying what they have seen to a new situation and shares it with the class (active and abstract styles)" (1999, p. 32).

Team norms. Carlsson, Keane, and Martin used the ELT learning cycle framework to analyze the biweekly reports of research and development project teams in a large consumer products corporation. Successful project teams had work process norms that supported a recursive cycling through the experiential learning cycle. Projects that deviated from this work process by skipping stages or being stuck in a stage "indicated problems deserving of management attention" (1976, p. 38).

Other studies of educational teams (Gardner & Korth, 1997; Pauleen, Marshall, & Egort, 2004) have found that interventions aimed at the introduction of experiential learning norms facilitated learning and transfer of learning. Gardner and Korth used ELT to design a course in group dynamics, group development, and group effectiveness. They taught student learning teams to use the experiential learning cycle to improve the transfer of learning. They concluded, "The use of learning groups in conjunction with the experiential learning model enhances the learning process, reinforces the link between theory and practice, and facilitates the transfer of learning to the workplace" (1997, p. 51). Pauleen, Marshall, and Egort used ELT to construct and implement web-based team-learning assignments in a graduate-level course in knowledge management. Students worked on projects in virtual teams. Follow-up student evaluations indicated that 75 percent "agreed or strongly agreed that experiential learning was a valuable way of experiencing and learning about a variety of communication channels in a team environment" (2004, p. 95); 99 percent found experiential learning to be more valuable than simply reading about something.

Two studies have explicitly examined team conversational learning spaces (see chapter 10) with norms that support the experiential learning cycle. Wyss-Flamm (2002) selected from a management assessment and development course three multicultural student teams who rated themselves as high in psychological safety, defined as the ability of the team to bring up and talk about difficult or potentially psychologically uncomfortable issues. Three of the teams rated themselves as low in psychological safety. Through intensive individual and team interviews, she analyzed the teams' semester-long experience. In teams with high psychological safety, the conversations followed a recursive experiential learning cycle: differences were experienced among team members, examined through reflective juxtaposition that articulated learning, and culminated in either an integration of the differences or an affirmation of the contrast. Teams with low psychological safety tended to have early disturbing incidents that limited conversation and made the conversational flow more turbulent and conflict filled. Lingham (2004) developed an instrument called the Conversational Space Inventory to assess the norms of conversational space as experienced by team members in a sample of forty-nine educational and work teams. Team members rated their experience of the "real" conversational space in their team and described their desired ideal for the team conversational space. One of his findings was that the more the teams supported the experiential learning cycle through norms that focused their conversation on interpersonal diverging (concrete experience and reflective observation) and task-oriented converging (abstract conceptualization and active experimentation), the better they performed, the more satisfied they were with their membership on the team, and the more they felt psychologically safe to take risks on the team.

Jules (2007) created an integrated model of the team-learning process and tested it in a survey of thirty-three work teams from six different industries (see figure 7.2). He examined the influence of members' demographic diversity and learning style diversity and the extent that the team followed experiential team-learning process norms using all four modes of the learning cycle. Overall both team-member learning style diversity and experiential learning work norms led to less process conflict and were positively related to a team's ability to make decisions, to achieve its goals, and to overall team performance. Demographic diversity by age, gender, and race tended to produce moderate levels of process conflict and impede team performance. Learning style diversity was related to team-learning process norms only in new teams suggesting that other factors than member composition such as team leadership, team task, or organization culture influence team norms in established teams. Learning style diversity was positively related to performance in teams with routine tasks; while experiential team norms were related to performance in teams with nonroutine tasks.

Figure 7.2
Team Membership and Team-Learning Process Model

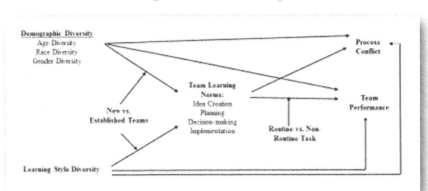

Education for team learning. Kayes, Kayes, and Kolb (2005a) have integrated the above research and other group theories into a theory of experiential learning in teams that focuses on six aspects of team functioning—purpose, membership, roles, context, process, and action (see figure 7.3). Based on this theory the Kolb Team-Learning Experience (KTLE—Kayes, Kayes, Kolb, & Kolb, 2004) was created as a structured simulation through which team members learn about team functions while engaging in the processes of knowledge creation, reflection, critical thinking, and action-taking. Thus, team members learn how to develop executive consciousness as the team progresses through activities and problems in the team-learning workbook. The team is encouraged to experience all stages of the learning cycle multiple times and reflect on its ability to continually experience these stages. As the team learns, it increases its ability to operate at higher developmental stages within the functional aspects of purpose, membership, roles, context, process, and action-taking (Kayes, Kayes, & Kolb, 2005b).

Figure 7.3
Arenas of Executive Consciousness in Teams

The KTLE helps teams work toward higher development through seven simulation modules:

1. *Team-learning overview:* Teams engage in an introductory exercise that encourages teamwork and requires the team to move through the learning cycle by engaging in a simulated product-development and marketing exercise. Teams then analyze their process and acquire their first exposure to the team-level learning cycle.

2. *Team purpose:* This module helps a team set its general direction by identifying individual purposes and how they relate to the team's overall purpose.

3. *Team membership:* Teams "map" the learning styles of individual members onto a specially designed learning space. They then

    develop a snapshot of team members' learning styles and can begin to see how the team as a whole learns best. Team members can identify the synergies and challenges relative to their individual learning styles.

4. *Roles*: Team members identify their role preferences and "map" them to identify gaps and potential strengths of team members and the team as a whole.

5. *Context*: The team identifies its primary contextual demands, including the nature of its task and the resources it needs to complete its task effectively.

6. *Team process*: The team once again visits the four-phase team-learning cycle. In this module the team diagnoses its own process and identifies its strengths and weaknesses in navigating the learning cycle.

7. *Action planning*: The team works through a detailed action-planning worksheet. In this final module, the team pulls together what it learned about itself from the other six modules. The planning process provides the team with a detailed but flexible action plan, including deadlines, expected results, and the necessary team processes to achieve these results.

Organizational Learning

"Most researchers would agree with defining organizational learning as a change in the organization's knowledge that occurs as a function of experience…Organizational learning is a process that occurs over time…an ongoing cycle through which task performance experience is converted into knowledge that in turn changes the organization's context and affects future experience" (Argote & Miron-Spektor, 2011, p. 1124). Since its first formulation (Kolb, 1976c), the ELT approach to organizational learning has been elaborated by a number of scholars (Dixon, 1999; Hayes & Allinson, 1998; Huczynski & Boddy, 1979; Kay & Bawden, 1996; Kayes, 2015; Kayes & Kayes, 2011; Kim, 1993; Lahteenmaki, Leroy, & Ramanantsoa,

2001; Mumford, 1991; Popper & Lipshitz, 2000; Ramnarayan & Reddy, 1989; Simonin, 1997; Thomas, 2002; Zhang, Macpherson, & Jones, 2006). Easterby-Smith (1997) in his typology of contemporary organizational learning theories classifies the ELT approach as a human, psychological, and organization development approach along with the theories of Argyris (1992), Dixon (1999), Kim (1993), Mumford (1991), Nonaka and Takeuchi (1995), and Revans (1971,1980). True to its Lewinian social psychology origins, organization learning in ELT is seen as a transactional process between individuals and their environment and between the organization and its environment.

A central issue for most organizational learning scholars is the relationship between individual learning and organizational learning. "Although individual learning is necessary for group and organizational learning, individual learning is not sufficient for group or organizational learning. For learning to occur at these higher levels of analysis, the knowledge the individual acquired would have to be embedded in a supra-individual repository so that others can access it. For example, the knowledge the individual acquired could be embedded in a routine or trans-active memory system." (Argote & Miron-Spektor, 2011, p. 1126). In *The Organizational Learning Cycle*, Nancy Dixon translates the individual learning cycle of experiential learning to the organizational level by introducing the concept of dialogue (Dixon, 1999) or conversational learning (Baker, Jensen, & Kolb, 2002) in the reflection and conceptualization phases of the individual learning cycle describing organizational learning as a cycle where employee direct experiences (Concrete Experience, Nonaka's [1995] tacit knowledge) and mental maps are shared in dialogue (Reflective Observation), interpreted collectively to create collectively shared meaning (Abstract Conceptualization, explicit knowledge) as the basis for responsible action (Active Experimentation). In this way the team learning from experience process described in the previous section becomes a pivotal linking pin between individual and organizational learning.

At the individual level, learning from experience leads to a "match" between the individual and their immediate organizational environment, that is, their work and functional work setting. Through learning from previous experiences that leads to choice of and/or placement into jobs and on the job learning to meet job demands, workers achieve a fit between their skills and their job demands that produces effective performance (Sims, 1980, 1981, 1983). The Learning Skills Profile (Boyatzis & Kolb, 1991, 1995, 1997) was developed as a holistic typology of learning skills associated with the phases of the experiential learning cycle to assess skills and job demands in commensurate terms. These job demand/learning skill profiles have been used to assess skill-development needs for management training and development programs. (Kolb, Lublin, Spoth, & Baker, 1986; Rainey Heckelman, Galazka, & Kolb, 1993; Smith, 1990).

At the organizational level, learning is a process of differentiation and integration focused on mastery of the organizational environment. The organization differentiates itself into specialized units charged with dealing with one aspect of the organizational environment; marketing deals with the market and customers, R&D with the academic and technological community, and so on. This creates a corresponding internal need to integrate and coordinate the specialized units.

Because specialized units need to relate to different aspects of the environment, they develop characteristic ways of working together, different styles of learning, problem-solving and decision-making. In fact, Lawrence and Lorsch define organizational differentiation as "the difference in cognitive and emotional orientation among managers in different functional departments" (1967, p. 11). From a learning perspective these represent differences in learning style. Previous research has shown that educational specialization is a primary determinant of learning style (Joy & Kolb, 2009; Kolb, 2015; Kolb & Kolb, 2005b). Interestingly, in these studies, business majors on the average tend to end up the middle of the learning style grid with no particular specialized style. However, research on the relationship between learning style and business functional specialty has shown consistent patterns of differentiation (Biberman & Buchanan, 1986; Jervis, 1983; Loo, 2002a, 2002b; Novin et al., 2003; Rowe & Waters, 1992). Results from these and other studies suggest that the concrete/active learning style is characteristic of entrepreneurs, of people in sales, and of general managers while the abstract/reflective style is characteristic of those in the planning, research and development, and finance specialties. Accountants, production managers, and engineers tend to be abstract and active in their learning style while people in marketing, human resources, and organization development tend to have concrete/reflective styles. These associations are of course not perfect; every function tends to have managers with different styles in it. This is important both for learning within the functional team and for integration and communication with other functions. For example, Kolb (1976c) found that those managers in marketing who deviated from the dominant concrete/active style by having an abstract/reflective style communicated better with the abstract/reflective R&D department. Concrete/ active managers in R&D also communicated better with marketing.

Organizations have numerous ways of achieving integration such as strategic management, vision, leadership, organization culture, and cross-functional teams. All of these mechanisms are designed to resolve conflicts between specialized units and achieve a coherent direction for the organization. Too often this integration is achieved through domination of one functional mentality in the organization culture. An example is the case of an electronics firm started by a group of entrepreneurial engineers who invented a unique product (Osland et al., 2007). For a number of years they had no competition and even when some competition appeared in the market they continued to dominate because of their superior engineering quality. It became a different story when stiff competition appeared and their very success created new problems when the management approaches of a small intimate company didn't work in a large organization with operations all over the world. The engineering mentality of the organization made specialists in marketing, finance, and human resources, who were brought in to help the organization, feel like second-class citizens. The organization's strength, its engineering expertise, had become its greatest weakness. Jervis (1983) provides other similar case examples from his studies of UK management teams. For example, in a senior manufacturing management team with managers who had concrete/active learning styles, the group was seen as pursuing a "butterfly" strategy, which concentrated on idea-generation and action but lacked systematic convergent evaluation of projects.

From the ELT perspective, organizational learning requires that the opposing perspectives of action/reflection and concrete involvement/analytical detachment are valued and integrated into a process that follows the whole learning cycle and is adaptive to changing environmental challenges (Ramnarayan & Reddy, 1989). Gemmell (2012) used the ELT organizational learning approach to study entrepreneurial organizations. He focused on organizational leadership using the "upper echelon theory" perspective where the innovation of a firm is driven by traits and actions of the CEO or top management who use strategies, structures, resource allocations, organizational learning processes, and organizational cultures to support and facilitate innovation in the organization.

He studied 172 technology entrepreneurs who were founders/CEOs of their current company, assessing the learning style of the founder/CEOs and the impact of their learning style on key metrics of company performance and innovation. As we reported in chapter 2, founder/CEOs with active learning styles led companies with an emphasis on iterative/experimentation (sometimes called Lean Entrepreneurship), which in turn was positively related to performance and innovation. Entrepreneurs with high learning flexibility were more likely to take longer to make key strategic decisions; however, in the process of doing so, they were more innovative. "Technology entrepreneurs who are flexible learners—in spite of the enormous environmental pressures—appear to achieve greater innovation by taking slightly longer to consider more alternatives, to reflect upon those alternatives and to ultimately converge to a solution and take action." (p. 90)

In a recent study, Gemmell (2017) compared the learning styles of the founder/CEOs in his sample to university business and engineering students. He found that 35 percent of his entrepreneur sample had either Initiating or Experiencing learning styles, a stylistic preference that scholars have argued is particularly suited to the opportunity seeking work of the entrepreneur (Corbett, 2005, 2007; Gemmell, Boland, & Kolb, 2011). In contrast, the engineering and business university students, a population similar to that from which many entrepreneurs are drawn, had exactly the opposite style preferences, with 33 to 38 percent identified as Thinking or Analyzing styles.

He wondered how entrepreneurs with styles other than the concrete/active style overcome what seem to be less effective learning styles for entrepreneurial work. He hypothesized that individuals with reflective and analytical styles will tend to partner with someone with the concrete/active style to complete the learning cycle and attain the cognitive diversity, action orientation, and cognitive agility to be successful. There are a number of high-profile partnerships where a market-oriented entrepreneur teams up with a technical expert such as Steve Jobs and Steve Wozniak or Bill Gates and Paul Allen; and recent data indicate that roughly half of start-ups in knowledge-based industries have this relationship between the cofounders (Gemmell, 2012; Gemmell, Boland, & Kolb, 2011).

To test his hypothesis he sent surveys to the half of the participants in his earlier study who had such partnership arrangements, asking them to ask their partners to complete a survey including the KLSI. Thirty-one respondent partners took the survey, with twenty-eight out of the thirty-one companies having at least one trusted partner with a Initiating or balancing style, lending support to his hypothesis that heterogeneous partnerships are formed to assure that the critical Initiating style is included in firm leadership and the learning cycle is fully represented in the top management team.

Part II

CREATING LEARNING SPACES

Eight

*To sit in a class where the teacher stuffs our minds with
information, organizes it with finality, insists on having
the answers while being utterly uninterested in our views,
and forces us into a grim competition for grades—to sit
in such a class is to experience a lack of space for learning.
But to study with a teacher who not only speaks but
listens, who not only gives answers but asks questions and
welcomes our insights, who provides information and
theories that do not close doors but open new ones, who
encourages students to help each other learn—to study with
such a teacher is to know the power of a learning space.*

—PARKER PALMER, *TO KNOW AS WE ARE KNOWN*

As experiential educators, we have come to recognize the importance
of creating and managing learning spaces. If learning is to occur, it
requires a conducive space. The physical dimensions of this realization were
driven home on numerous occasions as we arrived at our assigned classroom for the first day of class to find a dismal, poorly lit room with rows

of school-desk chairs in front of an instructor's table and dirty blackboard. The room had a timeless institutional feel to it, undoubtedly familiar to the students who came to our class, recreating their associations with their previous educational experiences. Some years later we moved to a new building where attention had been given to improving the classroom learning space. The chair desks were replaced with more comfortable chairs and worktables, the blackboard was now a white board and the lighting was better. But the institutional feel persisted. Classes were at night from 6 to 8 p.m. and then the dreaded second session from 8 to 10 p.m.; arranged so that working students could attend two courses after work in the evening. Everyone was tired after the day's work and for the most part they were just going through the motions. Students asked questions, but not about the course content. What do I have to do to get an A? (Their company would reimburse full tuition only if they got an A in the course.) How long should the paper be? And so on. Even intrinsically interesting and useful course material, inspired energetic lectures, and engaging experiential exercises had trouble breaking through. The upshot of it all was that there was very little space for learning to go on.

From the very beginning our work to introduce experiential learning in educational systems has been a struggle to make a space for learning to take place. Educational institutions, with their classrooms, credit hours, and time-blocked schedules, are learning spaces; but they are spaces constructed with a very different theory of learning than ELT. Based on an information-transfer model from teacher to student, classroom learning spaces are usually designed with seats often bolted down in concrete tiers. Students face the teacher in front in a structure that makes student-to-student interaction difficult. The university learning space of courses, broken down into block-scheduled bits of content that award credit hours for completion, supports the information-transfer model. When we were teaching at CWRU, we used to joke that we were more furniture movers than teachers because we always had to arrive an hour early to move the tables aside and arrange chairs in a circle with books, materials, flowers, music, and other "show and tell" items in the center for everyone to see and interact with. Our goal was to create an experiential learning space based on the principles described in the following chapters of this book.

What Is a Learning Space?

The above examples illustrate the multidimensional nature of a learning space. There are many factors that combine to create a space for learning that is either facilitative to the learning process or a hindrance—the physical space, the constraints of time, the person's psychological state, institutional constraints, and policies. While, for most, the concept of learning space first conjures up the image of the physical classroom environment, it is much broader and multidimensional. Figure 8.1 shows these dimensions of learning space that include physical, cultural, institutional, social, and psychological aspects.

Figure 8.1
Dimensions of Learning Space

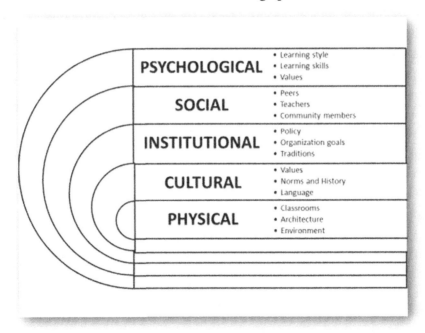

In ELT, these learning space dimensions all come together in the experience of the learner. In experiential learning terms, learning is conceived as a transaction between the person and the environment. This concept of learning space builds on Kurt Lewin's field theory and his concept of life space (1951). For Lewin, person and environment are interdependent variables, a concept Lewin translated into a mathematical formula, $B=f(p, e)$, where behavior is a function of person and environment. As Marrow puts it, "the life space is the total psychological environment which the person experiences subjectively" (1969, p. 35). It includes all facts that have existence for the person and excludes those that do not. It embraces needs, goals, unconscious influences, memories, and beliefs, events of a political, economic, and social nature, and other external factors that might have a direct effect on behavior. The various factors in a given life space are to some degree interdependent, and Lewin strongly maintains that only the dynamic concepts of tension and force can deal with these sets of interdependent facts. This is what led him to define psychological needs as tension systems and their topological representation as vectors to denote motion. He postulated that the particular organization of a person's life space was determined by a field of forces, both internal needs and external demands that positioned the individual in a life space composed of different regions. Using map-like representation, the life space could be depicted topologically. Life spaces can vary in a number of dimensions including extension, differentiation, integration, and level of conflict. Lewin introduced a number of concepts for analysis of the life space and a person's relationship to it that are applicable to the study of learning spaces, including position, region, locomotion, equilibrium of forces, positive and negative valence, barriers in the person and the world, conflict, and goal.

To take time as an example, in many organizations today employees are so busy doing their work that they feel that there is no time to learn how to do things better. This feeling is shaped by the objective conditions of a hectic work schedule along with the expectation that time spent reflecting will not be rewarded. Teachers objectively create learning spaces by the information and activities they offer in their course; but this space is also interpreted in the students' subjective experience through the lens of their learning style. One's position in a learning space defines their experience and thus defines their "reality."

Three other theoretical frameworks inform the ELT concept of learning space. Urie Bronfrenbrenner's (1977, 1979) work on the ecology of human development has made significant sociological contributions to Lewin's life-space concept. He defines the ecology of learning/development spaces as a topologically nested arrangement of structures each contained within the next. The learner's immediate setting such as a course or classroom is called the *microsystem*, while other concurrent settings in the person's life such as other courses, the dorm, or family are referred to as the *mesosystem*. The *exosystem* encompasses the formal and informal social structures that influence the person's immediate environment, such as institutional policies and procedures and campus culture. Finally, the *macrosystem* refers to the overarching institutional patterns and values of the wider culture, such as cultural values favoring abstract knowledge over practical knowledge, that influence actors in the person's immediate microsystem and mesosystem. This theory provides a framework for analysis of the social-system factors that influence learners' experience of their learning spaces.

Another important contribution to the learning-space concept is situated learning theory (Lave, 1988; Lave & Wenger, 1991). Like ELT, situated learning theory draws on Vygotsky's (1962, 1978) activity theory of social cognition for a conception of social knowledge that conceives of learning as a transaction between the person and the social environment. Situations in situated learning theory like life space and learning space are not necessarily physical places but constructs of the person's experience in the social environment. These situations are embedded in communities of practice that have a history, norms, tools, and traditions of practice. Knowledge resides not in the individual's head, but in communities of practice. Learning is thus a process of becoming a member of a community of practice through legitimate peripheral participation (e.g. apprenticeship). Situated learning theory enriches the learning-space concept by reminding us that learning spaces extend beyond the teacher and the classroom. They include socialization into a wider community of practice that involves membership, identity formation, transitioning from novice to expert through mentorship and experience in the activities of the practice, as well as the reproduction and development of the community of practice itself as newcomers replace old-timers.

Finally, in their theory of knowledge creation, Nonaka and Konno (1998) introduce the Japanese concept of "ba," a "context that harbors meaning," which is a shared space that is the foundation for knowledge creation. "Knowledge is embedded in *ba*, where it is then acquired through one's own experience or reflections on the experiences of others" (Nonaka & Konno, 1998, p. 40). Knowledge embedded in *ba* is tacit and can only be made explicit through sharing of feelings, thoughts, and experiences of persons in the space. For this to happen, the *ba* space requires that individuals remove barriers between one another in a climate that emphasizes "care, love, trust, and commitment." To promote learning, learning spaces similarly require norms of psychological safety, serious purpose, and respect.

Since a learning space is in the end what the learner experiences it to be, it is the psychological and social dimensions of learning spaces that have the most influence on learning. From this perspective, learning spaces can be viewed as aggregates of human characteristics. "Environments are transmitted through people and the dominant features of a particular environment are partially a function of the individuals who inhabit it" (Strange & Banning, 2001). Using the "human aggregate" approach, the experiential learning space is defined by the attracting and repelling forces (positive and negative valences) of the poles of the dual dialectics of action/reflection and experiencing/conceptualizing, creating a two-dimensional map of the regions of the learning space like that shown in figure 8.2. An individual's learning style positions him/her in one of these regions depending on the equilibrium of forces among action, reflection, experiencing, and conceptualizing. As with the concept of life space, this position is determined by a combination of individual learning style disposition and characteristics of the learning environment (Fry, 1978).

The ELT learning-space concept emphasizes that learning is not one universal process but a map of learning territories, a frame of reference within which many different ways of learning can flourish and interrelate. It is a holistic framework that orients the many different ways of learning to one another. As Lewin put it,

> Actually, the term learning refers to a multitude of different phenomena. The statement, "Democracy one has to learn; autocracy is imposed on the person," refers to one type of learning. If one says that the spastic child has to learn to relax one is speaking of a different type of learning. Both types probably have very little to do with learning French vocabulary, and this type again has little to do with learning to like spinach. Have we any right to classify learning to high-jump, to get along with alcohol, and to be friendly with people under the same term, and to expect identical laws to hold for any of these processes? (Cartwright, 1951, p. 65)

One's position in the learning space defines one's experience and thus defines one's "reality." Since a learning space is in the end what the learner experiences it to be, it is the psychological and social dimensions of learning spaces that have the most influence on learning. From this perspective learning spaces can be viewed as aggregates of the characteristics of the people in them. Strange & Banning (2001) argue that the people in a learning space are very powerful influences on the nature of the space. An individual's learning style positions him/her in one of these regions based on his or her unique equilibrium of forces among action, reflection, experiencing, and conceptualizing. A number of studies of learning spaces in higher education have been conducted using the human-aggregate approach by showing the percentage of students whose learning style places them in the different learning space regions (Eickmann, Kolb, & Kolb, 2004; Kolb & Kolb, 2005a).

Comparing Learning Spaces in Management and the Arts

Figures 8.2 and 8.3 show how the learning styles of management and art students are distributed in the learning regions. Art students are concentrated in the experiencing-oriented northern regions of the learning space while management students are concentrated in the thinking southern regions. The north regions have 42.1 percent of art students while the south regions have 23.6 percent. The south regions have 45.7 percent of management students while the north regions have 21.2 percent. There are more art students in the eastern reflecting regions than in the western acting regions (ranging from 35.2 to 26.3 percent). There are more management students in the western acting regions than the eastern reflecting regions (ranging from 36.3 to 30.4 percent). Among art students, the Deciding region is the least populated (3.7 percent) while the least-populated region for management students is imagining (5.1 percent). Among the management students, 10.2 percent are in the Balancing central region while 12.5 percent of art students are there. Boyatzis and Mainemelis found significant correlations between abstract learning styles and grades and GMAT, indicating a bias toward abstraction in evaluation and selection practices. For BFA graduates there was no relationship between grades and learning style.

Figure 8.2
Learning Styles of MBA Students (N = 1286)

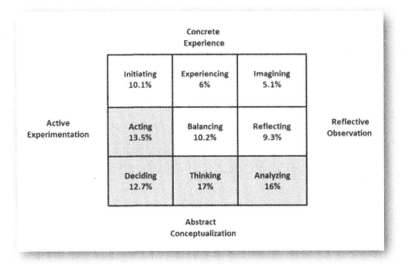

Figure 8.3
Learning Styles of CIA Graduating Students (N = 216)

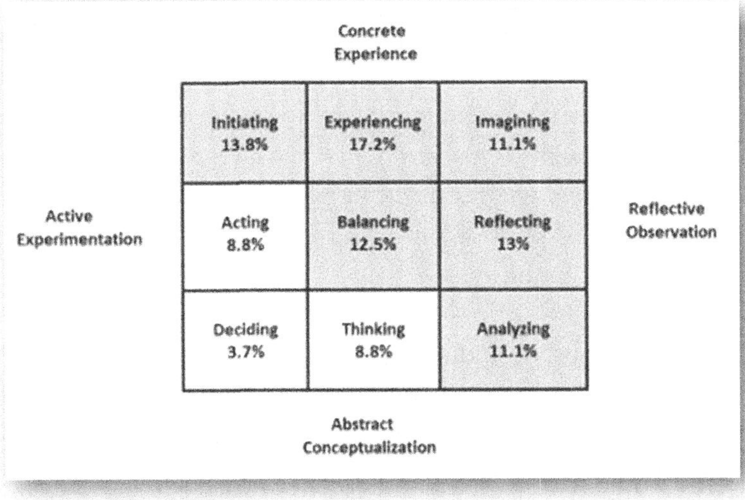

The way the educational process is conducted in art schools and management schools reveals some striking differences that give insight into the nature of learning in the different learning regions (see figure 8.4). Dewey's distinction between artistic and scientific learning helps us understand the difference between the kinds of learning that occur in art education and in management education:

The rhythm of loss of integration with environment and recovery of union not only persists in man, but becomes conscious with him; its conditions are material out of which he forms purposes. Emotion is the conscious sign of a break, actual or impending. The discord is the occasion that induces reflection. Desire for restoration of the union converts mere emotion into interest in objects as conditions of realization of harmony. With the realization, material of reflection is incorporated into objects as their meaning. Since the artist cares in a peculiar way for the phase of experience in which union is achieved, he does not shun moments of resistance and tension. He rather cultivates them, not for their own sake but because of their potentialities, bringing to living consciousness an experience that is unified and total. In contrast with the person whose purpose is esthetic, the scientific man is interested in problems, in situations wherein tension between the matter of observation and of thought is marked. Of course he cares for their resolution. But he does not rest in it; he passes on to another problem using an attained solution only as a stepping stone on which to set on foot further inquiries.

The difference between the esthetic and the intellectual is thus one of the places where emphasis falls in the constant rhythm that marks the interaction of the live creature with his surroundings...Because of the comparative remoteness of his end, the scientific worker operates with symbols, words and mathematical signs. The artist does his thinking in the very qualitative media he works in, and the terms lie so close to the object that he is producing that they merge directly into it. (Dewey, 1934, pp. 15–16)

Figure 8.4
Comparison of Arts Education and Management Education

ARTS EDUCATION	MANAGEMENT EDUCATION
Aesthetic	Scientific
Demo-practice-production-critique	Text driven
Recursive	Discursive
Theory and practice	Theory
Showing	Telling
Expression	Impression
Individualized	Batched
Diverse faculty	Abstract faculty

A first awareness of differences in the management and arts learning spaces came as we were preparing a learning style workshop for art students. We asked what readings we should give and the Provost, Paul Eickmann, said, "You know, for art students learning is not text driven." This stood in dramatic contrast with management education, which is almost entirely organized around texts that deliver an authoritative scientific discourse. The scientific basis of the management curriculum was established in 1959 by an influential Carnegie Foundation report that sought to improve the intellectual respectability of management education by grounding it in three scientific disciplines: economics, mathematics, and behavioral science.

The text-driven approach of management education contrasts with the experiential learning process of demonstration-practice-production-critique that is used in most art classes. This process is repeated recursively in art education while management education is primarily discursive with each topic covered in a linear sequence with little recursive repetition. Management education focuses on telling while art education emphasizes showing. Management education tends to emphasize theory while art education emphasizes integration of theory and practice. Art education focuses on the learners' inside-out expression while management education spends more time on outside-in impression. Most of the time in management classes is spent conveying information, with relatively little time spent on student performance, most of which occurs on tests and papers. In art classes the majority of the time is spent on student expression of ideas and skills. Art education tends to be individualized with small classes and individual attention while management education is organized into large classes with limited individualized attention. An assistant dean at the Columbus College of Art and Design who majored in music as an undergraduate and later got an MBA, contrasted the three-hours-a-week he spent in individual tutorial with his mentor with the shock he experienced in entering a tiered MBA classroom of two hundred students. Finally, art education tends to be represented by faculty members with diverse learning styles whereas management education tends to favor specialized faculty members with a primarily abstract learning orientation.

The comparison between the observed educational programs and teaching methods of CIA arts education and Case MBA education seems consistent with respective student LSI distributions in the nine-region learning space, with MBA students primarily in the Southern thinking and Western acting regions and arts students falling mainly in the Northern feeling and Eastern reflection regions. The corresponding discursive, telling educational methods of the MBA program and the recursive, showing techniques of the art school recall Dewey's description of the scientific worker who "operates with symbols, words and mathematical signs" and the artist who "does his thinking in the very qualitative media he works in."

Creating Learning Spaces for the Enhancement of Experiential Learning

The remaining chapters in Part II of the book focus on how educators can create effective spaces for learning. Chapter 9 is about how to create a hospitable, safe space for learning that achieves an optimal mix of challenge and support. Chapter 10 describes principles for the creation of good conversation and dialogue in the learning space. Chapter 11 is focused on the creation of learner-centered learning spaces. Chapter 12 is about the construction of learning spaces that foster reflection and critical thinking. Chapter 13 explores learning spaces that deepen and sustain learning.

Nine

CREATING A HOSPITABLE SPACE FOR LEARNING

True teachers are those who use themselves as bridges
Over which they invite their students to cross; then,
Having facilitated their crossing, joyfully collapse,
Encouraging them to create their own.

—NIKOS KAZANTZAKIS

One looks back with appreciation to the brilliant
teachers, but with gratitude to those who touched our
human feelings. The curriculum is so much necessary
raw material, but warmth is the vital element for
the growing plant and for the soul of the child.

—CARL JUNG

Engagement in learning is accompanied inevitably by emotions of hope and fear. The hope is for mastery and understanding and the empowerment it brings. The fear has many faces—to make a mistake, to fail, to look stupid, to be embarrassed and humiliated in front of others, even to question one's personal identity and self-worth. No one is immune from the tugs and pulls of hope and fear. The young child on the first day of school and the executive beginning a coaching relationship both experience this paradoxical blend of feelings about the unknown that lies ahead. While the child may be scarcely able to hide his terror, the mature executive is probably able to mask or even deny his fear. For both, however, not knowing is the doorway to knowing and to open the door is an act of courage.

We might call this the need to learn and the fear of learning; echoing the title of an essay by Abraham Maslow, the creator of the theory of self-actualization, called "The Need to Know and the Fear of Knowing." He describes it as follows:

> The need to know for its own sake, for the sheer delight and primitive satisfaction of knowledge and understanding *per se*. It makes the person bigger, wiser, richer, stronger, more evolved, more mature. It represents the actualization of a human potentiality, the fulfillment of the human destiny foreshadowed by human possibilities... But we know that curiosity and exploration are "higher" needs than safety, which is to say that the need to feel safe, secure, unanxious, unafraid is prepotent, stronger than curiosity...The cognitive needs show themselves most clearly in safe and non-anxious situations... We wind up with a dialectical back and forth relationship which is simultaneously a struggle between fear and courage. All those psychological and social factors that increase fear will cut our impulse to know; all factors that permit courage, freedom and boldness will thereby also free our need to know. (Maslow, 1968, pp. 63–67)

Maslow's hierarchy of needs theory, positing an innate motivation to actualize one's potential that can be thwarted by unsatisfied physiological and safety needs, was immensely popular in the mid-twentieth century. It was foundational for the wider human potential movement including the influential works of Douglas McGregor (2006), Chris Argyris (1957), Carl Rogers (1961), Edgar Schein and Warren Bennis (1965). It later lost some of its pragmatic appeal as many felt that hunger and physical and psychological safety were not great concerns in modern developed countries. Today it deserves a second look as many inner-city school children not only suffer from hunger and malnutrition (over 50 percent of US public-school children are eligible for federally subsidized meals at school), but they also fear for their physical safety on a daily basis and feel a lack of trust and psychological safety. When a learning space is dominated by hunger and violence, meaningful learning becomes extremely difficult.

Psychological Safety

In organizations, rather than fear for physical safety, the focus today is more on social and interpersonal *psychological* safety as a way to release innovation, team effectiveness, and productivity. As organizations have become more concerned about learning to cope with rapid change, diversity, and knowledge-intensive complexity, psychological safety has become an important focus of research and practice, being the most studied enabling condition in group dynamics and team learning (Edmondson & Lei, 2014). As a characteristic of a learning space, psychological safety is a norm that includes respect and caring for one another and trust in their good intentions. It is a climate where taking risks is possible and mistakes can be made. Differences are used for learning and difficult conversations can occur without reprisal. As a norm, psychological safety cannot be dictated but must be learned through experience. An educator can stress that such a norm is desired and supported; but learners need to create it together and experience it before they believe it.

Esther Wyss-Flamm's (2002) study of the impact of early pivotal experiences in a team illustrates how a group's experience together shapes psychological safety. In her qualitative study of year-long multicultural learning teams in a management course, she compared three multicultural teams that scored high on Edmondson's (1999) psychological safety scale with three teams that scored low on psychological safety. She developed narratives that told the story of the team's experience over time, based on extensive individual interviews with team members. She discovered that teams established conversational routines based on pivotal incidents that occurred early in the team's life. These routines were repeated in the conversational stream of the group, setting the tone for what she called the team's organizing principle. The safe teams established conversational routines that supported a shared team identity where members belonged and were valued. One high-psychological safety team, for example, got lost in an early orienteering exercise and lost the competition but was able to laugh together about it and have an important conversation about working together. The unsafe teams were fragmented and dominated by individualized perceptions and agendas. A low-safety team, for example, had a disturbing incident between two members early on that resulted in fear of expressing conflict and resulting difficulty in finding a common focus.

Maslow's self-actualization theory and the human potential movement in general are not without critics. Some years ago we were driving through upstate New York when our radio picked up a talk radio show where the host was in the middle of a rant about how permissiveness and lack of discipline were destroying American culture. We were surprised and shocked when he said, "And two men are responsible for this decline in values—Abraham Maslow and Carl Rogers!" This view that psychologically safe and supportive environments promote low standards and lack of discipline is, in our view, a misunderstanding of the theory. Amy Edmondson has responded to this critique this way, "Psychological safety is not about being nice—or about lowering performance standards. Quite the opposite: It's about recognizing that high performance *requires* the openness, flexibility, and interdependence that can be developed only in a psychologically safe environment, especially when the situation is changing or complex. Psychological safety makes it possible to give tough feedback and have difficult conversations which demand trust and respect—without the need to tiptoe around the truth" (Edmondson, 2008, p. 65).

Psychological safety is a necessary condition for meeting learning challenges, not a substitute for them. Sanner and Bunderson in their meta-analysis of research on the relationship between psychological safety and team learning and performance argue that, "Psychological safety creates a context in which team members feel safe to engage in the risky behaviors that promote experiential learning—experimentation, asking questions, and flagging/discussing errors—and these behaviors facilitate higher performance." (2015, p. 2) The results of their meta-analysis found that psychological safety was important for performance and learning only in situations where the work was knowledge-intensive, requiring complexity, creativity, and sense-making.

> It is precisely in such knowledge intensive tasks where experiential learning—that is, experimenting and sharing perspectives, reflecting on past actions—becomes particularly important for group performance…in settings where learning is critical…psychological safety becomes an essential performance requirement. (2015, p. 4)

A Hospitable Learning Space

As educators, our challenge is to recognize the hopes and fears of learners and to create a learning space that respects, supports, and empowers them to courageous action that overcomes fear and increases mastery. In defining our approach to the socioemotional factors in the creation of learning spaces (Jensen & Kolb, 2002) we have been inspired by the concept of hospitality as articulated by Henri Nouwen (1975) and Parker Palmer (1983, 1998). Calling on numerous biblical stories that emphasize welcoming the stranger, they describe this challenging and supportive learning space as one that welcomes the stranger in a spirit of hospitality where "students and teachers can enter into a fearless communication with each other and allow their respective life experiences to be their primary and most valuable source of growth and maturation" (Nouwen, 1975, p. 60).

Parker Palmer expands on Nouwen's work and its application in education:

> To be inhospitable to strangers or strange ideas, however unsettling they may be, is to be hostile to the possibility of truth; hospitality is not only an ethical virtue but an epistemological one as well… Hospitality is not an end in itself. It is offered for the sake of what

it can allow, permit, encourage, and yield. A learning space needs to be hospitable not to make learning painless, but to make the painful things possible, things without which no learning can occur—things like exposing ignorance, testing tentative hypotheses, challenging false or partial information, and mutual criticism of thought. Each of these is essential to obedience to truth. But none of them can happen in an atmosphere where people feel threatened and judged. (Palmer, 1983, p. 74)

To learn requires facing and embracing differences; be they differences between skilled expert performance and one's novice status, differences between one's deeply held ideas and beliefs and new ideas, or differences in the life experience and values of others. To be different is to be a stranger and different ideas are strange. The spirit of hospitality is to welcome the stranger and make the strange familiar, holding a space that respects difference while building bridges of understanding. In our own work we find it useful to welcome learners in the same way we strive to welcome guests in our home, with courtesy and friendly attention to each guest as an individual. We introduce everyone and invite them to share their stories, helping to build relationships and feel comfortable. Classrooms and workshop spaces can often be inhospitable and alienating physical spaces. In the next chapter on conversational learning we describe how we have experimented with ways to make the learning space more hospitable by rearranging seating or bringing music, flowers, books, and "show and tell" items related to the topic at hand.

Respect for Learners and Their Experience

In the introduction we spoke of parental love as the primal base of the educator relationship, while noting the limitations on love imposed by institutional and contractual relationships. If we cannot always love our students, we can at least respect them and their life experiences. To learn experientially one must first of all own and value their experience. Students will often say,

"But I don't have any experience," meaning that they don't believe that their experience is of any value or interest to the teacher or for learning the subject matter at hand.

If you think about the teachers who have had a great influence on your life, it is most likely that they paid attention to you as an individual and showed interest in your experiences and ideas. A basic way to show respect is to know and use students' names. Being known is the first step to feeling respected. We refer to this as the Cheers/Jeers experiential continuum. At one end, learners feel that they are members of a learning community who are known and respected by faculty and colleagues and whose experience is taken seriously, a space "where everybody knows your name." At the other extreme are learning environments where learners feel alienated, alone, un-recognized, and devalued. Learning and growth in the Jeers environment "where nobody knows your name" can be difficult.

In institutionalized educational systems with large classes and multiple courses to teach, knowing and naming our students can be a seemingly in-surmountable task for the educator, though one that is well worth the effort. President Lawrence Summers of Harvard dedicated his 2003 commence-ment address to the introduction of a comprehensive examination of the undergraduate program, motivated in part by a letter he received from a top science student that contained the statement, "I am in the eighth semester of college and there is not a single science professor here who could identify me by name." Summers concludes "The only true measure of a successful educational model is our students' experience of it" (Summers, 2003, p. 64).

In our teaching activities we have, in recent years, made learning of student names and using them regularly a priority. Remembering names is a significant challenge for both of us. As teachers we face a host of new students each semester and we have learned that it means a lot to students to have their teacher know them personally by name. As academics, our reflec-tive and abstract learning style doesn't help, because we tend to be so focused on the content that we want to deliver that we forget to connect personally with students. So after excusing ourselves for years with the bad-memory excuse, we adopted a learning attitude and applied the experiential learning cycle to the problem.

The technique is to apply a four-step learning process several times in interaction with the person—Attend, Reflect, Connect, and Act. While first meeting persons, Attend to the experience of being with them and hearing their name. Get a feeling for the person. If you miss the name, slow down the interaction and ask them to repeat it. Don't be embarrassed. Most people are flattered that you care to get their name right. Next, Reflect on your experience of the person and what their name means to you. Connect your reflections to related ideas you may have like, "This Betty is different than the other Bettys I know. My sister's name is Betty, too. " Finally, Act. Use their name several times in your conversation. And afterward mention their name to others. Be forewarned, however, that the first time you try this learning approach you may totally forget the person's name. You may have the steps of the technique in mind rather than meeting the person. Like any complex skill, deliberate learning requires practice and with practice the technique becomes automatic and fades into the background.

By practicing this approach we have significantly improved in our ability to remember names and we support each other in a friendly competition to test ourselves after class. We have also found that it is useful to share our objective with our class and enlist their help and forgiveness for mistakes we make. We encourage them to use the names of their fellow students and join us in creating an environment where we all know each other. When a class becomes a group of individuals who are known to one another and to the teacher, it can be transformed into a truly hospitable learning space.

Unconditional Positive Regard

Carl Rogers sets a somewhat higher goal for us as educators with his concept of unconditional positive regard. Of the three most important curative factors that research on nondirective therapy has identified—empathy, congruence or genuineness in the relationship, and unconditional positive regard—it is the latter that is arguably the most important (Rogers, 1961). Wilkins argues, "The communication of unconditional positive regard is a major curative factor in any approach to therapy; congruence and empathy merely provide the context in which it is credible...The limiting factor in the effectiveness of counseling and psychotherapy is the extent to which the therapist is able perceptibly to extend unconditional positive regard to the client" (2000, p. 23). Rogers describes unconditional positive regard as follows:

> The therapist experiences a warm caring for the client—a caring which is not possessive, which demands no personal gratification. It is an atmosphere which simply demonstrates "I care"; not "I care for you if you behave thus and so"...I have often used the term "acceptance" to describe this aspect of the therapeutic climate. It involves as much feeling for the client's expression of negative, "bad," painful, fearful, and abnormal feelings as for his expression of "good," positive, mature, confident and social feelings. It involves an acceptance of and a caring for the client as a *separate* person, with permission for him to have his own feelings and experiences, and to find his own meaning in them. To the degree that the therapist can provide this safety-creating climate of unconditional positive regard, significant learning is likely to take place. (1961, pp. 283–284)

Rogers himself admits that to show unconditional positive regard for everyone is extremely difficult; though it is essential to promote change and growth. One reason for the difficulty is that Rogers believes that such regard for oneself is essential to be able to give it to others. Not to mention that we often are involved with learners whose behavior conflicts with our values. Wilkins describes the difficulty of giving unconditional positive regard:

> Because it depends on the attitude individuals hold toward themselves, unconditional positive regard is the hardest therapeutic attitude to develop. It cannot be effectively faked, and tolerance (the

ability to patiently endure or "allow") is quite different...Because we have values and opinions, because few of us are without our own pain and shame, this is very difficult. Perhaps the first thing each of us needs to accept is that our ability to offer unconditional positive regard is limited; the second is to discover those limits and seek to expand them. (2000, pp. 30-34)

Why is it so important to strive to offer unconditional positive regard to learners? Most educators probably rely more often on conditional positive regard, given when expectations are met or performance is superior; and do their best to control unconditional disregard for the occasional student who is particularly annoying. When one is able to express warmth and caring for the whole person with all their limitations and shortcomings, that person is encouraged to bring their whole self into the learning space. This increases the probability that the person will be able to own his or her hopes and dreams and examine his or her personal weaknesses and insecurities, making possible conversation about committing to learning challenges and working on deficiencies, lack of knowledge, and feelings of inadequacy. This, after all, is the true work of learning.

A conditional positive regard learning space, on the other hand, encourages learners to show only their best face and hide their weak spots and mistakes. To ask questions or show weakness risks loss of the conditional praise and reward. At the group level it can silence and disenfranchise learners who are behind and need help, as attention is focused on the "best" students. Conditional regard increases dependency on the educator and over time can increase the learner's conformity and need for approval from others, stifling internal self-direction and creativity.

Holding a Space of Challenge and Support

A hospitable learning space is one that supports learners in taking on challenging learning goals. The concept of a learning space characterized by a blend of challenge and support was first proposed by the great personality and social psychologist Nevitt Sanford in *The American College* (1962). He later (1966) modified the theory to include consideration of a person's readiness for different levels of challenge. In 1981 he proposed a challenge/response theory of adult development. Development occurs primarily in response to the challenges of adult life. Those who, by choice or fate, do not face these challenges are less likely to develop mature responses to them. He argues that self-insight is critical. The absence of opportunity for self-examination and dialogue with others about life challenges and the appropriate responses to them is a significant barrier to development.

As educators it is important for us to set high standards and put forth challenging learning objectives. Yet, in the end it is the learner who must choose to accept the challenge. We can play an important role by providing a supportive learning space that stimulates conversation with us and their fellow learners, allowing learners to consider and commit themselves to challenging leaning goals. As Robert Kegan says, "People grow best where they continuously experience an ingenious blend of challenge and support" (1994, p. 42). As Kegan implies by his use of the term "ingenious blend," creating and holding this learning space is not easy. He notes that while educational institutions have been quite successful in challenging students, they have been much less successful in providing support. One reason for this may be that challenges tend to be specific and immediate while support must go beyond an immediate "You can do it" statement. It requires a climate or culture of support that the learner can trust to "hold" them over time. Kisfalvi and Oliver (2015) apply Winnicott's concept of holding, which includes "management of experiences that are inherent in existence" (1965, p. 44) to the experiential classroom as a safe container that provides students with the boundaries and limits that give a feeling "of being 'held together' and not in danger of chaotic disintegration in an emotionally charged but unmanaged situation" (Kisfalvi & Oliver, 2015, p. 724).

Ten

Making Space for Conversational Learning

*The more genuine the conversation is, the less its conduct
lies within the will of either partner. Thus, a genuine
conversation is never the one that we wanted to conduct...
[It is] more correct to say that we fall into conversation,
or even that we become involved in it...A conversation
has a spirit of its own, and the language in which it is
conducted bears its own truth within it—i.e., that it
allows something to "emerge" which henceforth exists.*

—Hans Georg Gadamer

A story that is often told about Herb Shepard, the founder of our department of Organizational Behavior at Case Western Reserve
University, describes a process consulting engagement that he had with the
Commandant of Wright/Patterson Air Force Base and his direct reporting
officers. The general began the meeting and proceeded to move through
the agenda with little comment from the other attendees. At one point
he turned to Herb and asked if he had any suggestions. Herb replied, "I
think we should have a break." The group got up and began talking among
themselves. Then they returned to the meeting and continued through the

agenda as before. Again the general asked Herb if he had any comment. And again Herb suggested a break. The group engaged in animated conversation before returning to hear the general proceed through the agenda. After a while, the general again asked Herb for comment and received the same request for a break. Exasperated, the general asked, "Why is it every time I ask you comment you suggest a break?" "Because the break is the only time that anything is happening," he replied.

The purpose of Herb's intervention was to address the restricted nature of the conversational learning space in the commandant's team meeting. A focus on proceeding efficiently through the agenda and the emphasis on hierarchical ranking were producing a meeting dominated by one-way communication from the general and little participation from his subordinates. When the break was taken, the solidarity among peers allowed comfortable active conversation. A similar dynamic often occurs in the traditional lecture classroom where genuine conversation can be extremely restricted or nonexistent. At the break or end of the class, the sometimes painfully silent classroom will suddenly come alive with spontaneous conversation among students. Significant learning can occur in these out-of-class conversations, although it may not always be the learning the teacher intended. In this chapter we will explore the nature of conversational learning spaces that produce such good conversation.

The Conversational Learning Cycle

Conversation is the most ubiquitous and common form of experiential learning. Indeed, one could say that the purpose of conversation is learning. In conversation, individual cycles of learning merge in a mutual exchange of speaking and listening. In listening we experience the other and reflect on what they are saying. In speaking we think and formulate intentions about how to respond and act to express them. Hunt (1987, 1991) suggests that this is a learning spiral shared between individuals in human interaction. People relate to one another in a pattern of alternating "reading" and "flexing" that mirrors the experiential learning process. When one person is *reading*—receiving feedback (CE) and formulating perceptions (RO), the other person is *flexing*—creating intentions based on those perceptions (AC) and acting on them (AE). As the exchange continues, both parties alternate between reading and flexing.

Figure 10.1

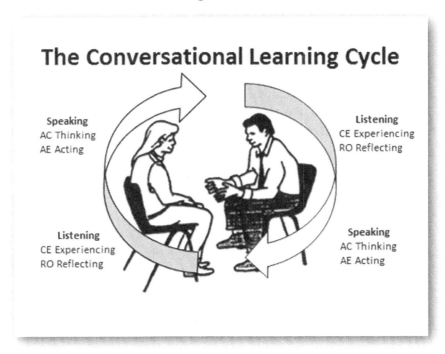

Although the great European philosophers of conversation Jürgen Habermas and Hans Georg Gadamer both see the conversational learning cycle as the way to resolve conflicts, solve social problems, and increase human understanding, their concept of the ideal conversational learning space differs in their emphasis on the thinking and talking vs. experiencing and listening.

Habermas describes his central idea as follows: "I think that a certain form of unrestrained communication brings to the fore the deepest force of reason, which enables us to overcome egocentric or ethnocentric perspectives and reach an expanded…view," (cited in Stephens, 1994, p. 30). He describes the desired conversational space as an "ideal speech situation" characterized by rational speech, symmetry, and reciprocal recognition in an environment free from coercion with participants motivated to reach rational agreement. Many credit Habermas for rescuing the great Enlightenment project of human emancipation through reason, which ushered in the modernist period in history. His "rescue" is accomplished by replacing Descartes's solitary reflection with rational reflection in relational conversation. In the relational perspective, meaning is intersubjective. It resides, not in the objectivity of what is said nor in the subjectivity of what is heard; but in the interaction of conversation—the validity of meaning is figured out by discussing with others.

Gadamer, whose approach to conversation is considered by many to be postmodern, is less sanguine about the potential of the methods and procedures of reason to produce universal truth. He views understanding as an ongoing process where historical, traditional understanding meets conditions in the present. This process is never completed. Since there is no final understanding or truth, Gadamer argues that there can be no method or technique for achieving understanding or arriving at truth. In his view, conversation is about experiencing the *Sache*, the situation or context and the problem or topic at hand. We approach the *Sache* with prejudice or prejudgments acquired from our traditions, which enable our understanding. This prejudice does not have the negative connotation of error in judgement; but rather is a starting point of understanding. In what Gadamer calls the hermeneutic circle of understanding, participants' prejudices meet the concrete experience of the *Sache* and the prejudgments of other participants in conversation. He describes experience as negative and open in that it involves a violation of expectations, casting doubt on our prejudices. In the hermeneutic cycle, we open ourselves to the experience of the *Sache* and the views of others, allowing these experiences to transform our consciousness and reconsider our prejudgments. The conversation encompasses self-understanding and understanding of the *Sache* as prejudices open up what is to be understood, and themselves become evident in that process.

Gadamer views understanding as a matter of negotiation between oneself and one's partners in the hermeneutical conversation. They come to an agreement about the Sache by resolving differences between individual prejudices and perspectives, which he refers to as horizons. This means establishing a common horizon or fusion of horizons of understanding. The goal of conversation is not universal truth but a consensus achieved through this fusion of horizons of understanding among participants. This hermeneutical circle of conversation helps individuals escape the "tyranny of hidden prejudices" as "each person opens himself up to the other, truly accepts his point of view as valid and transposes himself into the other to such an extent that he understands…what he says" (Gadamer, 1989, p. 385). With the fusion of horizons comes a new context of meaning, enabling integration of what before was strange or alien.

As educators we can draw from both Habermas and Gadamer. We can create procedures to ensure rational problem-solving and an "ideal speech situation" through such methods as formation of teams based on diversity and use of collaborative processes to ensure that all voices can be heard. We can also create a hospitable learning space based on principles described in the previous chapter to deepen experiencing and listening. Gadamer's hermeneutic circle of understanding is similar to the experiential learning cycle in that prejudices are dialectically related to concrete experiences of the *Sache* that challenge them.

The Conversational Learning Space

Making space for conversation can take many forms—making physical space, such as when a manager moves from behind his or her desk to join colleagues around a table; making temporal space, such as when a family sets aside weekly time for family conversation; or making emotional space through receptive listening. It is easy to become so focused on the conversation itself, on what is said, and how speech flows from one participant to another, that one fails to notice the bounded space that holds and shapes the conversation. Conversational cannot exist without a receptive space to hold it. A conversational learning space has two faces—boundaries that define and protect a conversational space and the internal processes such as group composition, rituals, and norms that shape the conversational interaction. As conversations progress, these processes shape the conversation and at the same time define boundaries that define the space. These processes determine what can be said and not said, what and who is heard and not heard, who has voice and who does not have voice in the conversation. At the same time, the processes create boundaries that define who is in and who is out of the conversation. There is a paradoxical quality to conversational boundaries. Conversation across boundaries is difficult and can block conversation; yet the space created inside the boundaries can create enough safety for the open exploration of differences across various dialectical continua. "From this perspective, boundaries are not confines but 'shape-givers' that can provide us with healthy space to grow…boundaries are not prisons, rather, they serve an essential function to make our existence more alive and vibrant" (Wyss-Flamm, 2002, p. 315).

In *Conversational Learning* (Baker, Jensen, & Kolb, 2002) we described the conversational learning space as defined by five dialectic dimensions. Good conversation is more likely to occur in spaces that integrate thinking and feeling, talking and listening, leadership and solidarity, recognition of individuality and relatedness, and discursive and recursive processes. When the conversational space is dominated by one extreme of these dimensions, for example, talking without listening, conversational learning is diminished.

The dialectic perspective on conversational learning suggests that conversation is a process of meaning-making whereby understanding is achieved through the interplay of opposites and contradictions. Dialectic inquiry can lead to the generation of new ideas and concepts through one's awareness of a tension and paradox between two or more opposites. It involves stating a point of view and questioning it from other points of view, eventually seeking consensual agreement that in turn is ultimately questioned from still other perspectives as in Gadamer's hermeneutic circle described previously. Dialectical inquiry aspires to *holism through the embracing of differences and contradictions.* It begins with contradictions, or literally opposing speeches. By taking the most opposite imaginable point of view, one increases the chance of encompassing the whole situation. The dialectical dimensions of the conversational space can open a conversational process where opposing ideas can be explored, resolved, or embraced. The five dialectics of a conversational space are described briefly here and again later in the chapter.

The Learning Cycle Dialectics of Experiencing/Thinking and Action/Reflection. For the conversational learning cycle to fully function, the conversational learning space must be open to experiencing and thinking and acting and reflecting. The dialectical relationship between concrete knowing and abstract knowing in the learning process is one of the central concepts of the ELT. James described this dialectic between concrete percepts and abstract concept as follows:

> We thus see clearly what is gained and what is lost when percepts are translated into concepts. Perception is solely of the here and now; conception is of the like and unlike, of the future, and of the past, and of the far away. But this map of what surrounds the present, like all maps, is only a surface; its features are but abstract signs and symbols of things that in themselves are concrete bits of sensible experience. We have but to weigh extent against content, thickness against spread, and we see that for some purposes the one, for other purposes the other has the higher value. Who can decide off hand which is absolutely better to live and to understand life? We must do both alternately, and a man can no more limit himself to either than a pair of scissors can cut with a single one of its blades. (1977, p. 243)

Concrete knowing involves experiencing the world primarily through sensing and feeling in an immediate, tacit, and subjective way, whereas abstract knowing is centered in a conceptual, linguistic, and objective interpretation of the world. Integrated knowing is achieved when learners equally engage in both dimensions of knowing in a given learning context. In conversational learning, concrete knowing manifests itself as learners engage emotionally in conversation, whereas abstract knowing is manifested in the learners' abstract and conceptual mode of engagement in conversation.

Action and reflection define the other major dialectic that drives the learning cycle; the idea that the creation of knowledge and meaning occurs through the active engagement in ideas and experiences in the external world and through internal reflection about the qualities of these experiences and ideas (Kolb, 1984, 2015). Thus, learning occurs through the dialectical movement of action and reflection as learners move outward into the external world and inward into themselves. The same principle applies to conversational learning. Knowledge is created through conversation as learners actively voice their ideas and experiences in conversation and make meaning of the experiences and ideas through reflection. The balancing of action and reflection is crucial to conducting a meaningful conversation, since suppression of one dimension will automatically hurt the other. Freire describes the dynamic interplay of this dialectic of reflection and action as follows:

> Within the word we find two dimensions, reflection and action, in such radical interaction that if one is sacrificed—even in part—the other immediately suffers…When…deprived…of action, reflection automatically suffers as well; and the word is changed into idle chatter, into verbalism, into an alienated "blah." On the other hand, if action is emphasized exclusively, to the detriment of reflection, the word is converted into activism…action for action's sake negates the true praxis and makes dialogue impossible. (1992, pp. 75, 78)

Discourse and Recourse. A central tenet of Gadamer's hermeneutics is the historicity of understanding, a concept that adds a temporal dimension to conversational learning. In his view, understanding is an ongoing process where prejudgments shaped by historical tradition meet in the immediate experience of conversation about the *Sache*, and where new understanding results in a modified tradition. Time in the conversation is thus twofold, the immediate experience of circular time in the here and now and the developing discourse in linear past-present-future time. Every conversational event is deepened by its traditional origins and its ongoing history.

In our formulation (Baker, Jensen, & Kolb, 2002) we describe this process as a dialectic between discourse and recourse. The discursive process is at work when learning is grounded in the *naming of the world*, whereas in a recursive process learners return to subjects that *reappear* anew through in-depth questioning and inquiry. The discursive process is often seen as logical and cognitive, giving the conversation momentum, and keeping it from becoming repetitive. The recursive process, on the other hand, is a more ontological and subjective desire to return over time to the deeply held ideas and experiences generated in conversation. In this sense, ontological recourse is cyclical in nature, where ideas and concepts acquire new meaning as individuals question and inquire anew about their experiences.

As illustrated in figure 10.2, the discursive process follows a linear progression over time from precourse, to discourse, to postcourse. Precourse is a manifestation of previous conversations, which sets up the assumptive frame for the discourse; the collective prejudgments that individuals bring into the conversation. In anticipation of joining a circle of conversation, individuals have assumptions, expectations, and agendas for the experience they will embark on that will ultimately influence and shape the discourse as they join and establish their positions in the conversation. At the conclusion of the conversation, the discourse continues as "postcourse," where there is a process of selecting what to keep from the conversation and what to throw away. The resulting story of the conversation becomes precourse for future conversations, thus transporting the discourse into other contexts in the future. Thus any conversational discourse is embedded in a complex network of previous and future conversations.

Figure 10.2
The Discourse/Recourse Dialectic in Conversation

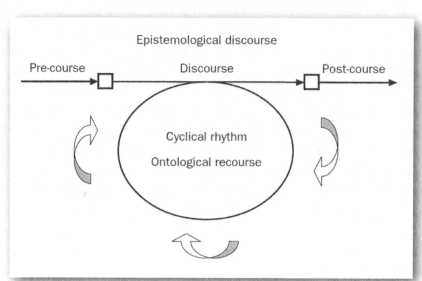

While discourse is an epistemological process of naming the world through language, recourse is a more tacit, ontological process of being in the world. It is a process whereby ideas and experiences in conversation have time to "sink in" and feelings and beliefs "bubble up" to consciousness. When the discourse is led by a high-status speaker or an urgent agenda, as in the organizational and classroom examples cited at the beginning of this chapter, the ontological process of recourse is often blocked. Baker (2010) describes the necessity of balancing the discursive process with its attendant fear of *losing time* with the recursive process of *taking time.*

For this reason silence in conversation, or more often its absence, is a powerful clue to whether the recursive process is operative in the conversation. In "Speech is Silver, Silence is Gold," Schweickart (1996) argues that Habermas's discourse ethics is too speech- and argumentation-oriented, and fails to take account of the importance of the silence of a listening perspective in a relational approach to understanding. An interesting study by Rowe (1974, reported in Jaworski, 1993) examined the quality of teacher instruction. She examined the silent wait time of teachers after asking a question and before responding to a question. Rowe found that in both cases the recorded wait time averaged one second. Teachers were then trained to wait longer, increasing the period of silence after a question and before responding to a student answer to three seconds. This resulted in higher-quality instruction as longer periods of silence between questions and answers produced longer student responses. The average number of student responses increased from five to seventeen and failures to respond dropped from seven to one. Inferences from evidence increased from six to fourteen and student-to-student interactions and student-initiated questions also increased.

In his philosophical analysis of Heidegger, Hans (1989) argues that humans tend to be driven primarily by the linear, epistemological discourse in what Heidegger called a "revenge against time," shying away from the recursive, ontological end of the dialectic. The accentuation of the linear discourse, says Hans, is caused by a fear of the *return of the same.* In returning to the same, one stands face-to-face with one's *being*—an ultimate ontological state that manifests itself in the cyclical passing of time. This fear of *being* drives some people to embrace the epistemological, sequential progression of events, where they find comfort in a sense of progress and absence of repetition. However, the regular return with a difference is at the core of all understanding, and it ultimately guides humans to attain a higher level of consciousness. Freire (1992) describes the understanding that is achieved through simultaneous engagement in the epistemological and ontological dimensions of the dialectics as follows: "To exist, humanly, is to name the world, to change it. Once named, the world in its turn reappears to the namers as a problem and requires of them a new naming" (p. 76).

As learners engage in conversation, they situate themselves within two qualitatively distinct, though closely interconnected, experiences that are specific to each temporal dimension. The discursive process unfolds progressively from the past, to present, to future in a continuous flow of activities. The weekly topic outlined in the course syllabus serves as the underlying structure that allows for these activities to unfold over time. Through the discursive process, learners become aware of what they know by explicitly voicing and sharing their thoughts and ideas related to their subject of interest to the larger group. What happens after the ideas and thoughts are voiced and heard is largely influenced and shaped by the recursive process of learning. During the conversation, learners arrive at choice points where they are faced with the decision to move on to a new topic of discussion or return to the previous subject that continues to intrigue, disturb, or capture their attention. Learners' choices to return to their topics of interest is largely dictated by intrinsic interest as well as emotional investment they have in the subjects of their choice. The intrinsic as well emotional engagements with the topic operate as primary motives for learners to go back in time and attend to the subject of their interest in a deeper way. In the absence of this recursive process, the discursive process would take over and drive the conversation in a predominantly linear fashion. The discursive process is a manifestation of learners' desire to move on and drive the conversation forward in an active way.

Individuality and Relationality: Inside Out and Outside In. According to evolutionary biology, humans have two biological prime directives—to preserve the self as an individual and to preserve the species as a whole. Individuality and relatedness in ELT are poles of a fundamental dialectic of development, "The capacities to form a mutual relationship with another, to participate in society, and to be dedicated to one's own self-interest and expression emerge out of the integration and consolidation of individuality and relatedness in the development of a self-identity" (Guisinger & Blatt, 1994, pp. 108–109). Similarly, Cook-Greuter (1999) and David Bakan (1966) argue that there is a human need to fulfill the double goals of autonomy (differentiation, independence, mastery) and homonomy (integration, participation, belonging).

The inside-out learning mode challenges learners to return to their reservoirs of life experience and stand face-to-face with their own deeply held values, feelings, and thoughts, and make them the starting points of their learning process. Each of us is deeply unique and we have an imperative to embrace and express that uniqueness, for the good of ourselves and for the world. Martha Graham said it well, "There is a vitality, a life force, an energy, a quickening, that is translated through you into action, and because there is only one of you in all time, this expression is unique, and if you block it, it will never exist through any other medium and will be lost." Inside-out learning finds its roots in the ideas of humanist thinkers such as Maslow(1968), Rogers(1961), Freire(1992), and Hunt(1987) for whom the process of individuation toward becoming a whole person cannot be achieved without valuing or owning one's own experience of who one is, regardless of how others construe what one is or should become.

The path toward becoming an authentic individual, however, is met with a paradox along the way, the outside-in process of learning that challenges the very process of inside-out learning. Outside-in learning refers to external socialization—the relationships, ideas, and events that act upon us and shape our knowing. Often, we find ourselves caught between the conflicting demands of the external world and the need to follow our true voice from within. How one integrates the paradoxes and conflicts generated by the tension between inside out and outside in ultimately determines one's success in becoming a whole person. If the journey toward becoming an authentic individual requires one to resist conformity to the outward expectations and conceptions of others, what is one to become at the end of the journey? As much as we may exert our own individuality and even claim the victory of having achieved it, the fully independent self will always remain one step ahead of us, for, contrary to our perceptions, our individuality is very much shaped in relationships with others. Paradoxically, the awakening of our own individuality is achieved by entering in conversation with others who in turn reinforce and acknowledge our freedom and existence as individuals. Carl Rogers's reflection on his professional and personal life is an insightful example of someone whose selfless act of extending oneself to others is drawn from his very capacity and willingness to be himself:

> Yet the paradoxical aspect of my experience is that the more I am simply willing to be myself, in all this complexity of life and the more I am willing to understand and accept the realities in myself and in the other person, the more change seems to be stirred up.

It is a very paradoxical thing—to the degree that each one of us is willing to be himself, then he finds not only himself changing; but he finds that other people to whom he relates are also changing. At least this is a very vivid part of my experience, and one of the deepest things I think I have learned in my personal and professional life. (1961, p. 22)

In *Women's Ways of Knowing*, Belenky et al. (1986) approach inter-subjectivity through the concepts of separate and connected knowing. According to their study, separate knowing operates in a primarily abstract mode assuming autonomy, extrication of self, and doubt; whereas connected knowing assumes relatedness, empathy, use of self, and connection. Their research revealed a more inter-subjective way of knowing, where learning is a process of:

Weaving together the strands of rational and emotive thought and of integrating objective and subjective knowing. Rather than extricating the self in the acquisition of knowledge, these women used themselves in rising to a new way of thinking. As Adele described it, "You let the inside out and the outside in." (1986, pp. 134–135)

Status and Solidarity: Ranking and Linking. Human relationships can be portrayed on a two-dimensional, interpersonal space of status and solidarity (Schwitzgabel & Kolb, 1974). Status is an asymmetrical relationship of ranking related to influencing and being influenced, while solidarity is a symmetrical relationship of linking related to mutual exchange and reciprocity. A conversational space is organized along these two dimensions such that a space characterized by ranking and low linking will produce top-down one-way communication while a space characterized by high linking and low ranking will produce conformity and agreement. The integration of the dialectics of ranking and linking opens the most satisfying and productive conversational space. Some measure of both status and solidarity is necessary to sustain conversational learning. Without some sense of status positioning, where one or more participants take the initiative and share expertise and experience, the conversation can lose direction. Without solidarity, where participants build on and link to each other, conversation can lose connection and relevance and not benefit from the diverse perspectives and expertise of each person. A space that combines linking and ranking allows for what is called functional role leadership (Kayes, Kayes, & Kolb, 2005a—also see chapter 7), where leadership and influence is granted to the person best qualified to handle the situation at hand.

Wilber (1995) argues that living system is made whole by a healthy interaction of hierarchy (ranking) and heterarchy (linking). A healthy hierarchy contributes to the wholeness and integrative capacity of a living system. Its ultimate goal is the actualization of each individual member as a valuable contributor. This kind of hierarchy turns pathological when its functioning is based on force or threat that results in suppression of individuals, groups, or individual actualization, thus undermining the good of the whole. In a normal heterarchy, no element is given special importance or dominant position; each element strives to contribute equally to the wholeness of the system. A normal heterarchy becomes pathological when an individual element "loses itself in others—and all distinctions, of value or identity are lost... Thus pathological heterarchy means not union but fusion; not integration but dissociation; not relating but dissolving" (Wilber, 1995, pp. 23–24).

The Learning and Development Seminar: The Evolution of a Conversational Learning Space

In 1988 we began an experiment in conversational learning by converting a traditional academic PhD seminar to a conversational learning format. The seminar on learning and development was created in 1988 to introduce PhD students to experiential learning and adult development perspectives on organizational behavior. The course description of the seminar was as follows:

This course provides an exploration of the learning and development paradigm underlying the human potential development approach to human resource development. The origins of this approach in the naturalist epistemologies—John Dewey's pragmatism, Kurt Lewin's Gestalt psychology, the works of James, Follett, Emerson, Piaget, Maslow, Rogers, and others—and the current research in adult development, in biology and brain/mind research, artificial intelligence, epistemology, and adult learning will be considered. The course will focus on applications of these ideas to current issues in human resource development such as adult learning in higher education, advanced professional development and organizational learning and development. (Kolb & Kolb, 2003)

The experiment continued for many years until 2004, allowing us to explore the historicity of conversational understanding by tracing the evolution of the conversational space over these years from tacit, intuitively felt notions of conversational learning to the explicit development of theory and practice of conversational learning reported in *Conversational Learning* (Baker, Jensen, & Kolb, 2002). This evolutionary process can be seen as experiential learning in conversation as learners in a given class move through the learning process of experiencing, reflecting, conceptualizing, and acting to create new experiences. Through this process each class became a self-organizing system by focusing on certain ideas and trends and turning away from others. The way each group organized itself was passed onto future generations of the course through several means: through modifications of readings in the syllabus to reflect and accommodate changes in participants' interests as well as the instructor's need to introduce new ideas and concepts; through conversation starters, a one-page summary of thoughts and reflections voluntarily written and shared by participants in the class on a rich array of topics and experiences of a particular interest to them; through introduction of various artifacts in the class that served as reminders of previously discussed topics and ideas; and, finally, through Kolb's position as transmitter of previous ideas, perspectives, and experiences over the course of the twelve-year life of the seminar.

Thus, one can distinguish between the personal knowledge that grew out of participants' personal experience and the social knowledge that grew out of explicit ideas generated through texts and experiences shared in conversations. This process can be equated with Nonaka's (Nonaka & Takeuchi, 1995) concept of explicit and tacit dimensions of knowledge-creation and transmission. We can trace the evolution of the larger conversational space by the analysis of the explicit records of participants' conversation starters. We can see how the experience of a given class session was shaped by the social knowledge of the preceding years. As the personal knowledge and the social knowledge continued to influence and shape each other through conversations, we can witness Gadamer's (1989) idea of "the conversation as larger than the consciousness of any single player"(p. 104). The conversation generated by a group of individuals in a given year is passed onto the next generation of players, perpetuating a dynamic flow of conversations over time. As the personal and social knowledge continued to be integrated and externalized thorough conversations, participants' deep interests also gained clarity and focus. Participants' pursuit of their personal interests led ultimately to substantial knowledge creation, as a significant number of doctoral dissertations were produced over the years as offspring of the multiple conversations conducted over time (e.g. Baker, 1995; Banaga, 2000; Fambrough, 2000; Hazelwood, 1999; Jensen, 1995; Kayes, 2001; Kolb, 2000; Mainemelis, 2001; Park, 1996; Steingard, 1997; Sullivan, 1997; White, 1993).

Participants in the seminar were adult learners with diverse professional backgrounds, nationalities, and life experiences, between twenty-five and sixty years of age. Prior to joining the organizational behavior department, many of the participants had held leadership and managerial positions at various for profit and not-for-profit organizations, as well as at several educational institutions nationally and internationally, with an extensive knowledge and expertise in their professional areas. The diverse and unique composition of the seminar participants mirror the long-held Organizational Behavior Department tradition and philosophy grounded on lifelong learning and fostering the unique human potential of the individual learners.

The twelve yearly course sessions can be grouped into in three broad phases: phase I (1988 to1989), phase II (1990 to1996), and phase III (1997 to1999). Phase I can be described as the exploratory period, in which both content and process of conversational learning was created and defined. In 1988, the course could be seen as a typical doctoral seminar covering interdisciplinary topics related to learning and development in psychology, philosophy, biology, neuroscience, and education. The primary text, *Experiential Learning* (Kolb, 1984, 2015), provided an intellectual backbone for the course with readings selected to explore current developments in topics covered in the book. The other text, *The Tree of Knowledge* (Maturana & Varela, 1987), described the biological roots of human understanding and the essence of life. In addition, there were readings specifically related to the topic of each week.

Two components of the seminar were explicitly related to conversational learning. The first was a paper by Michael Kahn (1981) that described four metaphors for conversation in a seminar: the free-for-all, the beauty contest, the distinguished house tour, and barn-raising, a fourth metaphor that served as a guide for functional intellectual conversation. The concept of the cooperative Amish barn raising was to become a normative ideal for the seminar process. The second component was the one-page conversation starter, an idea borrowed from Ronald Reagan, who insisted on one-page summaries of major issues, stating that no idea was so complex that it could not be summarized in one page. Seminar participants prepared a one-page conversation starter on the readings, their personal reflections, summaries of related topics, comments on the group's process, or anything else on their mind. On average, five to six conversation starters were voluntarily turned in during each seminar class. Copies of the conversation starters were passed around at the beginning of the class and were discussed one by one during the course of conversation.

Phase II, beginning in 1990, was a seven-year phase of a rapid growth in which the scholarly conversations explored by the readings increased in breadth and depth. Phase III can be characterized as a stable phase as the scholarly readings and ideas remained relatively unchanged but gained further depth and elaboration in conversation. These phases can be illustrated by the growth of the syllabus over time, as shown in Figure 10.3.

Figure 10.3
The Learning & Development Syllabus (Kolb & Kolb, 2003)

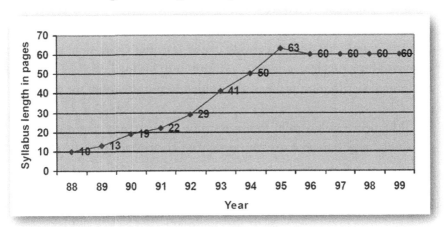

The overall characteristics of phases will be described within the five process dialectics of conversational space: the dialectics of concrete and abstract, inside out and outside in, status and solidarity, discursive and recursive time, and action and reflection. Overall, the learning space transitioned from a traditional discourse mode of learning to a conversational mode of learning.

Concrete Experiencing and Abstract Thinking. The gradual unfolding of the concrete pole of the concrete/abstract dialectic of conversational space was largely dependent upon how safe participants felt in fully engaging their physical, intellectual, emotional, and sensual experiences in the conversation. For the most part, participants' past experiences in the classroom were shaped by the traditional model of learning, where the primary emphasis was placed on the intellectual and abstract dimensions of learning.

Common to all conversation starters of phase I is a strong sense of commitment to produce a detailed, well-thought-out analysis and reflection on the assigned reading materials. A typical conversation starter would begin with a definition or a brief description of the main concept of the reading, followed by a summary of propositions and ending with several questions drawn from personal reflections. The preferred writing style tended to be very conceptual and abstract, taking up the full length of a page and, in many instances, far exceeding the one-page norm established early in the semester. Participants tended to emphasize the reflective and abstract dimensions of the experiential learning cycle, for the most part shying away from the emotional and active side of the learning cycle. One participant expressed his struggle to engage his emotions in his intellectual endeavor, as his former socialization processes prevented him from doing so:

> I thought how a formal education process constantly reminded me of the importance of separating emotional or personal aspects from the rational thought process. Especially in an intellectual setting, we were told time and time again that there would be no room for emotionalizing or personalizing. In this respect, experiential learning seemed to me anti-intellectual. (1989)

One of the marked characteristics of phase I was the acknowledgment of the importance of emotions and feelings in learning. Yet there was reluctance to embrace them fully at the personal as well as the group levels. In many instances the attempt to express emotions and feelings tended to be disguised in the form of vague questions, as if they were addressed to an unknown audience. In the early years, others are rarely mentioned in the conversation starters. The reflections are primarily drawn from individual readings and rarely from unique experiences of others or from interaction with other participants.

As the conversational learning space entered phase II there was a marked increase in the number of topics and reference materials discussed in the seminar. In addition, a significant change was witnessed in the language style of the conversation starters. During this phase the carefully measured words wrapped in highly abstract language of phase I gradually receded into the background and were replaced by emotional, highly charged tone of voices of men and women who were unafraid of being known for who they are. The conversation starters were no longer without a face. Participants' willingness to bring their diverse personal experiences and styles into the public life of the classroom further added to the richness and diversity of the conversation. The language became increasingly informal and personal, an indication of participants' willingness to move from the realm of the cognitive and the abstract to the realm of emotions and feelings. Graphics, drawings, and poetry became an integral part of the writing, and the overall length of the conversation starters saw a substantial reduction during the growth period. In his conversation starter titled "I am what I am—Popeye the Sailorman (among others)," one participant expressed his confusion and discomfort as he delved into the readings:

> I sit here at my desk having finished most of the reading—particularly on individuality (i.e. the "self-contained" self vs. the "ensembled" self or the "eco-self") and I realize that I am still having a quite visceral reaction to what I have read! I am upset, disturbed, no, more than that. I am angered by what I have been reading! As I read it, it challenges most of the basic foundations that I have built my life upon. Where do I start?!? (1993)

The collaborative effort to create a safe and welcoming learning space had a significant impact on the manner in which participants opened themselves up to different ways of being in conversation. As participants grew more comfortable in engaging their feelings and emotions in conversation, the learning space was enriched in a way that thought alone could not have achieved. A number of initiatives taken by the instructor and participants contributed to the significant shift in the tone of the conversation starters from an abstract to emotional mode of expression. In 1993 the instructor introduced music in the seminar as an acknowledgment of the sensual dimension of the learning space. In the same year, a Korean student brought flowers and placed them in the center of the circle as a way to honor nature. On another occasion the instructor distributed shells to the seminar participants as gifts from his winter retreat in Hawaii, a practice that became a ritual in the seminar during subsequent years. This invited a host of initiatives by students, who at different times brought various artifacts that symbolized concrete manifestations of seminar topics. One student brought a small doll as a souvenir from her trip, whereas on a different occasion a Turkish student brought a small rug from his home country. As a part of an ongoing effort to create a hospitable space for learning, the instructor placed the books, articles, handouts, and reading materials on the floor to allow participants to easily walk in the circle and reach out for the readings of their own choosing. In 1995 the instructor introduced the Amish wagon in the circle. The strong communal bond embedded in the Amish tradition was a reminder to all participants of the barn-raising article and the value of the equality and solidarity in the conversational space. In addition, the books, artifacts, and various objects stacked in the colorful wood wagon were an invitation for the participants to adopt a spontaneous and playful stance toward learning. In a letter to the instructor, a participant shared her experience with the physical space of the seminar as follows:

> I love flowers and books, and it made me feel warm and comfortable to have them around. It also gave me something to look at while I was deep in thought so the rest of the class did not know how far gone I was. The various objects that you passed around were interesting, and continued to remind me how little time I take to physically feel things. They allowed me to get in touch (no pun intended) with senses that are underutilized. I would always think to myself, I have to take more time to really explore things in depth. I see shells all over the beach but never really studied them, or pick them up. It's like taking time to really get to know something. I realize that I know a little about a lot of things, but I miss out on the richness of knowing something really deeply. (1995)

As the conversational learning space entered phase III, the physical, sensual, emotional, and intellectual dimensions of knowing were better integrated as learners' comfort grew in moving across the concrete-abstract continuum in a more flexible way. Learners' highly abstract and conceptual orientations of phase I, or the emotional and affect orientation that dominated phase II were replaced by a dynamic blend of these two dimensions of knowing. The atmosphere of the learning space as depicted in the conversation starters of phase III is dynamic, receptive to diversity of experiences and views, with attention and care devoted to the integration of the intellectual, sensual, and emotional dimensions of the learning process. The unique physical arrangement and design of the learning space that mirrored the multifaceted dimensions of the learning process encouraged learners to be adventurous, playful, and multidimensional in pursuit of their deeply held interests.

> In the center of our human circle there stood the wagon (fire?), a symbol of the mobilization and dynamism that learning involves. The flowers were there to remind us of the nature, its diversity, and its ability to (re)create life, harmony, and beauty. The feather and the stick were the metaphors for the mystery of life, whereas the books on the floor created an atmosphere of play—the Lila [free play] path to our original nature. (1997)

In stark contrast to the early phases, what emerged from the conversation starters of phase III was the profile of learners who are attracted to the idea of integration of opposites as they pursue their interests, balancing the dialectical tension between the objective and subjective, the conceptual and emotional dimensions of knowing.

> Must we function with either/or choices? Why not, instead, chose to utilize the most positive aspects for a wider band of options? Qualitative and quantitative evaluations? The scientific approach coupled with a constructionist science? If there are questions, why not find answers in a variety of ways? (1998)

> Each syllabus topic is a distinct facet of the social forces that influence me and other individuals...For example, I now see myself as being at a stage of moral development, in the conflict between women and men, of a style of learning and conversing, with multiple

meanings of adultness, and aboard the boat of spiritual self in the organizational world. I learned that I am of many things and all can be held simultaneously. (1999)

The evolutionary process of the dialectic of concrete and abstract illustrated thus far opened up yet another window of opportunity for participants to explore a new realm of learning experience that required a significant shift in their previously held basic assumptions and beliefs: the balancing of the inside-out and outside-in approaches to learning.

Individuality and Relationality: Inside Out and Outside In. When the inside-out approach was first introduced in the seminar, the idea was received with a mix of hesitation and anticipation. In one of the conversation starters of phase I, a participant expressed her dilemma in integrating herself as a whole person to pursue her own growth as well as that of others:

> What am I doing/thinking/feeling when I'm pursuing my own growth and that of my classmates? To what, to whom do I look to evaluate how I'm/we're developing skill in learning how to learn? Hunt suggests that we start with ourselves, that we take an inside-out approach. What do I/we know/think/feel/believe about learning?...How am I/are we shaping ways of interacting with one another that respect individual differences, challenge growth and create an environment that invites participation by all? (1989)

In phase II, the hesitation and tentativeness of phase I were replaced by full acceptance of the inside-out approach as participants eagerly shared their experiences with the encounter with the newly found idea:

> "Inside out Psychology" is most intriguing, and I should admit, a relatively new life value for me...I believe so strongly in the concept that I have come to believe that an inside out approach can arm one

with the potential for overcoming <u>any</u> difficulty if he or she chooses and is able to fully connect with his or her inner self. (1993)

When I read Rogers's "A Modern Approach to Values," I said, "Yes, here it is!!!" (Not the first and I'm sure not the last time that that will happen). I was one of those "usual adults" (slugs) running around corporate America in search of love, acceptance and esteem. I operated on a variety of introjected organizational values, which were in conflict, and which ultimately proved unsatisfactory and untenable…the "Is that all there is?" scene. (1996)

As liberating as the discovery of the inside-out approach was, this idea clashed with an apparently conflicting set of values that permeated the diverse topics introduced in the course over the semester. The course readings were structured and designed to introduce participants to a wide range of ideas and concepts beyond the confines of the Western concept of development. The broad reading assignments ranged from Eastern religion and spirituality, to the communal lifestyle of hunting and gathering cultures, to the postmodern philosophy that questions the capitalist and individualist way of modern life. They challenged participants to venture into the unfamiliar territory of a new learning experience and see their familiar world anew. These ideas stirred heated discussions and lively exchanges of diverse views and beliefs among participants. A male participant expressed his strong reactions and concerns as Western values came under intense scrutiny in conversation:

During last week's class I felt that the class had a growing movement/willingness/need to attack "Western culture." Whether it is capitalism, individualism, competition, rationality, functionalism, intellectualism, etc.…I know that I tend to take all this personally (probably too personally), but my personal values and beliefs are very closely tied to some of these concepts, and I often feel as if others are trying to change those beliefs so that I will be more closely aligned with some status quo. (1993)

In a different voice, another participant expressed her longing for relational values as she found herself moving toward a community-oriented life philosophy:

> For some time, I have been playing with the word "communitarian" as a descriptor for the lifestyle I tried to create for myself and encourage in others before coming to Case…Over the past few years, I have emerged from a career cocoon to become aware of, develop attitudes about (prize), and invest in the community around me…For me, that amorphous need for valuing, beauty, connectedness, however you wish to describe it, leads us to communitarianism. (1993)

As the inside-out learning rooted in the awakening of the individual values and beliefs met a host of concepts that redefine the conception of self, participants were challenged to reexamine their previously held conceptual frame. As the conversational learning space entered phase III, a shift was witnessed in the way learners approached the concepts of inside out and outside in. As learners delved into this dialectical dilemma with a deeper sense of reflection, the bipolar stance many participants exhibited in the early years toward diverse views gradually shifted to a more balanced conception of the self that coexists with one's surrounding environment. The following conversation starters reflect the gradual shift that took place in conversation during phase III. The conversation transitioned from a reflective stance toward deeply held issues to that of a desire to actively transform the ideas and concepts gained through reflections into a greater purpose for benefit of a larger community.

> What I found most intriguing about the readings for today was the variety of different ways in which the concept of "self" was presented. What is the self? Am I really an individual with unique properties, an intrinsically valuable, self-contained, self-determined unit?…Personally I think a concept of self that can encompass all of these thoughts makes the most sense. That is, I am unique, but my existence is intimately and inextricably tied to the people and

world around me. Coming from a culture that stresses individualism, where we feel that if we can just get people to value themselves, everything will work out well, I find it very tough to avoid dwelling on the individual aspect of "self." Which makes me wonder, do I really need more self-esteem training? Maybe what I need is to have more esteem for others! (1997)

I think there is more to be gained in "work" realms by taking in concepts from the outside...I'd like to explore the balance further, the balance between inside out and outside in. (1999)

Status and Solidarity: Ranking and Linking. The equality of status between the instructor and participants was a pivotal, albeit controversial issue in the seminar. The idea of "conversation among equals" that is a central idea of conversational learning could not go unexamined if the conversational space was to continue to thrive and flourish. The unique and diverse composition of the seminar participants played a significant role in creating and making the conversational learning space possible. Participants' rich lives and professional experiences further contributed to the richness and complexity of the learning process in the seminar. It is interesting to notice, however, how participants perceived themselves as learners upon entering the classroom setting. Regardless of their prior status as accomplished and autonomous individuals, lingering somewhere inside their minds was the idea that Freire (1992, 1973) described as "internalized oppression," a process whereby learners relinquish the valuable experience and knowledge they already possess in the name of the expert knowledge of the teacher. By surrendering their power to the teacher, learners relegate themselves to the position of passive recipients of information and knowledge. Perhaps a typical classroom scene commonly shared by most of the traditional educational institutions is the one in which, in a classroom of thirty students, only one person, the teacher, does most of the talking while the rest are left in silence. In the conversational, learning space however, the status of the teacher as the sole authority had to be reconsidered as the instructor deliberately shifted his position as a power figure to that of an equal participant in the seminar. Although the instructor provided syllabus and reading assignments early in the semester, he set no learning agenda or specific direction in the class discussions throughout the semester. The stance he maintained over the course of the semester was that of an equal participant who encouraged learners to have their voices in stark contrast to the traditional lecture format, where the instructor monopolizes the airtime in the classroom.

> One of the key concepts of conversational learning is a learning process where teachers and students come together as equal learners. When learning is viewed as a dialogue among equals, the teacher is no longer viewed as the sole provider of the expert knowledge. The status of the expert is equally shared among learners who actively take responsibility in offering expert knowledge when needed. Paulo Freire writes that you can't deny the fact that teachers know more in some regard. I think that it means that knowledge is a dynamic process which changes all the time. While I may know a lot about management, the others may happen to know a lot about engineering or some other kind of expert knowledge. Dialogue among equals doesn't mean that in any single conversation there isn't a point in which one person is an expert and the other person is not. (Kolb, 1998, p. 51)

Inevitably, participants faced a period of adjustment in order to become familiar with the new seminar concept and configuration. The lingering "internalized oppression" would resurface from time to time in the seminar, as participants looked to the instructor and asked for his voice and direction at crucial points during the conversation. Particularly during phase I of the seminar, the shift in perspective from a lecture format to the conversational mode was met with hesitation. By and large, the instructor appears to have been viewed as the primary purveyor of knowledge. The instructor is frequently personified as quotes, his physical presence far removed from the conversational space and for the most part clouded by an unspoken expectation participants attributed to him: the role of an ultimate knowledge provider.

In 1989, one event occurred several weeks into the seminar that was to give a new shape to the conversational learning space. An Asian student mentioned on several occasions that he was having trouble hearing and understanding what was being said. Finally someone suggested that the room be rearranged to bring the group closer together. However, eighteen people seated around a circle of tables placed people far away from each other. The tables were pushed away and the group sat in a circle inside the tables. This created a more informal and intimate conversational space. In addition, the group's action to improve members' ability to listen to and understand each other served to remind speakers that conversation is not just about speaking, but also about being understood. Particularly in this larger group this required some effort and discipline. In subsequent years this room arrangement was to become a norm and ultimately led to the physical arrangement and design of the learning space described in the previous section.

Coming together in a circle not only brought the participants closer physically but also challenged the hierarchical mentality embedded in the traditional classroom setting. It is safe to say that the change in physical configuration of the room played a significant role in promoting an egalitarian atmosphere in the learning space. As the conversational learning entered phase II, participants began to openly voice the need for a learning environment where all voices were equally heard and valued:

> A hierarchical approach to learning undermines the very concept of process and the prospect for dialogue among equals. It interferes with the spontaneous confrontation of different perspectives. (1990)

For the first time, the instructor is acknowledged and challenged as an equal member of the group: "Ok Dave...How is this course a demonstration of experiential learning?" (1990).

In 1990 the instructor introduced the Native American "talking stick" and the "listening feather" as a way to manage the flow of conversation in the group. The talking stick was used in tribal meetings as a form of parliamentary procedure, being passed from one speaker to the next as others listened and concentrated their attention on the holder of the stick. At the end of his speech, the speaker would hand the feather to a specific tribal member as an invitation to voice his opinion. A participant described her first encounter with the talking stick and the feather as follows:

> As David passed around the Native American talking stick and the response feather I imagined the differences in the type of dialogue that our desks and the stick/feather allowed. The stick, with its jagged edges and short branches, looked at first glance to be a weapon. But then as David spoke of its use the stick began to look like a hand—each little branch represented the individual fingers that come together into the collective unit. I saw it as an outstretched hand that at one time may offer assistance in the dialogue, and another time may slam down on the desk to strengthen the authority of the speaker. The feather, in contrast, offered a gentler and freer expression. I saw the bearer of the feather bringing a delicate and soft touch to the act of listening. Yet by its very function, assisting in flight, I also saw the feather helping the respondent to hover with the discussion or to lead the group into heights beyond normal reach of the hand. (1993)

Although the practice of the talking stick and the feather generated a certain level of discomfort and awkwardness, it helped participants to shift their focus from speaking to attentive listening. Over the years, the greater emphasis placed on deep listening further enhanced solidarity among participants who equally shared the privilege of speaking and being listened to. An example of such acknowledgment of the group solidarity is metaphorically expressed in the following conversation starter:

> To make music (knowledge) beautiful and whole we need to understand the various positions that are out there and be able to appreciate them; not just sing our verses over and over. When we nurture

and support each other a much more complete outcome is possible. We can't sing all the parts, and we have to recognize that there are other parts. Solos can be beautiful, but their beauty is enhanced if they are a part of a greater group piece. (1992)

It is important to emphasize, however, that the awakening process of group solidarity did not happen overnight. To better understand this process, it would be helpful to look into some patterns that kept resurfacing in the conversations starters over the years. Typically, around the third to fifth weeks into the semester, several participants began expressing frustration and discomfort as a reaction to their new experience of conversational learning. In a given year, a participant expressed her growing frustrations and anger directed toward the process and content of the seminar:

I'm not sure whether I want to continue being part of this class. Maybe if I just do the readings, discuss these with one or two other people, and then space out during our Wednesday morning together...but then I can't really handle sitting in class anymore. I left class yesterday feeling emotional, followed by feeling increasingly angry at my fellow classmates, our professor, and most of all (inevitably) myself. I played with the idea of dramatically walking into David's office during break announcing my desire to be excused from the class...or just getting up and stomping out of our cooped up place on the 5th floor of Sears. **Drama...**I wish I could convince myself that I wouldn't come across as too self-indulgent, egotistical, and morally superior by doing just that! Because a good kick in the butt may be just is needed...Why get so riled up? After all, it's only a class! But I have better ways of spending my time, I think, than watching us toy with ideas...I am accusing all of us flirting...with very complex and meaningful concepts in a cursory self-indulgent way, leaving our comments to a level of superficially befitting of a talk show, but not of a group of students committing themselves to questioning in depth. (1995)

During phase III the same frustration resurfaced in the seminar, as described in the following conversation starter:

> I don't know about you, but I am really frustrated with this class. I have reflected on the experience and developed a theory for how to make it more interesting for me.

> **Experience:** I've experienced frustration for three consecutive weeks during this class only.

> **Observations:** We come together in a room for three hours each week. There is lots of commentary on personal experiences. Our content has fleeting references to the reading and even fewer insights drawn about the personal experiences that are shared. 80 percent of the talking is done by 20 percent of the people. David has very little verbal involvement in the discussions. My experience of being in that circle is intensely frustrating for me; I feel like I'm missing out on the theoretical insights, the intellectual ah-has and David's experience for which I came to this doctoral program.

> **Concept/Theory:** I've tried on several theories, and two emerge as useful for me.

> 1. Content—If we (everyone!) anchor our insights and discussions in the core concepts and theory of the readings, then the theoretical insights and intellectual "ah-has will emerge. David's choices about how he shares his experiences and insights are his decision, although I think more input would help my process.
> 2. Process—If we (everyone!) were conscious of being concise, of listening and thinking before speaking, and of being mindful of the thrust of the speaker's point (rather than their tangents), then I

could more easily pay attention and more easily learn from everyone's ideas. (1999)

This insightful snapshot of the learning space offers a glimpse of critical
moments in the life of the seminar as participants struggle to redefine and
reexamine what is to be a self-organizing learning group and what it would
take for a group of adult learners to create a learning space that is hospitable
enough to welcome everyone's expectation, yet tight enough for a rigorous
learning and deep thinking to occur. Here the self-organizing nature of the
conversational learning space is put to an ultimate test, as its survival is
dependent upon how well the group will steer the oars of status and solidarity in a balanced fashion. In this regard, participants were left with several
conflicting issues. The welcoming of personal experiences creates a sense of
belonging in the learning space, yet an overdose of those moments runs the
risk of neglecting the readings by only touching them in a cursory and superficial way thus sacrificing the valuable learning one can gain from them.
Enthusiasm and passion toward one's interest leads to powerful learning;
however, too much of it will leave others powerless, sitting in silence.

Adding more frustration to an already complex situation, the instructor
seemed as though he had totally surrendered his authority as the ultimate
power figure and did not show any inkling in coming to the aid of the group
and steering the course of the conversation. The following comment by a
student reflects the instructor's persistent attitude and stance in the seminar:

David wants us to be a self-organizing class—he doesn't want to be
a typical lecturer. (1999).

Such was the atmosphere of the seminar that the group seems to have been
practically left with no choice other than discovering the way on their own if
they were to make their learning experience valuable and meaningful.

It is worth mentioning here yet another revealing pattern that emerged over
the years that sheds an important light on the group's self-organizing process.

During phase I, outbursts expressed in response to the uncertainty and ambiguity of the learning space did not surface in the conversation starters. During phase II, a clear emotional outburst made its appearance in the conversation starters eight to nine weeks into the seminar, whereas in phase III its occurrence was evidenced as early as three weeks into the life of the seminar. During phase I, participants' concerns seem to have been explicitly shared outside the seminar and only in an implicit way mentioned during the seminar. During phase II, however, participants seemed to have gained enough confidence to cast off any restraint and inhibition in voicing their concerns. As the learning space transitioned to phase III, not only did participants became more vocal in expressing their mounting frustrations, they also seemed to become keenly aware of the fact that it was up to them to make the learning space a productive and valuable place for all. As evidence of such awareness, participants began actively searching for ways to make the learning a meaningful experience to every member of the seminar by proposing detailed courses of action and inviting others to experiment with different processes and ways of being together in the classroom.

> Whether we do it implicitly or explicitly, we are developing through experiential learning during our class. I suggest—regardless of what we choose (or don't choose) to do during each class—that we make our mode of learning more explicit. I suggest that we explicitly do the following—we actively reflect on what works and what doesn't. We actively theorize. We actively propose new experiments. At a macro level, this is the essence of experiential learning. (1999)

A final observation of the dialectic of status and solidarity points to the emergence of a rather unique phenomenon that surfaced over time in the conversational learning space: the awakening of the gift cycle in conversational learning. Recall for a moment how the dialectic of status and solidarity evolved over time from phase I to phase III. In the early phase, when the conversational learning space was skewed toward the status end of the dialectic, the learners' overall tendency was to be primarily recipients of knowledge generated in the seminar. Their primary focus was on receiving rather than giving. As the conversational learning space transitioned to phase II and phase III, giving and receiving became reciprocal processes as the balancing of the dialectic of status and solidarity became more apparent in conversations. Participants' increased awareness of their own unique expertise and knowledge encouraged them to actively influence the process as well as the content of the conversation by means of sharing new concepts and ideas in the group. Many ideas and concepts offered in the seminar were eventually incorporated in the syllabus over the years in a continuous gift cycle of new knowledge that was passed on to the next generation of learners. The increase in the syllabus page numbers described earlier is a manifestation of such a gift cycle in the conversational learning space.

Discursive and Recursive. During phase I, with some rare exceptions, conversations were predominantly discursive, as learners tended to stick to the agenda assigned to the particular class and methodically follow the topics of discussion outlined in the syllabus throughout the semester. This phase coincided with the strong abstract and outside-in approaches learners preferred during the early years. Learners tended to have an intense intellectual engagement with the preassigned topics, came to closure at the end of the session, and moved on to the next subject of discussion. During phase II, as learners began to gravitate toward concrete and inside-out dimensions of the dialectical poles, the recursive process made its first appearance in the conversational learning space. Learners began frequently to regress in time and revisit the subjects discussed during the previous sessions:

Last week Paul related how his experiences made him angry with Habermas for using two-bit words too much. I agree, though I suspect it has to do with German semantics and word forms more than Habermas trying to show off. Although Emerson uses normal words and writes in English, my experiences make me mad at him. Emerson shows off by using ornate metaphors to make a mundane point sound richer than it is. (1992)

During last week's class, I realized a long-growing concern of mine. I sense that orthodoxy of thought seems to have crept into many of our class discussions. While this orthodoxy affects me in particular because I disagree with it, I hope that I would be concerned about it under any circumstances. (1993)

A closer look at individual conversation starters pointed to the rich array of trigger points, spontaneous and visceral reactions that prompted learners to return to a particular topic or experience in a deeper way. Furthermore, learners' inquiry and interests were triggered not only by personal reflections on the reading materials, but also from experiences largely drawn from class interactions. The urge to go back in time and revisit the subject of the previous conversation can be attributed to the emotional impact learners experienced through assigned readings or through memorable group interactions. To a great extent what drives the recursive process during this phase is the learners' tendency to rely heavily on the concrete dimension rather than the abstract dimension of the dialectics and to engage an inside-out approach as opposed to outside in as their predominant modes of conversation. It is worth pointing out that learners' preference for frequently going back in time and revisiting their topics of interest or their tendency to digress the conversation based on their personal motives undermined the discursive process of learning during phase II. The accentuation of the recursive process of learning often kept learners from exploring new topics of discussion and moving the conversation forward in a timely manner.

Toward the end of phase II, however, the discursive and recursive processes of learning faced a significant turning point in the life of the conversational learning space. In a particular year the discursive and recursive processes of conversational learning were for the first time explicitly acknowledged and voiced in a conversation starter:

What about the act of coming back again and again to the same bench in the same park to feed the sparrows—can this be called experience? Is the repetition of the same act indicative of experience or the denial thereof? Does the comfort of knowing the park, the bench, and the sparrows cover up a fear of venturing further into deeper and perhaps "unsafe" knowledge areas (i.e. Maslow) and becoming "stuck" in a place where we end up denying our talents and creativity? Or, is the repetition of the same act (leading perhaps to new understanding of the behavior of sparrows in their park environment) an attempt to probe more deeply, to deal head-on with the "shallowness that everyone threatens the true and the good" (Ken Wilber), an act of bravery, perseverance, and of appreciation of subtlety? I wonder. (1995)

In her metaphorical inquiry into the discursive and recursive processes of learning, the learner described her experience of tension and conflict as she inquired deep into the subject matter. The deeper one probes into the phenomenon at hand, the more heightened becomes one's awareness of the back-and-forth movement of these two distinct temporal dimensions of learning. The recognition of the discursive and recursive processes of conversational learning marks the transition from phase II to phase III of the conversational learning space.

During phase III the acknowledgment of the discursive and recursive process of learning became more deliberate and explicit as learners actively sought to pause and return to the subject of their interest by consciously redirecting the course of the conversation. The following conversation starter illustrates the state of the discursive and recursive processes of learning in phase III:

Last week I learned several lessons while observing and reflecting both about class content and about class members. Forgive me for a moment while I digress with an excerpt from my class notes and reflections…

Lessons about others and myself:

- Joanna likes to experiment
- Paul likes to experiment and he likes to discuss ideas through pictures

- Jane likes to think before she talks
- Tina sees this "unstructured" time as a release from her more structured work environment
- Tangents take air time—sometimes inappropriately
- It is good to take time to get in touch with one's inner self
- Sometimes it's hard to tell whether a tangent is a tangent or a good idea
- Carol and Helen feel like we need "something" more from class
- Sometimes we aren't always interested in the line of conversation and it is easy to tune out.
- Its OK to let Joyce know when I've gotten the idea.
- David wants us to be a self-organizing class—he doesn't want to be a typical lecturer.

Lessons about the process of experiential learning:

- Experiential learning is all about learning through processes
- If we are going to self-organize, we need to examine our process of learning.
- If we choose to focus on process, our approach needs to be loose enough to accommodate everyone's needs, yet tight enough to accomplish something of value to the members of the class. (1999)

The above conversation starter highlights a distinct portrait of the conversational learning space of phase III. In contrast to the previous phases, much of the learners' deliberate attempt to return to past class experiences was geared toward actively redirecting the course of the conversation for the purpose of urging and often challenging the group to inquire deeper into the subject or dynamics that emerged during the conversation. It is also true of this phase that participants often expressed a sense of weariness and concern toward tangential discussions that might have diverted the course of the core subject of the conversation. From this perspective, learners were also operating under the pressure to move forward by stressing the discursive mode of learning, thus emphasizing their need to engage in conversation in a more focused and meaningful manner. In order to balance this tension, there is a concerted effort to balance the recursive and discursive processes in conversation. When learners chose to refer back in time to a particular topic or group process, they consciously bridged the subject of their interest to the core topic of the ongoing conversation in the seminar.

As we turn to the last principle of conversational learning, the dialectic of action and reflection, the dynamic evolutionary trend described thus far becomes even more accentuated as the five dialectics diverge at times and converge at another in a highly organic manner.

Action and Reflection. This tenuous relationship between action and reflection is captured in one conversation starter written early in the life of the seminar:

> Boud, Keogh and Walker emphasize reflection as necessary to formulating informed action. Emerson emphasizes action as liberation: "The preamble of thought, the transition through which it passes form the unconscious to the conscious, is action." For BKW reflection precedes action, reflection implies action, for Emerson action precedes reflection but reflection is not in the driver's seat. What is the proper linkage between action and reflection? (1989)

The question regarding which comes first, reflection or action, or what connects the two was given focused attention during phase I of the seminar, as learners engaged in a series of reflective exploration into the evolutionary process of human consciousness and inquired into how language and the human's innate desire to communicate and engage in dialogue ultimately gave meaning to human existence.

> What connects—in an admittedly sketchy fashion—for me at this point is that new perceptions enter our awareness, and create new knowledge, when there exists an urge to know, and a capacity for empathy which allows dialogue, and there are others with whom

we can engage in dialogue who can help us to "grasp, name and share" new ideas. In order to create new knowledge, it is necessary to overcome, not only the fear of knowing which Maslow discusses, but the active hatred of learning from experience which Bion suggests is present in most adults...Perhaps learning occurs when we are able to transcend that fear in a dialogue with others where we let empathic understanding have free reign. (1989)

What comes through the early writings is a highly reflective stance that dominates the conversation starters of phase I. Much of what emerges from their writings is the acknowledgment of the process of dialogue and communication that is grasped and named but shared only in a tacit way. For the most part, learners' reflective tendencies and preferences appear to have kept the actual conversation within the confines of each individual's internalized monologue.

It is important to pause for a moment and reassess why learners' reflective and tacit tendencies became a predominant pattern in the early phase of the seminar. This phenomenon coincided with learners' tendency to be conscious of the status of the instructor. The idea of solidarity between the instructor and the seminar participants was not readily embraced during phase I of the conversational learning space. Learners' perceptions of the instructor as the primary purveyor of knowledge and thus the one who possibly would be the dominant voice in the conversation might have kept learners inclined toward the reflective side of the dialectic of action and reflection. As the instructor maintained his nondominant and nondirective posture over the years, the conversational learning space transitioned to phase II, where the idea of solidarity was explicitly verbalized in the seminar.

This also marks the transition of the learning space from the reflective to the active mode of conversation as learners searched for the meaning of conversation among equals. They struggled to make sense of the process of the seminar, perceived at that time to be unclear, ambiguous, and without a specific goal. The following conversation starter illustrates the learners' awakening process to conversational learning as they slowly emerged out of the reflective, internalized mode of dialogue and transitioned to a collective mode of exploration into the meaning of learning through conversations.

> Somehow education as learning needs to provide an environment where students and teachers both discover new realities that get beyond the current zero sum game between systems. Is the new curriculum doing this? Or is it just indoctrinating a different value set that makes the faculty feel better? How can we evaluate the dialogue about learning that we have here? Is this really a dialogue, or a multilogue, or a collection of monologues and dialogues? Is connectivity a multilogue, dialogue or a distributed monologue? How could we possibly tell the difference? (1992)

It is worth mentioning here yet another event that influenced the transition of the conversational learning space from a tacit and reflective mode to an active mode of conversation. In 1993 a significant event took place early in the semester that in many ways had a substantial impact in setting the course of future Learning and Development seminars on the path to conversational learning. During that year, Ann Baker and Patricia Jensen had begun their dissertation work on the topic of conversational learning, and the entire class of 1993 was invited to participate in their studies as part of the data- collection process. Both Ann and Patricia were present in the seminar during the entire semester as participants in the conversation. As part of their data-collection, each conversation session was tape recorded in addition to all participants being asked to participate in individual interviews at the beginning and at the end of the semester. The purpose of the interviews was to understand how participants learned through conversations by inviting them to explore and reflect on their learning experiences gained through conversation with someone at some point in their lives.

The simultaneous experience of being in conversation with one another in the seminar and being a part of a larger study on conversation learning appears to have had a significant influence on the life of the group. The scenario described in the following conversation starter mirrors the atmosphere of the seminar of that particular year:

> Last week I thought I saw a pattern emerging that seems very familiar to me from other classes, seminars, and workplace meetings: in class some people were very vocal and spoke often. Others spoke rather less often or almost never. I wondered about this recurring dynamic...I am intrigued by the power of silence and of listening. The gift of silence and listening is a great gift to a group. For starters, quiet creates the possibility of conversation; otherwise there is merely a free-for-all of competing voices. In addition, when I am speaking and I realize that my words are not just vanishing into thin air, but are being listened to with care by another human being, I am deeply moved and feel increased connection to the listener and to myself. Also, when I'm able to still my interior monologue and listen, truly listen to others, there is the pleasure of being taken outside my monologue and, paradoxically, I feel more centered. The gift of speaking is also a great gift to give to a group. Words are as fundamental to dialogue as quiet. However, as someone who tends to be pretty vocal, I wonder at my own need or tendency to be vocal. No doubt, my excitement and excitability play a part. I feel passionate about ideas and there is a pleasure to thinking out loud about them with others. Yet I sense there is another side to it: Am I afraid to be quiet? Am I afraid to give up control of the conversation for fear that my ideas will not be heard? Am I afraid to trust that my colleagues will take the conversation in promising directions? The gift of listening and the gift of speaking are necessary gifts for group function. But I wonder what will happen if we specialize in these gifts rather than each of us giving both to the group. Do we not run the risk of all specialization: lop-sided development, strong in one area, weak in another? Aren't we all tired to some extent of being specialists? (1993)

The clear articulation of the key elements and processes that ultimately would lead the group to conducting a meaningful conversation is the first indication that conversational learning left the realm of the tacit and reflective and entered the realm of the explicit and active side of the conversational dialectics. In this process conversation was acknowledged as a legitimate language and an active way to engage in learning. This trend continued through subsequent years during phase II as learners continued to explicitly articulate the meaning and values of different forms of conversations and how their learning experiences were impacted and shaped through conversation.

> This is a conversation starter about...conversation starters, and some reflections about our semester together. We began many conversations with each other during the past several months—some were in written form, and most were begun verbally. There were calm conversations, rational conversations, emotional conversations, exciting conversations and more exciting conversations. There were long periods of silence, too. Yet isn't silence a form of communicating? We talked about epistemology, biology, naturalism, education, morality, spirituality, learning and development. And we received many gifts each week—flowers, seashells from Hawaii, books, learning, and development. I anticipate that all those "unfinished" conversation starters will continue on and on...and they will evolve into many new conversation starters. Thanks for the new beginnings. (1995)

The conversation starters reviewed thus far are illustrative of how the conversational learning space transitioned from a primarily reflective and tacit mode to an explicit and active mode of conversation over the years. It is important to note, however, that knowledge-creation through conversation does not occur without simultaneous engagement in the active and reflective modes of the conversational dialectic. The movement from the tacit mode of phase I to the explicit mode of phase II was a substantial development in the seminar; however, it still left unfinished the integrative work of the dialectic of action and reflection that ultimately would result in generation of knowledge through conversations.

The following poem serves as the prelude to what marks the transition of the conversational learning space to phase III, where learners engage in conversation with a clear sense of purpose and intention to integrate action and reflection and the tacit and the explicit dimensions of the dialectic:

Shared separate loneliness
Days left me
I sit alone in person
Sharing only a passive life
Filled with lonely ideas
That few apprehend
And none will know
Share my loneliness?!
Come and listen to my ravings?!
Take a seat by half-cooked ideas
And the solitude of knowing
I too will listen to your loneliness
So that you will not remain,
Silently
Confined to ideas
We may not share love
Nor even resonation
But seldom do singing birds harmony
Always your children will cry
May we hear? Together different sounds
May we share? Separate loneliness.

Born from the proposition that we are always infinitely alone, that others can never completely know what we feel, this poem asks what might be gained from the activity of conversation. What might be gained from sharing this loneliness? It is actually an optimistic piece, both extending an invitation and asking the questions. (1996)

The question, "What might be gained from the activity of conversation" expressed in the poem continued to be articulated throughout phase III as conversation increasingly gained in complexity and richness. Learners chose to approach conversational learning from multiple perspectives and personal interests. For some participants conversation triggered in them a desire to act in the service of a cause they deeply cared about:

> Many times I leave class wondering how we can translate these great conversations into some action that will make a change for the better in some way, whether it's the academic world, the natural world, my world as a parent, or my world as a member of this department and this program. (1997)

Other times learners resorted to the exploration of the theoretical and conceptual side of conversation as they inquired into the connection of the theory and practice of conversational learning:

> Conversational learning: Learning occurs in many ways for many situations and for many people. I wish that I felt confident with when and how conversational learning is a good idea. Short of that, I am confident that it is a powerful learning mode. Now seeing myself as a lifelong learner, I can probably find more opportunities than I ever expected to learn through conversation with others. In so doing, I am inherently valuing what others have to offer me short of books, empirical findings and codified "knowledge." What actually is a conversation anyway? (1999)

The dynamic movement of the dialectic of action and reflection illustrated in the ebb and flow of the conversation starters reviewed thus far is indicative of how conversation evolved from the reflective to the active mode of learning during phases I and II and became more balanced during phase III. As the conversational learning space evolved, learners' distinct perspectives, interests, and styles shaped their integrative effort to make sense of the idea and the act of learning through conversations. Action-oriented learners were drawn to the active side of the conversation as a potential source of influencing change in the world, whereas philosophically and ideologically oriented learners chose to inquire into the meaning and impact of the conversation as they saw it manifest in life situations at large. Learners with a pragmatic orientation fell somewhere in the middle, as their interests were geared toward balancing the conceptual and theoretical framework of the conversational learning model against the practice of conversation.

Summary. It is important to emphasize that the evolution of the conversational learning space did not follow a linear progression, as the descriptions seem to convey. Rather, it evolved in an organic and recursive fashion as each year the learning space was influenced by the distinct composition of participants with multiplicity of views, interests, and unique life experiences. From phase I to phase III, the evolutionary process of the conversational learning space took a highly unpredictable and nonlinear path. The manifestations of these dialectics in each evolutionary phase were interdependent and organic, adding to the complexity and richness of the conversational learning space over time. At one time, conversations were highly abstract and discursive; other times, predominantly emotional and recursive. The five dialectical processes evolved in a highly interconnected manner, as one dialectic triggered another in an almost chain-like reaction. An example of such movement can be seen in the dialectical process of feeling and thinking as it ultimately influenced the dialectic of inside out and outside in. As learners moved toward the feeling end of the dialectic, there was also a gradual awakening and movement toward the inside-out approach to learning. The overall pattern identified throughout the three evolutionary phases within each of the five dialectics is the learners' tendency to move from one extreme of a dialectic continuum to the other during phase I phase II, until finally they settled somewhere in the middle of the dialectic during phase III upon reconciling the two extreme ends in a flexible manner.

The processes and factors that ultimately guided the conversational learning space deserve a closer attention. From the perspective of the course content and structure, the syllabus served as a guide to the destination; however, learners made their own choices as to how to proceed and what to focus and attend to. The manifestation of such a process can be witnessed in the dynamic change in topics and subjects over time, as topics that gained prominence in one particular generation are overshadowed by others in the generation that followed. The feminist voice that had prominent place in conversation during one year receded in the background as postmodernism gained central focus in the following year. In another year, naturalism and spirituality were the learners' choices until they were replaced by deep ecology in the subsequent generation. Learners' self-organizing tendencies became more accentuated over the years as the instructor maintained his nondirective posture and stayed away from a discursive, lecture format of class delivery throughout these years. Another key factor that appears to have impacted the evolutionary process was the instructor's choice in including the conversation starters of the previous years in the syllabus as part of the weekly focus readings. The knowledge and experience passed on to the next generation of learners through conversation starters gained significant historical value in the seminar over the years. The content as well as the process may have gained clarity and focus in the seminar as a result of the accumulated past experience and knowledge.

The dynamic movement of the dialectic of action and reflection illustrated in the ebb and flow of the conversation starters reviewed thus far is indicative of how conversation evolved from the reflective to the active mode of learning during phases I and II and became more balanced during phase III. As the conversational learning space evolved, learners' distinct perspectives, interests, and styles shaped their integrative effort to make sense of the idea and the act of learning through conversations. Learners' increased awareness of the past appears to have contributed to their confidence in making conscious choices in regard to content and process of the class. What comes through in the conversation starters of the pioneering generations is a collective experience of frustration and confusion, punctuated with moments of breakthroughs and excitements amid their struggles to make sense of the novel undertaking they have embarked on. Toward phase III, the novelty factor loses its power, as learners appear to have more or less gained control over the course of the conversation. One may argue that this "fusion of horizons" also poses a significant challenge to the conversational learning space in that it may eventually stagnate the conversation as a result of the shared sense of understanding and agreement jointly achieved by the learners. The challenge therefore resides in keeping the dialectical tensions alive thorough ongoing conversations in a hospitable learning space.

Eleven

To be a teacher in the right sense is to be a learner.
Instruction begins when you, the teacher, learn from the
learner, put yourself in his place so that you may understand
what he understands and in the way he understands it.

—KIERKEGAARD

As a learning-centered approach to education, ELT places a primary emphasis on the creation of learner-centered learning spaces. While ELT learning-centered education has a reform agenda that addresses other important stakeholders in the educational process such as teachers, educational institutions and organizations, and those that learners will eventually serve as employees and members of family and community; it is the learner who actually does the learning and is ultimately in charge of his or her learning. The movement to implement principles of learner-centered education takes place in educational institutions that have evolved in a long tradition of subject- and teacher-centered organizational practices. These systems deliver education through a system of specialized subject-matter courses organized in an introductory-to-advanced sequence through a batched processing model, usually lecture-based, where students in a class are assumed

237

to be equal recipients of the information, with little attention to individual differences.

This system has shown remarkable longevity and resistance to change. Laurentius de Voltolina must be considered one of the first reformist critics of this system. In the mid-1300s he created the painting of a Latin grammar school classroom at the University of Bologna in Italy, shown in figure 11.1. The creation of Latin grammar schools to train priests and monks to transcribe the Bible into Latin moved education away from the individualized apprentice model of education to the system that continues today. The learning space depicted in this classroom scene is familiar to us all. Many of the students appear disinterested, paying attention to things other than the lecturer. Aside from a couple of attentive listeners most are disengaged, daydreaming, sleeping, talking with one another, or staring at members of the opposite sex.

Figure 11.1
A Medieval Classroom at the University of Bologna

Learner-centered education attempts to address the problems of learner disengagement created in part by overreliance on the subject and teacher-centered educational approaches. Learner-centered learning spaces can empower learners by making them partners in learning from their experience. Accomplishing this requires teacher-learner relationships where together they can meet in experience; building on exploration of what students already know and believe and on the sense they have made of their previous concrete life experiences. Beginning with these and related concrete experiences allows the learners to reexamine and modify their previous sense-making in the light of new ideas. The constructivist developmental theories of Piaget and Vygotsky emphasize that people construct new knowledge and understanding from what they already know and believe based on their previous experience. Zull (2002) suggests that this prior knowledge exists in the brain as neuronal networks that cannot be erased by a teacher's cogent explanation.

Nancie Atwell is an excellent role model for the learner-centered approach. Called the "Best Teacher in the World," in 2015 she earned the Global Teacher Prize. The prize, called by some the Nobel Prize of teaching, was given in a process that chose her from among ten finalists selected from five thousand nominations in 120 countries around the world. What is the secret to her success? It is a learner-centered classroom that focuses learning on student interest. She founded the Center for Teaching and Learning in 1990, a K–8 school in rural Maine where students read an average of forty books a year, choose which books they read, and write constantly. It is based on the Writing Workshop method that focuses on student choice and self-expression. Children in her school choose their own books and writing topics, advance at their own pace and are coached one-on-one by teachers. Most students excel in high school and 97 percent go on to college. Atwell states that her goal is to make the classroom a place for "wisdom and happiness, rather than one of stress and frustration. Anybody's achievement is driven by interest. You know, adult, child, boy, girl, it doesn't matter. When I let go of my last bit of total control of everything in the classroom and let the students choose, they made wonderful choices, smart choices."

Learner-Centered Educator Relationships

In a comprehensive meta-analysis of studies examining learner-centered teacher-student relationships, Cornelius-White (2007) found that these positive teacher-student relationships were associated with optimal, holistic learning. The meta-analysis included 119 articles from two traditions of learner-centered teaching. Classical, humanistic education from the 1950s to the 1970s was inspired by Carl Rogers's *Freedom to Learn* emphasizing teacher empathy, unconditional positive regard, genuineness, nondirective teaching that emphasized self-regulated learning, and encouragement of critical thinking. The contemporary (1990–2000s) constructivist learner-centered model was summarized by the American Psychological Association (Lambert & McCombs, 1998) in a fourteen-point statement of learner-centered psychological principles that covered cognitive and metacognitive factors, motivational and affective factors, developmental and social factors, and individual difference factors. This constructivist learner-centered model focuses on learning spaces where learners have ownership and control over the learning process, learning with and from each other in the kind of hospitable learning space described in chapter 9. Cornelius-White summarizes the results of the meta-analysis as follows:

> Overall, learner-centered teacher variables have above-average associations with positive student outcomes. The classical and contemporary models as wholes both appear more supported than looking at variables in isolation. Positive relationships, non-directivity, empathy, warmth, and encouraging thinking and learning are the specific teacher variables that are above average compared with other educational innovations. Correlations for participation, critical thinking, satisfaction, math achievement, drop-out prevention, self-esteem, verbal achievement, positive motivation, social connection,

IQ, grades, reduction in disruptive behavior, attendance, and perceived achievement are all above average and are presented in de-
creasing order. (2007, p. 134)

The Importance of Experiencing

A distinctive characteristic of the ELT constructivist approach to learning
and development is the importance of joining with learners' experience to
provide the scaffolding necessary for learning to emerge from their experiencing process. A common error that educators make in applying experiential learning or constructivist principles to their teaching is to treat the
lesson plan, exercise, or simulation as a technique or method applied *to* rather than *with* the learner. The assumption is that if the principle and steps of
the method are applied, learning will be the result; notwithstanding the fact
that learners may be disengaged or experiencing something quite different
from the intended object of the lesson. We have observed numerous classes
and training programs where participants are marched through one exercise,
small-group discussion, and report one after another in a way that fails to
engage their experience sufficiently to allow for their learning to shape the
flow of the event. Often this is because of a fear of losing control on the part
of the educator, who is concerned about running off topic or overtime.

Edwards and Mercer (1987) have empirically documented this disconnect between constructivist method and the learner's experience in their
study of UK primary school teachers. The teachers they studied had been
trained in Piaget-inspired discovery-oriented education based on the influential Plowden report *Children and their Primary Schools* (1967), which had
a powerful influence on British primary education in the 70s and 80s. The
report emphasized experiential learning and teacher scaffolding guidance:

> The treatment of the subject matter may be summarized in the phrase
> "learning by discovery"...initial curiosity, often stimulated by the envi-
> ronment the teacher provides, leads to questions and to a consideration
> of what questions it is sensible to ask and how to find the answers. This

involves a great exercise of judgement on the part of the teacher. He will miss the whole point if he tells the students the answers or indicates too readily and completely how the answers may be found, but he must not let them flounder too long or helplessly, and can often come to the rescue by asking another question...Essential elements are enquiry, exploration and first-hand experience. (1967, p. 669)

Edwards and Mercer report the interactions between one teacher and her seven-and eight-year-old students in the debriefing session following a simulation in which students were told to pretend that they were castaways on a desert island and had to organize themselves, electing a leader and making rules for their life together on the island. The purpose of the simulation was to teach social studies concepts of power and authority, division of labor, conflict, and cooperation. The teacher began the debriefing session by asking students to use their experience on the desert island to consider how to change the country's compulsory schooling law:

T: Now can we leave the island for a moment and come back home? In this country there is a law that says all children when they reach the age of five must attend school. How could you change the law? What could you do, Angelina?

Angelina: You could say your child was a younger age.

T: Well if you were eleven, Angelina...Do you think you could get away with pretending that you are younger?

Angelina: No...

T: So you couldn't trick somebody that way could you, Jimmy?

Jimmy: Miss, if we are on the island anyway...you wouldn't get into trouble. There's no police or anything there.

T: Yes, but Jimmy you will remember that I have said that we have now left the island and are back home. And there is this law that says that you must attend school once you are five years old.

Jimmy: Miss we can just skive out of school Miss.

T: Well if you wanted to change the law what could you do Adam?

Adam: If you are a midget they will never find out.

T: But you're not you see...Rosemary?

Rosemary: Miss, if you pretend you are ill.

T: All the time?

Rosemary: Not all the time, Miss.

(The dialogue continues in this vein.)

T:...Have you got another idea Gary?

Gary: Yes Miss. Miss you could pretend you didn't exist.

T:: How would you do that?

Gary: Miss, make, pretend you did go to school Miss.

T: Well how would you pretend you did go to school?

Gary: Just go out every day to a certain place.

T: Who might know that you are not going to school? Anita?

Anita: The teacher.

T: How would the teacher know?

Anita: She calls the register.

T: She calls the register. Now if you think this is a good law that you come to school when you are five years old put your hand up. Sixteen people believe that it is a good law. If you disagree with that law put your hand up. One, two, three, four, thank you. Now I am going to ask you to very quietly get to your diaries please. (1987, pp. 50–51)

The conversation between the teacher and her students shows a disconnect between what the students were experiencing and what the teacher meant. Her questioning focused on making the conceptual connection between the island simulation experience and the rule of law in society. This sociological question appeared abstract and unconnected to what students had experienced in the simulation. It was mandated by the lesson's purpose created by the local project-advisory authority. Rather than asking students to talk about their experience in the simulation, she tried to use questions to guide students to the abstract concepts of the study purpose. Her questions seemed designed more to guide the class to the desired conclusion rather than explore students' experience of the desert-island simulation. Edwards and Mercer make the point that classroom conversation is paradoxical in the sense that the teacher is assumed to have all the answers yet also asks most of the questions. They argue that questioning is used as a means of controlling the discourse to reach the subject objectives:

> In no enterprise other than education is it held that questions stimulate and enhance thought. Interviewers, therapists, barristers and others whose job it is to ask questions are typically advised that

asking strings of direct questions is the surest means of shutting in-
terviewees up! Silences, declarative statements and other less direct
prompts are apparently more effective in getting people to talk...
Most of the questions that teachers ask do not, in the most straightforward sense, seek information. They are part of the discursive
weaponry available to teachers for controlling topics of discussion,
directing people's thought and action and establishing the extent of
shared attention, joint activity and common knowledge. (1987, p.
46)

We had the opportunity some years ago to observe a similar process in the
very different world of MBA education with the famous experiential approach of the case study method. A Harvard Business School professor
friend invited us to observe his discussion of a case study of a corporation's
marketing strategy. From the pit of a tiered classroom of fifty MBA students, our friend began calling on students, asking questions like "What
problem was the corporation facing?" "What were the challenges it faced
from competitors?" As students gave their answers, he began writing them
on the left-hand side of the board, continuing to the end of the class when
the board was filled under organized headings of Strengths, Weaknesses,
Opportunities, and Threats, a so-called SWOT analysis of the marketing
problem. It was a dazzling performance that appeared to draw the model
from the students' experience of analyzing the case. When we asked after
the class how he had been able to draw out students' understanding in such
an organized way he opened his notebook and showed us a page that dupli-
cated the material on the board almost exactly. "This is how we prepare a
case discussion analysis," he said.

These examples serve to illustrate how the ELT constructivist approach
of spiraling repeatedly through the learning process of continuously jux-
taposing and integrating experience and concept, action and reflection,
can easily be subverted by the domination of a subject-focused theoretical
discourse.

Alice Y. Kolb and David A. Kolb

Joining with the Learner's Experience: Attention, Interests, and Beliefs

In addition to the foundational status of Piaget's constructivist theory of learning and development for learner-centered education, there is another aspect of Piaget's work that is equally important. His methodology, the way in which he approached his research, was a marked departure from traditional psychological research methods. He began his work with Alfred Binet, the creator of the intelligence test; but unlike Binet, whose primary focus was on the answers given to test questions, Piaget was more interested in the process used to come up with answers. Capitalizing on the intimacy and trust of the primal parent/child educator relationship, he focused on conversations and observations of his children, presenting them with cleverly designed puzzles and problems, to understand the process they used to solve them. By joining with his children's experience of the problems and questioning them about their process of understanding, he was able to achieve remarkable insights into the process of cognitive development. Perhaps unintentionally he also provided a role model for how to create learner-centered learning spaces by joining with learners to create mutual understanding of their experience. As Duckworth points out:

> To the extent that one carries on a conversation with a child, as a way of trying to understand a child's understanding, the child's understanding increases in the very process. The questions the interlocutor asks in an attempt to clarify for herself what the child is thinking oblige the child to think a little further also…What do you mean? How did you do that? Why did you say that? How does that fit in with what you just said? Could you give me an example? How did you figure that? In every case these questions are primarily a way for the interlocutor to understand what the other is understanding. Yet in every case, also, they engage the other's thoughts and take them a step further. (1987, pp. 96–97, quoted in O'Laughlin, 1992, p. 798)

Joining with learners to understand their experience marks a starting point for learning for both the learner and the educator. At the most basic level this involves understanding the particulars of the learners' life experience and their understanding of it. More fundamentally, it involves understanding their process of experiencing that is shaped by what they attend to, their interests and beliefs.

Attention. The importance of attention in learning is of great concern in K–12 education, in large part due to what seems like an epidemic of Attention Deficit Hyperactivity Disorder (ADHD) in school children. The Center for Disease Control and Prevention estimates that around 10 percent of children have been diagnosed with ADHD. Though there is no definitive test for ADHD, it is considered to be a biological brain-based problem of executive functioning skills like planning, organizing, remembering, and sustaining voluntary attention on tasks. While ADHD treatment is focused primarily on the problems of individual learners, it is also important to examine the way in which learning spaces can either promote or inhibit attention to learning tasks.

William James emphasized the key role of attention in learning from experience. He described attention as playing its focus "like a spotlight" across the field of consciousness in a way that is sometimes involuntary, as when a bright light or loud noise "captures" our attention, but often voluntary. Voluntary attention is determined by one's interest in the object of attention. He defines a spiral of interest-attention-selection that creates a continuous ongoing flow of experience summarized in the pithy statement—"My experience is what I agree to attend to" (1890, p. 403). Interest directs attention and ultimately the selection of some experiences over others. Selection of an experience feeds back to refine and be integrated with a person's interests serving as "the very keel on which our mental ship is built" (James, cited in Leary 1992, p. 157).

We literally create our experience by attending to the sensations and feelings we take in. In chapter 3 we described how information received in the sensory receptors lasts only a few seconds unless attention passes it to working memory. Sensory experiences that are not attended to are lost forever. Experiences that are attended to are processed in working memory, which again requires continuing attention. James emphasizes the discipline that sustained attention requires, anticipating the later constructivist theories of Piaget and Vygotsky:

> There is no such thing as voluntary attention sustained for more than a few seconds at a time…No one can possibly attend continuously to an object that does not change…But, whether the attention comes by grace of genius or by dint of will, the longer one does attend to a topic the more mastery of it one has. And the faculty of voluntarily bringing back a wandering attention, over and over again, is the very root of judgment, character, and will…The only general pedagogic maxim bearing on attention is that the more interest the child has in advance in the subject, the better he will attend. Induct him therefore in such a way as to knit each new thing on to some acquisition already there; and if possible awaken curiosity, so that the new thing shall seem to come as an answer, or part of an answer, to a question pre-existing in his mind. (James, 1890, Vol 1, pp. 420–424)

Interest. James's emphasis on the foundational status of interest in learning and the development of what he calls an "intelligible perspective" is borne out by contemporary research on the role of interest in learning. Subramaniam's (2009) review of the role of interest in learning found that interests were more influential than achievement goals in predicting motivation and performance outcomes. In addition, he found that interest is the most important intrinsic motivation variable predicting future intentions; overriding extrinsic motivation and other sources of intrinsic motivation. A review by Ainley, Heidi, and Berndorff similarly found that, "the size of the relationship between interest and learning across a wide variety of studies has been documented as accounting for approximately 10% of the variance" (2002, p. 557). Shirey and Reynolds (1988) reviewed studies of fifth- and sixth-grade students showing that they had better learning and recall of interesting information than uninteresting information—a finding to which we can all relate. It can be very difficult to learn something you are not interested in. Tomkins goes further stating "There is no human competence which can be achieved in the absence of a sustaining interest" (cited in Silvia, 2001, p. 273).

Two hypotheses, both related to James's interest-attention-selection cycle, were suggested to explain why interest is related to learning. The first, called the "slot hypothesis," suggests that the selection of interest-related experiences develops more differentiated and elaborated cognitive structures and therefore the learner has more "slots" where material related to the interest can easily be stored in memory. The second hypothesis is that interesting information is allotted more attention. We pay more attention to topics we are interested in, and thus learn from them, creating more elaborated cognitive networks and slots for retaining even more about the interest.

Of particular importance for the creation of learner-centered learning spaces is the distinction between two types of interest—individual and situational. Individual interest is a relatively enduring orientation to engage in particular classes of objects, events, or ideas over time and is content-specific. It is an "intelligible perspective" related to the individual's previous experience, knowledge, and values. Situational interest is an immediate emotional reaction evoked by appealing aspects of the environment. Interest in a particular topic or activity is thought to be a combination of both individual and situational interest factors (Ainley et al., 2002; Subramaniam, 2009).

John Dewey carried forward James's emphasis on the key role of interest in learning in his 1913 book *Interest and Effort in Education*. He, too, distinguishes between individual interest and situational interest; but believed that education should focus on drawing out and developing learner interests by understanding learner interests and organizing subject matter to address them. For him, interest is not a stable "thing" but a dynamic motivating force similar to the ELT concept of "inside-out" learning and development described in the previous chapter and in chapter 5 on learning and development:

Interests, as we have noted, are very varied; every impulse and habit that generates a purpose having sufficient force to move a person to strive for its realization, becomes an interest. But in spite of this diversity, interests are one in principle. They all mark an identification in action, and hence in desire, effort, and thought, of self with objects; with, namely, the objects in which the activity terminates (ends) and with the objects by which it is carried forward to its end (means). Interest, in the emotional sense of the word, is the evidence of the way in which the self is engaged, occupied, taken up with, concerned in, absorbed by, and carried away by, this objective subject-matter. (1913, p. 91)

He argued that the subject-centered structure of traditional education has it backward from an inside-out interest-centered approach:

Here, and here only, have we the reality of the idea of "making things interesting." I know of no more demoralizing doctrine when taken literally than the assertion of some of the opponents of interest that after subject-matter has been selected, then the teacher should make it interesting. This combines in itself two thorough going errors. On one side, it makes the selection of subject-matter a matter quite independent of the question of interest, that is to say, of the child's native urgencies and needs ; and, further, it reduces method in instruction to more or less external and artificial devices for dressing up the unrelated materials, so that they will get some hold upon attention. In reality, the principle of "making things interesting" means that subjects be selected in relation to the child's present experience, powers, and needs; and that (in case he does not perceive or appreciate this relevancy) the new material be presented in such a way as to enable the child to appreciate its bearings, its relationships, its value in connection with what already has significance for him. It is this bringing to consciousness of the bearings of the new material which constitutes the reality, so often perverted both by friend and foe, in "making things interesting." In other words, the problem is one of intrinsic connection as a motive for attention. (1913, pp. 23–24)

He views situational interest as superficial and ultimately distracting attention from the process of deepening individual interests:

When things have to be made interesting, it is because interest itself is wanting. Moreover, the phrase is a misnomer. The thing, the object, is no more interesting than it was before. The appeal is simply made to the child's love of something else. He is excited in a given direction, with the hope that somehow or other during this excitation he will assimilate something otherwise repulsive. There are two types of pleasure. One is the accompaniment of activity. It is found wherever there is successful achievement, mastery, getting on. It is the personal phase of an outgoing energy. This sort of pleasure is always absorbed in the activity itself. It has no separate existence. This is the type of pleasure found in legitimate interest. Its source lies in meeting the needs of the organism. The other sort of pleasure arises from contact. It marks receptivity. Its stimuli are external. It exists by itself as a pleasure, not as the pleasure of activity. Being merely excited by some external stimulus, it is not a quality of any act in which an external object is constructively dealt with. When objects are made interesting, this latter type of pleasure comes into play. (1913, p. 13)

He argues that the attempt to make things interesting by situationally attention-getting "bells and whistles" produces a dysfunctional oscillation between the excitement of overstimulation and apathy that ultimately undermines learners' pursuit of their true interests:

The result is division of energies…there is oscillation of excitement and apathy. The child alternates between periods of overstimulation and of inertness, as is seen in some so-called kindergartens.

Moreover, this excitation of any particular organ, as eye or ear, by itself, creates a further demand for more stimulation of the same sort...Some children are as dependent upon the recurrent presence of bright colors or agreeable sounds as the drunkard is upon his dram. It is this which accounts for the distraction and dissipation of energy characteristic of such children, for their dependence upon external suggestion, and their lack of resources when left to themselves. (1913, p. 13)

At bottom all misconceptions of interest, whether in practice or in theory, come from ignoring or excluding its moving, developing nature; they bring an activity to a standstill, cut up its progressive growth into a series of static cross-sections. When this happens, nothing remains but to identify interest with the momentary excitation an object arouses. Such a relation of object and self is not only not educative, but it is worse than nothing. It dissipates energy, and forms a habit of dependence upon such meaningless excitations, a habit most adverse to sustained thought and endeavor. Wherever such practices are resorted to in the name of interest, they very properly bring it into disrepute. It is not enough to catch attention; it must be held. (1913, p. 91)

In the light of Dewey's obviously strong distaste for the use of situational interest to promote learning, it is surprising to see a strong trend in contemporary research on the use of situational interest to promote learning. The rationale given for this emphasis seems expedient but dubious—the subject-centered batch-processing structure of educational institutions makes individualized approaches that focus on learner interests impractical:

From an educational perspective, students come into the learning environment with a wide array of individual interests. It would be a mammoth task for teachers to cater to each learner's individual interest given the time constraints and class sizes teachers have to work with. Teachers, therefore, have little control over individual interest and student learning. But what teachers do have control over is the learning environment. Situational interest, therefore, offers an alternative to individualization of interest. (Subramaniam, 2009, p. 12)

From our perspective, this rationale represents a capitulation to existing educational structures and processes that are widely seen as dysfunctional, and an undermining of the central principle of learner-centered practice of connecting with the individual learner's experience. These structures can be changed as evidenced by such innovations as the flipped classroom, portfolio methods of assessment, and individualized approaches made possible by e-learning. To neglect the proven power of individual interest on learning makes no sense.

That being said, the substance of much of contemporary situational-interest research offers useful insights into how to create attractive learner-centered learning spaces and how to use situational interest to develop deeper long-term individual interests. This work goes somewhat deeper than the attention-getting "shiny objects" to which Dewey was apparently referring, examining characteristics of the learning space such as teaching strategies, task presentation, and the structure of learning experiences. Chen, Darst, and Pangrazi (2009), for example, have developed a measure of situational interest that identifies five dimensions of situational interest—novelty, challenge, exploration intention, instant enjoyment, and attention demand. The authors conclude:

Novelty and challenge are two necessary characteristics in an activity that facilitate perception of interest. On the other hand, an activity will not attract students without the two mental dispositions: high level of attention demand and exploration intention. In addition, students will be less likely to perceive the activity as interesting unless their engagement in it results in a positive and enjoyable interactive experience. (2009, p. 177)

A number of authors argue that engaging such situational interest can lead to the development of long-term individual interests (Silvia, 2001; Subramaniam, 2009). Hidi and Renninger (2006) have developed a four-phase model of how situational interests develop into long-term interests: "The first phase of interest development is a triggered situational interest. If sustained, this first phase evolves into the second phase, a maintained situational interest. The third phase, which is characterized by an emerging (or less-well developed) individual interest, may develop out of the second phase. The third phase of interest development can then lead to the fourth phase, a well-developed individual interest." (2006, p. 112) In the early stages of their model, teacher support to generate and sustain positive feelings about the interest and feelings of self-efficacy is critical. As the learner moves into stage three of developing individual interest, the teacher moves from external support to encouraging internal self-generated support for the interest:

> Some students may require the verbal scaffolding of teachers or support from the way in which a task is organized, such as using their well-developed individual interests as the topics of word problems or texts...Other students may respond well to cooperative project-based work that enables them to be scaffolded by the others and the task on which they work...In the shift from external to internal support, however, the knowledge, or basis of information (and skills) through which the student can begin generating curiosity questions, is of importance (Renninger, 2000). Such questions enable students to connect their present understanding of content to alternative perspectives that challenge them to reconsider what they do know and to seek additional information...While students are in early phases of interest development, providing them with questions to answer may be essential. However, as individual interest begins to emerge in the late phases, it is important that students also be encouraged to generate their own questions. (2006, p. 122)

Beliefs. In addition to joining with the learners' experience by knowing what they are attending to and what their interests are, there is a third important issue to address in creating a learner-centered learning space. This is understanding what learners believe about what they are learning. On one hand, belief must be considered a primary goal of education. The conviction of belief is a far greater determinant of action than the correct recall of declarative knowledge. This is because beliefs have, in addition to being a logical or factual statement, an emotional component of attachment to the truth of the statement. For this reason, a learner's beliefs can also be a great obstacle to learning. Beliefs are notoriously difficult to change and are often remarkably resistant to empirical evidence of their falsehood.

The primacy of belief. Michael Shermer, in *The Believing Brain* (2011), argues that humans have evolved to be believing animals. Early humanoids (and infants) rely on what he calls "patternicity" or associative learning:

> There was a natural selection for the cognitive process of assuming that all patterns are real and that all patternicities represent real and important phenomena. We are the descendants of the primates who most successfully employed patternicity. Note what I am arguing here. This is not just a theory to explain why people believe weird things. It is a theory to explain *why people believe things*. Full stop. Patternicity is the process of seeking and finding patterns, connecting the dots, linking A to B. Again, this is nothing more than association learning, and all animals do it. (2011, p. 60)

The associative learning process described in chapter 3 as the exploration/mimicry learning cycle automatically and unconsciously links stimulus and response without the intervention of critical reflection or abstract hypothesis formation and testing.

In an 1877 article in *Popular Science Monthly*, Charles Sanders Peirce, a cofounder of pragmatism with Dewey and James, wrote about how beliefs become fixed; arguing that the primacy of belief was due to the fact that it is a more satisfying state than doubt: "On the contrary, we cling tena-ciously, not merely to believing, but to believing just what we do believe" (1877, p. 6).

For Peirce, the logical scientific method was a superior way to determine belief over three other ways that beliefs can become fixed in the mind—the *a priori* method of assuming first principles, the method of obedience to authority, and the method of tenacity—although he cannot resist a tongue-in-cheek admiration for the latter:

> But most of all I admire the method of tenacity for its strength, simplicity, and directness. Men who pursue it are distinguished for their decisive character, which becomes very easy with such a mental rule. They do not waste time in trying to make up their minds what they want, but, fastening like lightning upon whatever alternative comes first, they hold to it to the end, whatever happens, without an instant's irresolution. This is one of the splendid qualities which generally accompany brilliant, unlasting success. It is impossible not to envy the man who can dismiss reason, although we know how it must turn out at last. (1877, p. 14)

Shermer concurs, offering a great educational challenge:

> Research supports what I call Spinoza's conjecture: belief comes quickly and naturally, skepticism is slow and unnatural, and most people have a low tolerance for ambiguity. The scientific principle that a claim is untrue unless proven otherwise runs counter to our natural tendency to accept as true that which we can comprehend quickly. Thus it is that we should reward skepticism and disbelief, and champion those willing to change their mind in the teeth of new evidence. Instead, most social institutions—most notably those in religion, politics, and economics—reward belief in the doctrines of the faith or party or ideology, punish those who challenge the

authority of the leaders, and discourage uncertainty and especially skepticism. (Shermer, 2011, p. 135)

The persistence of belief. In addition to their primacy, beliefs have long been known to persist in the face of evidence that contradicts them. Francis Bacon in the *New Organon* said:

> The human understanding when it has once adopted an opinion draws all things else to support and agree with it. And though there be a greater number and weight of instances to be found on the other side, yet these it either neglects and despises, or else by some distinction sets aside and rejects, in order that by this great and pernicious redetermination the authority of its former conclusion may remain inviolate. (Cited in Godden, 2012, p. 56)

Recent psychological experiments using what is known as the "debriefing paradigm" have confirmed Bacon's observation. In it, subjects are prompted to form beliefs based on evidence that is later determined to be false. Following this false information, they then report on the status of their belief. Godden describes the results of one such study:

> A standard experimental paradigm involves getting participants to distinguish between supposedly authentic and fake suicide notes. During the task, participants are given false feedback which ranks their success as either above average, average, or below average. Following the task each participant is completely debriefed: the false and predetermined nature of the feedback is thoroughly explained. On the (standard) outcome debriefing condition, participants are told that the feedback was contrived and not in any way linked to their actual performance; they are shown the experimenter's instructions specifying the details of the feedback to be given and assigning them to the success, average or failure group. Finally, as part of an

ostensibly unrelated questionnaire, participants are asked to estimate their actual performance on the task they completed, and their
prospects for future success both in similar tasks and in general.

The result is that even following debriefing, participants assigned
to the success group (and their observers) ranked their abilities
more highly than those assigned to the average or failing groups.
(Godden, 2012, p. 57)

Numerous variations of the debriefing paradigm show the same results.
Even when subjects are told before they receive the feedback that it is false,
the persistence of belief persists. Three psychological processes are thought
to explain the belief persistence in the face of negative evidence:

The availability heuristic (where only memorable confirming or disconfirming cases are considered); illusory correlation (where more
confirming cases and fewer confirming ones are remembered than
actually exist); and data distortions (where confirming cases are in-
advertently created and disconfirming cases are ignored)…When
we acquire a new piece of information we synthesize it with our
existing beliefs by finding ways that it can serve as a premise or
conclusion from our existing beliefs. As we find new ways that the
belief can be a conclusion of our existing beliefs, it becomes further
entrenched in our overall web of belief. (Godden, 2012, p. 60)

In addition to these cognitive psychological biases, there are also powerful
social/relational factors that contribute to the persistence of belief. Balance
theories of attitude change show how our networks of relationships shape
our beliefs. If Mary and Jim are becoming close friends and Mary is a liberal
and Jim is a conservative, their difference in beliefs will either have to be
modified to some agreement or they will become less close. A most powerful
form of the associative learning of beliefs originates in our relationships with
significant others. Beliefs held by those who give us love, acceptance, and

esteem are associated with them and adopted as our own through a process of introjection. Rogers argues that, for most adults:

> these conceived preferences are either not related at all, or not clearly related to their own process of experiencing. Often there is a wide and unrecognized discrepancy between the evidence supplied by their own experience and these conceived values. Because these conceptions are not open to testing in experience, they must hold them in a rigid and unchanging fashion. (1964, p. 162)

A powerful example of the way in which the cognitive biases and social relationships described above influence the persistence of belief in the face of belief disconfirming evidence is found in Leon Festinger's classic book, *When Prophecy Fails* (Festinger, Reicken, & Schachter, 1956). With his coauthors, he investigated the real-life story of a UFO prophet and practitioner of automatic writing and her followers, who believed that automatic-writing responses from the planet Clarion indicated that the world was coming to an end by a great flood on December 21, 1954. When the date passed with no flood, the group gathered at the woman's house at first experienced great distress; but soon was "saved" by an automatic writing message from Clarion that said their dedication had spared the earth. Rather than disbanding after this failure of the prophecy, the group gained greater solidarity and promoted their cause more fervently. Festinger argued that the group's increased commitment to their beliefs was consistent with his theory of cognitive dissonance that states that when two ideas are in conflict (belief in the flood prediction and the fact it didn't happen), there is a motivation to reduce the inconsistency in the easiest way, which in this case was promoting their cause to gain wider social support.

Beliefs and learning. As educators we are often faced with situations in which learners have strong beliefs that are potentially in conflict with our educational objectives. Many college freshmen arrive at college bringing with them belief systems that have been formed and reinforced by their relationships in family and community. In many cases they meet other students who come from diverse backgrounds with similarly diverse belief systems. This can, of course, become an occasion for considerable emotional and intellectual turmoil; as previous belief are challenged and changed along with repercussions on the relationships from which they were formed. From this turmoil emerge new beliefs and relationships. William Perry (1970), whose work we will describe in detail in the next chapter, has beautifully documented these changes as Harvard students progressed through their college years, in his groundbreaking theory of adult development, *Forms of Intellectual and Ethical Development in the College Years: A Scheme.* He showed that freshmen entered college with absolutist beliefs about knowledge and ethics, which, in the sophomore year, moved to a relativistic perspective as they were challenged by exposure to the diverse ideas and beliefs they experienced. Some reacted to this diversity by retreating back to the security of absolutism. In the later years some students emerged from an "everything is relative" perspective to a stage of conscious and deliberate commitment to beliefs forged through reflection and critical thinking. Others had more difficulty in finding principles to live by in the face of the complex and diverse choices before them.

Robert Kegan (1982, 1994) has made it his life's work to explore and define these adult levels of mental complexity. In the course of his career he has created a five-stage theory of adult development that traces qualitiative changes in how one makes meaning from experience in the cognitive affective, interpersonal, and intrapersonal realms. The system is an elegant and persuasive theory based on subject-object relations that describes how the subjective framework that one is embedded in that is used to view the object at one level becomes itself the object of a new more encompassing subjective framework at the next level. Kegan describes this growth as making what was subject into object so that we can "have it" rather than "be had by it." In his latest work *Immunity to Change* (Kegan & Lahey, 2009) he applies the insights from his work to the problem of why people find it so difficult to change beliefs and behavior.

He gives an example of how developing higher levels of mental complexity from socialized mind to self-authoring mind can free one to reexamine and freely choose beliefs and values rather that be "had" by them:

A person who perceives the world through a socialized mind is subject to the values and expectations of his "surround" (be it family of origin, his religious or political reference group or the leaders of his work setting who set the terms on his professional and financial reality). The perceived risks and dangers that arise for such a person have to do with being unaligned or out of faith with that mediating surround; being excluded from it and thereby cut off from its protections; or being evaluated poorly by those whose regard directly translates into his regard for himself.

At the next level of mental complexity, the self-authoring mind, a person is able to distinguish the opinion of others (even important others) from her own self-opinion. She might certainly take other views into account, but she can *choose* how much, and in what way, to let them influence her. People who advance to this more complex mental capacity can take the whole meaning-making category of others' opinions as a kind of tool, or something they have, rather than something that has them. (Kegan & Lahey, 2009, pp. 52–53)

The self-authoring mind describes individuals who see themselves as autonomous independent selves who are responsible for their actions and in control of their lives. Operating in Piaget's formal operations stage they rationally analyze variables to determine cause-and-effect and solve problems. Kegan says these individuals, "can coordinate, integrate, act upon or invent values, beliefs, convictions, generalizations, ideals, abstractions, interpersonal loyalties and intrapersonal states. It is no longer *authored* by them, it *authors them* and thereby achieves a personal authority" (1994, p. 185).

Baxter-Magolda advocates the self-authoring mind as the foundation of higher education, "Twenty-first century learning outcomes require self-authorship: the internal capacity to define one's beliefs system, identity and relationships" (2007, p. 69). Based on her extensive research (1992, 1999), including a twenty-one year longitudinal study of young adults from eighteen to thirty-nine years of age (2001), she has identified three components of self-authorship—trusting one's internal voice, building an internal foundation of beliefs, and securing internal commitments to strengthen personal identity (2008). The self-authoring mind seems a good fit for the challenges of living in a highly individualistic society such as the United States, where responsibility for the course of one's life including health care, retirement, and education are left to the individual.

We educators want to have a constructive influence on this process of belief examination and choice; but often are unable to engage the necessary conversations because of the restrictions imposed by the traditional classroom. A learner-centered learning space can make room for learners' beliefs to be "on the table" for examination and discussion. By joining with learners' experience to discover what they are attending to, their interests and beliefs, it becomes possible to remove the barriers that beliefs can pose for learning and also engage the positive commitment that beliefs can provide to what one knows.

Angelo and Cross (1993) provide an illuminating case study of how students' beliefs about astronomy and science in general influenced their learning in an astronomy class. The instructor gave students a questionnaire asking to distinguish facts from opinions in astronomy and other areas. To the instructor's surprise, the result revealed that her students mis-categorized astronomy-related statements far more frequently than statements about everyday life problems, even after they have been exposed to the information in the astronomy course. The instructor learned from follow-up interviews with students that they held highly negative and skeptical attitudes toward science, explaining the high degree of incorrect responses even from some of the brightest students. Several A and B students "simply did not believe that astronomers could judge the temperature of a star from its brightness, even though they knew that the statement 'Brighter stars are generally hotter ones' is considered in astronomy to be a fact"(p. 67). The instructor was surprised that, "students could do well in her class on most objective measures, and could succeed in distinguishing facts from theories without necessarily accepting the general premises of fundamental values of the discipline. In other words, they could play the game without believing in it" (p. 67).

Many of us may have encountered similar situations in our teaching. Faced with such challenges, our inclination is to review what went wrong and focus on improving teaching strategies to correct such future students' misunderstanding. That was precisely what the astronomy professor did. She was convinced that she needed to "devote more class time to making explicit the similarities and differences—between distinguishing facts form opinions in 'everyday' settings and the more explicit and rigorous rules used by scientists" (p. 67). The challenge here, however, is not to speak more clearly about the facts but to be able to engage the underlying conversation about student beliefs and feelings about science in a way that opens them to a reexamination of those beliefs.

Empowering Learners to Become Partners in the Learning Process
In addition to joining with learners to understand their experience, a learner-centered learning space enables learners to take charge of their own learning and become partners with the teacher in the learning process. There are those who oppose the idea of student-centered learning, arguing that it gives the false impression that the teacher is not an expert in the subject under study who knows more than the students. In most cases teachers *are* the subject-matter experts; but they still need the learner to be a partner in learning; because it is learners who hold the ultimate power, the power to give or withhold their participation in learning. There is the potential here for a powerful partnership where learner and educator have different arenas of responsibility and expertise joining together to create a greater competence in learning. To realize this potential, however, requires communication and trust between the partners (Gemmell, 2012) and learner expertise in taking charge of their own learning. A first step in this process is for learners and educators to share their respective expectations about their desires and responsibilities in learning together, a process we call establishing a "psychological contract" for learning (Osland, Kolb, Rubin, & Turner, 2007). Ideally the psychological contract is established in a collaborative way where everything about the course is not dictated by the teacher, but where learners can have some input and control about what is learned and how they go about it.

Alice Y. Kolb and David A. Kolb

Many learners, however, are not prepared for the learning partnership required in a learner-centered learning space. In many cases this is because their previous educational experiences have led them to believe that the teacher is in charge and their role is just to follow instructions. Often they have given little thought to what the process of learning is about and to the way they learn in particular. For this reason a learner-centered learning space needs to provide learners with the opportunity to learn about learning, their approach to learning and strategies they can use to learn more effectively. For the experiential educator this means that their educational goals need to be broader than learning the specifics of the subject matter at hand. Variously termed "learning how to learn" or "meta-learning" (Vanhear, 2013), this educational agenda is about fostering in learners the understanding, desire, and skills required to intentionally and deliberately manage their own learning; preparing them to better master and apply the knowledge of the current course and to continue to learn and renew themselves throughout their lifetime.

In chapter 6 "Deliberate Experiential Learning," we have described the specifics of this agenda, outlining the important issues to be addressed in this process. The central focus of deliberate learning is metacognition, the capacity to reflect on how one learns and to evaluate and implement strategies to increase one's learning effectiveness. In the chapter, we identified six metacognitive practices that can awaken and enhance learners' capacity to learn effectively. The six areas of metacognitive regulation are mindful experiencing, learning style, learning identity, learning spaces, learning relationships, and deliberate practice (see figure 6.1). These practices encompass skills that enable learners to become aware of how they learn and to evaluate and adapt these skills to become increasingly effective at learning.

Twelve

CREATING SPACE FOR REFLECTIVE THINKING

I don't want to believe. I want to know.

—CARL SAGAN

In the current educational environment, there is an urgent call for an "educated mind" capable of navigating a complex global, socioeconomic environment. Yet, as data comparing sixty-five global educational systems from the OECD 2012 triennial Program for International Student Assessment (PISA) indicate, American teenagers continue to lag behind in all study areas—reading, math, and science literacy (OECD, 2012). Unlike other international assessments designed to measure how well students have memorized what they have been taught in classrooms, the PISA test has a different purpose. As the creator of the test, Andreas Schleicher explained, it was designed "not looking for students' answers to equations or to multiple choice questions; it was designed to look for their ability to think creatively" (Ripley, 2013, p. 15). Why then, are American students falling behind in ability to think creatively? "Our most privileged teenagers," Ripley writes, "had highly educated parents and attended the richest schools in the world, yet they ranked eighteenth in math compared to their privileged peers around the world" (Ripley, 2013, p. 4).

As it turned out, countries with children with the highest level of creative thinking abilities recognized that the world had changed and their educational system needed to adapt to changing times. While the path chosen for educational reform and transformation varied enormously in each country, they navigated politics, bureaucracy, conflicts with unions, and parental opposition to embrace a learner-centered philosophy as the underlying framework of their education. In contrast, as we discussed in Chapter 11, the mainstream educational system in this country has been stubbornly slow in embracing a learner-centered model of education suited to the nurturing of an empowered, lively, and creative mind.

More than a century ago, when John Dewey wrote *How We Think* (1910), an inquiry into the nature and the formation of an educated mind, he was facing similar challenges and oppositions from the traditional institutions and educational practices that he saw as ill-suited for the development of a truly creative mind. As Richard Rorty noted in the preface of Dewey's 1933 revision of the book:

> *How We Think* was written precisely because Dewey's intention was to encourage teachers to educate children not to be dogmatic in their worldviews, but to be critical in their understanding of the traditional educational practices of the time. Rejecting a parochial and prescriptive way of thinking he saw prevalent in traditional school system, Dewey was convinced educators could teach students to become better thinkers with sound judgment and reasoning, free of dogmatism and prejudice. Dewey defined this particular way of thinking as "reflective thought," *an active, persistent, and careful consideration of any belief or supposed form of knowledge in the light of the grounds that support it and the further conclusions to which it tends.* (Dewey, 1933, p. 118)

Earlier Dewey (1910) distinguished reflective thought from ordinary thinking:

Thinking signifies everything that is "in our heads" or that "goes through our minds"...More of our waking life than we should care to admit, even to ourselves, is likely to be whiled away in this inconsequential trifling with idle fancy and unsubstantial hope...Now reflective thought is like this random coursing of things through the mind in that it consists of a succession of things thought of; but it is unlike, in that the mere chance occurrence of any chance "something or other" in an irregular sequence does not suffice. Reflection involves not simply a sequence of ideas, but a con-sequence—a consecutive ordering in such a way that each determines the next as its proper outcome, while each in turn leans back on its predecessors (pp. 2–3).

While humans naturally engage in all kinds of thoughts, the attitudes and habits of a thoughtful mind are not a gift from nature. Dispositions and the inquiry methods to arrive at a reasoned conclusion needs to be cultivated by providing conditions suitable for nurturing of the mental discipline required for true reflective thought.

Humans can never be trained to think, says Dewey. One can only learn to think *well.* (Dewey, 1910, p. 29). With those emphatic words, Dewey challenges us to learn and nurture within us an educational stance and approach that will encourage the "formation of wide-awake, careful, thorough habits of thinking" in our students (1933, p. 177).

During our work with implementation of SAGES learner-centered seminar program at CASE to be described in Chapter 14, we had the opportunity to talk to several faculty members about their role in the SAGES program. Here is how Professor James, a physics professor, beautifully summarized his commitment to help his students become the kind of thinker Dewey had envisioned:

My role is to get my students to develop critical thinking. To teach my students how to calculate the amount of energy required to burn a gallon of oil is one type of critical thinking. My responsibility also is to teach them to think about the social responsibility of burning that oil. (Kolb et al., 2003, SAGES Interview)

Professor James's words encapsulate the kind of reflective thinking a learner-centered education aspires to develop in students. In learner-centered education, our critical role is to provide students with a point of departure for their intellectual journey, equipped with skills and dispositions to inquire in depth. We want students' actions and commitments in all areas of their lives to be the outcome of a reflective, thorough, and deliberate thought process.

Development of Reflective Thinking

Between the two types of reflective thinking that Professor James alluded to, the first type is a domain-specific thinking mode required to master the knowledge and the problem-solving skills within a discipline. While the nature, goal, and the outcome of a discipline-specific knowledge may vary among academic domains, for the most part the "text book approach" favored by the subject-centered model of education has proven to be ineffective in developing the kind of thinking Dewey thought was essential to solve problems of real consequence.

As Huba and Freed (2000) noted, textbook problems, even those constructed to mimic the real-world context, were only useful to promote students' automaticity and habitual thinking. The problems were highly structured and carefully written to help students develop skills to arrive at right answers in the classrooms, but limited in providing opportunity for practical application and encouragement for students to ask insightful questions about solving real-world problems. In the real world, King and Kitchner (1994) argued, the problems students will likely face are *ill-structured*, with no clear cut answers and solutions. They need to wrestle with often uncertain, ambiguous, and conflicting situations and make reasonable judgment in the face of such complexity. Professor James's second type of problem falls within the ill-structured problem category. *What are the social implications of burning a gallon of oil?* No preexisting formulas or algorithms will help students answer such an ethical dilemma; they need to rely on their moral compass and construct for themselves a thoughtful, just, and viable solution.

It is our responsibility to develop in students the intellectual capacity to solve both well-structured and ill-structured problems. King and Kitchner (1994) described the contrasting characteristics of these two types of problems: well-structured problems can be described with a high degree of completeness and certainty and experts will usually agree on the solution. Ill-structured problems, on the other hand, cannot be described with a high degree of completeness and certainty and experts will disagree on solutions. With well-structured problems, the educational goal is to learn how to reason to a correct solution while for ill-structured problems the goal is to learn how to construct and defend reasonable solutions.

While the two types of problems may differ in terms of definition, content, and educational goals, it is no less important to consider how students' intellectual processes evolve over time toward mastery of reflective thinking and learning strategies appropriate to both types. How do students develop intellectually and ethically? This was the epistemological question William Perry pursued in his study of Harvard and Radcliffe students in the 1950s and 1960s. Perry's work, inspired by Dewey's ideas about the development of reflective thought, provided a foundation for a provocative scholarly dialogue about the nature of late adolescent and adult development and the role of higher education in fostering intellectual and ethical development in students. The assumptions a person holds about the knowledge and origins of knowledge, observed Perry, go through a structural change over time. As students move from adolescence into adulthood, they advance from a simplistic, categorical view of knowledge to a more complex, contextual view of the world and themselves. Perry identified nine such developmental stages grouped into four major categories. As we describe the stages below (Kolb, Godwin, Murphy, Joy, Ghazal, & Coombe, 2005), notice that the distinctions between them are subtle and not as clear as one might expect. This is particularly true of the later stages of development, where students are asked to deal with increasingly complex sets of problems and challenges before they make a thoughtful, conscious choice about an issue in a given context.

Dualism—The world is viewed in absolute, right-and-wrong terms. The students believe that right answers exist to all questions and that authorities have these answers. It is the instructor's job to provide these answers and the students' job to learn them.

Examples:

- I'm lost in this class; the professor lacks a clue.
- Every lecture course, no matter how bad, has taught me more than any seminar, no matter how good. In a lecture, you get taught by an expert, which means the information is credible. But in a seminar, most of the information is from other students like me, which leads to discussion that is irrelevant and suspect in accuracy. In seminars, professors don't like to tell students directly that they are "wrong" or "correct," so one can leave a seminar confused and not knowing any more than when one entered.
- When I came here, I didn't think any question could have more than one answer.

How students view the instructor's role:

Students expect the instructor to provide the answer to every question. In their minds, good teachers know the answers; bad ones don't. When you ask questions, especially open-ended ones, they are wondering, **"What is the correct answer? Why should we bother with the wrong ones? Can't you just tell us the answer?"**

Multiplicity—In some areas, knowledge is certain. In most areas, nobody knows anything for sure. In those areas where the authorities have yet to find the answers, uncertainty is viewed as temporary. In the meantime, everyone's opinions are just as valid as everyone else's.

Examples:

- You know, it seems to me that there are two different kinds of things we study—things where there are answers and things where there aren't any!
- I like that there are many ways to solve or code a program. Since the material tends to be subjective, it helps to see the reasoning of another person sometimes.
- If there are no right answers, I think my ideas are as good as anyone's and I do not see why I got a "C" on my midterm.

How students view the instructor's role:

Students begin to realize that the instructor will not provide all the answers to their questions. As they seek to discover the solution on their own, they struggle with the realization that there is generally more than one solution to a complex problem. Since there are many ways to look at an issue, they conclude that their view is as good as anybody else's.

Relativism—Students come to view knowledge as contextual and relative in nature. Right and wrong answers exist within a specific context and are judged by how well one is able to construct a well-reasoned point of view.

Examples:

- I love our class discussions because they help me figure out what I think about things.

- I always thought I knew what I thought about politics, but after hearing others and thinking more, I realize that there are so many ways of looking at the same thing!

How students view the instructor's role:

Students realize that there is more than one solution to a dilemma and that the solutions must be examined based on evidence and sound thought processes. Students also become aware of the strengths and weaknesses in their lines of reasoning. They expect instructors to help them see alternatives more clearly. When exploring multiple theories or answers to a problem, they begin thinking, **"What principles underlie each of them? Which is the most efficient?"**

Commitment—Students are able to test out and evaluate various alternatives and commit to the most well-reasoned theory, solution, or interpretation. The commitment leads to the development of a personalized set of values, lifestyle, and identity.

- As the president of student council I have chosen to embrace and promote the value of diversity. As a leader I have the extraordinary opportunity and responsibility to maintain a climate that affirms diversity of persons and diversity of views.
- For the purpose of my dissertation I have chosen to pursue the topic of peace in the Middle East and the use of dialogue as a means to promote peace. I believe that the creation of a peaceful environment in which to function is vital to survival. The creation of a means to create that peace through dialogue has applications beyond the Middle East and perhaps will help create more peaceful social structures and organizations in which people can flourish.

How students view the instructor's role:

> Students are capable of integrating personal experience with the complex set of skills and knowledge they have mastered. Students commit to a choice or viewpoint and become aware of the consequences of that commitment. They also realize that commitment is an ongoing, unfolding, evolving activity. They may seek instructors' guidance to evaluate different choices they are about to make and the implications of their decision to adhere to a particular viewpoint.

Patricia King at the University of Michigan, who has devoted three decades to researching this subject, once wrote that students in college move from ignorant certainty to intelligent confusion. Since certainty is more gratifying and tranquil than confusion, students may find the uncertain and complex developmental path bewildering and painful at times. As a seasoned professor in the Case SAGES program explained, students' progress from one stage to another is anything but orderly or direct:

> We want the students to move steadily and quickly through the stages; however, students do not develop in a linear fashion. It takes time. In practice, the developmental path is much more convoluted than we might expect. We should celebrate every small incremental improvement that students make in their intellectual and ethical reasoning.

This statement finds support in Perry's study. The journey through these stages is not necessarily linear, and sometimes students move back and forth between stages. Under certain conditions during the developmental process, Perry found that students may hesitate in taking the next step or retreat to a dualistic, dogmatic world view. Dewey also highlighted the turbulent nature of the developmental path toward becoming a true reflective thinker:

> Reflective thinking is always more or less troublesome because it involves overcoming the inertia that inclines one to accept suggestions at their face value; it involves willingness to endure conditions of mental unrest and disturbance. Reflective thought, in short, means judgment suspended during further inquiry; and suspense is likely to be somewhat painful. (Dewey, 1910, p. 13)

Supporting the Development of Reflective Thinking

While we spend a great deal of time talking about the qualities we want our students to have when they leave our classrooms, we cannot overlook the importance of understanding who our students are when they first arrive, especially in terms of their intellectual and ethical development. As we craft our teaching practices, an awareness of students' different levels of development will enhance our ability to help them make sense of their experiences, become able to reconcile contradictions, understand why others might hold different views, and take responsibility for their actions.

At each stage of development, students have particular learning needs and if the examples of students' statements above serve as an indication, their view of the role of instructors and their peers in the learning process are substantially different from one stage to another. Those in the early stages require highly structured experiential learning strategies. Those in the later stages value more flexible experiential learning opportunities, as they do not need as much structure in order to make full use of new concepts presented in the course. As we create an environment to help move students forward in their reasoning, the following suggestions from veteran CASE seminar instructors may be useful. While the suggestions were crafted specifically within the seminar context, they may be applicable to other learning contexts where the learning goal is to advance learners' capacity for reflective thinking.

Helping Students Move from Dualism to Multiplicity

- Draw out students' own views and experiences; reinforce their legitimate arguments.
- Use structured, small-group discussions to create space for students to explore their own ideas and the ideas of others.
- Include your own ideas and responses as feedback on their assignments.
- Consider role plays or debates to help students "try on" different points of view.
- Focus on helping students develop strategies to pick out major concepts or the most relevant information in a section of text. This will aid them in learning *how* to learn, as opposed to merely learning answers.
- Create situations where students can experience two or three conflicting views.
- When students reject a viewpoint, encourage them to be *concrete about their basis for rejection.*
- If students appeal to authority or overgeneralize, ask them about instances when the authority's opinion might be challenged or the generalization might not hold.
- Reinforce the notion that authorities can and do disagree.
- Invite students to identify and evaluate their own assumptions.
- After evidence and rational arguments are presented, reinforce the possibility of changing one's mind.

Statements and questions you may try:

- What view does the author take? What other position could she/he have taken?
- Who has a different perspective?
- Changing your mind is not a sign of weakness.

Helping Students Move from Multiplicity to Relativism

- Let students take responsibility for structuring their own learning. This may involve some negotiation on syllabus, course content, and due dates; the creation of individual contracts; and use of the teacher as a resource rather than as an authority figure.
- Create assignments or discussions that invite students to evaluate the relative merits of an argument via nonabsolute or imaginative criteria.
- Use readings, guest speakers, and field trips to introduce paradoxes or conflicting themes and ideas.
- Let students explicitly identify bases for disagreements among authorities and their different viewpoints.
- Invite students to continually identify and evaluate their own assumptions.

Statements and questions you may try:

- Under what circumstances would you change your mind?
- What have other people thought about this topic throughout history?
- When have you changed your mind about something and why?
- How have your life experiences influenced your views?

Helping Students Move from Relativism to Commitment

- Encourage students to structure their own learning experiences.
- Design situations that invite students to give alternative new ways of looking at complex problems.
- Have students encounter several views and take a reasoned stance.
- Reinforce that commitment can be—and usually is—reassessed and changed.

Statements and questions you may try:

- If you choose that career path, what will your life look like?
- How can you link this theory with the others we have discussed?
- What do you want to research and why?

Creating Space for Reflective Thinking—Unifying Principles

Part of our role as educators is not only to provide students with the accumulated knowledge in a given field, but more importantly, to help students develop their power to inquire in depth; to master reasoning abilities to integrate what they have learned with larger concepts and understand the consequences of application of those ideas and information broadly. As we work to help our students to become reflective thinkers, the following common principles may serve as a guide to create conditions for our students to realize their intellectual growth and become independent thinkers.

Use Yourself as a Model. More often than we care to admit, our tendency is to present ourselves as "the ultimate expert" or, as one teacher humorously put it, "We teach like we were god" (Bain, 2004, p. 142). We expect our students to reflect and think but we rarely make explicit to them how we came to make sense of our lives and think the way we do. If we look back on our intellectual journey, we would easily recognize that our developmental path was anything but as logical and orderly as we may communicate to our students. We tend to hide from them those very experiences of setbacks, disappointments, failures, and triumphs that have shaped our thinking and our lives. In our SAGES research at Case we uncovered an interesting finding in this regard. Students were very interested in how instructors created meaning in their own lives, whether professionally or personally. Instructors who were open and personal about their life journey were far more successful in establishing trust and a safe learning space that invited students to openly explore new questions and interests in depth. Bain (2004) reported a similar finding in his study of exceptional teachers. When a student heard her chemistry professor share the difficulty she first had with chemistry, this was her response:

> [That] gave me the confidence I needed to learn it. I used to think these people were just born with all this knowledge. That's the way a lot of them act. (Bain, 2004, p. 141)

Your End-Point is not Your Students' Point of Departure. We have a tendency to organize the subject matter "chronologically" and "logically" in hopes to stimulate understanding of scientific thought process in our students. We want them to learn how to organize, classify, and make sense of information coherently the way experts do. However, as we learned from the stages of intellectual development, students' thought processes have distinct logic at each stage that may contradict the logical path we want them to follow. Furthermore, regardless of their developmental stage, the unique learning pathway each student may choose may be influenced by their learning style. They construct meaning following their own learning cycle, not necessarily ours. Dewey warns us about the pitfall of imposing the expert's mature thinking process to a novice mind:

> That which is strictly logical from the standpoint of subject matter really represents the conclusions of an expert, trained mind. The definitions, and classifications of the conventional text represent these conclusions boiled down…Some kind of intellectual organization must be required, or else habits of vagueness, disorder, and incoherent "thinking" will be formed. But the organization need not be that which would satisfy the mature expert. For the immature mind is still in process of gaining the intellectual skill that the latter has already achieved. It is absurd to suppose that the beginner can commence where the adept stops. (Dewey, 1933, p. 182)

Teaching with Your Mouth Shut. Don Finkel's (2000) insightful suggestion to shut our mouths when we teach may be on target. Teachers, somehow, internalized the habit of filling up the learning space with long monologues, almost oblivious to where their students may be in their thought process. We need to listen more and speak less. While lectures may be effective to deliver content for students to absorb, the intake of information by itself is not sufficient to develop their reflective thinking capacity. Instead, create a learning space rich in opportunities for them to listen to their own voices and the voices of their peers; this will help you identify where they are in terms of their reasoning and meaning-making. Resist the temptation to jump in and save your students by providing answers; instead, as Rilke (2012) suggests, guide them to live their questions into their own answers.

Master the Art of Questioning. Asking thoughtful and meaningful questions is critical to foster a learning mind-set in our students. Do I encourage rich and meaningful discussions to expand their reasoning? Do I motivate my students to carefully reflect and examine their assumptions? What are the defining qualities of questions that stimulate intellectual growth in our students? This was precisely the main topic of discussion of the faculty development seminar offered at CASE in preparation for the launching of the new undergraduate SAGES program. In the midst of a lively exchange among faculty from diverse disciplines around the campus, the physics professor, Joe Thomas, who was the lead facilitator of the session, said the following: "If you only ask questions you already have answers for, you are being unfair to your students. You have to make sure you ask questions you yourself do not yet have answers." A brief moment of silence descended in the seminar room, followed by rumbling voices mixed with disapproval and surprise. Finally, a math professor blurted out in almost disbelief: "You are being unreasonable, Joe. We have responsibility to teach our kids how to do science and you know that. There are certain scientific knowledge and procedures they have to know that are not worth questioning: the earth is not flat and two plus two always equals four." Other science faculty joined forces in support of the math professor's view. Professor Thomas did not budge. He pushed back asking, "Is that always true? As you go deep into the math world the assertion that two plus two equals always four may not hold." True, science teachers in particular need to help students understand that in the scientific arena there are some governing laws so well verified by experiment over the centuries that it is not fruitful to question them. One might say that these areas are "nonnegotiable." It is also true many areas of scientific discovery are not yet settled. In fact, science is not certain; what exists are conflicting facts and theories—and, sometimes no theories at all, merely questions that have yet to be answered.

Professor Thomas's statement gets to the heart of art of questioning. Consciously and unconsciously, the kind of questions teachers ask in the classrooms are overwhelmingly the ones to which they themselves already know the answers. Edward and Mercer's (1987) study described in the previous chapter underscores this point. As well-intentioned as they may be, teachers, they found, had a tendency to ask specific questions to guide students to arrive at predetermined conclusions within the time frame allocated to teaching a particular subject. Their approach to questioning, the authors observed, was that while it afforded larger control over their subject, it robbed the students of the ability to apply their own thought to arrive at an idea. As Professor Thomas suggests, we need from time to time to surrender control of our teaching agendas, time constraints, or content to be covered and venture into "unknown" topics together with our students and let the inquiry take its own course, and experience the unfolding of our students' minds.

A good question, Dewey suggests, is what directs students to guide their own inquiry and form in them the habit and discipline to think by themselves. Here are Dewey's insightful suggestions to develop the art of questioning (Dewey, 1933, pp. 331–332):

a. ***Direct students to apply the knowledge in a different context.*** Avoid questions that make students regurgitate back and simply reproduce what they have learned. A good question requires students to use the knowledge to solve different problems. Even if the solution to the problem at hand is well known, what matters the most is the nurturing of originality and creativity in students to find the path to the problem on their own.

b. ***Direct the mind of students to the subject matter and not to the teacher.*** If the main purpose of the question is to draw "correct answers" from the students, then we have denied our students the capacity to conduct serious inquiry and reflection. It is simpler and quicker to provide answers than to ask questions to develop their inquiry process. We need to be mindful of the risk of turning our students' intellectual pursuit into a mindless guessing game as to what the teacher is after. Here is how Professor T from CASE redirected his students' attention from him back to the topic of discussion:

Early in the semester, I noticed that the conversation always kept coming back to me. Students would often talk to me, but rarely addressed one another. I was becoming the center of the conversation. I realized that I needed to do something to divert the attention from me and have them engage with one another. Whenever a student asked me a question, I tried first to address the same question to the group: "That is an interesting question. What do you all think?" They gradually came to understand that I was not there to provide answers to all the questions; they needed to work together to come up with an answer.

c. ***Keep the subject "developing."*** Good questions promote continuity and development of ideas. They expand the learning space enough to encourage movement and flow of thoughts and ideas from one point to the next in a consecutive manner. Questions that disrupt the continuity of discussion and thought invite a disorderly and haphazard thinking process.

d. ***Require a mindful pause.*** What are the key concepts we have learned? Can you summarize the author's main points? Such questions will require students to review, summarize, and highlight the essential meaning of what they have learned. It is natural for students to digress or "wander all over" when they are learning, in attempts to hold on to something meaningful. Well-crafted questions will help students discriminate significant information and concepts from side issues and exploratory remarks. It will also bring coherence to what they have learned and help them view the subject from a new perspective.

e. *In summary...leave their minds "wanting more."* What will I tackle next? I wonder where this idea might take me? When you hear students ask such self-directed questions, you have succeeded in awakening their minds. What they have learned and accomplished serves as a fertile ground to fuel their curiosity and desire to pursue their inquiry further toward the mastery of true reflective thought.

Thirteen

The *Ludic* Learning Space

Men do not quit playing because they grow old;
they grow old because they quit playing.

—Oliver Wendell Holmes Sr.

The late paleontologist and evolutionary biologist Steve Jay Gould (1977) argued that play may rescue humans from overspecialization. Gould's words point to a concept developed by the early evolutionary biologists called *paedomorphosis* or *neoteny*, a process whereby humans retain the ability to play throughout their lives, thus avoiding detrimental effects of *gerontomorphism*, a form of evolution of adult stages of successive and independent development responsible for extreme specialization and the loss of brain plasticity and adaptive flexibility (Montagu, 1984). Montagu argued that one of the crucial human neotenic traits is the capacity to learn. Play allows humans great flexibility and adaptability to learn and retain nonspecialized traits unique to humans such as open mindedness, malleability, questioning, seeking, curiosity, humor, and laughter. Montagu writes:

> The child's play is a leap of the imagination far beyond the capability of any other creature. It is the vaulting capacity of the imagination

in play that is one of the most valuable traits of the human species. This sort of play of imagination, the challenge to "take a giant leap," has been responsible for much of the invention, discovery, and great ideas which have benefited humanity. (Montagu, 1984, p. 31)

Many foundational scholars of experiential learning, Piaget, Dewey, and Vygotsky in particular, recognized the importance of play in the holistic process of learning and development. For them, play serves as a critical scaffolding mechanism for healthy human development from early childhood into adulthood giving us the capacity to "escape from overspecialization" by retaining the neotenic mind-set and attitude throughout our lives.

From an experiential learning perspective, we view play and learning as a unified and integral process of human learning and development. We introduce in this chapter the concept of the *ludic* learning space, wherein learners achieve deep learning through the integration of intellectual, physical, moral, and spiritual values in a free and safe space that provides the opportunity for individuals to play with their potential and ultimately commit themselves to learn, develop, and grow.

The Concept of Play

The cultural historian Huizinga (1950) contends that from the very beginning, cultures evolved in forms of play. The instinct of play pervades all human endeavors: in law, science, war, philosophy, and in the arts. Through the eyes of Huizinga, a human emerges not as *Homo Sapiens*, the man who knows, but primarily as *Homo Ludens*, the man who plays. Play encompasses a wide range of activities and forms in both the human and animal world. From the play-fight of kittens, imaginary play of a child, to the more abstract play of adult games and organized sports, it permeates our lives as a significant source of creativity, imagination, and fun. While play has undoubtedly been a unique and universal human experience across cultures, it has also been the subject of scholarly inquiry across diverse fields of social science with a focus on its significance in the process of individual expression and adaptation (Callois, 2001; Dewey, 1990; Erikson, 1950; Freud, 1965; Gadamer, 1989; Mainemelis & Ronson, 2006; Miller, 1974; Piaget, 1962; Sutton-Smith, 1997; Turner, 1974; Vygotsky, 1966; Winnicott, 1971).

With the bold statement "play = learning" Singer et al. (2006) emphasized the importance of play in human cognitive and social-emotional growth. While play has been characterized as "older and more original than civilization" Huizinga (1950, p. 1), and has been defined as a distinct form of behavior possessing serious biological, developmental, functional, and evolutionary implications in animal life (Bekoff and Byers, 1998; Darwin, 1965, 1981; Fagen, 1981, 1984, 1994; Goodall, 1995; Groos, 1898; Lorenz, 1971), in reality play has been devalued and continues to be squeezed out of our formal educational institutions and under the misguided view that learning is reserved for the classrooms and play should be confined to smaller and smaller playgrounds without consideration of the detrimental effect that such a distorted separation of play and learning might have on human growth and development (Dewey, 1910, 1933; Elkind, 1988, 2007; Hannaford, 1995; Healey, 1990; Russ, 2004; Singer et al., 2006).

There are wide conceptions regarding the nature, purpose, and the way in which play manifests itself. Play is defined as purposeless activity (Bekoff & Byers, 1981), fundamentally different from earnest activity (Lorenz, 1994), amphibolous (going simultaneously in both directions) (Spariosu, 1989), a vacation from reality (Erikson, 1950), any activity a body is not obliged to do (Twain, 1988), or an intrinsically driven activity without a clear goal other than its own activities (Brown, 1995). Despite such multitude of definitions and characterizations, our multidisciplinary review of play literature (Kolb, 2000) reveals three interconnected streams of play concepts that provide a useful framework from which to understand play— the dialectics of play, its role in learning and development, and the *ludic* play space.

Dialectics of Play. Play exists precariously between the two dialectic poles variously labeled the irrational and rational, playful and serious, imaginary and real, and arbitrary and rule bound (Huizinga, 1950; Hutt, 1981; Spariosu, 1989; Sutton-Smith, 1997; Turner, 1974). For the most part, playful situations occur in a narrow space and time when the rational and irrational reach a tenuous balance, with neither dimension overshadowing the other.

As Erikson puts it, in order to experience play, one needs to be "free from the compulsions of conscience and from impulsions of irrationality" Erikson (1950, p. 187). According to Huizinga (1950), the dual worldview embedded in the dialectics of rational and irrational play is shared by many cultures, where play and earnest, serious and nonserious, represent two diametrically opposing concepts. In his view, the Greek terms *agon* (contest) and *paidia* (play) which surfaced in his cross-cultural comparison of play language best describe this antithetical relationship. Huizinga observed that in many forms of play in theater, music, or in group games, competitiveness can become its primary pursuit, tilting the balance of the dialectical relationship toward *agon*. Building on works of Huizinga, Callois (2001) categorized *agon* as all activities that involve competition. From ancient Greek era to the present, the dialectical struggle of *agon* and *paidia* finds its resting point along the continuum of the two polarities at different points in time (Spariosu, 1989).

Once a basketball player and later a philosopher, Hyland's (1984) world of play is experiential in nature, where the dialectic of play is lived firsthand within the confines of a basketball court. Hyland contends that play cannot be understood within a rigid dichotomy of rational and irrational, playful and nonplayful, or serious and nonserious activity. Rather, one needs to fully embrace the duality embedded in play. In his view, the duality commonly experienced in play is related to the tension between dominance and submission dynamics that coexist in a very precarious fashion in that, "excessive responsiveness easily devolves into dominance and excessive openness into submission" Hyland (1984, p. 52). In his own experience, this tension is easily seen in the basketball game when excessive domination and aggressiveness aimed primarily at "beating the opponent" drive the spirit of play out of the game.

The Role of Play in Learning and Development. Studies in education, psychology, and ethology suggest that the dialectical tension between *agon* and *paidia* is deeply ingrained in the learning process. From childhood to maturity, play has a central place at each stage of development in its different forms, styles, and meanings (Erikson, 1950; Piaget, 1962; Vygotsky, 1978; Wolf, 1984). The theory known as arousal modulation theories of play (Berlyne, 1960; Ellis, 1973; Hutt, 1981), uncovered stimulus-seeking activity that leads to two distinctive modes of play behavior: epistemic and ludic modes of play. Hutt (1981) uncovered substantial behavioral differences when children are in the epistemic mode versus when they are in the ludic mode. In the epistemic period of play, the children's attitude is that of seriousness and focus, followed by intense, attentive investigation of all aspects of a toy. Once their investigation is over, they then proceed to handle the toy playfully. As children transition to the ludic mode, in a relaxed manner they proceed to apply the knowledge gained through investigation in their play.

Developments in neuroscience reveal how the external manifestation of play is connected to the internal functioning of the brain. Hannaford (1995) contends that play operates as an integrative process between the limbic system and the frontal lobe of the neocortex, by transforming and integrating the sensory stimuli into meaningful thoughts and behaviors. This is similar to Zull's (2002: see chapter 3) description of how brain functioning follows the process of experiential learning. The studies of animal play in neuroethology suggest that humans and other mammals share similar play behaviors associated with their neural plasticity (Height & Black, 2000). Cross species' comparative studies suggest that play has a central role in brain development, facilitating the integration of cognitive, social, affective, and sensorimotor systems in mammals (Bekoff & Byers, 1998; Fagen, 1981; Smith, 1982, 1984).

The psychodynamic theory of play (Erikson, 1950; Freud, 1965) focuses on the role of play in the individual's emotional development. Play facilitates the expression of positive and negative emotions through engagement in fantasy and play. Play fulfills the need of the child's ego to master different aspects of his life and helps integrate his body, spirit, and mind in a nonthreatening way (Erikson, 1950).

The cognitive developmental theories of play (Piaget, 1962; Vygotsky, 1966) explain the role of play in the children's cognitive development, creativity, innovation, and adaptive flexibility. Through an extensive observation of children's play, Piaget (1962) contended that in early childhood, cognitive development occurred through two complementary processes of adaptation: imitation and play. At a later stage of cognitive development imitation would evolve into accommodation, where one molds oneself to the context; and play evolves into assimilation, as when, for example, a child uses her concept of house to build with blocks. For Piaget, play provides a rich context in which children interact with the environment and create their own knowledge about the world.

For Vygotsky (1978), play constitutes a primary context for cognitive development whereby children create their own zone of proximal development. Children develop capacity for self-regulation, by learning to create a constraint-free situation, molded to their own ego. By doing so, they subordinate themselves to their own rules, since from this surrendering to the rules and controlling their impulsive actions they derive enormous pleasure and joy. As Vygostsky observed, a child in playacts "as though he were a head taller than himself" (Vygotsky, 1978, p. 102).

Epistemic and ludic behaviors are distinct and complementary forms of play inherent in the developmental process. Epistemic behavior is essentially characterized by efficient, economical, and goal-specific behavior, whereas ludic behavior concentrates on means rather than ends. A healthy adaptation requires the harmonious integration of both modes of play (Piaget, 1962).

Ludic **Space.** What characterizes the spaces where playful behaviors thrive? What are the core principles that sustain the livelihood of such a space? We will examine the central concepts of play space from ethological, anthropological, psychological, and philosophical perspectives.

For Huizinga (1950), play has three central characteristics; it is free, it is stepping out of the "real" life, and it is bounded in space and time. Contrary to the widely held view of play as nonserious activity, Huizinga contends that play is an activity of utmost seriousness that is played out within a "consecrated spot" mentally and physically, with strict rules of its own. Since it begins and ends within a limited time, it demands order, and a slight deviation from it will collapse the play space. The rules of play are internalized and transmitted through repetition and practice, which in turn becomes the inner structure of the play itself. The play space can expand beyond its limited existence in time and space to form a self-organizing community with a tradition of its own.

Building on Huizinga's concept of the closed world of play, Gadamer (1989) contends that the *spielraum* (play space) is a bounded space created from within, by the nature and the structure of the game and by the conduct of the players themselves who are responsible for ordering and shaping the fate of the game. The players join the game by choice and by sheer desire to play, imposing on themselves rules of conduct and constraints they vow to observe in order to continue to play. The player is drawn to and kept captive by the game itself, in what Gadamer describes as the acknowledgement of "the primacy of play over the consciousness of the player" Gadamer (1989, p. 104).

Building on Maturana and Varela's (1987) concept of *autopoiesis*, whereby a living organism, whether physical, mental, or social, becomes a self-organized, autonomous system by specifying its own laws of existence, Nachmanovitch (1990) contends that free play enables the creation of a self-organizing system. In his view, the ludic space is similar to an *autopoietic* system whereby its existence is generated from within, "questioning and answering itself about its own identity" Nachmanovitch (1990, p. 102).

From an anthropological perspective, the play space is defined as a liminal zone (Turner, 1974), a sacred transitional phase observed in primitive societies, where cultural and communal practices take place free from the normative social structure. Within liminal space and time, tribal members are granted temporary freedom to explore the ludic, sacred, and profane in the forms of rituals and myths. As Turner puts it, "In liminality people 'play' with the elements of the familiar and de-familiarize them. Novelty emerges from unprecedented combinations of familiar elements" Turner (1974, p. 60).

In psychological terms, play happens within the safety of a transitional space where children can explore and express themselves, unchallenged by the pressure of defining an inner or outer reality. These early experiences that intensely shape the child's life manifest themselves throughout adulthood in the forms of art, religion, and creative scientific work (Winnicott, 1971). Similarly, Moustakas (1997) contends that the most essential element in play therapy is a safe play space, bounded by the therapist's consistency, firmness, courage, and love.

Among many forms of animal play identified by ethologists, the particular play form of great interest to us is social play, one of the play behaviors through which animals send a play signal, a message exchanged among animals to communicate a desire to create a play space where they can freely engage in play and not in an aggressive fight (Bekoff & Allen, 1992; Brown, 1995; Goodall, 1995; Hole & Einon, 1984; West, 1974). Most mammals have identifiable visual, auditory, tactile, or olfactory signals that serve to initiate or maintain social play or denote that "what follows is play" (Fagen, 1981, pp. 414–418). Play signals are usually clear, unambiguous, powerful, and capable of crossing species lines (Brown, 1995).

Ludic Learning Space and Deep Learning

Playfulness does not cease with childhood; it continues throughout adult lives. While such an assertion may be true, for many, the spontaneity and openness experienced as a child takes a back seat in their adult years. Unlike children who can turn almost anything into a playground and animals who can create a play space by simply exchanging play signals, as Erikson once said, the playing adult needs to step sideward into another reality in order to rediscover play (Erikson, 1950, p. 194). Similarly, Dewey (1990) says the adult can play only after being free from economic pressure and the fixed demands of adult responsibilities. We are skilled at "playing" social and professional roles, which, ironically, discourage us from playing. The social conventions imposed on adult life block our ability to exchange human play signals and create a shared understanding that it is "OK to play."

Our case study of the Free Play Softball League illustrates a pick-up softball league formed to create an alternative space to our university intermural league where *agon* ruled the games, as *macho* fraternity teams found great pleasure in humiliating our department's diverse team of faculty and students with wide variation in their skill and familiarity with the game. Created in the spirit of *paidia* or free play, for twenty-five years a group of individuals diverse in age, gender, level of education, and ethnic background have come together to play softball and sustain a *ludic* learning space conducive to deep and transformative learning. Here are the seven key conditions that sustained the livelihood of this space. (For a detailed description of the case study, see Kolb & Kolb, 2010).

Play is Free. Intrinsic motivation is at the foundation of any authentic learning worth pursuing. The intrinsic love of the game and the desire to play was what made the game fun. The voluntary commitment of the players was the key to the sustenance and survival of the league.

Autopoietic **Play Boundary.** The rules of the game that were created served as the boundary that sustained and held the space together. The rules regulated the flow and the structure of the game as well as the players' behaviors within the space. The chaos generated by the uncertainty of the game fueled improvisation and creativity in dealing with the game in the moment, encouraging players to learn to re-create and monitor themselves in order to maintain the integrity of the space. Over time, players became aware of the space as something larger than their individual needs and desires. The space boundary would eventually discourage those players whose temperament and style did not conform to the rules of the game or the spirit of the space from coming back to the game.

Celebrating Foolishness. Since the players' skill levels varied enormously, it was particularly important to set a positive tone to encourage players to develop softball skills and discover their love for the game without the fear of external judgment or self- induced criticism. As Nachmanovitch (1990) asserts, the "fear of appearing foolish" to others blocks our ability to be a "fool," a necessary state of mind for being able to fully engage in play.

Stepping out of Real Life. Sunday morning from 10:00 a.m. to 12:00 p.m. was a special time when players would leave their "real life" behind and enter the world of the softball game. Regardless of the role one played in real life, a therapist, a forest ranger, a nurse, an unemployed person, or a college professor, this was a time to play ball. Play requires discipline to remove oneself from the burden of social and professional life.

Balancing the Tension of *Agon* and *Paidia.* Competition is at the heart of any organized sport or game. While it is possible to engage in softball with playfulness and fun, the intense rivalry between two teams can drive fun out of the game. While *agon* (contest) and *paidia* (fun) would ideally coexist in the game, often the balance tips toward aggressive pursuit of the final victory. In the Free Play game, *agon* and *paidia* needed to coexist in equal balance if it was to survive as an inclusive league, since players joined the league for a variety of motives and reasons. The excessive pursuit of outcome can collapse the play space from within.

Play Signals. This highly developed skill among mammals to send signal to one another to engage in play was replicated in the game. The play signals were not artificially imposed from outside, but emerged within the natural course of the game. Play signals were transmitted by observation and mimicry and operated at many levels in the game. For example, newcomers were never told what to do; they picked up the flow of the game, participated in the game at their own skill level and learned the rules of the game while playing. The positive and carefree nature of the game was critical to the process of learning to send and receive play signals. On another level, play signals regulated the tension between *agon* and *paidia.* The disposition and temperament of each player, whether it tips toward the extreme end of competition or fun, determined whether a player would stay in the game or eventually decide to leave. Every time someone would go "off the deep end" of competitiveness, voices would erupt from the field playfully teasing the player to "ease off" on their aggressive streak.

Replication of the Space through Recursiveness. Play space is fragile and finite. The game emerged and vanished every Sunday morning, with no guarantee or certainty that it will be there the following week. A league member described the unique nature of the space:

> Every year, in the last game of the season, I look around the field and say to myself, some of us will not be here next year. We don't even know what is going to happen next week. So why not give it all when I am here. (Interview with a player. Kolb & Kolb, 2010, p. 41)

Yet, the game managed to reemerge week after week, season after season, for twenty-five years in a surprising display of resilience and perseverance. The replication of the space occurred at different levels. On one level, the space survived through the persistence of a core group of players who consistently showed up to play and modeled behaviors and practices that set the exemplary tone of the game. The welcoming spirit extended to all newcomers; respect and solidarity expressed among the players, and weekly rituals of setting up the field, are examples of behaviors and attitudes espoused by the founders of the league in a recursive manner and replicated to the next generation of players. For example, since the field needed to be prepared for the game every Sunday, the equipment manager arrived half-an-hour earlier to set-up the field. The equipment manager felt there was almost a sense of sacredness in the act of preparing the game field:

> Every Sunday morning, I feel a sense of responsibility for the game. When I come to the field, I can't help but play in my mind a few possible scenarios that may happen that morning. What if some other sport team had the field reserved in advance? On a different level, I also feel a sense of magic in setting up the field for the game. You put the bases around, haul the bats, balls, and gloves, and lo and behold, people show up to play. (Interview with a player, Kolb & Kolb, 2010, p. 42)

In the free-play league, the recursive nature of the play activities not only sustained the structure and flow of the game, but also had profound impact on players' inner lives as they recursively came back to confront their "true selves" in the process. When players joined the league for the first time, it was natural for them to wear a "game face," rarely revealing their personal side during the game. Over time, players gradually began to peel off their game faces and freely express their authentic selves.

Play Community. Over the years, despite the informal, ad hoc nature of the game, there was a sense of shared communal identity that developed among players that extended beyond the ludic space. It provided a wide range of disposition of personality and expressions of emotions, while, at the same time, it elevated cooperation, sense of community, and shared experience. The temporary suspension of the reality that is fully acknowledged in the play space invites individuals to "play for real" in the game. Stripped off from real-life roles, players stand naked in play, expressing a wide range of emotions and behaviors for all to see. The unique dispositions and personalities of the players are openly exposed in the space in the various forms of spontaneous display of joy, anger, selfishness, generosity, and courage. The true self that emerges through play evokes the ontological nature of human frailty as well as the limitless possibility for growth and self-discovery. The shared understanding and acceptance of each player's vulnerabilities may be what bound the members together as a play-community.

The *Ludic* Learning Space and Experiential Learning

Huizinga notes that play is about stepping out of common reality into a "higher order," where one can imagine oneself as someone different, more beautiful, courageous, and daring Huizinga (1950, pp. 13–14). One imagines oneself in the game as the great hitter, or fast runner. The power of play is about the symbolic representation of self as the embodiment and actualization of what one has imagined oneself to be and become. Our case study suggests that most of the regular players reported significant deep learning from their participation in the game. Some of the learning involved development of the basic skills of hitting, fielding, running, and throwing and greater understanding of position play, game strategy, and teamwork. Many, however, reported learning that was deeper and more personal, contributing to their personal growth and development in all areas of their life. They spoke of courage to fail, of controlling negative emotions and competitiveness, of developing empathy and personal authenticity.

The case study suggests that play exemplifies one of the highest forms of experiential learning in three fundamental ways: first, because learners are intrinsically motivated to create their own learning path, it encourages learners to take charge of their own learning based on their own standards of excellence. In play, learners achieve authentic and higher-order learning by creating their own rules and conduct. Second, an equal value is placed on the process and the outcome of learning. Play does not happen by staring at the scoring board. An outcome acquires meaning only if equal attention is paid to the experience and the process of play. As Dewey (1933) says, a truly educative experience sees no difference between utility and fun, the process and outcome. Third, in play, the experiential learning cycle is fully engaged by allowing learners to come back to the familiar experience with a fresh perspective. The recursive nature of the play activity gives continuity for the individual's experience to mature and deepen moment-to-moment and stage-by-stage. Taken together, these three factors are the key principles of a ludic learning space conducive to deep learning.

Formal educational and organizational institutions are faced with the dilemma of balancing two seemingly contradicting goals: high productivity and efficiency versus creativity and learning. As the case study suggests, these goals are in fact complementary and need to coexist harmoniously if schools and organizations are to create an environment where members can be creative and productive. The reality is, most schools and organizations tend to overemphasize control and demand for accountability through an excessive use of extrinsic rewards and ignore the detrimental effects this has on members' creativity and productivity. The case study suggests that deep learning can be promoted by allowing members to self-organize, creating boundaries for recursive, timeless play, and allow their intrinsic interests and authenticity to come alive. As for the Free Play Softball League, it continues to hold and sustain the ludic learning space, as it celebrated its twenty-fifth anniversary in 2016.

Fourteen

CREATING SPACES TO DEVELOP AND SUSTAIN DEEP LEARNING

Concepts can never be presented to me merely,
they must be knitted into the structure of my being,
and this can only be done through my own activity.

—MARY PARKER FOLLETT

The traditional classroom structure with its time-block scheduling of un-related courses is a learning space designed for the transmission and assessment of declarative knowledge. The courses follow a syllabus, with the subject topics covered class-by-class in a one-time-through fashion. Assessment is usually based on recall of the information presented, often with multiple-choice tests. This fact-based educational space is unsuited for the deeper learning and development required to progress from novice to expert in any subject. To create learning spaces that deepen and sustain learning requires a different kind of learning environment, one that is ex-tended in time to allow for repeated cycles of deliberate learning, applied in different contexts, aided by educators who are skilled in nurturing develop-ment. The focus in deep-learning spaces is on completing the learning cycle through performance, actions that generate feedback and reinforcement for continued improvement and learning. Deep-learning spaces need to hold and stimulate the learner's interest by providing support and reward for the required long-term commitment and continuing practice needed to develop high levels of expertise. These spaces must also sustain and renew a process of lifelong learning through the development of the learner's positive learning identity, learning flexibility, and skills in deliberate learning.

Deep Learning

The concept of *deep learning* describes the developmental process of learning that fully integrates the four modes of the experiential learning cycle—experiencing, reflecting, thinking, and acting (Border, 2007; Jensen & Kolb, 1994). In ELT, this holistic process is called full-cycle learning, referring to the kind of learning that leads to development. A number of scholars have addressed the issue of deep learning. For example, in the tradition of research initiated by Marton and Saljo (1976) and further developed by Ramsden (1992), Biggs (1987, 1992), and Entwistle (1981), deep learning is contrasted with surface learning. In this framework, surface learning is focused on accumulation of information and memorization for extrinsic reasons such as getting a good grade. Deep learning is more intrinsically motivated, integrated, reflective, and complex. Border (2007) has argued that the terms "surface" and "deep" have often been used superficially in education and that use of ELT (Kolb, 1984) can provide a definition of deep learning that can be used to help learners learn deeply.

Development toward deep learning is divided into three levels paralleling the three stages of the ELT developmental model described in chapter 4—Acquisition, Specialization, and Integration. In the first level, learning is registrative and performance-oriented, emphasizing the two learning modes of specialized learning styles that are limited ways of learning. The second level is interpretative and learning-oriented, involving three learning modes. The third level is integrative and development-oriented involving all four learning modes in a holistic learning process called full-cycle learning. In his foundational work, *Learning from Experience toward Consciousness*, William Torbert (1972) described these levels of learning as a three-tiered system of feedback loops; work that has been adopted and applied by Chris Argyris, Donald Schön, Peter Senge, and others in the concepts of single- and double-loop learning (Argyris & Schön, 1978; Kim, 1993; Senge, 1990). Single-loop learning describes learning that does not modify functional frameworks for action or fundamental beliefs. To learn deeply, assumptions need to be called into question, which is the basis of "double-loop learning." The third level of learning is referred to as either "triple-loop learning" (Bateson, 1972; Isaacs, 1993; Romme & van Witteloostruijn, 1999) or "transcendent learning" (Pauchant, 1995). It involves intentional examination of conventional mind-sets, values, and paradigms; identifying and transcending arbitrary and outmoded conventions. Bateson (1972) and Pauchant (1995) claim that accessing new levels of intelligence and creativity depend on freeing up energies normally restrained by rigid thought patterns. Learning at this level can involve a profound redefinition of one's personal identity.

Differing dynamics promote and constrain movement from one level of feedback to another. When the hypotheses that underpin our approach to a given situation cease to be valid or effective, we come to the limits of effective single-loop learning. The transition from single-loop to double-loop learning can be accompanied by anxiety and fear. Double-loop learning requires challenging accepted assumptions, attitudes, and thought patterns. Learners may impulsively use defense mechanisms or seek refuge in deeply rooted routines (Argyris, 1974). The obstacles that inhibit accessing triple-loop learning are of a different order. The search for meaning and deep learning subjects people to paradoxical pressures and the sacrifice entails letting go of attitudes that blind awareness and limit behavior. Learners are confronted by the paradox of learning, that is, doubt and anxiety generates reticence and justification for not learning while doubt and anxiety are also driving forces for learning. Level-three learning is not a matter of removing doubt and anxiety but rather of engaging them to learn at a deeper level.

Alice Y. Kolb and David A. Kolb

Deep-Learning Spaces and the Development of Expertise

The complex and dynamic nature of deep-learning spaces, the educator's role in them, and the way they are embedded in the lifelong development of expertise is shown in the classic studies of the Development of Talent Research Project directed by Benjamin Bloom at the University of Chicago (Bloom, 1985). The project involved retrospective interviews of twenty exceptionally accomplished persons in each of six different fields—concert pianists and sculptors in the artistic field, Olympic swimmers and tennis players in the psychomotor field, and research mathematicians and neurologists in the cognitive area.

The process of talent development involved a long-term commitment with the average time from one's first formal lesson to international recognition lasting seventeen years. The different learning spaces that the talented individuals experienced over this time were described in three phases: the early years of childhood, the middle years as early teenagers, and the later years from late teens to adulthood. These phases parallel the stages of development in the ELT theory of development—acquisition, specialization, and integration.

The Early Years of Acquisition. The early stage of skill acquisition has been called the romance period. The focus was on developing basic skills in a fun atmosphere that rewarded the development of interest from family members who themselves were skilled in the field. First teachers were described as warm and enthusiastic but not highly skilled experts, often a neighborhood teacher or a friend of the family. Parents had a great influence: giving a lot of attention to the child, setting high standards, and emphasizing the importance of hard work.

Sosniak (1987) reported how the budding concert pianists described the learning space:

> Initial music instruction also typically was playful, enticing and encouraging...Lessons with first teachers reportedly were "fun" experiences. "It was an event." "I looked forward to them." Instruction

was informal, personal and filled with immediate rewards. The teacher was likely to "indicate when a piece was finished by putting a star at the top of the page."…The first period of instruction emphasized engaging in lots of musical activity and exploring possibilities. (1987, p. 281)

The Middle Years of Specialization. The specialization middle period marked the beginning of serious concentrated learning, though Bloom (1985) remarked that this intense, serious period of learning may well have been feeble and barren without the early period of play and interest development. This period was marked by precision, attention to detail, and skill-building. Teachers were more accomplished and strict and demanding. Student relationships with them shifted from love to respect. As skill developed, motivation shifted from extrinsic reward to intrinsic satisfaction.

Sosniak's description of the second phase for pianists describes a process similar to the deliberate practice process described in chapter 6:

In the second phase of learning, instruction became more rational and less informal and personal than it had been earlier. Technical skills and vocabulary were the core of lessons. The rules and logic of music-making were dealt with in a very disciplined and systematic way…Lessons changed dramatically. "(They) were very long. Very, very detailed. Always working on the shape of my hand and all these little tiny things. She had me phrase things. Had me do things over and over to make them as beautiful as possible. With great attention to detail." (1987, p. 282)

The Later Years of Integration. Those who reached the third stage of integration could not succeed without the specialized accomplishments of the second. Yet, even for the highly accomplished respondents to the talent-development survey, the transition to the third phase proved to be the most challenging, uncertain, and difficult. One can only imagine the difficulties encountered by the many who had achieved specialized technical competence but did not meet the accomplishment criteria for inclusion in the study.

In the integration stage the emphasis shifts from disciplined skill mastery to a broader development of self that incorporates a professional identity in the field. Motivation at this stage is primarily intrinsic. They love the process of continued improvement and become dedicated to the calling of a lifelong career. Sosniak describes development to the third phase this way:

> Reviewing the pianists' experience with instruction, practice, and performance, we might find major changes over time in the pianists' perception of musical activities, in their ways of working at music-making, and in their reasons for their continued efforts. The piano shifted from being a toy to being a tool. The pianists' interests were at first in "playing around," later in mastery of the machine, and still later in making music. What seemed like a game at first became hard work; still later it became what one aspired to do for a living; eventually it defined who one was. The pianists reported growing into the perception of themselves as pianists, and then outgrowing even that as they learned to think of themselves as musicians. They were transformed and reoriented and their experiences were reinterpreted again and again as they learned to be as good as they are today. (1987, pp. 285–286)

Educators in the third stage tended to be chosen mentors from the elite in the field who were tough and demanding master teachers. Sosniak's pianists:

> spoke with awe about the opportunity to study with such outstanding musicians. "The idea that this man was willing to teach me, to give me his time, overwhelmed me." "What she said to me was like the voice of God."…Let two pianists summarize for themselves the third period of instruction with a master teacher. "He didn't teach you how to play the piano; he teaches you…integrity, devotion, and a complete dedication to music-making." "He made me think and

he made me experience and he made me understand that you have to find your own way. You have to know what's right and what's wrong, but the possibilities and tonal color are absolutely endless." (1987, p. 285)

The Educator's Role in Fostering Deep Learning

In the introduction we called for those of us who work in educational roles as teachers, consultants, coaches, managers, parents, and citizens to raise our self-definition to think more broadly of ourselves as educators. Bloom and Sosniak's work on the deep learning and development of accomplished individuals in many fields offers many insights into the dimensions of such an expanded view. Most importantly, their study reinforces the profound importance of our role as educators. There is a common view that highly successful and accomplished individuals were genetically endowed with superior talents, were child prodigies, and were self-made men or women. Bloom's studies and the expertise-development research of Eriksson and Charness (1994) both found that this is rarely the case:

The vast majority of exceptional adult performers were never child prodigies, but instead they started instruction early and increased their performance due to a sustained high level of training. (Bloom, 1985). The role of early instruction and maximal parental support appears to be much more important than innate talent, and there are many examples of parents of exceptional performers who successfully designed optimal environments for their children without any concern about innate talent. (Ericsson & Charness, 1994, p. 729)

The talented individuals we studied got a lot of help—sometimes from parents, sometimes from teachers, sometimes from other family or family friends. For a good number of years they worked with or had close personal contact with people they felt were "very sincere...very interested in seeing me develop," with people they felt really believed in them, with people from whom they "got the feeling it was worth trying," people who were "openly encouraging... no question about that." (Sosniak, 1987, p. 289)

When we work with a learner as a parent or family member, or as a teacher in a course, or facilitating a training program, or as a coach, it is worth thinking about the fact that we meet that person at a particular moment in their developmental life journey. We can make a difference by igniting the spark of deep learning or passing the flame that will light their way to reach their full potential, recognizing that our contribution is but one part of a longer journey to which many will contribute as educators.

By knowing where they are in the developmental phases for the subject matter at hand we can adopt the appropriate educator role to promote their progress (see chapter 16). In the initial acquisition phase, a facilitator role that stimulates imagination, play, and enjoyment and elicits and focuses interest is most appropriate. In the specialization phase, the role of standard-setter and evaluator in a regimen of deliberate practice aimed at developing mastery is key. For learners entering the integration stage of making creative contributions one can act as a mentor, role model, or coach.

Talent Development vs. Traditional Schooling. Bloom and Sosniak (1981) also found that the learning approaches used in the talent-development process offered innovative alternatives to traditional schooling methods. They found similarities in the learning spaces in every field that they contrasted with the traditional school learning spaces we described at the beginning of this chapter.

Most obvious was the continuous life-span process of development contrasted with the block-scheduled, batch-processing course approach that dominates formal education. Another was the great importance of interest development in the acquisition phase, often through the encouragement of a talented family member or other relative; and the creation of a fun, playful, and exploratory learning space as described in the previous chapter. Without the development of a deep and sustained interest in this phase, it was difficult to attain the persistence necessary to succeed in the hard work of the specialization phase of deep practice.

In talent development, each person was seen as unique and instruction was tailored to where the learner was at the time. Rather than group instruction, the talent-development process was highly individualized with educators who diagnosed what the learner needed, set appropriate goals, and provided feedback, corrective instruction, and reward and encouragement in a cycle of learning that was repeated over and over. Another distinguishing characteristic was the emphasis on public performances and competition events that spurred learning in preparation for them and garnered rewards and recognition for excellent performance. These events integrated the individual's expertise into the context of the wider community.

Lave's Situated Learning Theory and Legitimate Peripheral Participation. The deep learning approaches of talent development identified by Bloom and Sosniak are in many ways consistent with the sociocultural activity theories of Lev Vygotsky and Jean Lave. Lave and Wenger's situated learning theory (1991) offers a sociological theory of learning that emphasizes learning from the direct experience of activities in context. Knowledge is co-constructed in relationships such as legitimate peripheral participation in apprenticeship roles or social interaction between novices and experts in communities of practice. This is opposed to a what they call a "cognitivist" theory of learning that separates knowing and doing:

> The theory of sociocultural order discussed here encourages a rethinking of the nature of direct experience…dichotomous mind/body schemes assign emotions to the negatively valued body as part of the devaluation of immediate, sensuous experience. Correspondingly, higher cognitive functions are presumed to be further away from the body and from "intuitive, concrete, context embedded experience. The only "good" experience was distanced and generalized, removed from the debilitating influence of immediate time and place in the form of abstract accounts of action. (Lave, 1988, p. 182)

Lave argues that the traditional educational structure is based on a function-alist sociology of education that emphasizes abstract generalized knowledge:

> The functionalist position contains a theory of learning: in particular, that children can be taught general cognitive skills (e.g. reading writing mathematics, logic, critical thinking) if these "skills" are disembedded from the routine contexts of their use. Extraction of knowledge from the particulars of experience, of activity from its context, is the condition for making knowledge available for general application in all situations. Schooling reflects these ideas at a broad organizational level, as it separates children from the contexts of their own and their families' daily lives. At a more specific level, classroom tests put the principle to work: they serve as the measures of individual "out of context" success, for the test-taker must rely on memory alone and may not use books, classmates, or other resources for information. Arguably examinations are also condensed, symbolic, ritual ordeals which inculcate the essence of the theory. (Lave, 1988, pp. 8–9)

The deep-learning strategies of talent development are embedded in a large multi-dimensional learning space with a long time horizon emphasizing the learner's action and performance in a social context involving multiple educators and settings from the intimate family to international professional competitions and training with master teachers. Generalized knowledge is always transferred and integrated into these contexts through recursive cycles of deliberate practice.

Vygotsky's Proximal Zone of Development and Scaffolding. Vygotsky's (1962, 1978) cultural/historical approach to the development of higher mental functions, like Lave, emphasizes learning through action in a social/relational context. He particularly emphasizes the mediational role that "tools of culture," most importantly language, play in learning and development. For example, he maintained that speech is a major psychological tool in the child's development of thinking. He is critical of the traditional educational view and that of Piaget that development is solely an individual internal process of maturation:

> Education is seen as a kind of superstructure over maturation...A one-sided relationship is thus conceded: Learning depends on development but the course of development is not affected by learning...This view characteristic of old-fashioned educational theory, also colors the writings of Piaget, who believes that the child's thinking goes through certain phases and stages regardless of any instruction he may receive; instruction remains an extraneous factor. The gauge of the child's level of development is not what he has learned through instruction but the manner in which he thinks on subjects about which he has been taught nothing. Here the separation—indeed, the opposition—of instruction and development is carried to its extreme. (Vygotsky, 1962, p. 94)

The Proximal Zone of Development. The ZPD is perhaps the most influential of all of Vygotsky's concepts. It is the zone in which the activity responsible for the creation of higher mental development occurs. It is measured by the difference between a learner's "actual developmental level as determined by independent problem solving and the level of potential development as determined through problem-solving under adult guidance or in collaboration with more capable peers" (Vygotsky, 1978, p. 86). The ZPD is based on his law of internalization, stating that the child's novel capacities begin in the interpersonal realm and are gradually transferred into the intrapersonal realm. What is internalized is "mediational means" or tools of culture, the most important of which is language.

Scaffolding. The educational technique most associated with Vygotsky's ZPD is called scaffolding. Vygotsky apparently never used the term, which was created by Jerome Bruner who was instrumental in introducing the cognitive development theories of Piaget and Vygotsky in the United States. The scaffolding approach, however, is directly related to ZPD, in that it is the support mechanism that helps learners successfully perform a task within their zone of potential.

Wood, Bruner, and Ross (1978) first used the term to describe the role of a tutor (or coach):

> Discussions of problem solving or skill acquisition are usually premised on the assumption that the learner is alone and unassisted. If the social context is taken into account, it is usually treated as an instance of modelling or imitation. But the intervention of a tutor may involve much more than this. More often than not, it involves a kind of "scaffolding" process that enables a child or novice to solve a problem, carry out a task or achieve a goal which would be beyond his unassisted efforts. The scaffolding consists essentially of the adult "controlling" those elements of the task that are initially beyond the learners' capacity, thus permitting him to concentrate upon and complete only those elements that are within his range of competence. The task thus proceeds to a successful conclusion. We assume, however, that the process can potentially achieve much more for the learner than the completion of the task. It may result, eventually in development of task competence by the learner at a pace that would far outstrip his unassisted efforts. (1978, p. 90)

They describe six functions of the educator in the scaffolding process:

- *Recruitment*—Developing the learner's interest and attention to the task.
- *Reduction of degrees of freedom*—Simplifying the task to eliminate learner overload.
- *Direction maintenance*—Providing support and motivation to keep the learner on task.
- *Marking critical features*—Focusing on and giving performance feedback on critical features of the task.

- *Frustration control*—Reducing stress and embarrassment about errors.
- *Demonstration*—Modelling solutions for the learner to observe and imitate.

Shotter offers an interesting critique of Bruner's scaffolding techniques, suggesting that it differs from Vygotsky's ZPD by introducing an individualistic frame. Citing Vygotsky's statement that learning is a process by which children grow into the intellectual life of those around them, he says

> I take that to mean, not that the consciousness of the instructor and of the child can be located and defined independently of one another but that instruction is an activity in which they are both involved and in which the consciousness of each is formed within the activity. In other words, the adult being an instructor is "invited" by the child being amenable to instruction, and vice-versa; both act "into" the situation between them.

> In other words, Bruner still offers a far too inter-individualistic view of instruction, in which language seems to function solely as a medium of communication between two people who are already individuals, except that one possesses a much less well articulated consciousness than the other…it also ignores the affective motivational nature of that context in "inviting" not only the child but also the adult instructor, to act "into" it. (Shotter, 1989, p. 200)

In our reading of Vygotsky, he is describing an intersubjective joining together in the direct experience of the problem activity and context, where the learner gains access to the greater understanding of the educator and the educator gains an understanding of what the learner understands. This co-immersion in direct experience is a precursor to the application of the six scaffolding techniques described by Wood, Bruner, and Ross (see chapter 11).

Implementing Deep Learning. As educators, deep learning can be difficult to implement, given the institutional constraints of courses or the limited learning spaces that training programs and workshops provide. However, we can use the concepts of deep learning to enrich learning even within these limitations. The major implication of ELT for education is to design educational programs in a way that teaches around the learning cycle so that learners can use and develop all learning styles in a way that completes the learning cycle for them and promotes deep learning. As we described in chapter 2, this process of engaging all learning styles is called full-cycle learning. The flexibility to move from one learning style to another in the learning cycle is important for deep learning. Learning flexibility can help us master different learning problems by capitalizing on the strengths of each learning style. Educators can empower learners toward full-cycle learning by designing their courses with attention to which of the nine styles they intend to develop in each of their educational activities. Appendix 3 gives examples of this approach.

The traditional lecture course, for example, emphasizes first level, registrative learning, emphasizing the learning modes of reflection and abstraction involving little action (often multiple-choice tests that assess registration of declarative knowledge in memory) and little relation to personal experience. Adding more extensive learning assessments that involve practical application of concepts covered (see Appendix 4) can create second-level learning involving the three learning modes where reflection supplemented by action serve to further deepen conceptual understanding. Further addition of learning experiences that involve personal experience such as internships or field projects create the potential for third-level integrative learning. As a counter example, an internship emphasizes registrative learning via the modes of action and experience. Deeper interpretative learning can be enhanced by the addition of activities to stimulate reflection such as team conversation about the internship experience and/or student journals. Linking these to the conceptual material related to the experience adds the fourth learning mode, abstraction and integration, thereby completing the learning spiral. Collective reflection through team conversations in teams with diverse learning styles can also stimulate deep learning by integrating the different perspectives that different learning styles bring.

Deep learning in medical education. The medical profession has long recognized the limitations of generalized factual declarative knowledge acquired in the classroom. For example, Schmidmaier et al. (2013) found that medical students had problems applying conceptual knowledge to clinical cases. Conceptual knowledge that is generally thought to be a requirement for procedural knowledge in making clinical decisions and solving clinical problems was unrelated to performance on clinical decision and problem-solving tasks. This performance was however significantly predicted by prior in-context clinical experience. As a result, medicine has developed complex systems of contextualized experiential learning such as internships, residencies, morning rounds, mentoring, shadowing, and a host of other learning in-context opportunities, including a rigorous program of continuing medical education. Development of expertise in compassionate care, diagnosis, and execution of complex medical procedures requires deep learning acquired through recursive learning cycles in these different contexts.

A recent example of a deep-learning approach in medicine is a widely adopted innovation called the longitudinal integrated clerkship (LIC—Poncelet & Hirsh, 2014). The LIC is designed to overcome the limitations of the traditional block-scheduled clerkship and the "silo" nature of traditional medical-school instruction. Organized around the comprehensive care of patients over time in relationship with patients' care providers, the longitudinal clerkships are designed to address the multidisciplinary core clinical-education competencies. These clerkships emphasize continuity of patients, faculty preceptors, peers, and settings over time, enabling learners to participate more fully in patient care and learn from the mentoring of expert physicians. The LICs are thought to reduce "ethical erosion," the loss of professionalism that arises as a result of medical training by a hidden curriculum of witnessing demeaning behavior and lack of empathy. This is accomplished through,

The formations of trusting student-patient relationships, thereby enabling students to play more significant roles in providing care. In turn, this level of engagement fosters caring and learning, responsibility and a sense of duty. Students grow to understand and emphasize with their patient's experience of illness. Students also gain first-hand on understanding providers' decisions and roles, and on the functioning of health care delivery systems. Students also become better able to appreciate the ways in which socioeconomic conditions impact patients' access to care. (Poncelet & Hirsh, 2014, p. 180)

Sustaining Lifelong Deep Learning

The difficulties that the accomplished experts in Bloom's study had in making the transition from the second stage of specialized technical development to the third integrative stage of unique creative contributions point to a paradox of specialized learning and development. Highly specialized learning in one domain can also lead to what might be called the shadow side of expertise that results in one being closed off to renewal and development as a whole person. The path of deep learning and development is not a linear one. The recursive deliberate learning process of single-loop learning that moves toward matching one's behavior to the ideal model can lead to a state of technical perfection that ultimately can lack purpose and direction. It is here that double-loop examination of assumptions and triple-loop transcendent learning can precipitate a course change. Jung viewed deep learning and development in the context of the life course, comparing it to the course of the rising and setting sun with the noon of life, midlife, marking a reexamination and adjustment of purpose.

Take for comparison the daily course of the sun—but a sun that is endowed with human feeling and man's limited consciousness. In the morning it rises from the nocturnal sea of unconsciousness and looks upon the wide, bright world which lies before it in an expanse that steadily widens the higher it climbs in the firmament. In this extension of its field of action caused by its own rising, the sun will discover its significance; it will see the attainment of the greatest possible height, and the widest possible dissemination of its blessings, as its goal. In this conviction the sun pursues its course to the unforeseen zenith—unforeseen, because its career is unique and individual, and the culminating point could not be calculated in advance. At the stroke of noon the descent begins. And the descent means the reversal of all the ideals and values that were cherished in the morning. (Jung, 1930, p. 778)

Jung believed that the afternoon of life had a different developmental task, an integration of conscious and unconscious aspects of personality that brings a perspective and understanding of what one's life is about:

But it is a great mistake to suppose that the meaning of life is exhausted with the period of youth and expansion; that, for example, a woman who has passed the menopause is "finished." The afternoon of life is just as full of meaning as the morning; only, its meaning and purpose are different. (Jung, 1912, p. 114)

The obstacles encountered in moving to the "triple loop learning" of integrative development make its achievement, for most of us, more a worthwhile aspiration than an accomplished reality. Adult-development research suggests that only a minority of us move beyond the conventional stage of development characteristic of specialized development. Cook-Grueter (1999, 2000) estimates that about 10 percent of adults are in the preconventional stages, 80 percent are in the conventional stages and 10 percent are in the postconventional, integrative stages of adult development. Less than 1 percent of Kegan and Lahey's sample (2009) achieve the highest integrative level of self-transforming mind and fewer than 2 percent achieve Cook-Greuter's similar construct, aware and unitive stages (Loevinger's Integrated stage). In their research on expertise,

Eriksson and Charness make a similar point about the highest levels of development:

> Eminent scientists make major discoveries and propose new theories that permanently change the concepts and knowledge in the domain. Similarly eminent artists generate new techniques and interpretations that extend the boundaries for future art. The process of generating innovations differs from the acquisition of expertise and mastery. Major innovations by definition go beyond anything even the master teachers know and could possibly teach. Furthermore, innovations are rare, and it is unusual that eminent individuals make more than a single major innovation during their entire lives. (Ericsson & Charness, 1994, p. 740)

Although most of us won't make breakthrough innovations or profoundly change the course of history, we nonetheless will experience the challenges of integrative development at some point in the context and course of our own lives. To the extent that we have undergone intensive specialization in one area, our knowledge and interests tend to focus there, often at the expense of other areas of our lives. Recall the spiral of learning and development described in chapter 4 and Maturana and Varela's concept of self-making or *autopoiesis*, a closed-circular process that is self-referential and self-organizing. The closure of the autopoietic process creates boundaries that allows the system autonomy but at the same time these boundaries shape what information is excluded or included in the system. In ELT terms, the recursive spiral of the learning cycle circles around a spine of the person's self-referential attention and interest. In William James's metaphor, interest is "the very keel on which our mental ship is built." On the one hand, the learning spirals around interest cast the brighter and brighter light of attention on the subjects of interest; yet, at the same time, they exclude everything else that is of no interest. As James put it:

Millions of items of the outward order are present to my senses which never properly enter into my experience. Why? Because they have no interest for me...Only those items which I *notice* shape my mind—without selective interest, experience is an utter chaos. Interest alone gives accent and emphasis, light and shade, background and foreground—intelligible perspective, in a word. (James, 1890, p. 402)

Thus the paradox of specialized development; what is of interest becomes more valued and attended to, while everything outside of the specialized interest is bound to receive less attention, respect, and admiration. Developmental pathways are the product of the process of *accentuation*, the interaction between choices and socialization experiences in a field of specialization such that choice dispositions lead to choices of experiences that match these dispositions, and the resulting experiences further reinforce the same choice disposition for later experiences. This accentuating process of specialization can result in professional deformation—in the intensive overlearning of a specialized-professional mentality that actively hinders integrative development.

In a highly cited review of expertise literature, Erik Dane argued that, "as one acquires domain expertise, one loses flexibility with regard to problem-solving adaptation and creative idea generation...For example, experts may have difficulty viewing domain-related problems from the perspectives of others and adapting to new rules and conditions within their domain" (2010, p. 579). Dane based his analysis on cognitive psychology theories that suggest that experts have more complex cognitive schemas than novices. They are larger and more interconnected. They are more stable and resistant to change, leading to what he calls "cognitive entrenchment."

His cognition-based explanation for cognitive entrenchment is supported by the neuroscience research we described in chapter 3. Here Dane's cognitive schemas are neural networks that are strengthened and interconnected through the associative learning process of the exploration/mimicry learning cycle of procedural learning. Repeated firing of the neuronal connections in these networks strengthens connections through growth of receptors at the synapses, chemical facilitators (Zull, 2011) and myelination, the growth of insulation around the neurons that increases stability, resistance to change, and efficiency of the connection (Coyle, 2009).

Dane does not consider the considerable social forces that also promote entrenchment, such as the "When Prophecy Fails" example of belief fixation described in chapter 11 or the vested interests and conformity pressures of professional groups and organizations. These, too, also can lead to entrenchment that is both cognitive and emotional. With specialized development of expertise comes a sense that one is special, which is reinforced by the respect given by others to expert status. Specialized professionals also tend to associate with other specialists who share similar beliefs, creating a shared social entrenchment.

Ottati and colleagues (Ottati et al., 2015) have demonstrated support for what they call the Earned Dogmatism Hypothesis: social norms dictate that experts are entitled to adopt a relatively dogmatic, closed-minded orientation. Experts are seen to possess extensive knowledge, and are entitled to adopt a more dogmatic or forceful orientation. In the first of a series of experiments they found that dogmatic assertions by experts were more likely to be approved of than similar assertions from novices. Other experiments found that experimentally induced self-perceived expertise engenders closed-minded thinking. The relationship between expertise and closed-minded thinking was mediated by ratings of the expert's normative entitlement to be closed-minded.

In addition to closed-minded thinking, there is evidence that expertise can result in "overclaiming," in particular, claiming to know about impossible, nonexistent knowledge. Beginning with a quote from Daniel Boorstein, "The menace to understanding [is] not so much ignorance as the illusion of knowledge," Atir, Rosenzweig, and Dunning (2015) found in four studies that self-perceived knowledge in a domain (personal finance) was positively related to claiming knowledge of nonexistent terms in the domain and that this effect was independent of genuine knowledge in the domain. The overclaiming tended to be domain-specific; the more individuals knew about a domain, the more likely they were to claim impossible knowledge in that domain. It appeared that the self-perceived knowledge/overclaiming relationship was not due to the desire to make a good impression, but to honest but mistaken claims of knowledge. The final study induced self-perceived knowledge of geography experimentally and found increased overclaiming knowledge of nonexistent places. Since some of the studies reported above involved experimentally induced self-perceptions of expertise, it appears that these social effects of overclaiming and closed-mindedness are independent of Dane's cognitive network factors that influence cognitive entrenchment.

Another consequence of expertise acquired through the procedural learning process of the exploration/mimicry learning cycle is that the expert skills learned become unconscious and automatic to the point where an expert "intuitively" knows, for example, how to make a complex medical diagnosis, but cannot explicitly say how he or she did it. This phenomenon has been called "expert amnesia." Beilock and Carr (2001), for example, found that expert golfers recalled fewer of the mechanics of their putts than novices, but were much more extensive in their abstract descriptions of how to putt in general. The authors concluded:

> This pattern follows the prediction of expertise-induced amnesia derived from current theories of skill acquisition and automaticity. According to this idea, experts' extensive generic knowledge of putting is declaratively accessible during off-line reflection, but it is not used during real-time performance, which is controlled by automated procedural knowledge. Because proceduralization reduces the need to attend to the processes by which skill execution unfolds, episodic recollection of step-by-step real-time performance is impoverished. (2001, pp. 707–708)

These results may in part explain why experts do more poorly than novices in predicting novice performance times in learning a task (Hinds, 1999). Hinds and colleagues (Hinds, Patterson, & Pfeffer, 2001) found that experts used more abstract ideas and fewer concrete examples in a teaching task than novices and that novice-instructed novices performed better than expert-instructed novices. However expert-instructed novices performed better on a task requiring knowledge transfer, presumably because of the abstract-teaching approach the experts used.

Educating for Integration: The Challenges of Adult Development. The research cited above suggests an agenda for lifelong learning that goes beyond "more of the same" when it comes to education. Most professions have mandated programs of continuing education to insure that professionals keep up to date on the latest development in their field and to promote lifelong learning. Few of these continuing education programs, however, have successfully addressed successful transition to the integrative development stage and reduction of the cognitive and social/emotional entrenchment that accompanies the development of specialized expertise. Carl Jung spoke eloquently about the challenges of learning in adult life:

> The worst of it all is that intelligent and cultivated people live their lives without even knowing of the possibility of such transformations. Wholly unprepared, they embark upon the second half of life. Or are there perhaps colleges for forty-year-olds which prepare them for their coming life and its demands as the ordinary colleges introduce our young people to a knowledge of the world? No, thoroughly unprepared we take the step into the afternoon of life; worse still, we take this step with the false assumption that our truths and ideals will serve us as hitherto. But we cannot live the afternoon of life according to the programme of life's morning; for what was great in the morning will be little at evening, and what in the morning was true will at evening have become a lie. (Jung, 1930, p. 784)

Inspired by Jung's challenge, we created, with our late colleague and dear friend, Donald Wolfe, a Lifelong Learning and Development Project at Case Western Reserve University. The National Institute for Education supported us in our study of advanced professional learning and development, and the Spencer Foundation helped fund our investigation of midlife transitions in professional men and women. Over a four-year period, these projects included more than twenty researchers and seventy men and women in midlife who engaged with us as co-inquirers in a continuing dialogue about their life situation and development. The studies also included questionaire data, interviews, and psychological testing with a cross sectional sample of four hundred professional engineers and social workers who became alumni of CWRU in five-year intervals from 1955 to 1975.

From the many research projects our team conducted (Kolb & Wolfe, 1981; Wolfe & Kolb, 1982) there emerged a perspective on the process of lifelong leaning in the second half of life and a learning agenda for adult development. We were influenced in this perspective by Nevitt Sanford's (1981) challenge/response theory of adult development. He argued that development occurs primarily in response to the challenges of adult life. Those who, by choice or fate, do not face these challenges are less likely to respond to them in a way that is growth-producing. Our studies identified eight areas of adult development challenge and positive growth response at midlife and beyond—wholeness, generativity, complexity, time, moral leadership, interdependence, ordinary life, and facing challenge itself as we age (Kolb, 1991).

These challenges are not simple problems to solve but involve one's perspective on life as a whole. They are game-changing dilemmas. The challenges may happen in the form of career change or disruption, divorce, unexpected death of family or friend, or some out-of-the-blue blindsiding event that you cannot ignore. Or they may be subtler shifts, such as dissatisfaction with a part of your life that you took for granted. This awareness may create a yearning for a change. Successful responses result from a process of engagement and deliberate experiential learning.

The challenge of wholeness and the response of centering. As we have seen, the process of specialization and expertise development can have the unintended consequence of creating a one-sided and encapsulated sense of self that can result in an unbalanced life structure and a myopic view of the world. Dane's prescription for ameliorating this cognitive entrenchment was experiences that expand the expert's flexibility and world view. He first suggests that involvement in dynamic, unpredictable conditions within one's domain of expertise can of necessity increase flexibility and the adaptive skill to remain open to possibilities, information, and options for action. He also suggests that experts deliberately focus some attention outside of their domain of expertise. By participating in dynamic environments and performing tasks in other domains:

> individuals are likely to encounter doubt-inducing exceptions to what they believe to be true to their domain of expertise, thus preserving their potential for flexible thinking within their expertise domain...Although excessive doubt can be problematic in that it reduces conviction, some level of doubt can be useful in certain respects. Researchers argue that doubt helps generate new perspectives by reducing habitual behavior, fostering creativity, and motivating a search for discovery. Indeed, some have pointed to doubt as a critical feature of "wisdom." (Dane, 2010, p. 590)

The developmental response to the challenge of wholeness is to center oneself by bringing life and work into balance, bringing vitality and energy to all areas of one's life. The balance between body and mind becomes important, particularly when physical health becomes an issue or when work is stressful "mind work." Often there is a need to break the confines of the technological, fast paced, civilized world and reestablish connection with the organic beauty of the natural world. We can expand our specialized learning style by becoming more flexible in our approach to learning and appreciation of those with different learning styles. The response of centering comes with an appreciation of the different parts that make up the whole; freeing us from implicit assumptions and opening new possibilities and perspectives.

The challenge of generativity and the response of caring. The first part of life is primarily concerned with "finding" oneself, establishing identity, and achieving independence, competence, and success. This preoccupation with oneself can be particularly intense in individualistic cultures like the

United States. With maturity there also emerges a generative challenge to empathize and care for others, usually first with family and children and later in the wider community and the world at large. With increasing competence and power there comes the responsibility to contribute more to the greater good.

Erikson warned in graphic terms the dangers of failing to address the challenge of generativity observing that, "we need to be needed lest we suffer the mental deformation of self-absorption in which we become our own infant and pet." (1961, p. 160). More positively, empathy and caring for others brings a powerful sense of purpose and meaning. Caring also means careful work that ensures quality in the services and products we provide others.

The challenge of moral leadership and the response of valuing. With increasing power and responsibility come challenges of moral leadership. These moral challenges are among the most difficult of advanced professional life—to be a role model for others, to be a public person, to represent others, to create a culture with inspiring values, to choose right from wrong in the most complex of circumstances. All of these require development of a sophisticated valuing process that is often neglected in early career preparation focused on factual and technical knowledge. The tasks of moral leadership are to make judgments about value priorities, to promote them in one's activities, and to preserve these values through the creation of a culture that sustains them. It is important to distinguish the process of valuing from the dogmatic imposition of one's own values on others. Valuing is a creative process based on open and receptive dialogue with others. Valuing is the medium for caring. In caring relationships one values and prizes the other, creating value in the relationship and feelings of self-worth in the other. The goal of careful work is to create value, to make a contribution.

The challenge of interdependence and the response of teamwork. Still persisting is the myth of the solitary all-powerful individual leader who, by virtue of extraordinary competence, brilliance, and expertise, is able to command preeminence. This is in spite of the fact that, while anecdotal stories can be mustered to prove the point, research shows only weak or nonexistent relationships between individual leader characteristics and performance. Specialized experts who become leaders in their field can easily fall prey to this myth, believing that their accomplishments and status are the result of their efforts, neglecting the many ways that others have been instrumental in their success.

Leadership is a relational concept and leaders are made by their followers as much as they make their followers do their bidding. They are shaped to the "leadership" of followers, reacting to their wishes and opinions and reflecting their values. In today's world, little is accomplished alone and most work requires interdependent relationships and teamwork. The challenge of interdependence is in many ways a challenge to recognize the relational nature of the leadership concept and to recognize that there are many different forms of leadership that are required to be effective (see the functional theory of leadership in teams described in chapter 7). Teamwork emphasizes the horizontal integrative dimension of leadership where leadership is the collective responsibility of the group. Working together in this interdependent way can produce synergy—where the product of the whole team is greater than the sum of the accomplishments of the team leader and individual team members.

The challenge of ordinary life and the response of humility. We have described the paradox of specialized expertise where prowess within one's specialty becomes all-consuming. To become specialized is also to become special, and with that sense of specialness there comes a tendency to see specialized knowledge as universal knowledge, to see knowledge as wisdom. There is a danger of a kind of hubris that extends specialized knowledge beyond its appropriate boundaries with dogmatic certainty. One becomes extraordinary; while others are ordinary "laymen," even though we are all ordinary laypersons outside of our specialty. The humble simplicity of ordinary life is humanity's common meeting ground.

In recent years there has been a resurgence of research on the ancient virtue of humility (Tangney, 2000, 2002) redefining the contemporary view that humble people are modest, simple, weak, and insecure. A recent study of humility in Chinese CEOs by Amy Ou and associates (Ou et al., 2014) defined humility as follows:

> First, humble people, in their experience of reflexive consciousness, are willing to seek accurate self-knowledge and are open to feedback…By recognizing something greater than the self, humble people accept their imperfections…Such self-acceptance, however, does not imply self-abasement or self-degradation. To the contrary, humble people are fully aware of their talents and abilities. Knowing their limitations helps them put their strengths in perspective…allowing them to avoid arrogance or self-contempt. Self-acceptance allows them to willingly disclose themselves, admit their limitations or mistakes, and actively seek feedback. Thus, through reflective consciousness, humility is associated with open-mindedness and willingness to learn from others…

> Second, in their experience of interpersonal being, humble people appreciate others as being like themselves, with strengths and weaknesses…Humble people appreciate others' positive worth, strengths, and contribution…Such appreciation is grounded in the understanding of their own strengths and thus generates no need for entitlement or dominance over others…

> Third, in their experience of executive functions, humble people are less self-focused and more engaged in self-transcendent pursuits. Humility is regarded as a virtue leading to growth…Being aware of something greater than the self, humble people understand that they fall short of a standard that they are striving to reach. Their life pursuits are less about themselves than about the larger community, the greater whole, moral principles, or ultimate universal truth… causing them to forget the self. Self-transcendence protects them from excessive ego and pursuits of materialism or excessive luxury…

Overall, humility is grounded in a self-view of accepting that something is greater than the self and manifests in self-awareness, openness to feedback, appreciation of others, low self-focus, and self-transcendent pursuit (Ou et al., 2014, pp. 37–38).

Their study found that, in contrast to self-aggrandizing CEOs, who tend to make riskier investments, pay higher acquisition premiums, and pursue grandiose schemes with volatile performance results, humble CEOs engaged in empowering leadership behaviors that resulted in greater integration among members of the top management team. This led to perception of an empowering organizational climate among middle managers, leading to greater work engagement, affective commitment, and good job performance.

The challenge of time and the response of visioning. The afternoon of life brings an acute awareness of the fact that "the clock is ticking." Time becomes a more precious commodity. Paradoxically, the more successful one is and the more one is paid for their time, the less one seems to have of it. "Free time" to explore new experiences and interests becomes more expensive and scarce. We can lose control of our lives, becoming a slave to our calendar and commitments.

Creating and committing oneself to a personal vision and life purpose can be a way to find a guide star for life priorities. "Getting our priorities straight" can be a bulwark against the inexorable demands of a hectic life. Whillans, Weidman, and Dunn (2016) in a study of a representative sample of five thousand Americans found that those who prioritized time over money were happier and had a greater sense of well-being.

The challenge of change and complexity and the response of learning. A paramount challenge for all of us is the dizzying rate of increasing complexity and change. Ray Kurzweil, the renowned futurist has proposed what the calls the Law of Accelerating Returns, an exponential growth in the rate of exponential growth. A corollary of this rapid change and attendant increased complexity is rapid increases in professional obsolesce in nearly every field and discipline. Specialized experts, perhaps appropriately, are squarely focused on performance; yet, this focus in many ways can inhibit the necessary learning required to keep up with the state of the art. High performance is often achieved by simplicity and predictability, while learning requires a search for requisite complexity to match the complexity of emerging problems and circumstances.

Time becomes a critical issue in moving from a performance orientation to a learning perspective. For example, the choice of an appropriate time span in which to view a problem is perhaps the most important decision in defining a problem and finding a solution for it. A learning perspective enlarges the time frame through two processes. Proto-learning, the formulation of scenarios, hypotheses, and intentions, anticipates the future. The more articulated these expectations and models of the future are, the more quickly course deviations can be signaled. Retro-learning, the reexamination and debriefing of past experiences, establishes and refines general operating principles, adding a cumulative quality and historical continuity to work. These processes require that we make the space and time for the necessary reflection and analysis to take place. The principles of deliberate experiential learning described in Chapter 6 provide guidelines for the adoption of a learning perspective in one's life.

The challenge of facing challenge and the response of courage. Life brings many challenges and in later life the challenges increase. As we have said, facing challenge is how we grow, learn, and develop, although doing so can be more difficult as we grow older. In general, aging is accompanied by a retreat in many aspects of life. Social engagement decreases as solitary reflection increases. Physically there is a tendency to close up, with stooped posture, folded arms, and closed chest. Mentally there is a retreat from activities that sharpen memory and mental activity.

Courage is considered to be one of the four cardinal virtues, since it is required for persistent action on behalf of all the other virtues. Mustering the courage to face life challenges is itself growth-producing, what Maddi and Kobasa (1984) have called the hardiness response to stress. Their studies show that individuals who see themselves as in control of their lives, committed to the world around them, and challenged by life are less debilitated by stressful life events than those who feel alienated and controlled by fate.

The Professional Fellows Program. At the CWRU Weatherhead School of Management we created a program that was designed to help advanced professionals engage with the above challenges and develop positive responses to them (Ballou, Bowers, Boyatzis, & Kolb, 1999). Growing out of the co-inquiry self-assessment and development workshops of the Spencer Mid-life Transition Research, in the Professional Fellows Program we sought to create a learning space for the establishment of a community of lifelong learners. The workshops, projects, courses, and seminars were designed to prepare fellows for membership in the Society of Professional Fellows—a self-managed organization of program alumni dedicated to supporting sustained lifelong learning and development for its members and the larger community.

The men and women in the program were lawyers, physicians, and other health-care professionals, business executives, teachers, academics, and independent individuals seeking personal development. The unique nature of the program seemed to attract many with a strong learning identity, a love of learning, and desire for continuing personal development. There was also a shared generativity theme, a desire to "give back" to the community through their projects and activities. The fellows were particularly attracted to the collaborative learning design of the program that engaged everyone's expertise in working together.

The components of the program included workshops modeled after the co-inquiry life-assessment and planning workshops of the Spencer Lifelong Learning Project. The workshops examined the challenges of adult development described above and engaged the fellows in a comprehensive life-assessment process modeled after the popular Weatherhead MBA management assessment and development course (Boyatzis, Cowen, & Kolb, 1995). From this work, fellows developed a five-to-seven-year Learning Plan related to their emerging career and life direction.

Other components were seminars on current "hot" topics chosen by fellows and faculty, an elective course from the Weatherhead Management courses and individual and group projects. At the fellows' graduation in May, they were inducted into the Society of Fellows, organized with officers and program activities selected by society members and offering informal social, networking, and mentoring activities.

A comprehensive assessment of the participants in the first four iterations of the fellows program was conducted (Ballou, Bowers, Boyatzis, & Kolb, 1999) with the surprising result that most fellows reported great increases in self-confidence; surprising because most entered the program as already highly successful professionals. It seems that the program gave space for reflection and resolution of private concerns and insecurities. The component of the program rated most helpful was the Learning Plan, which brought their thinking together and empowered the fellows to take control of their lives. Fellows valued the learning space created to discuss life transitions without competition about success and shame about failure, placing these transitions in the context of their life journey. They also found the interdisciplinary, cross-professional relationships established in the Fellows Society to be a rare opportunity for learning.

Part III

THE PRACTICE OF EXPERIENTIAL EDUCATION

Fifteen

CURRICULUM CHANGE THROUGH THE
APPLICATION OF EXPERIENTIAL LEARNING
PRINCIPLES AND LEARNING-SPACE CONCEPTS

*Robert Hutchins (1953) called college "the great continuing
conversation." The idea was, of course, that it made no
sense for all of you to sit silently side by side in the library
or the lecture hall being "taught" by the books and the
faculty, but rather that a college was an opportunity to
engage in a fantastic dialogue, trialogue, multilogue with
a fantastically varied assortment of consciousnesses. The
books and the lectures were to be the material from which
such conversation was launched. Professors were to be
expert in facilitating such conversation till you got on to
the knack of it and could fly on your own. You had to come
here because this is where other seekers were gathered and
where all those extraordinary conversations could be had.*

—MICHAEL KAHN, *THE SEMINAR*

In Parts I and II of the book we have described the principles of experiential learning and the characteristics of experiential learning spaces. Part

III of the book is focused on the application of these ideas in educational practice. In this chapter we focus on the institution-wide introduction of an experiential seminar-based curriculum for undergraduates at Case Western Reserve University. Introduced in 2002, the program, known as SAGES (Seminar Approach to General Education and Scholarship), was an ambitious undergraduate reform initiative based on the philosophy of experiential learning. The reform was not a radical change; but for better or worse, was introduced within the confines of the traditional block-scheduled course/credit-hour curricular system. Like most major curricular-reform projects, it initially was met with resistance from various stakeholders of the university. For example, the expanded general education requirements of the SAGES program cut into credit hours that professional schools and departmental majors wanted to keep in their control for their programs. The change process required major negotiation and compromise to gain approval, but was eventually fully implemented in the university-wide undergraduate education curriculum at Case in the fall of 2005. Thanks to an inclusive and respectful planning process that stayed squarely focused on the SAGES vision, the curriculum has continued to evolve from the specifics of the pilot program described below. It continues in its basic outlines to this day.

CWRU President Hundert, in his address to the SAGES faculty in 2005, summarized the educational vision and philosophy embraced by core SAGES faculty reformers and their rationale for embracing an experiential learning approach to seminar education.

> Achieving higher-order intellectual skills is not easy to do alone or even in peer groups, whether in science or the humanities. Students need support and confidence-building to master and apply abstract concepts, to question familiar ideas, and to solve complex problems. Too often, traditional university teaching encourages students to "borrow" understanding from the professor or textbook long enough to pass an exam. At Case, we want the students to build

understandings and cultivate skills that they will retain for the rest of their lives. This kind of knowledge cannot be acquired passively, by listening to lectures.

Students create knowledge for themselves by building on what they already know. They each have their own personal ecology of learning, their individual toolkit of learning skills. But their continuing development as learners and thinkers requires active engagement in a supportive social setting. Hence the seminar format. For most students, the traditional lecture format supplies answers too readily, short-circuiting their need to coordinate their own performance and cognition. Although students welcome it, traditional, authoritative, "professorial" intervention unwittingly undermines most students' efforts to develop the patience, self-confidence, and persistence they need to create complex representations and abstractions. (Kolb et al., 2005)

The seminar structure of the SAGES program consists of:

- A freshman seminar taken in the first semester where students can choose from a menu of about eighty courses. The seminar includes a fourth credit hour for experiential place-based learning exploring Cleveland's scientific and cultural institutions.
- Two university seminars, which have to be completed by the end of a student's second year. Like the freshman seminars, these are small classes with an intensive writing requirement. Over a hundred and fifty courses are offered over the academic year ranging from fuel cells to fly fishing, Gothic literature to the business aspects of professional sports. The courses fall into three different thematic areas: The Natural/Technological World, The Social World, and The Symbolic World.
- After these seminars, students submit a writing portfolio of work from those classes. This is a requirement for graduation.

- In a student's third year, they take one departmental seminar, in which they bring the writing and critical thinking skills they have learned to bear on a topic that is related to their major.
- In a student's senior year, the culmination of the SAGES program is the *Capstone*, a semester-long project ending in a public presentation.

The SAGES seminar was structured around four main competency areas:

- Development of writing competencies—Regardless of the field students may pursue, they need to be proficient writers. To achieve this goal, faculty were assigned a co-instructor from English department who was charged with the responsibility of developing students' scholarly writing skills.
- Development of oral communications—SAGES seminars provide a forum where students can learn to articulate their thoughts coherently and powerfully. Seminar discussions and oral presentations give students the opportunity to practice essential communication skills while getting constructive feedback from faculty and peers.
- Development of critical/ethical reasoning skills—Seminars help students begin to conceive of knowledge as something to be gathered from multiple sources, and then subjected to rigorous scrutiny through testing and comparative analysis. An ultimate goal is to prepare students to define a problem and learn to develop a thoughtful response to that problem.
- Development of appreciation of diversity—Students are exposed to a wide range of ideas and approaches to scholarship. The seminar is designed to be a space where a diversity of thought and opinion is not only offered, but also welcomed and valued. Thus, it provides a rich learning opportunity, allowing students not only to explore why others believe what they do, but also to examine their own beliefs and assumptions about the world.

In addition, as a key component of the SAGES program, seminar leaders serve as advisors to students for their first two years of general education. They serve as mentors to the students they teach, introducing them to the culture and resources of the research university and establishing close relationships with them from the very beginning of their college career.

Our Study of the SAGES Pilot Program

As local experiential learning "experts," we were asked to design and implement a study to investigate the effectiveness of the SAGES pilot program as a new model for undergraduate education that builds the foundation for multidisciplinary academic inquiry using small classes and a seminar approach. The SAGES committee commissioned our SAGES Research and Learning Team in 2002, and for the next three years the team extensively interviewed faculty and students about their experiences with SAGES and conducted many classrooms observations to capture the overall climate of the SAGES learning environment.

Our approach was not a traditional outcome evaluation but a search for those exemplary practices in seminar design and instructor approach that led to seminars that were successful learning experiences. The study had two specific objectives. First, we wanted to understand the relationship between students' learning experiences and the learning environment fostered by the SAGES initiative, and to assess the impact of the program on student performance, development, and overall satisfaction. Second, it was crucial for us to understand the faculty members' experiences of teaching the SAGES seminars and to assess how those experiences fostered student learning and the overall climate of the seminar environment (Kolb et al., 2003).

What makes an engaging seminar experience? This question guided our inquiry throughout the program, helping us to illustrate the dynamic nature of the seminar learning space and the key contributing factors necessary to deepen the participants' seminar experience. We describe this dynamic process from two distinct but interconnected vantage points; the first illustrates the dynamic interplay of the four foundational pillars of the seminar activities in a learning cycle of experiencing, reading, writing, and discussing. The second examines the key components of the generative and creative seminar learning space that emerged in the seminars.

The Seminar Learning Cycle

The SAGES seminar competency areas were heavily focused on development of student writing, reading, and discussion abilities. As such, those competencies became focal points for the instructors in designing the structure and the content of their seminars. Seminar participants, both instructors and students, reported positive seminar experiences when discussions, reading materials, and writing assignments were dynamically interconnected with student experiences as depicted in figure 15.1.

Figure 15.1

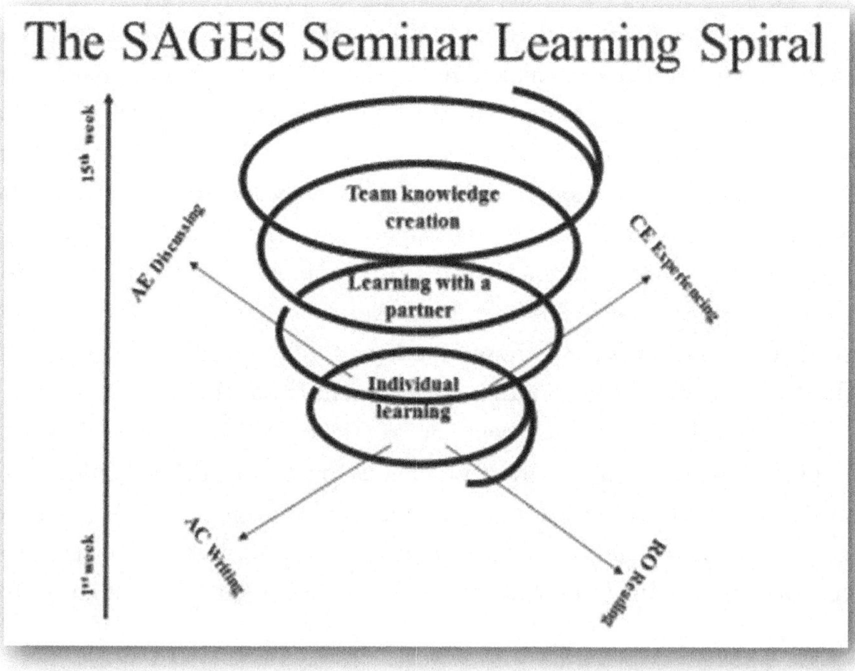

The SAGES Seminar Learning Spiral

The dynamic interactions among the four seminar activities of experiencing, reading, writing, and discussing created the seminar learning space. The activities did not necessarily occur simultaneously, but one or two at a time depending on the focus of the seminar on a particular day. The four activities defined an experiential learning cycle where the dynamic tensions among these activities drove learning that was essential for the livelihood and the sustenance of the seminars. Experiencing refers to being exposed to a particular activity or situation related to the ideas under consideration in the seminar. Reading refers to observation and reflection upon a particular content derived from a book, a film, or through a visit to the museum. Writing was focused on conceptual sense-making of ideas discussed in the seminar, to be presented to the instructors for feedback and shared with peers for review. Active discussion describes seminar conversations around questions, ideas, experiences generated within the seminar or outside of class.

Through classroom observations and conversations with instructors and students, we saw three levels of learning opportunities in the seminar—individual learning, learning with a partner, and team learning involving the entire class. We describe these three distinct learning situations below beginning with an individual learning experience. Each situation is narrated by participants' experiences within the seminar context, combined with in-class observation by a research team member.

An Individual Learning Experience. In her preparation for the SAGES seminar, Marianne read the assigned book by Oliver Sacks, *An Anthropologist on Mars: Seven Paradoxical Tales*, consisting of discussions of medical case studies of patients with neurological conditions such as autism. The assignment was to write a critical essay about the book and, intrigued by the topic, Marianne conducted additional readings about the subject. In one of the readings, she came across a research paper that, in her mind, totally disproved Sacks's reasoning about autism. Marianne had an autistic cousin, and this particular paper finding was in alignment with her own experience with her cousin's autistic behaviors and symptoms. Reading a research paper that contradicted Sacks's argument, but affirmed her own experience about her cousin's autistic conditions triggered a strong response in Marianne and she felt compelled to discuss her discovery and experience with her writing instructor.

> I did not put what I found in the draft but I brought it up in my conversation with the writing instructor and it really moved him and he encouraged me to include that in the paper. He said, "You have to put that in the paper!"

The tension generated between reading and experiencing prompted Marianne to engage in conversation about her ideas with the writing instructor, who in turn encouraged her to formalize her ideas in writing.

> That experience gave me an idea about how to address my audiences in writing.

As Marianne attests, discussing her idea with the instructor gave her the confidence to find her own voice in her writing, a valuable experience she carried over to future assignments. Her unique seminar experience is filled with excitement, conflicting discoveries, and sense-making process to resolve those tensions. The final integration of her experiences through writing was mediated by a critical conversation with her instructor who guided her to articulate her voice. As Marianne acknowledged in the interview, she was able to carry this experience into her different reading and writing assignments.

Learning with a Partner. The seminar learning cycle was also identified in dyadic learning situations. The goal of the activity set for this particular seminar activity was to read and explore the nature of creativity with a partner. The voices of the students uncover the quality of their engagement with the reading materials, the nature of their conversations, and the final learning outcome attained.

> A lot of excitement and critical thought came out when we were told not to report biographical details of the book but rather explore

something about creativity. Given that assignment there was wonderful moment like epiphany when you say "Hey look at this! This is pretty cool! I came up with this."

Reading with a partner with specific goal in mind immediately led to lively discussions and exchange of ideas about the reading material.

> And then you toss it back and forth with your partner and you have different perspectives. You come up with a larger idea that may not have to do with T. S. Eliot but it is a generic idea that can be applied across the board.

The focused engagement and discussion of the material continues to be carried out outside the classroom. As they continue to dig into the materials, their understanding of the material attains refinement and depth and their ideas continue to deepen and mature through the preparation of a written document to be presented in the seminar.

> Just the feeling that we can say: "Hey, we came up with an idea!" It wasn't put in our heads by our instructors or stated in the book. It was something we came up with. That was just a cool feeling.

By discussing and writing together about their ideas, it is clear students experienced the feeling of accomplishment and self-confidence that they were capable of generating new knowledge together. In this particular case we can identify the dynamic movement between reading and discussing, experiencing and discussing, and finally a movement from writing to experiencing. The engagement and interest in the assignment fueled by this experience may further influence their attitude toward future collaborative projects, expanding their skill and capacity for learning together.

Team Learning. What SAGES instructors aspired to from the very beginning was to create an opportunity where the entire seminar participants worked together to produce a collective team product. It required significant time and effort from all the seminar participants for such a teamwork experience to emerge. As the following case illustrates, when it happened, the seminar space was alive, with every participant engaged and hard at work to produce a high-quality product. As the instructor describes, a turning point in the seminar may happen unexpectedly and by seizing that opportunity he was able to build the momentum and stir participants to engage in lively discussions:

> Between Monday and Wednesday aliens seemed to have abducted my students and replaced them with the people that were in the classroom on Wednesday, because they were totally different on Wednesday than on Monday. That day they had a deep scholarly discussion in which they questioned all of their previous beliefs as far as I can tell. I had them bring questions about a chapter of Bertrand Russell's book. The chapter itself has very little to do with logic, but a lot to do with general soul searching. It had a lot of letters in it, too. Letters from when he was a little bit older than our students.

The conversation continues to deepen as participants brought written questions about the book to be discussed in the seminar.

> In this chapter he makes statements that struck the students as aggressive and imperialistic. I think it's because they have already come to admire him and they were hearing things that were totally out of the blue for them. Really beyond the spectrum of what one would think about Russell. So we talked about why he would say some of these things and his internal struggle with English Imperialism.

These questions further fueled the discussions and helped expose the incongruence in author's stances and views.

> At this point our talk about Gandhi from Gardner's book came in very useful. So we talked about Russell's position in the aristocracy and his struggle with it.

Previous readings and discussions were reintroduced into the discussions, further expanding and enriching the conversation. As the instructor observes,

> Some of the students said "England was just a bully, they were powerful not because they have special qualities, but because they happened to be in the right time in the right place to do these things." These comments made by students were foreign to anything that they had said before. Then a student who has been a strong supporter of the US attacks on Afghanistan said that "we are not really in a very different situation right now" and the class discussed what was different and what was similar.

In the instructor's mind, the discussions challenged students to experience the current political situation from a very different perspective and forced them critically reexamine their previously held political views;

> Then this student also said, that "other countries are jealous of the US because we are the best, and someone has to be the best." Other students pushed back on that statement, and he compared it to sports, which he often did. The others replied that in sports you can tell who won, and there are these criteria of what being the best would be...and that the US is not the best on many indicators of human development. And he had to admit that they were right.

This case exemplifies the ideal SAGES seminar and, as the model suggests, such dynamic learning space was kept alive and sustained by continuous back-and-forth movement of all four seminar components as students committed themselves to creating knowledge together, building on each other's ideas and perspectives. The instructor of this seminar acknowledged that this was by far her best seminar experience of the semester. She enthusiastically declared, "This is what SAGES seminar is supposed to be about."

Alice Y. Kolb and David A. Kolb

The Seminar Learning Space

What makes an engaging seminar experience? This question guided our inquiry into the developmental process of the seminar learning space from within. Building a successful seminar experience happened over time and from ground up through participants' engagement with seminar materials, discussions, and experiences. The factors that contributed to successful, engaging seminars are described below in two categories, the seminar learning-space boundaries and the instructor's role.

The Boundary of the Seminar Space. The boundary of the seminar space refers to those specific components that held and sustained the seminar activities. Those components served more or less as operating norms of the seminar and seminar participants expressed positive experience in those seminar sections where those norms were put in place.

Sense of intimacy. Intimacy emerged as one of the key characteristics of a successful seminar experience. The seminar sections that reported the highest level of satisfaction were those where the physical configuration was arranged in such a way that participants were able to make eye contact with one another. Arranging chairs in circles or desks in rectangular configuration seem to increase participation and engagement at verbal and nonverbal level.

A small class size. There was almost a unanimous perception among students that the class size of ten to fifteen participants in the seminar was one of the decisive factors in the quality of their experience. According to their experience, a small class size where everybody knows each other's name provided a familiar and intimate ambience and facilitated active class participation. Both faculty and students appreciated the opportunity of close classroom interactions and the added flexibility of rearranging the class into pair interactions or small group discussions.

> They also liked when I divided them into small groups (groups of six, three or four) for discussion about something. I did that four or five times and they liked those better. The small groups worked well, it got them into conversations, especially the quiet ones. Everyone was talking to each other. (Instructor)

A small class makes it very personable. Everyone listened and talked.

Often when we would split up into smaller groups I really felt involved. This was probably because I could hear everyone's responses and reactions and give mine more freely. (Student)

An open learning environment. An "open learning environment" refers to a broad range of forms of engagement participants perceived as allowed or acceptable in the seminar. These forms of engagement were broadly of two kinds: an example of the first kind was specific learning contracts that participants collectively created and agreed to abide by during the class; the second type was not necessarily articulated or made explicit in the seminar but emerged from within in each specific seminar section and over time they evolved into implicit norms that guided the conversation. We found that seminar sections that reported the highest level of engagement had the opportunities for participants to: (1) voice their own opinions; (2) engage in free-flow conversations; (3) have a chance to discuss issues beyond he required readings and assignments; and finally, (4) allow instructors to give short lectures.

Voicing their opinions. Students reported that the opportunity to voice their own opinions was a great stimulus to engage in conversation and learn from one another:

I liked the fact that the teachers were not telling us what to think. Instead we were drawing from each other's views. Everybody could hear me and I did not have the teacher tell me "OK you are off the topic." I could have been slightly off the topic but it was all right. (Student)

Exposure to diverse points of view. Seeing things out of the box. The instructor obviously has lots of knowledge but we were able to express our points of view. (Student)

Instructors also saw a good opportunity to voice their opinions and promote learning about particular issues or foster students' engagement:

I was able to get students to think more structurally about the issues Sacks was raising, how they personally conceptualize, and use personal metaphors to understand the aspects of the mind. Not only do writers use rhetorical structure to think about a mental event but they also use those all the time to write; not only how they conceptualize the aspect of the mind, but also how they use the metaphors to conceptualize. They are not blank slates coming to class without any idea how the mind works, but often with quite complex and invested theories about how their mind works. (Instructor)

Free-flowing conversation. While a structured discussion helps conversations to stay on target and focused, participants reported being more engaged during free-flow discussions when they were able to bring their own unique ideas and experiences into the conversation unrestricted by the subject of discussion. In our class observations, students were more engaged in discussions when tangential conversations were welcomed and instructors made room for divergent topics to flow in and out of the main topic of discussion.

All of our discussions were exciting because it was very much an open forum for exchange of knowledge. (Student)

I also became really involved and enjoyed the discussions that, while they were more based on the readings and information that might come from the readings, were not only about the readings. Free-form discussion was the best. (Student)

Additionally, free-flow conversations decentralized the conversation from the instructors, giving more opportunities for students to voice their opinions and ideas.

We were free to talk. In the beginning of the class we set few contact rules. We were free to talk without raising our hands because the instructors wanted to avoid a hierarchy where they are the one who are running the class, unless there were people interrupting each other in the class discussion. (Student)

Beyond the readings. "You can bring points from all over the place," said one student, who was referring to her freedom to engage in seminar in multiple ways. This view was shared by many students, who valued the conversations and discussions that were drawn from many different sources such as personal experiences, outside readings, other classes, and visits to outside institutions. The possibility of bringing comments, ideas, and questions from outside the seminar gave students multiple entry points into the seminar conversations.

> The best times in this class were when the instructor would take what we are learning and relate it to our own lives, sometimes sacrificing discussion of the book to do so. The success of the class was left up to us and we could do with it what we wanted. (Student)

> [Howard] Gardner talks a lot about childhood and we come from a very different childhood background and so we were able to bring a lot of that in the class discussion. (Student)

> Unlike High School English, it was much more than just writing a paper. There were other experiences that can't be described through print media. You have actually to go out there to explore UCI (University Circle Institutions) for example. The exciting thing was to bring all those outside experiences into the class. In normal classrooms you just read the books given to you and discuss about them but here you can bring outside information in to the discussion that is relevant but has not been discussed. (Student)

Lecturing. Lectures do not belong in seminars. At least this was our preconceived notion about what should or should not be included in the seminar activities. It turns out that in the SAGES seminars, students welcomed and valued small lectures when delivered in appropriate doses and occasions. Lectures often provided new insights for further discussion, or grounded and brought focus to a seemingly divergent seminar discussions. It also served as venue for the instructors to engage in conversation from their own areas of expertise.

> One day in particular, when the instructor was writing notes on the whiteboard and we still were discussing things on the market sector, I thought it went well. I felt we were learning something well and at the same time examining what we're learning. (Student)

> My favorite times in the seminar were the ones when the instructor did some lecturing, that is, she would discuss evolution and its mechanisms, and implications. During these days I felt as if I am learning so much. The instructor can explain ideas very clearly and during these days. I was excited and interested in learning about evolution and Charles Darwin. (Student)

Diversity of participants. Diversity in the seminar context included broad individual characteristics such as major areas of expertise, age, experience, gender, and ethnicity. In general, participants valued the diverse composition of students in the seminar. Diversity afforded students opportunities to be exposed to a wide range of opinions and perspectives about a subject matter.

> We had different educational backgrounds. We don't know a lot of things about each other. People learn differently and think differently. At home the circle of people I knew was family, friends, and church. We pretty much agreed on everything. Exposure to diverse points of views...Seeing things out of the box. (Student)

> The diversity of chosen majors...Different people generate more learning because of the diverse perspectives and areas of expertise. (Student)

The Role of a Caring Instructor. We begin with a close look at specific actions instructors demonstrated in the seminars that contributed to the students' positive learning experience. These actions were—not being at the center of the class, treating students as equals, sustaining the seminar, knowing students, being knowledgeable, and being challenging and supportive.

Not at the center of class. Participants reported having a positive experience in the seminars where instructors were not at the center of the class. In our observations, effective instructors were fully present in the class, skillfully deflected attention from themselves and focused in opening and freeing the space for students' expression of ideas and opinions.

The instructors were not the focal point. (Student)

Student centered discussions allowed us to learn what is important to us, and to explore diverse opinions. (Student)

The instructor treats us as equals. In an engaging seminar, instructors maintained an egalitarian stance toward students. In the students' view, equality was related to the degree to which their opinions and point of views were respected and valued on various decision-making process of the course such as defining the readings and assignments. Instructors who treated students as equals expressed genuine interest in students' personal lives and ideas.

The instructors treated us as equals and I think the mutual respect really helped us open up and be able to express our views and learn from each other. (Student)

Students were empowered to make decisions. They were treated as peers [by the instructors]. (Student)

It wasn't just from me to them but back and forth, like a delightful conversation. What was good about it is that we both [instructors and students] talked. I like hearing your ideas and you like hearing mine. (Instructor)

Challenging and supportive. During the seminar sessions, it was very common for students to be hesitant in their first attempt to introduce a controversial idea or diverging opinion. In an engaging seminar, students reported that the instructor challenged them and held them accountable for their statements or questions in a supportive manner. The challenge and support were expressed as questions, demands, or encouragement for the students to dig deeper into an idea or think through their line of arguments. As one instructor shared his view,

> I tried to get them to make a point out of what they were saying. I would ask them something like "Does that mean that this is the same thing as that?" I encourage students not to back off the point of view they were trying to make, because very often they lose confidence after sometime and do not continue their argument. (Instructor)

From the student perspective, this act by the instructor fueled the discussion and enriched the seminar learning experience:

> A lot of instructors take students' answers and are ambiguous about that. They may say, "Well, you may be wrong, or you may be right." Instructor F is not like that. He sometimes plays devil's advocate and challenges our thinking. He created controversies. Whenever there were controversies there were far more opportunities to learn. (Student)

The instructor knows me. A typical undergraduate class is conducted in large lecture halls. Such a learning environment makes it virtually impossible for the instructors and students to engage in a one-on-one interaction. In contrast, the small-size SAGES seminars provided opportunities for instructors and students to relate in a much closer and intimate manner. Such close instructor-student relationship was further enhanced by the intense advising process built into the SAGES curriculum. SAGES instructors not only could identify their students by their names, but they also came to know their students' personal lives and aspirations at a much deeper level. Our findings suggest that there is a strong educational benefit that flows from a direct and sustained engagement among faculty and students.

> I think it was an excellent idea to have the freshman adviser as someone who teaches your class, besides the fact that you foster a stronger relationship with your adviser. He is the one who will help you to pick the right course and make sure you graduate. Case is a big environment and as a freshman, you do not know anybody. If you are sitting in the back of a lecture hall with five hundred students, nobody knows you. It is nice to be known by your name and not just as a number. (Student)

> Partly because I know who they are and I know what they are doing, and what their plans are, we are more comfortable with each other than we would otherwise be. The fact that I am a teacher helps me in advising and also helps me in teaching them in the course. Through one-to-one interaction the advising appointment gives me a good insight and information about the student I would not have otherwise. (Instructor)

The instructor is knowledgeable. "Ms. K is very knowledgeable." In our conversations with the SAGES students, this is a comment that came up many times. It mattered a lot for students that their teachers be knowledgeable. While the seminar format did not require instructors to give lectures or to deliver a specific content on a regular basis, students greatly valued instructors' command of areas of expertise that enhanced the quality of discussions.

> I was always very interested by the detailed background information that instructor F was able to provide. She was able to provide theories of many other scientists as well. I really enjoyed all the discussions about the science and the scientific history of Darwin's theories and scientific related theories. (Student)

For example, in one session of the seminar, the instructor's knowledgeable comments played a crucial role in guiding the conversation by expanding the topics of discussion or by providing relevant information that could support or challenge the ideas under scrutiny.

> When they looked a little bit daunted I said something that would help, or add a couple of critical things on particular ideas. (Instructor)

Sustaining the seminar. It is not an easy task to maintain a high level of student engagement for a prolonged period of time in a seminar. Students' energy level, interests, and attention span naturally tend to fluctuate over the life of the seminar. In this sense, an engaging seminar experience is an ephemeral phenomenon that needs to be recreated and maintained each time the class meets. Seminar instructors played a fundamental role in sustaining a lively seminar atmosphere by providing a basic structure, guiding and sustaining students' attention and focus by punctuating their experience, and finally by modeling an ideal seminar behavior. In our observation, in an engaging seminar section, while instructors had a hands-on approach as opposed to laissez-faire attitude toward the preservation of the seminar learning space, they managed to maintain the integrity of the seminar in a nonthreatening manner.

Providing a basic structure. A common complaint among SAGES students was the lack of structure they perceived in some of the seminar sessions. Several students wanted a more formal structure where students were held accountable to complete readings on time for the discussion, turn in assignments on due dates, and actively participate in the class discussions. In engaging seminar sections, instructors provided a basic structure by providing a clear syllabus, a clear assignment, an explicit purpose of the seminar and clearly articulated class norms to be followed by all. While instructors succeeded in holding students accountable to this structure, the basic structure functioned more as a reference point, a tool to bring participants in, rather than a rigid boundary for conversations. For example, in one seminar section, full participation was a requirement and this norm often challenged the quiet ones to speak up and share their views. As one student recounts, the instructor skillfully brought in a quiet student into the conversation and the entire class benefited from student's participation:

> Nobody was allowed to hide in the back corner. We opened up a big circle but still we had people who would not talk. Instructor G tried to say "So and so, what do you think of this?" I liked that because too many people were passive participants. They may have some great point they have written in the paper, which would have taken the discussion in a whole different direction if had they spoken up in the class. Because those people do have important things to say and they have to realize that. (Student)

Punctuating the experience. When participants experienced seminar discussions as lacking in purpose and direction, there was a marked decline in participants' willingness to engage in discussions. Instructors who managed to keep students' attention focused on the direction and outcome of the conversation were more able to sustain a lively seminar throughout the semester. Participants had a sense of accomplishment when instructors purposefully punctuated the direction, shifts, outcomes, or conclusions of a particular class discussion. Such conscious interventions in the process of the seminar led to more disciplined, focused, and lively conversations in the following sessions. We observed in one particular seminar section an example of such an act when the instructors purposefully tried to bring to focus what the students had accomplished through discussions. The instructor's intervention prompted students' reaction that ranged from surprise, to excitement, and to pride in having accomplished something significant.

> The writing co-instructor made the observation that the barn rais-
> ing method is a good idea but unless at the end we stop to observe
> the kind of barn we have raised, unless we stop to admire what
> we have built, then we missed the point. An important part of the
> group barn raising experience it is to have a party at the end and
> enjoy the barn. Sometime at the end of our discussions everybody
> is holding on to a board, or the nails. Or maybe we built this thing
> that nobody can figure out. So we wanted to provide more time,
> more focus at the end on trying to draw architecturally what we
> have built, or maybe to map how the discussion went and to think
> about that as our final product. So at the end, each one of the in-
> structors (we were three) put on the board his or her representation
> of the discussion, each of us in our own way. Something about see-
> ing it, something about how we visualized and represented what
> they have done made them think, feel more proud about what they
> had accomplished on the discussion. So it was a great dynamic be-
> tween the teachers and students in that way because we were able
> to show them at the end "this is what you did. This is what this dis-
> cussion looked like to me." And they said "Wow, that looks pretty
> cool, that looks pretty complex, we sure did something here." So
> that was one kind of a neat moment because people refer back to
> the drawings on the board as representations of what they have ac-
> complished. (Instructor)

Modeling. Our classroom observations suggest that modeling a desirable seminar behavior by instructors was one of the most effective ways to create and sustain the seminar. Instructors accomplished this in multiple ways, with specific goals in mind to influence students' behaviors in a positive way. In one class session, the instructor gave students a scholarly piece of writing and asked them to analyze the style, critique it, and offer alternatives. This the students did with great fervor, picking the paper into pieces, just to discover that it was one of the instructor's own published pieces of work, which caused a cascade of laughter and delight at the instructor's capacity to laugh at himself, his comfort to self-disclosure, and openness to criticism. One of our research team members recounted a memorable seminar session where the instructor demonstrated a great capacity for enduring student silences. Rather than cutting the silence short by introducing another question or an opinion, he waited for the students to reply, which they did after careful reflection. In this class, he observed, the students built on other students' ideas, which resulted in an ideal seminar format, with the students largely shaping the class content. The instructor said he considered himself as a "catalyst for eliciting students' ideas and voices."

The Internal Process of Seminar Activities. The analysis below identifies a number of processes that emerged in seminars from the creative tension between participants' diverse views that enabled a lively discussion, active participation defined by seminar members' high level of engagement, and engaging content that stirred students' attention and interest in the subject matter or seminar activities.

Diversity of views. Participants' multiple perspectives about a seminar topic or a specific activity (a reading, a movie, or an event that occurred in the seminar) fueled intense interactions among students. If those differences were sustained in a healthy manner, over time, students were able to build on each other's ideas, experience the convergence of an idea into concepts or theories, and thus gain deep understanding of a given phenomenon and the process by which the knowledge is attained.

Disagreement. Often, disagreement was the source of energy that fueled the initial phase of the discussion. Disagreements were born out of conflicting points of view held by participants or subgroups of students about a discussion topic, or it could also be triggered by their reaction to a particular text, event, or ideas generated in the seminar.

> As I listened to people's opinion, I noticed that somebody said something totally opposite of my thinking. This person said that

Alice Y. Kolb and David A. Kolb

Early American Literature was a copy of European literature and I thought he was wrong. I voiced my opinion and I could back up with evidence and I felt comfortable with that. It was something that I had knowledge about because history and literature are the some of the things I enjoy. (Student)

An instructor's observation about how a joint seminar session with a different class generated a lively interaction about differences illustrates the point;

[The most engaging sessions was the] joint session with section XX. We compared two books each section has taken on. Maya Angelou and Barbara Macintosh. We separated the group in two and had a discussion. It was a very successful session. Again, his students were intrinsically livelier than mine. A little rivalry there and a good learning experience. My students were the most intense of all the sessions. There was creative tension. (FS instructor)

Controversy. Controversial issues or topics with no clear-cut answers generated heated discussions among students. Students felt strongly about their positions, and if the instructors encouraged the exploration of those differences, they challenged and questioned the positions held by others while defending their views. Many participants described this as a "back and forth discussion," and considered this experience in the seminar as one of those moments they felt engaged and energized.

I felt energized those days when we have had back and forth discussion. That is when people argued, tried to clarify their points more, etcetera. This happened mostly when we were talking about controversial issues such as the nature of life. (Student)

Whenever there were controversies there were far more opportunities to learn. This by far was the most engaging discussion I ever had. The class did not always agree. And we did not agree with the Instructor either. (Student)

Building together. In the process of grappling with differences and controversial issues, there were times in the seminar when, through the instructor's guidance and students' collaborative effort, participants were able to build ideas as a group, through a careful and thoughtful consideration of divers points of view. While such moments were rare in the first year of the SAGES seminars, when the convergence of ideas occurred, students reported great satisfaction derived from the experience of creating ideas together.

It was engaging because we did it together. It wasn't just me telling them what to do. So I hope they would be more interested in doing it. They control what they are doing. That is one of the collaborative things that I would like to see in the seminar. (Instructor)

This was about a particular chapter on Gardner. Gardner's book generated a lot of criticism. We were encouraged to look at the creative minds in a more general fashion and so my partner and I worked on Elliot on duality of creativity about how the actual ideas for him were created out of a feeling of ostracism. So flushing out these ideas with my partner going back and forth and presenting our ideas in the class and receiving feedback from my classmates was a big highlight for me. (Student)

Active participation. Students' high level of engagement was another cornerstone of an engaging seminar. Such engagement was characterized by equal balance of intense talking and listening by all participants. They were very attentive and responsive to one another—as many students said, "everyone was listening and talking."

In this class everybody was talking. Everybody had great ideas, relating to the book, to their personal experiences. Everybody was talking and listening intensely, discussing about the creativity and how the mind works to create an idea. This is what I enjoyed the most. (Student)

It wasn't just from me to them but back and forth, like a delightful conversation. What was good about it is that we both talked. I like hearing your ideas and you like hearing mine. (Instructor)

Hearing everyone's point of view. In our observation, active listening was one of the key indicators of a successful seminar. Conversations were richer and deeper when there was opportunity for students to actively make meaning, draw conclusions from somebody else's experiences.

Over time, I've gotten different points of view and different ideas. I was watching and listening to other people's opinions. Group dynamic that day was such that everybody was involved in the discussion. (Student)

It was quite engaging and it was interesting to hear everyone's point of view. (Student)

They were allowing the space for people to explore ideas without having to be right off the bat. They were letting people say things that they disagreed with without feeling they had to talk them over or immediately refute them. (Instructor)

Giving input. Students' willingness to contribute to the seminar discussion was a clear indication of an engaging seminar. As many participants reported, "people were contributing to the discussions and not just talking out loud." Students asked questions to each other to gain better understanding about a subject, provided examples to support or challenge each other's ideas, or presented new information to the conversation.

Everyone got to give their input, and the discussion kept fueling itself. Like someone would bring up a topic and there would be a counter point to a topic that would lead to a new topic and you wanted extra time at the end of the class to keep discussing it. You did not want the class to end. (Student)

The day when I gave a presentation I felt energized too, inspired, and interested. We talked about the nature of science and had a discussion about fame in science. (Instructor)

Engaging content. The nature of the seminar content was the third pole of the seminar component that fueled lively conversations. Our findings suggest that the most appealing contents were of two kinds: the first was related to students' deep interests and the second was a content related to their own experiences. Equally important as the nature of the contents themselves, were the diverse ways in which students were able to engage with the seminar contents. Several students reported that one aspect of the seminar they valued the most was having "multiple modes of involvement like writing, reading, presenting, which led to engagement of people with different modes of learning." The preferred ways to engage with the content varied among students; for some it was through readings, or a critique of those readings; for others were through an engaging assignment; or it was a question or an idea that emerged during the discussion or a lecture given by instructors.

Related to my interest. Participants clearly had personal preference for the subject matter, and their interests influenced their level of engagement in the discussions. However, as the students' voices suggest, the diverse seminar processes made available for the students to engage in the specific topics of their interest determined the depth of their inquiry.

I was quite often very interested in the science of evolution that the instructor was talking about. I was glad she went into so much detail about the biology and appreciated how knowledgeable she was. (Student)

I liked the discussions about the mind and about diseases. I enjoyed sharing experiences about different people with different ailments and obstacles. I felt they inspired me to talk about my views on diseases and how to define diseases. (Student)

Related to my experience. When participants were able to relate the readings, assignments, or discussions to their own experience, the content became more real and meaningful:

The best times in this class where when the instructor would take what we are learning and relate it to our own lives, sometimes sacrificing discussion of the book to do so in the class...We were allowed to talk about things that are going on in our lives today rather than always take them back to the book. This allowed us to explore ourselves within the context of the book, and sometimes even dismiss any relation to the book. But always we seem to be able to connect any conversation back to an aspect of the book. (Student)

In this class everybody was talking. Everybody had great ideas, relating to the book, to their personal experiences. [I am engaged when] connections between the academic, philosophical and personal come together in the classroom. (Student)

Generative readings. The quality of readings was one of the determining factors of students' engagement in the seminar and they were primarily of two kinds: the first, books they liked and found inspiring, and second, books they disliked because they were not aligned with their ideas or experiences, or books they considered poorly written. A common trait that these books shared was the arousal of strong interest and motivation for the students to voice their reactions and opinions thus generating a lively and rich discussion.

> I was interested while reading the Oliver Sacks book. That was my favorite selection. It was very inspiring to read real-life stories about people having to deal with unique problems. (Student)

> The class was liveliest when there was something engaging on the table. This happened with the assignment I gave them on Maya Angelou's book, "I know why the caged bird sings." I think they enjoyed this book better than anything else. And it is not a coincidence for it is a very well written book. She is a poet. She writes about what the kids could really care about. (Instructor)

> In general I did not like the book. The books are assigned because as a general rule the books are chosen because the instructors like it. It came as a surprise that L. did not like the book either. We were able to draw a lot out of this book in terms of learning from his mistakes. How could he have been more successful in his analysis and arguments? I learned more from this discussion than I might have learned from reading a good book. The instructor was excellent in drawing that from the reading. (Student)

Generative assignments. The nature of the assignment significantly influenced the quality of students' seminar experience. An engaging assignment encouraged students to dig deeper into the content, allowed them to be creative, and inspired them to go beyond the specifics of what was required. These assignments ranged from a simple question, to a complex analysis of a particular text, to a small research project about a topic of their interest. Furthermore, these assignments shared two elements in common: they required students to bring either their personal experience or their own ideas.

So for the following class I invited them to choose a paragraph or half a page from the text that they especially liked. In class each student read out lout his or hers excerpt and explained why they like it. They brought wonderful metaphors and emotions and they said: "Boy this is the best." (Instructor)

I felt energized when working on the paper on Picasso because of the independent thought and responsibility I had. I was able to use my own human nature to interpret how Picasso arrived at his creations. (Student)

I find the assignment I gave them in writing a five-page screenplay based on their biography was an enormous success. I learned so much about the students. It was wonderfully freeing. It was an assignment that was true to the spirit of the syllabus that engaged them with the material. (Instructor)

Generative questions and ideas. There were special kinds of questions and ideas that emerged during the class that enriched the conversations. Engaging questions, comments, or ideas were those that challenged the common understanding of a particular issue, bringing a new perspective to the issue under discussion. For the most part, these questions or ideas consisted of remarks based on personal experiences or interests.

The really good seminar discussions we had were the ones in which we were all very much focused on trying to understand and deal with some particular question. We had a very engaging discussion around the starting question "Where do ideas come from?" (Instructor)

It was early on when we read Sacks and we were discussing whether the mind is part of the brain or whether the mind is a purely physical thing, or whether the mind is spiritual, a part of soul. (Student)

The Seminar Outcomes

Seminar sections that reported a high level of satisfaction at the end of the semester shared a common trait; students could point to the specific learning outcomes derived from their participation in the seminars. Those outcomes were broadly of three distinct levels; first, they became able to look at the world at large or at a particular phenomenon from different perspectives; second, the seminar experience helped them discover their own interests and they felt inspired to pursue their line of inquiry on their own or continue to explore the topic in conversation with others; the third outcome was collective in nature and it was achieved when the entire class worked collaboratively to created knowledge together.

Looking at the world in a different way. Perhaps this was the most impactful outcome of all and it influenced students at many levels. For some students it was an eye-opening discovery about a topic they had never thought about before. As one student said, "I have never thought about most of the stuff in Oliver Sacks's book like autism." On other occasions, students gradually came to gain a richer understanding about a subject—as one instructor explained, "Their opinions and ideas were developing along the way, often coming to a more refined point or several points. They were able to articulate things they were not able to articulate before." The seminar also challenged students to look at a familiar topic in a new way:

> We had been discussing about something to do with hominid evolution and how viewing the human species in this context changed our perception of humanity. It was really intriguing and mind opening to look at the world in a different way. Conversation seemed to be fairly intense and everyone seemed interested in discussing this tangential subject. (Student)

> There was one specific time in which I felt that the program was completely worth it. Instructor Z brought in a guest speaker who spoke about learning styles, although I do recall that he was a

physics instructor. The topic that he spoke about hit my mind and completely revised my way of thinking. (Student)

Pursuing one's interest. Whenever there was an inspiring conversation, students left the seminar with the desire to further pursue the topic of discussion outside the seminar. They researched the topic in the library or through the internet, or through conversations with peers. Often, their findings and explorations were brought back into the seminar in the following sessions.

[The conversation in class] made me think more about the relationships between species and the mechanisms by which life evolves. When I got back to my room, I started looking up more information on theories on evolution and talking with other people about it. It was a rare occasion of inspiration,when I went out and sought knowledge. (Student)

Collaborative Teamwork to Create of Knowledge. "Hey, we came up with an idea!" This statement by a student supports this outcome, when students left the seminar feeling they had accomplished something together as a group. The collaborative accomplishment came in different forms; students may have come up with a new idea, reached a new level of understanding about a topic, gained capacity to look at a subject matter in a different way. From our perspective, this collective endeavor may constitute one of the most significant learning outcomes achieved in a seminar learning space. As one instructor described about the best seminar session of the semester, "It was really a situation where ideas were developed. It was as if the [students] had a critical mass of information and ideas, and they were to do something with it in a consistent manner during the entire class." According to the instructor, this session occurred during the tenth week of the course. Participants form another section reported a similar experience after the sixth or seventh week of the seminar.

As the instructor above suggests, this type of learning outcome cannot be achieved overnight, for it requires the creation of a common ground by recursive acts of sustaining the foundations of the seminar each time the seminar meets. A high level of seminar outcome requires that a social norm be established early on in the life of the seminar and the entire group needs to adhere to the agreed-upon social contract in terms of commitment and responsibility to personal as well as collective learning.

Sixteen

*My observations suggested that college teachers used some styles
more often than others. Thus, each cluster reflects the fact that
some blends of styles are dominant and others are secondary.
The primary or dominant styles are like the foreground in a
painting. They are easily seen and central to understanding
the artist's vision. The other qualities are like the background.
In effect, each individual style was like a different color on
an artist's palette. Like those colors, they could be blended
together. When teachers lecture, one sees the expert and
formal authority side of them much more easily than the
modeling, facilitative, or delegative parts of their styles.*

—ANTHONY GRASHA

B ecoming an experiential educator is a high art; and you the educator are
its prime instrument. How are we to conduct ourselves as educators,

keeping squarely focused on the goal of promoting learning for our students and clients? Should we be learner-centered and love our students into learning by creating hospitable learning spaces to draw out their budding interests? Should be we subject-centered and fully deliver the richness and depth of our special knowledge, developing learners' capacity for reflective thinking about our field? Should we focus on the pragmatic applications and implications of the ideas we present for the learner and the world; or should the emphasis be on the deep meaning of these ideas and concepts, their origins, and their connections to other ideas and fields of study? In the abstract we would probably answer all four questions affirmatively, but in a practical context there are very real constraints that require trade-offs between the learner-and-subject focus and the action-and-meaning focus—time limitations, learner needs, the amount of subject matter to be "covered," its complexity, and required evaluation standards to name a few. In addition, as educators we have different philosophies of education and priorities for the four perspectives based on our personalities, values, and job responsibilities.

Educator Roles and the Dynamic-Matching Model

One way we address these dilemmas as educators is by the role we adopt with learners. We play educator roles in educational institutions as teachers and administrators; in organizations as leaders, managers, and human-resource specialists; and in our personal lives as parents, spouses, and friends. We have created an educator-role framework to assist educators in the application of the ELT concepts of the learning cycle and learning style in a dynamic-matching model of teaching around the learning cycle (see figure 16.1). It describes four common educator roles—Facilitator, Subject Expert, Standard-Setter/Evaluator and Coach. Most of us adopt each of these roles to some extent in our educational and teaching activities.

Figure 16.1
Educator Roles and the Learning Cycle

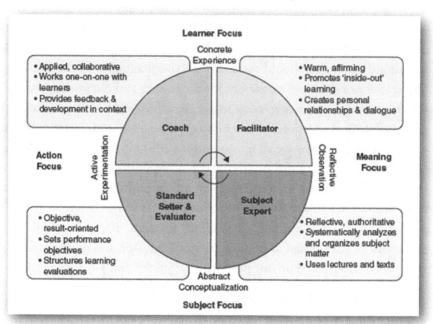

The Facilitator Role. When facilitating, educators help learners get in touch with their personal experience and reflect on it. They adopt a warm affirming style to draw out learners' interests, intrinsic motivation, and self-knowledge. They often do this by facilitating conversation in small groups. They create personal and trusting relationships with learners.

The Subject-Expert Role. In their role as subject expert, educators help learners organize and connect their reflections to the knowledge base of the subject matter. They adopt an authoritative, reflective style. They often teach by example, modeling and encouraging critical thinking as they systematically organize and analyze the subject-matter knowledge. This knowledge is often communicated through lectures and texts.

The Standard-Setter/Evaluator Role. As a standard-setter and evaluator, educators help learners master the application of knowledge and skill in order to meet performance requirements. They adopt an objective results-oriented style as they set the knowledge requirements needed for quality performance. They create performance activities for learners to evaluate their learning.

The Coaching Role. In the coaching role, educators help learners apply knowledge to achieve their goals. They adopt a collaborative, encouraging style, often working one-on-one with individuals to help them learn from experiences in their life context. They assist in the creation of personal development plans and provide ways of getting feedback on performance.

The Kolb Educator Role Profile (KERP), created as a self-assessment instrument, is designed to help educators sharpen their awareness of their educator-role preferences and to make deliberate choices about what works best in a specific situation using the dynamic-matching model. (For a detailed description of the KERP self-report instrument and its psychometrics see Kolb, Kolb, Passarelli, & Sharma, 2014. The KERP is a free assessment available at http://survey.learningfromexperience.com/.)

Most previous research on individual differences in educational approaches to education has focused on the concept of teaching style, conceived as personal characteristics and teaching methods in classroom teaching (e.g., Grasha, 1994; Kember & Gow, 1994; Trigwell & Prosser, 1996). To emphasize the relational perspective of experiential learning, the educator-role framework goes beyond individual teaching style to shift the educational paradigm from the educator acting *on* the learner to the educator acting *with* the learner. Because the learner and the educator are intertwined, the teacher must behave in ways that elicit or respond to the desired mode of the students. Educator roles do not directly correspond to the four learning modes, but are defined as bridging strategies between learning modes. Just as students can gain proficiency in integrating multiple learning modes, educators can gain flexibility in enacting the four educator roles.

The educator roles of coach, facilitator, subject expert, and standard-setter/evaluator are a patterned set of behaviors that emerge in response to the learning environment, including students and the learning task demands. Educator roles include teaching style, beliefs about teaching and learning, goals for the educational process, and instructional practices. To help learners move around the learning cycle, educators must adapt their role —moving from Facilitator, to Subject-Matter Expert, to Standard-Setter/Evaluator, to Coach. Each educator role helps students to learn through a specific part of the learning cycle. In the facilitator role, educators draw on the modes of concrete experience and reflective observation to help learners get in touch with their own experience and reflect on it. Subject-matter experts, using the modes of reflective observation and abstract conceptualization, help learners organize and connect their reflection to think about the knowledge base of the subject matter. They may provide models or theories for learners to use in subsequent analysis. The standard-setting and evaluating role uses abstract conceptualization and active experimentation to help students apply knowledge toward performance goals. In this role, educators closely monitor the quality of student performance toward the standards they set, and provide consistent feedback. Finally, in the coaching role they draw on concrete experience and active experimentation to help learners take action on personally meaningful goals. These roles can also be organized by their relative focus on the student vs. the subject and action vs. knowledge, as illustrated in figure 16.1.

How Successful Educators Use the Different Educator Roles

We have found that highly experienced and successful educators focus not solely on one of the educator roles but find a way to blend all of them into their work. In our interviews and observations of highly successful educators, we find that they tend to organize their educational activities in such a manner that they address all four learning cycle modes—experiencing, reflecting, thinking, and acting. As they do this, they lead learners around the cycle, shifting the role they play depending on which stage of the cycle they are addressing. In effect, the role they adopt helps to create a learning space designed to facilitate the transition from one learning mode to the other as shown in figure 16.1. Often this is done in a recursive fashion, repeating the cycle many times in a learning program as the learners gain secure footing at their current level, to use a scaffolding metaphor. The cycle then becomes a spiral with each passage through the cycle deepening and extending learners' understanding of the subject. On the basis of the actions that they take, educators can activate different learning modes in learners.

The Case of Professor King. We saw in Chapter 15 how the SAGES seminar instructors, who played such a central role in the success of the seminar, skillfully applied many of the experiential learning principles and learning-space concepts in the way they designed and conducted their courses. They did so, not by following a cookbook recipe, but by artfully applying these ideas in a way that was attuned to their unique personality and talents, the individual members of the seminar, the vital features of the subject matter, and the opportunities of the moment. Consider the case of one of the very best instructors we studied. Professor King was a law professor with a distinguished publication record and several teaching awards under his belt. When on one occasion one of our research team members visited his class, she observed an enthusiastic professor deliver an animated and content-rich lecture on epistemology. The students were intensely listening and totally absorbed in his lecture. She noticed that his lecture, while fascinating, lasted for no more than five to ten minutes; he abruptly stopped the talk and pivoted to the class and begin asking provocative questions related to the topic. Often he would offer controversial point of view and challenge students to offer a counter argument. He would freely move around the classroom, stand in front of the student who was talking to the class, nodding, making clear eye contact and eliciting more thoughts from the student through follow up questions.

In another class, a very quiet student who rarely spoke, raised his hand and offered his view in a very soft-spoken manner hardly audible to the rest of the class. Professor King immediately crossed the room, stood in front of his seat, bent over to hear him better, and repeated his points of view to the class so everyone could hear his opinion. His sensitive approach to students, as it turned out, was rooted in a bitter experience he had had as a young undergraduate student when in one class, his professor humiliated him by publicly criticizing his opinion as superficial and poorly constructed. "I was so devastated and ashamed, that I vowed to myself I will never, ever put my students through that kind of humiliation," said Professor King in one of the faculty meetings.

On her regular visit to the class, the research team member witnessed Professor King standing by the classroom door greeting and welcoming each student as they arrived. When we interviewed his students, they unanimously agreed that "Mr. King was very knowledgeable" and "caring." We could understand why students would respect him for his deep knowledge of the subject matter but were curious about his specific action and behavior that made students feel Professor King cared about them. One female student shared her experience of being overwhelmed by the course requirements, electives, and extracurricular activities and reached out to Professor King for help. Professor King immediately picked up the phone, made several phone calls to specific departments and effectively helped her make the course plan for the semester. "Now I know I don't have to worry about a thing. If I have a problem, I go to Mr. King," said the student. He valued nurturing strong and trusting relationships with his students. When Thanksgiving was around the corner, he invited the entire class to his house for a Thanksgiving dinner with his family, devoting part of the class to organize carpools to make sure all students were included.

When students claimed "Professor King was knowledgeable," we looked for the evidence of his knowledge and how he used his subject-matter expertise to help students think rigorously. The evidence of the depth of his knowledge was revealed during class discussions centered on a famous psychology book written by a well-known author in the field. While psychology was not his knowledge domain, Professor King pointed to the several flaws in the author's arguments. His inferences were based on the book's ill-formed and faulty assumptions that led the author to a flawed set of conclusions. As a result, what he claimed to be a ground-breaking finding, Professor King argued, was a speculative and unfounded description of unrelated facts. Professor King led students to come to this conclusion by alternating short and focused lectures on how scholars build their case, questioning students' understanding, and engaging the entire class to think and reason rigorously. This was no easy task. Students were challenged to work hard to develop a sound scholarly reasoning. As the research member observed, students' attention was focused and fully engaged the entire class session.

Professor King was very explicit about the academic standards he set for students. In the beginning of the semester, he told students they would learn how to think and write academically and to do so they were required to master the skill of scholarly reading and writing. He made available to them papers his students had written throughout the semester, with his comments included. By the end of the semester, it was clear that students had made substantial progress in their writing, from a superficial and simplistic thought process seen in their early writing to a more reasoned, nuanced, complex grasp of an idea backed by rich academic sources. We suspect this progress had a lot to do with the time and effort Professor King put into writing comments on the papers. His comments were not merely a letter grade "A" or "B" or cursory comments such as "good," "not clear," "be more specific." It had a prologue, middle, and epilogue, beginning with the initial assessment of student writing, how he or she could further improve his or her thinking and writing, and explicit words of encouragement assuring the student would be able to achieve the desired high-quality writing.

In the faculty community meeting we attended, we saw a very opinionated, impassioned, and almost combative Professor King arguing for educational reform, expressing frustration and impatience toward the politics of the university and forces operating against the innovative educational initiative. How Professor King saw his role as a professor became apparent in our one-on-one conversation. He cared deeply about teaching. He believed students can learn and succeed academically and his role was to make sure they achieved those goals. He communicated his belief in students' potentials clearly and loudly in his class. In one particular session devoted to Einstein, Professor King passionately told students they had potential to achieve what Einstein had accomplished. He was also aware how important it was for him to model a desirable behavior. He wanted his students to read broadly and think deeply about wide issues the world faces. "I share with my students the newspapers and magazines that I read outside my academic readings. I hope students would think, 'If King reads *New York Times* and *Atlantic Monthly* maybe I should try to read them too.'"

In one particular class toward the end of the semester, a few students were gathered around the white board scribbling what looked like a cartoon character. On a close examination it was a drawing of a mouse with a moustache and round framed eyeglasses, wearing oversized baggy shorts. One student drew an arrow out from the mouse's face and wrote: "Mr. King." A few minutes later Professor King walked into the classroom, looked at the drawing and said with a grin, "This is a darn good drawing."

The King case shows a highly skilled teacher who addressed all four perspectives—the subject-matter-and-learner focus and the action-and-meaning focus by fluidly shifting the role he took with students. Clearly his role as a *subject-matter expert* was his strong suit. However, his command of expert knowledge would have had little impact on his students' learning had he not also adopted a *facilitator* role, establishing trusting relationships with them. He attended to their level of conceptual understanding through skillful facilitation of discussion about their interests, thoughts, and ideas. Adopting a *standard-setter/evaluator* role, he set clear learning objectives and expected high-standard work from his students. He also established a *coaching* role with his students, providing frequent feedback and consistent coaching and guidance on how to achieve their learning goals. Without this coaching, his students may have shifted their effort to merely "memorizing" the concepts and "making the grade" as their primary goal, with little change in the way they felt about themselves and thought about his ideas at a deeper level. By successively taking the roles of facilitator, subject-matter expert, standard-setter/evaluator, and coach with students at the appropriate moment, Professor King helped them to spiral through numerous turns around the learning cycle developing their confidence, deep understanding, and scholarly skills.

The Practice of Dynamic Matching

The ELT principle of dynamic-matching offers the experiential educator a more complex, but more realistic model for guiding educational practice than the stereotypical characterization of the experiential educator as a facilitator whose role is often parodied with phrases like "What I hear you saying" or dodging questions with "What do you think?" The experiential learning facilitator is often seen as a sharply contrasting approach to traditional education where a teacher is a subject-matter expert who transmits information and knowledge to the student. This "outside-in" approach is contrasted with the "inside-out" approach of experiential learning that seeks to tap the internal interest and intrinsic motivation of learners and builds on their prior knowledge and experience. The educator's role is to facilitate this process of "drawing out" (the root meaning of the word educate) by creating a hospitable, safe space for learners to reflect on and make meaning from their experiences. Facilitators believe that learners can learn on their own and that their role is to remove obstacles and create conditions where learners can do so. Their role is not to instruct, provide answers and personal advice, or tell people what they should learn.

However, the simple notion that to become an experiential educator one must become a nondirective facilitator who eschews lectures, evaluation, and advice is an oversimplification of the complexities of the educator-learner relationship. The techniques of facilitation such as debriefing learning experiences, drawing out and building on the prior knowledge of learners, and facilitating a climate of trust and open communication are but one facet of a holistic process of learning from experience that also includes expert knowledge input, evaluation, and coaching on learning strategies.

The ELT concepts of the learning cycle and learning style suggest a dynamic-matching model of "teaching around the learning cycle" where learners, regardless of their style, are sometimes matched with the learning activity and are sometimes challenged to stretch themselves to use a less-preferred style. Perini and Silver (in Varlas, 2010) argue that learning style assessments should not be used to match the teaching approach with a learner's style but instead should follow the dynamic-matching model:

> In our experience, learning-style assessments have proven to be wonderful tools for promoting conversations about learning, building teachers' and students' metacognitive capacities, increasing student engagement, and helping teachers find hooks into content for struggling students. We've also found benefits for differentiation: teachers who assess their own and students' styles are typically more

willing and able to implement a wide variety of instructional strategies in their classrooms…Along with Bernice McCarthy and David
Kolb, and supported by Robert Sternberg's research, we've long argued that teaching to the full range of styles is far better and more
consistently leads to higher achievement across grade and content
levels than confining students to a single style of instruction. (p. 2)

Figure 16.2 shows the nine-style experiential learning styles and the corresponding educator roles that match them; for example, the coach role is
most appropriate for the experiencing, imagining, and reflecting styles.

Figure 16.2
Educator Roles and the Nine Learning Styles

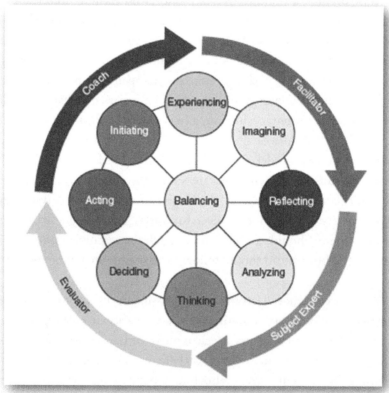

The dynamic-matching model suggests that matching style with role is important to connect with and engage learners. Raschick, Maypole, and Day (1998) find that social-work students whose learning styles were similar to their field supervisors along the active experimentation-reflective observation continuum rate their field experience with them more positively. The finding is most relevant for the supervisors at the beginning point of the learning cycle, when matching their teaching techniques to learners' preferences offers encouragement to move through the rest of the learning cycle. Individual learning styles can be an entry point through which learners enter a particular learning space, but most learning requires that they continue to actively move around the learning cycle using other learning styles to acquire increasingly complex knowledge and skills and capacity to adapt to the wider demands of a given learning environment.

While Figure 16.2 depicts an idealized sequential progression through the educator roles and learning styles in most cases, a curriculum design will be based on a sequence of activities and instructional techniques that fits the subject matter and learning objectives that may or may not fit such an orderly progression. In considering a design, it is useful to consider for each segment the teaching role to adopt, the learning style that to engage, and the choice of instructional technique best suited to the learning style and the role (see Appendix 3).

In addition to considering the relationship between educator role and the learning style of the learner, one must also consider the match of learning approach with the subject matter. Willingham (2005, 2009), in fact, considers this more important than matching learning and teaching style. All of this must be determined in the light of the multiple performance, learning, and development objectives we have for most educational activities. Professions with precise performance requirements such as surgery or software development make the standard-setter/evaluator role paramount and require development of thinking, deciding, and acting learning styles. Art education, on the other hand, may make the facilitator role paramount and require development of experiencing, imagining, and reflecting learning styles (Eickmann, Kolb, & Kolb, 2004).

Along with specialized academic training, teachers often have objectives concerning the growth and creativity of their students. In making students more well-rounded, the aim is to take care of the weaknesses in the students' learning styles to stimulate growth in their ability to learn from a variety of learning perspectives. Educating is holistic. It is about developing the whole person. Educating the whole person means that the goal of education is not solely the cognitive knowledge of facts, but also includes development of social and emotional maturity. In ELT terms, our primary role as educators is to facilitate learners' integrated development in affective, perceptual, cognitive, and behavioral realms.

Our primary role as educators then, is to guide learners around the learning cycle and transform the way they feel, perceive, think, and act in a sustained manner. Scaffolding is the key technique for accomplishing this transition. In scaffolding, the educator tailors the learning process to the individual needs and developmental level of the learner. Scaffolding provides the structure and support necessary to progressively build knowledge. The model of teaching around the cycle described above provides a framework for this scaffolding process. When an educator has a personal relationship with a learner, he or she can skillfully intervene to reinforce or alter a learner's pattern of interaction with the world. This approach requires competence in relating to learners in complex ways—ways that help them feel, perceive, think, and behave differently. These ways of relating are characterized in the multiple roles an educator plays in relationship to the learners and the objective of the learning endeavor.

Learning Flexibility and Dynamic Matching

The dynamic-matching model recognizes that not only do educators have individual role preferences, and learners have preferred learning styles, but also that both can develop the capacity to adapt their respective roles and styles to one another and to the learning situation at hand.

Educator Role Flexibility. It is widely believed that educators teach the way they learn (Davidson, 1990; Hartel, 1995). Some studies even use style measures to assess teaching approach (Allinson, Hayes, & Davis, 1994; Onwuegbuzie & Daley, 1998). In our research examining the relationship between the educators' role preferences and their learning styles as measured by the KLSI 4.0 (Kolb & Kolb, 2011) and KERP, we found a highly significant relationship (p <.0001) between the abstract learning styles of Analyzing, Thinking and Deciding, and subject-matter orientation as indicated by preferences for the Expert and Evaluator roles. Concrete learners, on the other hand, are learner-oriented, preferring the Facilitator role in particular (Kolb, Kolb, Passarelli, & Sharma, 2014). These results are consistent with predictions that concrete feeling-oriented educators connect more with individual learners while abstract educators connect more with ideas.

Kosower and Berman (1996), however, argue that faculty members are capable of learning to teach in ways that are incongruent with their own learning styles: "Because we all engage in all of the strategies to some degree, it seems to be more a matter of willingness to learn rather than ability" (p. 217). Baker, Simon, and Bazeli (1987) contend that teaching is an art requiring the instructor to select from among a wide variety of instructional strategies to reach students with a diversity of learning preferences.

Milne, James, Keegan, and Dudley (2002) develop an observational method to assess mental health trainers' transaction patterns along with their impact on student learning and a training program designed to enable trainers to teach to all learning modes. The results of the study indicate that during the baseline phase, the observed teaching method was primarily didactic in nature and accounted for the greatest impact (46.4 percent) on learner behavior in the reflection mode of the learning cycle, followed by smaller overall impacts on the remaining phases of the cycle. In the intervention phase by contrast, the greatest impact of the trainer's behavior was on learners' concrete experience (59.5 percent), followed by reflective observation (33 percent), and active experimentation (4.5 percent) phases of the learning cycle. They concluded that the intervention phase produced trainers's behaviors that promoted learners' ability to take advantage of the full range of the experiential learning cycle thus maximizing their learning outcomes.

As education becomes more learner-centered, Harrelson and Leaver-Dunn (2002) suggest that experiential learning requires traditional subject-centered teachers to assume a facilitator mind-set, which might be difficult for some. Lipshitz (1983) underscores the complexity of roles for an experiential educator who needs to have a firm grasp of the relevant conceptual material, and develop sensitivity and skill in managing learners' emotional reactions to the learning process. Learners may also react to the shifting role of the educator from that of knowledge purveyor to one that creates a learning environment that facilitates a student-centered learning process. Lindblom-Ylanne, Trigwell, Nevgi, and Ashwin (2006) in their study of higher education teachers in Finland found that teachers do change their approach to teaching from a teacher-centered information-transfer model to a learner-centered conceptual-development approach, depending on the educational context. Specifically, they found that teachers were more teacher-centered in their usual teaching context of mainstream courses and more learner-centered in their less usual teaching contexts. They conclude, "In the less usual teaching contexts teachers are possibly more open to new ideas and new teaching methods. Furthermore, the class size might be smaller, giving teachers more possibilities for using student-centered methods" (2006, p. 295).

McGoldrick, Battle, and Gallagher (2000) indicate that the less control instructors exert on the students' experiences, the more effective the learning outcome will be. However, instructors may run the risk of losing control over course structure and failing to keep the learning activities bounded within a specific time frame. Most of the risks associated with the experiential method, contend the authors, can be mitigated through careful planning, unambiguous course structure, establishing of clear expectations, and maintaining a firm deadline for each class activity. Furthermore, learners will have differing levels of interest as well as difficulties with certain stages of the learning cycle. It is incumbent upon the educator to grasp the diverse needs of learners and be aware of the challenges that some will face in the various phases of the cycle.

Learners' Learning Flexibility. Studies also show that learners are able to flex their learning styles according to the demands of different learning tasks. Several studies suggest that students shift their learning strategies to match the learning demands of a particular discipline (Cornett, 1983; Entwistle, 1981; Kolb, 1984; Ornstein, 1977). Jones, Mokhtari, & Reichard (2003) examined the extent to which community-college students' learning style preferences vary as a function of discipline. They found significant differences in students' learning style preference across four different subject-area disciplines: English, math, science, and social studies. The results indicate that 83 percent of the 103 participants switched learning styles for two or more disciplines, suggesting that students are capable of flexing their learning strategies to respond to the discipline-specific learning requirements. By understanding the dynamic-matching model, they may become more capable of deliberate experiential learning (see chapter 6).

Summary

The KERP and the dynamic-matching model offer experiential educators a framework to guide their practice. Becoming an experiential educator involves more than just being a facilitator or matching learning style with teaching style. Experiential education is a complex relational process that involves balancing attention to the learner and to the subject matter while also balancing reflection on the deep meaning of ideas with the skill of applying them. The dynamic-matching model for "teaching around the learning cycle" describes four roles that educators can adopt to do so—Facilitator, Subject Expert, Standard-Setter/Evaluator, and Coach. Using the KERP, we find that to some extent educators do tend to teach the way they learn, finding that those with concrete learning styles are more learner-centered, preferring the facilitator role; while those with abstract learning styles are more subject-centered, preferring the expert and evaluator roles. However, with practice, both learners and educators can develop the flexibility to use all roles and styles to create a more powerful and effective process of teaching and learning.

Seventeen

EDUCATOR ROLE BEST PRACTICES

*Passion, hope, doubt, fear, exhilaration, weariness,
colleagueship, loneliness, glorious defeat, hollow victories—
how can one begin to capture the reality of teaching in a
single word or phrase? The truth is that teaching is frequently
a gloriously messy pursuit in which surprise, shock and risk
are endemic. Teaching is the equivalent of white water
rafting. Periods of apparent calm are interspersed with
sudden frenetic turbulence…In the midst of teaching,
teachers make a dazzlingly quick series of judgments about
what to do next…These intuitive and immediate judgments
are based not only on calmly reasoned discussions but on
viscerally felt, "gut" instincts concerning which actions best
fit certain situations. They are informed by recollections of
similar situations…This process occurs almost simultaneously
so that reflection is perceived as concurrent with action.*

—STEVEN BROOKFIELD

In the previous chapter we described a dynamic-matching model for teaching around the experiential learning cycle where learners, regardless of their style, are sometimes matched with the learning activity and are sometimes challenged to stretch themselves to use a less-preferred style. By successively taking the roles of facilitator, subject-matter expert, standard-setter/evaluator, and coach with students at the appropriate moment, the experiential educator helps learners address all four learning modes—experiencing, reflecting, thinking, and acting—by leading them around the learning cycle; shifting the role they play depending on which stage of the cycle they are addressing. In effect, the role they adopt helps to create a learning space designed to facilitate the transition from one learning mode to the other. Often this is done in a recursive fashion, repeating the cycle many times in a learning program. The cycle then becomes a spiral with each passage through the cycle deepening and extending learners' understanding of the subject.

In the hands of experienced educators, this role-shifting can become an art form choreographed for student learning, with each learning activity springing from the educator's deliberate choice as to what role may be most suited to respond to students' unique learning needs in a specific context. From the perspective of the experiential learning cycle, the four roles have a nested and interconnected relationship, each supporting the other, and the absence of one role may disrupt the integrity of the holistic learning practices that flow out of the creative tension among the four roles.

How can we develop and sustain such a creative tension in our practice to ensure that our students develop attitude, intellectual curiosity, and discipline to inquire in depth? Achieving this creative tension may not be easy. As powerful as the concept of dynamic matching may be, in practice the craft of teaching around the learning cycle by adjusting one's roles to guide student learning may not come naturally at first. It involves examining one's educational values and adopting a deliberate learning approach to improving teaching practices and skills in taking on the four roles.

How does my awareness of the different educational roles I play impact students' learning? What can I do to improve my craft of teaching around the learning cycle? We will explore these questions by looking into the distinct nature and the characteristics of each of the four educational roles and how they come together as a unified whole. The sections below contain the best advice we have been able to find about the best practices for conduct of each role. It is interesting to note, in relation to the holistic interconnectedness of the roles, that in most cases we see that the best practice within a given role includes use of other roles. So, for example, the subject-matter expert role works best when it includes an awareness of the learners' perspectives on the subject. The coaching role would be more effective if learners understand that the standard by which their work would be judged is clear, fair, and just.

The Subject-Matter Expert

An expert is someone who has an extensive knowledge and experience about a specific domain. This expertise is a prerequisite to qualify as a teacher, as Dewey emphasized when he invited educators to be equipped with "an abundance of knowledge in the subject matter to the point of overflow." (1933, p. 338). Yet, an extensive knowledge about one's area of expertise by itself would not meet the criterion of becoming a true expert experiential educator. The intellectual preparation of teachers, says Dewey, should cover much wider ground beyond knowledge of textbooks or fixed lesson plans; it should encompass the knowledge and understanding of how students organize and create meaning of their experiences:

> The problem of the pupils is found in the subject matter; the problem of teachers is what the minds of pupils are doing with the subject matter. Unless the teacher's mind has mastered the subject matter in advance, unless it is thoroughly at home in it, he will not be free to give full time and attention to observation and interpretation of the pupil's intellectual reactions. The teacher must be alive to all forms of bodily expression of mental condition—to puzzlement, boredom, mastery, the dawn of an idea, feigned attention, tendency to show off, etc. He must be aware not only of their meaning; but of their meaning as indicative of the state of mind of the pupil,

his degree of observation and comprehension. (Dewey, 1933, pp. 338–339)

The exceptional college teachers Bain (2004) identified in his study embody Dewey's vision of subject-matter experts who rely on two kinds of knowledge to help their students learn. First, they are well-versed in the knowledge of their disciplines and have a deep understanding of the nature of thinking within their fields. Second, they use their ability to "think about their own thinking" as a starting point to understand how their students might learn. They put their metacognitive skills to use in organizing the subject matter from basic to complex concepts, raise provocative questions to stimulate students' thinking and use effective strategies to simplify and clarify students' comprehension of subjects.

Bain also found several accomplished scholars in their fields who were squarely focused on preparing lectures that reflected the highest standard and cutting-edge knowledge in their field with no regard as to whether their students grasped the concept or not. Those sophisticated lectures, Bain observed, were of little help for developing a complex intellectual and scientific understanding in their students. One may argue that these accomplished experts have successfully created a learning space where they could methodically and rigorously craft their own thinking but ironically, they were the only ones in it; their students were barely at the margin of the learning space, if not totally outside it.

Bain's insightful description about these experts who were totally absorbed in their subject matter and oblivious to their students begs the question as to why and how they came to acquire such a mind-set. The study on expertise knowledge transfer by Hinds, Patterson, and Pfeffer (2001) described in Chapter 14 suggests an answer. The very process of expertise acquisition, the authors suggest, points to the challenges subject-matter experts may confront in the process of conveying their superior knowledge to the novice learners. Unlike novices, experts have a far more sophisticated way of organizing and accessing knowledge coupled with extensive experience in applying this knowledge to solve a variety of problems in their domain. When it comes to transferring this knowledge to novice learners, however, experts may suffer from an "availability bias," noted Hinds (1999) in a different study, where she describes a process whereby experts attempt to predict the experience of novices based on the recall of their own novice experiences. As it turned out their prediction was disrupted by their inability to recall their own novice experiences accurately. Experts relied heavily on their current experience and were unable to connect to the experiences of the novice minds compared to those with less expertise with experiences that were closer to the novice learners.

It is worth noting that one of the key findings in the Hinds et al. (2001) study points to the crucial role subject-matter experts play in educating the novices: while those with less expertise were more effective in training novices to perform concrete, specific tasks, experts were more successful in preparing novices to function in a variety of contexts and environments subject to volatility and frequent changes. Under such conditions, when novices were called to adjust their tasks across different dimensions, experts were able to convey their abstract and sophisticated knowledge that can be better transferred between different tasks.

This brings us back to Dewey's critical idea of the dual-knowledge subject-matter experts need to embody in the educational process: first, being totally at home with their abstract critical-domain knowledge and second, having a solid mastery of pedagogical-content knowledge about how their students acquire and master those abstract concepts. Dewey reminds us of the power of abstraction and the pivotal roles subject-matter experts play in instilling in our students the value of abstract meaning making:

> Abstracting gets the mind emancipated from the conspicuous familiar traits that hold it fixed by their very familiarity. Thereby it acquires ability to dig underneath the already known to some unfamiliar property or relation that is intellectually much more significant because it makes possible a more analytic and more extensive inference. (1933, p. 277)

Abstraction frees learners from a fixed and naïve worldview. This freedom is obtained by the capacity to generalize one's experience to a broader life context. If the role of education, as Dewey defines, is *"an emancipation and enlargement of experience,"* then, subject-matter experts are in a powerful position to expand their students' worldview by getting closer to their students' experiences. In order to do so, as we discussed in Chapter 12, experts cannot make their mature and trained mind the starting point of their students' education. The subjects matter needs to be organized, reconceptualized, and communicated in the language closer to the learner's experiences and their appropriate stage of intellectual development. A subject matter will come to fruition in the lives of the learners in a truly transformative way only if educators adopt a holistic stance toward their role as subject-matter experts.

Shulman (cited in Artzt & Armour-Thomas, 1998) articulated this holistic stance by proposing a unified concept of teacher knowledge as a multifaceted construct that encompassed subject-matter knowledge, pedagogical knowledge, and knowledge about how students learn. Building on Shuman's concept, Artzt and Armour-Thomas developed the Teacher Metacognitive Framework to better understand the role of metacognition in teachers' classroom practice in mathematics. They used the instrument to investigate the difference between experienced and novice math teachers' metacognitive thought processes as they were applied to plan instruction, monitor students' learning, and adapt their teaching methods in the classroom. The study also compared teachers' underlying belief system about student role, teacher role, and learning goals and how those belief systems influenced their approach to teaching and learning.

The experienced teachers planned their lessons with a focus on problem-solving to promote both procedural and conceptual understanding of the subject matter. In order to achieve their learning goal, they organized the learning tasks based on students' prior knowledge, and focused their attention to arouse their interests and curiosity. Examples of teachers' comments reveal their thought process:

In general, they have difficulties with proofs. So I thought I'd start with simple diagrams and deal with things they knew and were pretty confident with already.

I wanted students to really understand the logarithmic rules and understand their important uses. (1998, p. 14)

During instruction, these teachers made sure the content, pedagogy, and the knowledge about their students had unity and integrity. As a result, most students were on task and actively involved in the learning activities. They enacted a learner-centered approach to teaching by encouraging their students to think and reason well, articulate their thoughts, and listen to each other's ideas. As one teacher commented:

The idea is I would like them to talk more than I do. Let them listen to each other because that's how you learn. I didn't want just an answer. I wanted an explanation and I wanted an explanation that everyone would hear. (1998, p. 14)

Finally, they assessed their own teaching based on students' understanding of the subject matter, and were willing to revise and improve their instructional methods to make the materials interesting and accessible:

By their feedback, I thought they understood what I was talking about.

I didn't get to walk around enough to help. Some students were left confused.

I should have shown that some expressions are really very difficult to handle without logs. (1998, p. 15)

The novice teachers showed a remarkably different metacognitive process toward planning, delivery, and revision of their instructions. Their knowledge, learning goals, and beliefs were directed toward covering the content sorely for the purpose of skill development. They exhibited limited knowledge of the mathematical content and vague understanding about teaching methods and how students learned.

> They have to learn the characteristics of a parabola, mainly the turning point, axis of symmetry, and do the formula for the parabola.

> It is an average class with good students.

> I just wanted to do one example and get right into the graphing. (1998, p. 15)

The instructional sequences were poorly organized, the level of difficulty of the learning tasks unbalanced. The class atmosphere was tense and students appeared to be most of the time disengaged. They were more interested in telling students when they were right or wrong and readily provided the correct answers without engaging students in exploring the questions in depth. They were inattentive to how students were learning and failed to monitor and adjust their teaching strategy from their original instructional plan, even when it was clear students were confused and lost.

Their assessments of their instruction delivery were simplistic and focused primarily on inadequate content and student behavior. Several teachers suggested they would have been more effective if they had "covered more."

> I think we went too slow. I should have done more.

> Some kids were still not paying as much attention as I'd like. (1998, p. 16)

Another poignant finding of their study came from teachers who espoused metacognitive beliefs about the goals of student learning with understanding, but whose instructional practice was not conducive to accomplishing this goal. They often asked low-level questions that required simple one-word answers, they judged student responses based on right or wrong answers and ended up solving the problems themselves without including students' input. These teachers believed it was more efficient to provide the answer to the students rather than having them discover it on their own. Similarly, other teachers articulated the importance of developing both procedural and conceptual knowledge and believed in actively involving students in their own learning, yet in practice demonstrated insufficient and superficial knowledge of the content, teaching method, and understanding of student learning. As result, their content was poorly organized and delivered at a fast pace, leaving students confused and lost. They expressed the belief that when time is at a premium, covering the content must take precedence over student learning with understanding.

Finally, the authors noted that many of the teachers who lacked metacognitive skills were unaware of the importance of monitoring and regulating student understanding during class instruction. Unless teachers accurately assess what the students are "getting" or "not getting" in the here and now, it makes it difficult to change and adjust their instructional plan and teaching strategies to enhance student learning.

Tips for the Subject-Matter Expert Role. As subject-matter experts, we are constantly required to grapple with the multiple demands of our knowledge domain, state-of-the-art educational methods, and a deep understanding about how students learn. While there may not be a magic bullet to master our role as the subject-matter expert, we certainly can take an incremental stance toward getting closer to our vision. The following are some tips we have gleaned from the literature about how to be an effective subject-matter expert.

Connect subject matter to students' interests. Outstanding teachers extend their curiosity and interest beyond their areas of expertise hoping to find an entry point into their students' passions and deeply held interests. While their ultimate goal may be to get their students to develop capacity to make accurate diagnosis or to master a thinking process required in an engineering field, they are open to draw their knowledge from diverse fields in their constant search for ways to capture students' attention and gradually direct their interest to the subject matter at hand (Bain, 2004).

Organize subject matter around concepts central to the discipline. Regardless of academic disciplines or professions learners decide to choose, they need to nurture abstract-thinking abilities required to succeed in the specific field or profession they are about to enter. How can I develop in my students the conceptual ability to think like a physician, writer, mathematician, or anthropologist? To help learners progressively achieve higher-order reasoning abilities, it is important to organize the subject matter sequentially from fundamental concepts to complex ones. For example, unless students fully grasp the concept of algebra it is impossible for them to tackle calculus in the future. Students will be able to clear each milestone if they are provided with meaningful and rich experiences that will enhance their abilities to reason at a higher level of complexity.

Imagine students' minds. In preparation for his class, a history teacher made it a common practice to imagine the mental steps his students would need to take to reach the learning goal. He would mentally visualize and walk through the content himself first. When the time came to work with students in real time, this strategy would give him the freedom and opportunity to grasp how their mind worked, where they may stumble to understand, bringing to the surface what needed to be adjusted to meet the students' learning needs (Green, 2014, p. 221).

Less is more. Learning is about creating meaning. "Covering" more content does not automatically translate into learners' ability to think in depth. As we described in Chapter 3, working memory is limited and too much information input causes the unprocessed information in working memory to be lost. The time it takes to create episodic memory through experiential learning brings the benefits of full-cycle learning.

Draw out mistakes. Excellent teachers treat students' mistakes as a golden opportunity for understanding how they learn. The best teachers, in fact, make drawing out mistakes as one of the primary purposes of their teaching. This view is widely shared among Japanese teachers who adopted a unique two-step teaching strategy to correct students' misunderstanding. Teachers adopt a first strategy, *kikan-shido* (between-desks instruction), by observing students' effort to solve problems, and provide them with extra help to clear their confusions and mistakes. The second approach, *kikan-junshin* (between-desk patrolling), involves observing students' work in silence, without comment. When mistakes or confusion arise, teachers simply make a note and let the students see their misunderstanding on their own. As a next step, teachers make sure all students see the mistakes by opening up the subject to class discussions (Green, 2014, pp. 277–278).

Punctuate the experience. Excellent teachers routinely incorporate a summary of the main learning point in their teaching activities. Their approaches may vary, but they have their own unique approach to highlight the main ideas or pivotal questions in order to bring into focus what they have learned in each class session. Several SAGES professors skillfully accomplished this by making sure students summarized their main thoughts and ideas coherently and understood what they had accomplished at the end of each session. Japanese teachers instituted the practice of *matome* (summary of main points) having students write down what they have learned at the end of the class and share that with the group. Through sharing, students were given the opportunity to learn from each other and have the chance to revise their learning points. Summarizing helps students tie their thoughts and concepts together, giving continuity and direction to their ideas to be explored in the following sessions (Green, 2014).

Study learning. Outstanding teachers approach their craft of teaching with a scientific mind-set. Finnish teachers allocate more time researching teaching methods and student learning than classroom time. They believe they would be far more effective as teachers if their teaching were backed with well-researched educational theories, methods, and practices. Their training involves observing experienced teachers in classrooms and delivering lessons to different groups of students under the supervision and guidance of experienced mentors and supervisors (Sahlberg, 2010).

Japanese teachers approach teaching as a collaborative endeavor, rigorously studying and critiquing each other's teaching practices. They conceptualize and test what practices may work in the classroom and create a bucket list of successful activities labeled by the learning objectives they are supposed to accomplish. For example, *neriage* describes the process of effectively using students' ideas to achieve the learning goal, whereas *tsuma-zuki* points to the mistakes to be shared in class to generate rich learning opportunities (Green, 2010).

The Facilitator

"I am not a facilitator. I am a teacher, trying to facilitate my students' learning," said Paulo Freire during the panel discussion at the 1994 ICEL conference. It was obvious that Freire was troubled and concerned about the way in which the word "facilitator" has been routinely uttered and often misused in the educational circles as the ultimate gold standard of experiential education, with little understanding about the vital relationship that exists between facilitation and learning. As Freire's words suggest, facilitation is the critical starting point of our dynamic engagement and effort to promote significant change and learning in our students.

A true facilitator of learning, says Carl Rogers (1969), is someone who sets learners free to live and learn as individuals in process. Such facilitation of significant learning is not achieved through lectures, class plans, or teaching techniques, but rather it is born out of a "certain attitudinal quality which exists in the personal *relationship* between the facilitator and the learner." (Roger, 1969, p. 106). Rogers first came upon this finding in the client-therapist relationship in the field of psychotherapy and later he found the same relationship existed in teacher-student interactions in the field of education. Here are the three qualities that Roger found to be essential for facilitators to establish a trusting relationship with the learners:

Genuineness. Facilitators are much more likely to be effective when they enter into relationship with learners as real persons. This means being themselves, genuinely being able to live and accept what they are experiencing. From this vantage point, one is free to experience both negative and positive feelings; one can be enthusiastic, disappointed, empathetic, or frustrated, without imposing those feelings on students. If one is aware and accepting of those feelings, one can communicate them to one's students in a sensible and appropriate manner.

Rogers once came to know a teacher who expressed genuine frustration toward her students' inability to maintain order and cleanliness in the classroom. This is how she expressed her feelings:

> I told the children that I am a neat, orderly person by nature and that mess was driving me to distraction. Did they have a solution? (1969, p. 108)

Students readily responded to her frustration and request to come up with a solution and found a way to keep the room clean and neat. The teacher later acknowledged, "I used to get upset and feel guilty when I became angry. I finally realized children could accept *my* feeling too" (1969, p. 108).

Prizing the Learner. Successful facilitators have developed a trusting attitude toward their students, prizing their feelings and opinions as separate individuals with worth in their own right. As Rogers observed, the facilitators who possess this quality care deeply for learners but in a nonpossessive manner. They accept and value learners for their imperfections as well as their many potentialities. Here is how a student described her experience of being "prized" by such a teacher:

> I still feel close to you, as though there were some tacit understanding between us, almost a conspiracy. This adds to the in-class participation on my part because I feel that at least one person in the group will react, even when I am not sure of others. It does not matter really whether your reaction is positive or negative, it just IS. Thank you. (1969, p. 110)

Empathic Understanding. When facilitators have an empathic understanding, they are able to see how a student feels and reacts from inside. Such sensitivity helps establish a climate where students' change is self-initiated. From this vantage point, empathic understanding is sharply different from evaluative understanding that often hides underneath a judgmental undertone. Facilitators with a deep sense of empathic understanding do not approach learners with the aim of "correcting," "analyzing," or "judging" their behaviors or attitudes. In the presence of a sensitive and empathic teacher, learners experience freedom to grow and learn, charting their own learning path.

How do students who experienced genuineness, positive regard, and empathy from teachers learn, change, and grow? Rogers found evidence for this question in numerous research studies. As one study suggests, when teacher attitudes were real and accepting, students' responses were "productive" with their attention focused on discovery, exploration, and experimentation. When teacher behaviors were perceived to be judging, directing, or reproving, students' responses tended to be "reproductive," limited to parroting, guessing, memorizing, and eager to please the teachers (McDonald & Zarett, 1966. Cited in Rogers, 1969).

The unconditional positive regard Rogers proposes rests upon teacher's deep trust in learners' potentialities to grow, learn, and make choices to live their lives toward self-actualization. Being real, accepting, and empathic is not easy. As we act from a place of a deep trust, we may confront our students' cynicism, as well as our own skepticism and mistrust for the possibilities and change that these qualities promise to bring about in our students. We can only learn and slowly grow into our genuineness, says Rogers, by living our feelings, being aware of them, and taking the risk of sharing them as they are:

> I can only state that I started my career with the firm view that individuals must be manipulated for their own good; I only came to the attitudes I described, and the trust in the individual which is implicit in them, because I found that these attitudes were so much more potent in producing learning and constructive change. Hence, I believe it is only by risking himself in these new ways that the teacher can *discover*, for himself, whether or not they are effective, whether or not they are for him. (1969, p. 115)

Tips for the Facilitator Role. In Rogers's terms, a true facilitation born out of those intrinsic qualities can be incorporated into the following concrete actions:

Establish a climate of trust and safety. In creative ways, communicate to the learners your fundamental trust in their genuine desire to learn and grow. Your trust will help unleash in them a positive learning identity and give them freedom to pursue their deeply held interests. Recall in Chapter 5 how Sam Devries, the math teacher, transformed his students' math-learning identity from a negative-self ("I don't do math") to a confident-self ("I can totally do math").

Elicit and support a meaningful purpose of learning. Learners need to feel free to embrace learning purposes worth pursuing. Accept diversity of purposes even it means to be open to contradictory and conflicting aims of the individual learners. It is counterproductive to force a unified purpose upon an individual or a group if such unity does not exist. A far more significant learning can be generated if each learner is self-motivated to pursue his or her own interest.

Promote inside-out learning. Provide rich resources and opportunities for learners to find their interests from inside out. We often run the risk of "making things interesting" from outside in, after the subject matter has been thoroughly organized from the teacher's perspective and expect learners to "get interested" in the materials or activities. As we learned from Dewey (see Chapter 11), this approach is misguided in two ways. First, the content or activities are organized independently from the learners' genuine interests. Second, it reduces the activities into a mere "shiny objects" to keep hold of learners' attention for a brief moment. Meaningful learning activities should help learners make connections and appreciate the relationships with what they already value.

Encourage expressions of thoughts, feelings, and emotions. Allow learners to express their deep feelings of conflict, pain, joy, and sorrow. A rich climate of learning will be enhanced if learners are able to freely express those strong emotions. Thoughts and feelings are not disconnected.

Intellectual maturity is supported by authentic expression of feelings and emotions.

Make yourself available as a learner. As the trust and acceptance becomes established in the learning space, share your feelings and thoughts as a member of the class. Your comments or views of learners' experiences should be accepted as genuine reactions free of judgments or evaluations.

Accept your own limitations. Be honest with yourself. You can only give freedom to learners to the extent that you are prepared and willing to give such freedom. Do not take risks if you feel you are not ready. In many instances, you may find your actions and attitudes to be incongruent with a learner-centered approach. At times, you may find yourself unable to trust your students' motivation to learn, or you may feel angry, resentful, and judgmental toward their attitudes. When those feelings arise, stay close to them and own them, as they are without guilt or judgment. Only then, you can engage in an authentic and growth-promoting interaction with your students.

The Coach

In the coaching role, educators' primary objective is to help learners apply knowledge to achieve their goals within a specific learning context. In this sense the coaching role is perhaps the most emergent and active role among the four educator roles. This is where the rubber meets the road so to speak, as educators are required to balance the creative tension among four key interconnected learning components: the coaching relationship, the content, the learning goal, and the learning context, to guide learners to achieve their purposes. To be effective in this role, the educator needs to adjust the content to the individual learner's current skill level while monitoring her progress toward acquiring and demonstrating higher-order skills within a specific learning context. In this sense, in the coaching role the educators find themselves continuously cycling through the learning cycle with the learners while actively exploring and experimenting with effective ways to transfer knowledge, the best way to apply domain-specific skills and help learners achieve their learning goals.

Coaching around the Learning Cycle. In fact, Chapman (2006) proposed the integrated experiential coaching model based on ELT framework as the best approach to promote sustained change in his clients. Within this framework, an open and explicit conversation about self-regulatory "learn-how-to-learn" process serves as an entry point into the learning cycle. The essential purpose of coaching, says Chapman, is to equip learners with self-regulatory skills to use a variety of resources to change and develop in all aspects of their lives. As a next step, educator and the learner share their perspectives (concrete experience) about the learning agenda to be accomplished, followed by joint reflection (reflective observation) about what the process of achieving the learning objective might entail. The learner may at this point engage in meaning-making process and develop a personal theory about her direct experience (abstract conceptualization). At this point, the educator may offer a conceptual understanding of her experience from an expert point of view. Once the learning expectations are made explicit, the final step involves deciding on a course of action (active experimentation) to achieve the learning goal.

The active process of coaching around the learning cycle is further elaborated by Matsuo (2014) in his study of instructional skills of 715 OJT instructors covering twenty-two Japanese firms. The study results suggest that excellent OJT trainers promote the experiential learning cycle by consistently using four types of instructional skills associated with four modes of learning cycle: stretching trainees' objectives (AE), monitoring their progress (CE), providing positive feedback (AC), and promoting reflection on results (RO).

The study also found that superior trainers facilitate the experiential learning process by promoting deliberate practice and reflective practice on an ongoing basis according to the skill level of the trainees. Working with novice trainees, trainers emphasized monitoring the progress phase of the learning cycle, while de-emphasizing reflection on results and stretching objectives phases to reduce stress and pressure on trainees who are new to the learning situations. Dealing with more experienced trainees, trainers encourage them to set goals slightly higher than their current skill level, urging them to reflect and evaluate the reasons for successes or failures and set the next goals. To help trainees attain their learning goals, excellent trainers provide positive feedback by finding strengths while explicitly pointing out areas in need of improvement.

Both studies cited above offer a useful coaching process structured around the learning cycle, transferable to varieties of learning contexts and knowledge domains. In reality, regardless of the knowledge domain, the coaching learning space in which educators operate in real life is very fluid, dynamic, and highly contextual. As we stated in the beginning of the section, the dynamic nature of the coaching landscape requires educators to manage and hold the dialectic tension among four key components: the coaching relationship, content, learning objectives, and context.

For example, the skill-development strategy that may work with a concrete learner may be ineffective with an abstract learner; the learning goals need to be revisited and realigned with the learner's specific learning needs while steering her progress to meet the external requirements and standards; the educator-learner relationship needs to be established and nurtured on an ongoing basis to motivate learners to achieve their learning objectives and potential. Finally, effective coaching occurs in context. Whether in the surgical room, art studio, or in the basketball court, real learning occurs where the action is.

From this vantage point, educators in the coaching role may be required to function with a high level of flexibility and ingenuity to navigate the often uncertain and unpredictable coaching territory in a given time. How to prepare ourselves for this role becomes, then, an essential endeavour for us as educators to effect sustained change in our students. As several studies suggest, outstanding educators in diverse fields demonstrate such superior coaching skills and invest significant time and resource to master those capabilities.

A study by Schemp et al. (2006) of expert sport coaches reveals key characteristics of superior coaches that differentiate them from less competent ones. First, they have an extensive knowledge base of the sport they coach and of the athlete they train, and they have mastered coaching principles and skills by drawing their knowledge from variety of sources. Second, they have the ability to adjust the delivery of information at the athlete's level of understanding. Third, they frequently employ intuition in the decision-making process drawing from years of practical experience and extensive knowledge of their area of expertise. Their extensive preparation affords them ability to act on "gut feelings," even when "feelings run counter to accepted logic or convention" (Schemp et al., 2006, p. 157). Fourth, regardless of their years of accumulated experience, they invest considerable time and effort for preparation and planning to correctly "identifying, defining and analyzing a problem before searching for a solution," as they are aware that "if they don't get the problem right, they have no hope of getting the solution right" (p. 159).

As a result, expert coaches are equipped with superior ability to pull together coaching principles and actions through which "practice openings, closings, demonstrations, explanations, activities, player movement, equipment distribution and even interactions with athletes are performed with seemingly little effort, but result in remarkable outcomes" (p. 158).

Perhaps there is no better model of a master coach then John Wooden, the basketball coach, who embodied these coaching principles, values, and actions to successfully lead his team to win seven NCAA consecutive championships from 1967 to 1973. Gallimore and Tharp (2004) conducted an extensive empirical study of Coach Wooden in action inside and outside the basketball court in the hope to find lessons from his coaching practices that educators from other fields could learn.

> "I think everyone is a teacher. *Everyone!*" Maybe it is your children, maybe it's a neighbor, maybe it's someone under your supervision in some other way. In one way or another, you're teaching them by your action. (Gallimore & Tharp, 2004 p. 119)

From these words flow his unified teaching beliefs and practices he consistently demonstrated in his teaching, which transformed his athletes inside and outside the basketball court in significant ways.

Coach Wooden studied individuals as well as the group intensely. He recognized they were all different and there was no single formula that worked for all. He studied and analyzed each player and created a detailed individualized practice plan to the point that "he could track the practice routines of every single player for every practice session" (Gallimore & Tharp, 2004, p. 126).

His own learning approach to improve his knowledge base and skills included researching about specific areas of basketball, library search and reading, and interviewing successful coaches and players to learn their effective principles and practices he could adapt to his own team. As Tharp and Gallimore noted, Coach Wooden did not look for big and quick improvement; he focused on small, incremental change each day, believing "that's the only way it happens—and when it happens, it lasts" (p. 127).

Wooden spent as much time as planning each practice session as the practice itself. He would set aside two hours every morning with his assistants planning the practice sessions even though the practice lasted less than two hours. In the court, the planned session was executed with remarkable precision and speed, with players quickly and efficiently moving from drill to drill. As a NCAA college player of the year once noted, his experience of the practices was so intense, nonstop, and demanding, he thought in retrospect, that the actual speed of the games was much slower, because everything that happened in practice was much faster in pace.

Contrary to the educational psychology perspective on teaching, observed the authors, Wooden's approach to instruction was unique and unconventional. He would blend specific instructions, feedback, and modeling into a distinctive pattern that he delivered with remarkable accuracy, timeliness, and brevity. For example, Wooden would say:

I have been telling some of you for three years not to wind up when you pass the ball: Pass from the Chest. (p. 123)

This statement was followed by a specific three-step instruction through modeling; the correct way to perform, followed by imitation of an incorrect way a player had just performed, and back to demonstration of a correct act. Wooden called this method of instruction "sandwich approach" and as the authors observed with a sense of awe, it was performed with remarkable artistry and had "such clarity they leave an image in memory much like a text-book sketch" although it lasted no longer than three seconds (p. 123).

Here are how the authors summed up their experience of Coach Wooden's teaching in action:

> He made decisions "on the fly" at a pace equal to his players, in response to the detail of his players' actions. Yet his teaching was in no sense ad hoc. Down to the specific words he used, his planning included specific goals both for the team and individuals. Thus, he could pack into practice a rich basketball curriculum and deliver information at precisely the moments it would help his student learn the most. It was, he always said, the teaching in practice that he valued, more than the games and the winning, and it was practice that he was so reluctant to leave behind when he retired. (p. 124)

One may wonder if in fact Wooden's coaching style and approach would be transferable to other educational environments. The irony is, Wooden learned the principles and skills of coaching basketball from his experience as a high school English teacher. He learned the importance of detailed planning and over the years, he developed and perfected the teaching strategies that best suited the basketball learning environment.

In fact, another exemplary coaching practice aligned with Wooden's approach comes from a surgical room. Gawande (2011) describes in great detail how a medical professor made him a better surgeon through his superior coaching skills. Here is an excerpt of his experience in surgical room:

> Year after year, the senior residents chose him for their annual teaching award. He was an unusual teacher. He never quite told

you what to do. As an intern, I did my first splenectomy with him. He did not draw the skin incision to be made with the sterile marking pen the way the other professors did. He just stood there, waiting. Finally, I took the pen, put the felt tip on the skin somewhere, and looked up at him to see if I could make out a glimmer of approval or disapproval. He gave me nothing. I drew a line down the patient's middle, from just below the sternum to just above the navel. "Is that really where you want it?" he said… it took me a couple of years to realize that it was not his voice that scared me but his questions. He was invariably trying to get residents to think—to think like surgeons—and his questions exposed how much we had to learn. "Yes," I answered. We proceeded with the operation. Ten minutes into the case, it became obvious that I'd made the incision too small to expose the spleen. "I should have taken the incision down below the navel, huh?" He grunted in the affirmative, and we stopped to extend the incision. (Gawande, 2011)

Much later in his medical career as an experienced surgeon, Gawande invited his mentor back into the surgical room to improve his surgical skills. As the surgery went on, the mentor quietly watched and took intense notes:

He saw only small things, he said, but, if I were trying to keep a problem from happening even once in my next hundred operations, it's the small things I had to worry about. He noticed that I'd positioned and draped the patient perfectly for me, standing on his left side, but not for anyone else. The draping hemmed in the surgical assistant across the table on the patient's right side, restricting his left arm, and hampering his ability to pull the wound upward. At one point in the operation, we found ourselves struggling to see up high enough in the neck on that side. The draping also pushed the medical student off to the surgical assistant's right, where he couldn't help at all. I should have made more room to the left, which would have allowed the student to hold the retractor and freed the surgical assistant's left hand. (Gawande, 2011)

Through his coaching, Gawande also improved his ability to coach novice residents more effectively:

He wanted me to let the residents struggle thirty seconds more when I asked them to help with a task. I tended to give them precise instructions as soon as progress slowed. "No, use the DeBakey forceps," I'd say, or "Move the retractor first." Osteen's advice: "Get them to think." It's the only way people learn. (Gawande, 2011)

Three critical learning points can be drawn from the medical professor's coaching practice. First, his highly developed observational skills helped him accurately assess the learner's strengths and weaknesses and identify skill areas in need of development. Second, by delaying his expert input and feedback, he forced the learner to think hard to identify and define the problem on his own; otherwise the learner would have attempted to solve a wrong problem, putting the patient's well-being at risk. Third, his contextual understanding about what goes on in the operating room gave him the ability to analyse the learner's surgical behaviour with an expert eye.

Tips for the Coaching Role. While the coaching role may be influenced and constrained by the unique learning space requirements in which educators operate, there are fundamental coaching principles applicable to diverse learning contexts worth considering when planning and designing a practice or a lesson.

Establish a trusting learning relationship. Trust is the cornerstone of a genuine learning relationship. The educator and learner enter into a learning relationship based upon a mutual agreement and understanding about the specific purpose or objective a learner is required to achieve. The process of leading a learner toward achieving a specific goal can be personal, intense, and demanding. You can only get the commitment from a learner to enter into an authentic learning relationship if a learner trusts your genuine desire and commitment toward helping her achieve the learning goal.

Create a learning contract in conversation. As Chapman (2006) suggests, creating a learning contract in conversation with the learner navigating around the learning cycle may be an effective way to establish a learning goal and agenda. It makes the learning goal and learning tasks explicit and the process of creating action steps a shared responsibility. By clarifying the process of "learn-how-to-learn," it provides an opportunity for educators to introduce the idea of learning as an incremental and ongoing effort to achieve mastery of knowledge and skills. Create space for conversation on an ongoing basis to revisit the learning contract and monitor progress.

Define learning goals. Clarifying the learning goals is a critical first step in planning any learning activities. Here is an example:

> At the end of the (semester, training season) my (class, training session) will be a success if the (students, athletes, clients) have explored _____ and learned _____.

Clear articulation of the learning goals establishes the learner's expectation for the learning task and will help you keep the content and the learning process in alignment when you plan your lessons and activities. A clear learning goal will also give you and the learner effective ways to monitor progress toward achieving those goals.

Get to know the learner. As Dewey (1933) noted, "the teacher has to be a student of the pupil's mind" (p. 339). Whether teaching an individual learner or a group, you need to know the learners well. As Coach Wooden suggested, "you've got to study and analyse each individual and find out what makes them tick and how you can get them under control" (p. 126). Learners are all different in learning styles, temperaments, attitudes, skill levels, and mental readiness. Spending time and energy in getting to know the learners individually gives you a critical entry point into their minds and hearts. Once learners understand that you value them as individuals they are more likely to accept and endure the challenges a learning task might entail. In fact, as a seasoned CASE faculty once said, "Once you get to know your students well, you can make them learn practically anything."

Help learners identify and define the problem. As the medical coaching case indicates, learners' ability to identify and define the problem accurately will determine their capacity to solve the right problems. Resist the temptation to offer immediate help to guide the learners in the right direction; let them struggle for moment; create an opportunity for them to find their way out on their own.

Be a disciplined observer. The best way to accurately diagnose learners' skill level is to watch carefully what they do. Observation is the best tool for you to identify the problem areas in need for improvement and plan for right teaching strategy to help learners achieve quality work.

You haven't taught until they have learned (John Wooden, in Nater & Gallimore, 2008). In the coaching role, your primary objective is to help learners demonstrate the specific knowledge they have learned through performance in a specific context. Your role is much more than simply "delivering the content." Unless his players demonstrated a tangible sign of learning, Coach Wooden was never satisfied that what he "taught" was learned. As he said, "Fundamentals and conditioning are important…but since I'm preparing them to play, I must have them play, compete, and test things being presented. In other words, I must put them in competition to see if I've taught them" (p. 109). From this vantage point, your preparation and mastery of knowledge-transfer skills that produce a tangible student-learning outcome becomes the central focus of your role as a coach. This brings us to the next coaching principle.

Failure to prepare is preparing to fail. The above insightful words that Nater and Gallimore (2008) used to describe Coach Wooden's dedication to preparation and planning sums up the importance of studying learning. Bain (2004) found outstanding educators across diverse knowledge domains spend as much time studying, researching, and testing the best pedagogy that maximizes student learning outcomes as they spend mastering and deepening their domain expertise. For example, a CASE physics professor shared with us how he prepares himself to deliver information in his seminar class. In his view, not all content information is made equal in terms of its relevance:

> Many times we as teachers fall into a *"just-in-case"* mode of teaching, where we try to give students all the information about a subject they may ever need, just in case they need it. Instead, I try to teach using the *"just-in-time"* approach; meaning that I interject content materials when it becomes relevant to the conversation. I watch the conversation unfold and then, when I see that a piece of information will help inform the conversation—providing an alternative point of view or an important fact the students need to know—then I offer it up in the context of the current conversation. (Interview with SAGES professor, 2003)

Green (2014) documented the standard practice, *jugyokenkyu*, that Japanese teachers use on an ongoing basis to hone their craft of teaching. Translated as "lesson study," it is a bucket of practices teachers have developed by watching and critiquing each other's teaching practices, closely studying students' reactions and responses toward their teaching methods, and intensely studying and revising their curriculum materials.

Modeling. Teaching by your actions is a strategy you can capitalize on in the coaching role. Whether modeling a correct way to pass the ball in the basketball court, demonstrate how to think like a scholar, or write like a great novelist, modeling is a powerful way educators can change and expand learners' intellectual, affective, and behavioral framework. For example, in the case study we described early in the chapter, Professor King demonstrated how a scholar built an idea by turning assumptions into hypothesis, evaluating the validity of the idea by testing it in the real context. By breaking the researcher's thought process into parts, identifying his conceptual flaws and pointing to the erroneous conclusions he derived as result of an ill-defined question, Professor King was able to model how scholars think. Coach Wooden's flawless demonstration of a correct way to pass the ball is another example of how an expert knowledge is transferred into the real context in real time and has consistently produced remarkable results in his athletes.

Encourage deliberate practice. Many say "drill is a way to kill" students' interest and motivation. There is a common misconception about the role of drill or repetitive practice in learning. In learner-centered education, drill cannot be equated with mind-numbing mechanical activity aimed at subjugating the learner's mind or body into obedience and passivity. Dewey warned educators not to misunderstand drill with discipline. Through discipline, says Dewey (1910), learners master methods and skills in a specific domain so that they are free to exercise control over their mental, emotional, or physical capacities unhindered by external forces. The genuine purpose of deliberate practice, then, is to free our students. In Dewey's mind, learning activities, tools, materials, and equipment not purposefully organized and aimed at the attainment of such freedom are useless and harmful. For Coach Wooden, deliberate practice was a means to an end, not an end in itself. As Gallimore and Tharp observed, "drilling was intended to achieve an automaticity or mastery of fundamentals that opens up opportunities for individual creativity and initiative" (2004, p. 133).

The Standard-Setter/Evaluator

During his research on exceptional teachers, Bain (2004) encountered a traditional teacher who clearly thought about grades as a way to "separate the sheep from the goats." To Bain's amazement, many traditional teachers he interviewed shared the same dogmatic and narrow view of learning assessment and evaluation. We all know too well that this view of education is shared by many teachers, not through any fault of their own, but because for many years they were forced to function in educational systems in which the pervasive conception of teaching and learning has been centered around rank-ordering the students into "winners" and "losers" based on a simplistic measurement of how well they were able to parrot back what they were taught.

Not too long ago, influenced by such traditional view of education, critiques of experiential learning initiatives tended to question its pedagogical methodology and validity of the teaching and learning experiences they provide (Hickcox, 2002). Such criticism that put into question the legitimacy of learner-centered philosophy was particularly aimed at the outcome assessment component of experiential education. In contrast to a lecture-based traditional education that relies primarily on the one-size-fit-all evaluation of the abstract dimension of the students' performance outcomes, experiential learning conceives learning as a holistic process in which the evaluation of the learning outcomes need to be based upon students' effective integration of affective, perceptual, cognitive, and behavioral dimensions of learning. The multidimensional teaching and learning strategies applied in experiential classrooms requires equally diverse and complex assessment methods that adequately and fairly evaluate students' integrated functioning in the learning process (Kolb & Kolb, 2006).

While this brings us back to century-old debate about traditional versus progressive education, what has significantly changed in recent years is the accumulation of palpable evidence that traditional outcome measures based on subject-centered education are no longer suited to properly assess knowledge and skills needed to meet the challenges of the twenty-first century.

As schools and universities shift their educational initiatives toward learner-centered education with focus placed on creativity and problem-solving, there is also a growing awareness that it necessitates innovative and more comprehensive methods of assessment of teaching and learning outcomes (Litchfield & Dempsey, 2015). As a result, the call for research on authentic assessment has seen a substantial increase over the years (Angelo & Cross, 1993; Boud, 2013; Boud & Falchikov, 2006; Santos et al., 2015; Wiggins, 1989). One of the many challenges the authentic assessment movement faces is, Boyle & Hutchinson (2009) attest, when outcome-based skill development is included in educational curriculum or training programs but the assessment methods are inappropriate and misaligned with what it is intended to measure.

In Asia, China, Hong Kong, Macao, Singapore, Japan, Taiwan, and South Korea are leading the initiative toward learner-centered education with particular focus on creating a holistic and relevant assessment to replace the traditional methods of evaluation (Koh & Luke, 2009). For example, ever since the launching of the vision of "Thinking Schools" by the Ministry of Education in 1997, Singapore has spent considerable energy and effort to move from test-based conventional assessment to authentic assessment that adequately measures higher-order thinking skills in their students (Koh, Tan, & Ng, 2012).

Tips for the Standard-Setter/Evaluator Role. The following are some tips for the experiential educator when taking the standard-setter/evaluator role:

Authentic outcome assessment. If a music teacher wants to know how well her student has learned to play the piano, it would be unthinkable for her to use multiple-choice test to see whether her student had met the standard. She would have her play the piano in the "real life context" of a performance stage to demonstrate her skills. The same rationale applies to assessment in schools. As the psychological assessment literature indicates, "the best predictor of the ability to do something is the actual doing of it—not multiple-choice answers about what to do, or knowing what to do, saying what I would do" (Boyatzis, Cowen, & Kolb, 1995).

"Authentic" in this context means learners should demonstrate knowledge and skills in real-life context. The goal of authentic evaluation then, is to draw education close to real life. If we want our assessment of our students to be authentic, the subject centered question, "*What should my students know?*" can only be appropriately addressed in conjunction with the learner-centered question "*How can I help my students learn skills and knowledge and be able to transfer what they have learned in real-life context?*"

In our role as the standard-setter/evaluator, we need to understand three core principles of an authentic assessment to help us direct our teaching to maximize student learning. When we set learning standards, create learning activities, and examine our own teaching practices it is helpful to keep these core principles in mind.

Learner focused. The ultimate goal of education is to help students become independent learners. Students must learn to take full responsibility of their own learning if they are to become autonomous and lifelong learners. We can best help our students pursue their lifelong goals and objectives by teaching them meta-learning skills to understand the way they learn. Understanding their learning styles and skills, being aware of their own attitudes, beliefs, and habits will equip learners with skills transferable to a wide range of life contexts. Because learning is the primary focus, students should be actively involved in the self- and peer-assessment process. As Kearney and Perkins (2014) found, when students were actively engaged in every step of the process of creation of the criteria from which they would be evaluated, they understood the learning objectives more clearly and were able to effectively utilize peers' and teachers' feedback in their future work.

Teacher-focused. Regardless of the learning context, educators are the knowledge experts in any profession or a given subject area. As someone who is in close contact with learners, educators should be given full control and freedom of the assessment process and use the information to monitor their teaching and student learning. The following guiding questions may be helpful to evaluate their own teaching: (1) Is the material worth learning? (2) Are my students learning what I am teaching? (3) Am I encouraging my students to learn? (4) Am I encouraging my students to trust their own experiences? These questions will bring their teaching to a clear focus, improving their ability to set meaningful learning objectives and authentic standards from which to evaluate students' work.

Context-specific. Learner-centered education takes place in a specific context. A truly authentic assessment promotes high-quality learning by strengthening the connection between content knowledge and the real-life application (Brown, Collins, & Duguid, 1989; Darling-Hammond & Snyder, 2000; Kearney & Perkins, 2014). Learning that occurs closer to the real-life context is inevitably messy and complex. The organization of learning tasks, selection of materials, or time allocation of the activities require careful and yet flexible planning. Students' unique learning styles, attitudes, beliefs, and skill levels may come to the surface, and each individual student may achieve the learning objectives at a different time. The quality of student learning in real-life context can be greatly enhanced by the educators' ability to flexibly adjust their teaching to meet the students' needs and contextual demands.

Ongoing. The purpose of the assessment in learner-centered education is to improve the quality of student learning and not to grade or evaluate student performance at a fixed point in time. If grading and testing are used, they need to be used carefully and purposefully within the context of a holistic learning development of the learner. As Wiggins's (1989) insightful comments suggest, the confusion over the use of the standardized test is akin to using the pulse rate as the only measure of a patient's overall health. If a standardized test is to be authentic, it needs to inform learners about themselves and how well they are able to apply a subject matter in the field. An ongoing assessment follows the feedback movement of the learning cycle; it continually informs educators about what and how students are learning. Using the information, educators can improve their teaching to make it more relevant to meet the students' needs on an ongoing basis. Because its aim is to develop individual learner as the whole person, an ongoing assessment is labor intensive and time consuming but ultimately effective in grasping how students are developing emotionally, physically, and intellectually.

Setting authentic standards. A truly educative assessment prepares and motivates students to meet the real-world challenges. A simplistic measure of student performance does not meet the standard of an authentic assessment. As Wiggins (1989) noted, an authentic standard replicates or simulates what writers, mathematicians, business people, scientists, and historians do, not just what they know. Not only it should reveal to the educators what students have learned but it also should inform students the actual standard of the field they are about to enter. This brings to the surface the tension between the conventional and authentic assessment and therefore the need to understand the fundamental distinction between the two.

According to Moss, Girard, and Haniford (2006) (cited in Koh & Luke, 2009), conventional assessment of student achievement historically has focused on the reproduction of students' factual and procedural knowledge with focus on retrieval of facts and application of routine formulas and procedures. In contrast, an authentic assessment that Newmann et al. (1996) proposed (cited in Koh & Luke, 2009) consists of meeting three criteria: ability to construct knowledge, disciplinary inquiry, and value beyond school. In their minds, authentic learning tasks enable students to develop higher-order thinking through real-world problem-solving, rather than absorption of facts and procedures.

Koh and Luke (2009) set out to study the relationship between teacher assignments and assessment tasks and the student learning outcomes in fifty-nine Singapore schools from grade 5 through 9 in English, social studies, mathematics, and science based on the authentic assessment criteria suggested by Newmann et al. The findings reveal that in social science in particular, the students of teachers who implemented learning tasks closer to daily real-world problems were required to engage in higher-order thinking, evaluation, and reconstruction of knowledge in order to arrive at the answers. Furthermore, in those classrooms where high-stakes testing was eliminated altogether, teachers were able to create learning conditions that enabled the setting of more intellectually challenging tasks. As a result, students "rose to the challenge" and produced higher-quality products. Joe Miller offers rich authentic assessment tools at http://jfmueller.faculty.noctrl.edu/toolbox/glossary.htm#standard.

Summary

Considering art as a metaphor, shifting educator roles is comparable to an artist mixing primary colors in a palette to achieve the desirable effect or mood on canvas. We have all the colors at our disposal but we tend to favor one or two colors over others. Awareness of our preferred educator roles will enhance our ability to expand our repertoire of pedagogical methods and understand how our deeply held values influence our teaching. An example will help illustrate this point.

Recently we conducted a workshop with experiential educators at the ISEEN (Independent Schools Experiential Education Network) using KERP as a way to address the importance of teaching around the learning cycle and understand how role preferences impact their ability to help

411

students learn. We created four groups of educators based on KERP profile and asked them to discuss how their dominant role preference influenced their teaching.

The facilitator group raised an insightful learning point. The strong value they placed on their students' ability to pursue their passion and interests became sometimes a hindrance to help students set goals and develop necessary skills to achieve their purposes. As one participant noted,

> We are not good at the coaching role. When students ask questions, we tend to focus too much in letting them find their own answers but we don't spend enough time teaching them how to set goals, define action steps to help them answer their questions. (ISEEN workshop participant, January 2016)

The standard-setter/evaluator group raised another critical issue related to assessment of learning outcome in learner-centered education. As one participant said:

> We are the accountants of the learning cycle. What the students are asking is, "why should I learn this stuff?" As educators we have the responsibility to answer this question and evaluate our teaching against it. No matter what we do in other roles, at the end, it comes to this bottom line.

It became clear to the participants that an overreliance on one or two roles may hinder their ability to guide learners around the learning cycle. Facilitating role is a powerful way to develop a sense of learning identity in learners. It is very difficult to pursue one's interest with passion and determination unless one has a strong learning identity to fuel those deeply held interests. Interests need to be purposefully directed and connected to an existing framework of inquiry, ideas, or pragmatic world of diverse professions. It is the role of the subject-matter expert to provide that valuable connection through the development of intellectual rigor and discipline to think like surgeons, artists, teachers, accountants, scientists, or writers. In the coaching role, educators work with students in context, in the art studio, in the operating room, or in the basketball court to develop the specific skills needed to succeed in those arenas. Finally, in the standard-setter/evaluator role, educators help learners master the ability to judge their own quality of work against the standard of the field they are about to enter.

Because learning occurs close to life in learner-centered education, the role shifting becomes very highly context dependent, and therefore challenging. The role combination that worked with one set of students may not work with another given the messy, unpredictable, and complex nature of the learning space. However, the more we engage in deliberate practice to adopt the four roles, the more we enhance our ability to create lively, supportive, and growth-promoting learning space where students willingly set high standards to produce quality work. As Rogers suggests, they "will live and learn as individuals in process" by asking themselves: "What should I explore next?" "Where will this question lead me?"

Appendix 1

The KLSI differs from other tests of learning style and personality used in education by being based on a comprehensive theory of learning and development that develops a holistic model of the experiential learning process and a multidimensional model of adult development.

Purpose

The KLSI was created to fulfill two purposes:

1. To serve as an educational tool to increase individuals' understanding of the process of learning from experience and their unique individual approach to learning. By increasing awareness of how they learn, the aim is to increase learners' capacity for metacognitive control of their learning process; enabling them to monitor and select learning approaches that work best for them in different learning situations. By providing a language for talking about learning styles and the learning process, the inventory can foster conversation among learners and educators about how to create the most effective learning environment for those involved. For this purpose

415

the inventory is best presented, not as a test, but as an experience in understanding how one learns. Scores on the inventory should not be interpreted as definitive, but as a starting point for exploration of how one learns best. To facilitate this purpose, a self-scoring and interpretation book that explains the experiential learning cycle and the characteristics of the different learning styles along with scoring and profiling instructions is included with the inventory.

2. To provide a research tool for investigating ELT and the characteristics of individual learning styles. This research can contribute to the broad advancement of experiential learning and specifically to the validity of interpretations of individual learning style scores. A research version of the instrument including only the inventory to be scored by the researcher is available for this purpose.

The KLSI is not a criterion-referenced test and is not intended for use to predict behavior for purposes of selection, placement, job assignment, or selective treatment. This includes not using the instrument to assign learners to different educational treatments, a process sometimes referred to as "tracking." Such categorizations based on a single test score amounts to stereotyping that runs counter to the philosophy of experiential learning that emphasizes individual uniqueness. "When it is used in the simple, straightforward, and open way intended, the LSI usually provides a valuable self-examination and discussion that recognizes the uniqueness, complexity and variability in individual approaches to learning. The danger lies in the reification of learning styles into fixed traits, such that learning styles become stereotypes used to pigeonhole individuals and their behavior" (Kolb, 1981a, pp. 290–291).

The LSI is constructed as a self-assessment exercise and tool for construct validation of ELT. Tests designed for predictive validity typically begin with a criterion like academic achievement and work backward to identify items or tests with high criterion correlations. Even so, even the most sophisticated of these tests rarely rises above a .5 correlation with the criterion. For example, while Graduate Record Examination Subject Test scores are better predictors of first-year graduate school grades than either the General Test score or undergraduate GPA, the combination of these three measures only produces multiple correlations with grades ranging from .4 to .6 in various fields (Annastasi & Urbina, 1997).

Construct validation is not focused on an outcome criterion, but on the theory or construct that the test measures. Here the emphasis is on the pattern of convergent and discriminant theoretical predictions made by the theory. Failure to confirm predictions calls into question the test and the theory. "However, even if each of the correlations proved to be quite low, their cumulative effect would be to support the validity of the test and the underlying theory" (Selltiz, Jahoda, Deutsch, & Cook, 1960, p. 160). Judged by the standards of construct validity, ELT has been widely accepted as a useful framework for learning-centered educational innovation, including instructional design, curriculum development, and lifelong learning. Field and job classification studies viewed as a whole also show a pattern of results consistent with the ELT structure of knowledge theory.

History

There have been six versions of the Learning Style Inventory published over the last forty years. Through this time attempts have been made to openly share information about the inventory, its scoring, and technical characteristics with other interested researchers. The results of their research have been instrumental in the continuous improvement of the inventory.

Learning Style Inventory—Version 1 (Kolb, 1971, 1976a). The original Learning Style Inventory (LSI 1) was created in 1969 as part of a MIT curriculum-development project that resulted in the first management textbook based on experiential learning (Kolb, Rubin, & McIntyre, 1971). It was originally developed as an experiential educational exercise designed to help learners understand the process of experiential learning and their unique individual style of learning from experience. The term "learning style" was coined to describe these individual differences in how people learn.

Items for the inventory were selected from a longer list of words and phrases developed for each learning mode by a panel of four behavioral scientists familiar with ELT. This list was given to a group of twenty graduate students, asking them to rate each word or phrase for social desirability. Attempting to select words that were of equal social desirability, a final set of twelve items, including a word or phrase for each learning mode, was selected for pretesting. Analysis showed that three of these sets produced nearly random responses and were thus eliminated, resulting in a final version of the LSI with nine items. These items were further refined through item-whole correlation analysis to include six scored items for each learning mode.

Research with the inventory was stimulated by classroom discussions with students who found the LSI to be helpful to them in understanding the process of experiential learning and how they learn. From 1971 until it was revised in 1985, there were over 350 published research studies using the LSI. Validity for the LSI 1 was established in a number of fields including education, management, psychology, computer science, medicine, and nursing (Hickcox, 1990; Iliff, 1994). The results of this research with LSI 1 provided empirical support for the most complete and systematic statement of ELT, *Experiential Learning: Experience as the Source of Learning and Development* (Kolb, 1984). There were several studies of the LSI 1 that identified psychometric weaknesses of the instrument, particularly low internal consistency reliability and test-retest reliability.

Learning Style Inventory—Version 2 (Kolb, 1985a). Low reliability coefficients and other concerns about the LSI 1 led to a revision of the inventory in 1985 (LSI 2). Six new items chosen to increase internal reliability (alpha) were added to each scale, making twelve scored items on each scale. These changes increased scale alphas to an average of .81 ranging from .73 to .88. Wording of all items was simplified to a seventh-grade reading level and the format was changed to include sentence stems (e.g. "When I learn"). Correlations between the LSI 1 and LSI 2 scales averaged .91 and ranged from .87 to .93. A new more diverse normative reference group of 1,446 men and women was created. Research with the LSI 2 continued to establish validity for the instrument. From 1985 until the publication of the

LSI 3 1999, over 630 studies were published, most using the LSI 2. While internal reliability estimates for the LSI 2 remained high in independent studies, test-retest reliability remained low.

Learning Style Inventory—Version 2a (Kolb, 1993). In 1991 Veres, Sims, and Locklear published a reliability study of a randomized version of the LSI 2 that showed a small decrease in internal reliability but a dramatic increase in test-retest reliability with the random scoring format. To study this format, a research version of the random format inventory (LSI 2a) was published in 1993.

Kolb Learning Style Inventory (KLSI)—Version 3 (Kolb, 1999a). In 1999, the randomized format was adopted in a revised self-scoring and interpretation booklet (KLSI 3) that included a color-coded scoring sheet to simplify scoring. The new booklet was organized to follow the learning cycle emphasizing the LSI as an "experience in learning how you learn." New application information on teamwork, managing conflict, personal and professional communication, and career choice and development were added. The KLSI 3 continued to use the LSI 2 normative reference group until norms for the randomized version could be created.

KLSI—Version 3.1 (Kolb, 2005). The KLSI 3.1 modified the LSI 3 to include a new normative data sample of 6,977 LSI users. The format, items, scoring, and interpretative booklet remain identical with KLSI 3. The only change in the KLSI 3.1 is in the norm charts used to convert raw LSI scores.

KLSI—Version 3.2 (Kolb & Kolb, 2013b). The KLSI 3.2 was created in 2013 to incorporate the new nine-learning style typology of the KLSI 4.0 in a paper version. The instrument and normative sample are identical to the KLSI 3.1. The self-scoring and interpretation booklet was changed to explain the nine learning styles and their application to problem-solving, relationships, and so on.

KLSI—Version 4.0 (Kolb & Kolb, 2011). The KLSI 4.0 is the first major revision of the KLSI since 1999 and the third since the original LSI was published in 1971. Based on many years of research involving scholars around the world and data from many thousands of respondents, the KLSI 4.0 includes four major additions:

A new nine-learning style typology. Data from empirical and clinical studies over the years has shown that the original four learning style types—Accommodating, Assimilating, Converging, and Diverging—can be refined further into a nine-style typology that better defines the unique patterns of individual learning styles and reduces the confusions introduced by borderline cases in the old four-style typology. The new nine styles are Initiating, Experiencing, Imagining, Reflecting, Analyzing, Thinking, Deciding, Acting, and Balancing.

Assessment of Learning Flexibility. The experiential learning styles are not fixed traits but dynamic states that can "flex" to meet the demands of different learning situations. For the first time, the KLSI 4.0 includes a personal assessment of the degree to which a person changes his or her style in different learning contexts. The flexibility score also shows which learning style types the individual uses in addition to his or her dominant learning style type. This information can help individuals improve their ability to move freely around the learning cycle and improve their learning effectiveness.

An Expanded Personal Report Focused on Improving Learning Effectiveness. The new personal interpretative report has been redesigned to focus on improving personal-learning effectiveness based on a detailed profile of how the person prefers to learn and his or her learning strength and weaknesses. It helps learners take charge of their learning, with a planning guide for learning and tips for application in work and personal life.

Improved Psychometrics. This revision includes new norms that are based on a larger, more diverse, and representative sample of 10,423 LSI users. The KLSI 4.0 maintains the high scale reliability of the KLSI 3.1 while offering higher internal validity. Scores on the KLSI 4.0 are highly correlated with scores on the previous KLSI 3.1 thus maintaining the external validity that the instrument has shown over the years.

Format

The LSI is designed to measure the degree to which individuals display the different learning styles derived from ELT. The form of the inventory is determined by three design parameters. First, the test is brief and straightforward, making it useful both for research and for discussing the learning process with individuals and providing feedback. Second, the test is constructed in such a way that individuals respond to it as they would respond to a learning situation: it requires them to resolve the tensions between the abstract-concrete an active-reflective orientations. For this reason, the LSI format requires them to rank order their preferences for the abstract, concrete, active, and reflective orientations. Third, and most obviously, it was hoped that the measures of learning styles would predict behavior in a way consistent with the theory of experiential learning.

All previous versions of the LSI have had the same format—a short questionnaire (nine items for LSI 1 and twelve items for subsequent versions) that asks respondents to rank four sentence endings that correspond to the four learning modes—Concrete Experience (e.g., experiencing), Reflective Observation (reflecting), Abstract Conceptualization (thinking), and Active Experimentation (doing). The KLSI 4.0 has twenty items in this format—twelve that are similar to the items in the 3.1 and eight additional items that are about learning in different contexts. These eight items are used to assess learning flexibility. The KLSI 4.0 is only available online due to the complex scoring formula for learning flexibility.

Items in the LSI are geared to a seventh-grade reading level. The inventory is intended for use by teens and adults. It is not intended for use by younger children. The LSI has been translated into many languages, including, Arabic, Chinese, French, Japanese, Italian, Portuguese, Spanish, Swedish, and Thai; and there have been many cross-cultural studies using it (Joy & Kolb, 2009).

The Forced-Choice Format of the LSI. The format of the LSI is a forced choice format that ranks an individual's relative choice preferences among the four modes of the learning cycle. This is in contrast to the more common normative or free-choice format, such as the widely used Likert scale that rates absolute preferences on independent dimensions. The forced-choice format of the LSI was dictated by the theory of experiential learning and by the primary purpose of the instrument.

Alice Y. Kolb and David A. Kolb

ELT is a holistic, dynamic, and dialectic theory of learning. Because it is holistic, the four modes that comprise the experiential learning cycle, CE, RO, AC, and AE are conceived as interdependent. Learning involves resolving the creative tension among these learning modes in response to the specific learning situation. Since the two learning dimensions AC-CE and AE-RO are related dialectically, the choice of one pole involves not choosing the opposite pole. Therefore, because ELT postulates that learning in life situations requires the resolution of conflicts among interdependent learning modes, to be ecologically valid, the learning style-assessment process should require a similar process of conflict resolution in the choice of one's preferred learning approach.

The primary purpose of the LSI is to provide learners with information about their preferred approach to learning. The most relevant information for the learner is about intraindividual differences, his or her relative preference for the four learning modes, not interindividual comparisons. Ranking relative preferences among the four modes in a forced-choice format is the most direct way to provide this information. While individuals who take the inventory sometimes report difficulty in making these ranking choices, they report that the feedback they get from the LSI gives them more insight than has been the case when we use a normative Likert rating scale version. This is because the social desirability response bias in the rating scales fails to define a clear learning style, that is, they say they prefer all learning modes. This is supported by Harland's (2002) finding that feedback from a forced-choice test format was perceived as more accurate, valuable, and useful than feedback from a normative version.

The adoption of the forced-choice method for the LSI has at times placed it in the center of an ongoing debate in the research literature about the merits of forced-choice instruments between what might be called "rigorous statisticians" and "pragmatic empiricists." Statisticians have questioned the use of the forced-choice format because of statistical limitations, called ipsativity, that are the result of the ranking procedure. Since ipsative scores represent the relative strength of a variable compared to others in the ranked set, the resulting dependence among scores produces method-induced negative correlations among variables and violates a fundamental assumption of classical test theory required for use of techniques such as analysis of variance and factor analysis—independence of error variance. Cornwell and Dunlap (1994) stated that ipsative scores cannot be factored and that correlation-based analysis of ipsative data produced uninterpretable and invalid results (c.f. Hicks, 1970; Johnson et al., 1988). Other criticisms include the point that ipsative scores are technically ordinal, not the interval scales required for parametric statistical analysis; that they produce lower internal reliability estimates and lower validity coefficients (Baron, 1996). While critics of forced-choice instruments acknowledge that these criticisms do not take away from the validity of intraindividual comparisons (LSI purpose one), they argue that ipsative scores are not appropriate for interindividual comparisons since interindividual comparisons on a ranked variable are not independent absolute preferences but preferences that are relative to the other ranked variables in the set (Baron, 1996; Karpatschof & Elkjaer, 2000). However, since ELT argues that a given learning mode preference is relative to the other three modes, it is the comparison of relative not absolute preferences that the theory seeks to assess.

The "pragmatic empiricists" argue that in spite of theoretical statistical arguments, normative and forced-choice variations of the same instrument can produce empirically comparable results. Karpatschof and Elkjaer (2000) advance this case in their metaphorically titled paper "Yet the Bumblebee Flies." With theory, simulation, and empirical data they present evidence for the comparability of ipsative and normative data. Saville and Wilson (1991) found a high correspondence between ipsative and normative scores when forced choice involved a large number of alternative dimensions.

Normative tests also have serious limitations that the forced-choice format was originally created to deal with (Sisson, 1948). Normative scales are subject to numerous response biases—central tendency bias where respondents avoid extreme responses, acquiescence response, and social desirability responding—and are easy to fake. Forced-choice instruments are designed to avoid these biases by forcing choice among alternatives in a way that reflects real live choice making (Baron, 1996; Hicks, 1970). Matthews and

Oddy found large bias in the extremeness of positive and negative responses in normative tests and conclude that when sources of artifact are controlled, "individual differences in ipsative scores can be used to rank individuals meaningfully" (1997, p. 179). Pickworth and Shoeman (2000) found significant response bias in two normative LSI formats developed by Marshall and Merritt (1986) and Geiger and Boyle (1993). Conversely, Beutell and Kressel (1984) found that social desirability contributed less than 4 percent of the variance in LSI scores in spite of the fact that individual LSI items all had very high social desirability.

In addition, ipsative tests can provide external validity evidence comparable to normative data (Baron, 1996) or in some cases even better (Hicks, 1970). For example, attempts to use normative rating versions of the LSI report reliability and internal validity data but little or no external validity (Geiger & Boyle, 1993; Marshall & Merritt, 1986; Merritt & Marshall, 1984; Pickworth & Shoeman, 2000; Romero et al., 1992). Jamieson (2010) also found no external validity in her study comparing the KLSI 3.1 with semantic differential and Likert scale versions of the instrument. Her results suggest caution in comparing research results from the KLSI and these other formats since she found only a 47 percent match between style classifications and the three instruments and learning mode correlations "only explained 13% to 16% of the variance and the bi-polar dimensions explained 24% to 41% of the variance" between instruments (p. 73).

Characteristics of the LSI Scales

The LSI assesses six variables, four primary scores that measure an individual's relative emphasis on the four learning orientations—Concrete Experience (CE), Reflective Observation (RO), Abstract Conceptualization (AC), and Active Experimentation (AE), and two combination scores measure an individual's preference for abstractness over concreteness (AC-CE) and action over reflection (AE-RO). The four primary scales of the LSI are ipsative because of the forced-choice format of the instrument. This results in negative correlations among the four scales, the mean magnitude of which can be estimated (assuming no underlying correlations among them) by the formula $-1/(m - 1)$ where m is the number of variables (Johnson et al., 1988). This results in a predicted average method induced correlation of -.33 among the four primary LSI scales.

The combination scores AC-CE and AE-RO, however, are not ipsative. Forced-choice instruments can produce scales that are not ipsative (Hicks, 1970; Pathi, Manning, & Kolb, 1989). To demonstrate the independence of the combination scores and interdependence of the primary scores, Pathi, Manning, and Kolb (1989) had SPSS-X randomly fill out and analyze 1,000 LSIs according to the ranking instructions. While the mean intercorrelation among the primary scales was -.33 as predicted; the correlation between AC-CE and AE-RO was +.038. In addition, if AC-CE and AE-RO were ipsative scales the correlation between the two scales would be -1.0 according to the above formula. Observed empirical relationships are always much smaller, for example, +.13 for a sample of 1,591 graduate students (Freedman & Stumpf, 1978), -.09 for the LSI 2 normative sample of 1,446 respondents (Kolb, 1999b), -.19 for a sample of 1,296 MBA students (Boyatzis & Mainemelis, 2000) and -.21 for the normative sample of 6,977 LSI for the KLSI 3.1 (Kolb, 2005). The independence of the two combination scores can be seen by examining some example scoring results. For example, when AC-CE or AE-RO on a given item takes a value of +2 (from, say, AC = 4 and CE = 2 or AC = 3 and CE = 1) the other score can take a value of +2 or -2. Similarly when either score takes a value of +1 (from 4 -3, 3-2, or 2-1) the other can take the values of +3, +1, -1, or -3. In other words, when AC-CE takes a particular value, AE-RO can take two to four different values, and the score on one dimension does not determine the score on the other.

In the new KLSI 4.0, we introduce two new non-ipsative continuous combination scores in addition to the primary learning cycle dialectics of AC-CE and AE-RO. These scores assess the combination dialectics of Assimilation-Accommodation and Converging-Diverging assessed by the four learning style types in previous LSI versions:

Assimilation - Accommodation = (AC+RO) - (AE+CE)

A high score on this dimension indicates a learning preference for assimilation or generalized, conceptual learning, while a low score indicates a learning preference for accommodation or active contextual learning. The concepts of assimilation and accommodation are central to Piaget's (1952) definition of intelligence as the balance of adapting concepts to fit the external world (accommodation) and the process of fitting observations of the external world into existing concepts (assimilation). This measure was used in the validation of the Learning Flexibility Index (Sharma & Kolb, 2010— see Chapter 6) and has been used by other researchers in previous studies (Allinson & Hayes, 1996; Weirsta & de Jong, 2002).

Converging – Diverging = (AC+AE) – (CE+RO)

A high score on this dimension indicates a learning preference for converging or evaluative decision-making that closes down on the best solution to a problem vs. diverging to open up new imaginative possibilities and alternatives. The concepts of converging and diverging originated in Guilford's structure of intellect model as the central dialectic of the creative process. This dialectic concept has been used in research on ELT by Gemmell (2012) and Kolb (1983).

Continuous Balance Scores. Some studies have used continuous balance scores for AC-CE and AE-RO to assess balanced learning style scores (Mainemelis, Boyatzis, and Kolb, 2002, Sharma & Kolb, 2010). These variables compute the absolute values of the AC-CE and AE-RO scores adjusted to center on the fiftieth percentile of the normative comparison group, in this case the KLSI 4.0.

Balance AC-CE = ABS [AC – (CE + 9)]
Balance AE-RO = ABS [AE – (RO + 6)]

Appendix 2

O n the Cycle of Learning, target scores form a "kite" shape defined by the combination of preferences for the four modes of the learning cycle. Because each person's learning style is unique, everyone's kite shape is a little different. Years of research on the learning styles of many thousands of individuals have led to the identification of nine distinct kite types or clusters of learning styles in the KLSI 4.0. These learning style types can be systematically arranged on a two-dimensional learning space defined by AC-CE and AE-RO.

Figure A2.1
The Nine Learning Styles of the KLSI 4

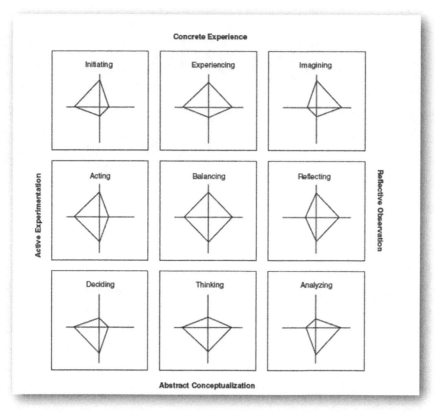

Previous versions of the KLSI divided this learning space into four regions defining four learning style types—accommodating, diverging, assimilating, and converging. Research and feedback from individual users indicated that the division of the space into four regions was problematic for some and categorized their learning style in a way that was misleading. Individuals who scored near the middle of the space reported that their style description was inaccurate while those who scored near the line between two styles were not comfortable with being typed into just one of the two styles. Further investigation revealed that these borderline cases were actually distinct styles in themselves resulting in the creation of the following nine-style typology.

- The **Initiating** style is distinguished by the ability to initiate action to deal with experiences and situations.
- The **Experiencing** style is distinguished by the ability to find meaning from deep involvement in experience.
- The **Creating** style is distinguished by the ability to create meaning by observing and reflecting on experiences.
- The **Reflecting** style is distinguished by the ability to connect experience and ideas through sustained reflection.
- The **Analyzing** style is distinguished by the ability to integrate and systematize ideas through reflection.
- The **Thinking** style is distinguished by the capacity for disciplined involvement in abstract reasoning, mathematics, and logic.
- The **Deciding** style is distinguished by the ability to use theories and models to decide on problem solutions and courses of action.
- The **Acting** style is distinguished by a strong motivation for goal-directed action that integrates people and tasks.
- The **Balancing** style is distinguished by the ability to flexibly adapt by weighing the pros and cons of acting versus reflecting and experiencing versus thinking.

These nine style types are described in detail below. Each description shows the characteristics of the style type and its learning space region based on previous research and clinical observation. Learning strengths and challenges for individuals with the style type are summarized. Finally, individuals with the style type describe themselves in their own words.

The Initiating Learning Style

Emphasizes the learning modes of **AE** and **CE**. The Initiating style is distinguished by the ability to initiate action in order to deal with experiences and situations.

Learning Strengths

- Committing yourself to objectives
- Seeking new opportunities
- Influencing and leading others

Learning Challenges

- Controlling the impulse to act
- Listening to others views
- Impatience

If your learning style is **Initiating,** you prefer to learn from "hands-on" experience and real-life situations. You are willing to jump in and try out new and challenging experiences and will volunteer for leadership on tasks. You are able to act quickly and decisively in a changing environment without being caught in excessive deliberations. Because of your style you are comfortable thinking on your feet. Because you are willing to take risks, you are able to identify new opportunities and generate possibilities for success at work and in life in general. You have the ability to take initiative to start new projects, put ideas into practice, and identify a course of action.

You learn best by tuning into the present circumstances and less from reflections about past events or planning for future actions. Your tendency may be to act on "gut" feelings rather than on logical analysis. In solving problems, you may rely more heavily on people for information than on your own technical analysis.

Others may see you as spontaneous, energetic, persuasive, and courageous.

Preferred Learning Space

You thrive in dynamic learning spaces where you can work with others to get assignments done, to set goals and to try out different approaches to completing a project. You prefer teachers who take the role of coaches or mentors in helping you learn from your life experiences.

Initiating—In Their Own Words

Jodie—college student

I can see why my learning style is "Initiating" because I do have strong preference for action over reflection. For example, I enjoy lab courses but do not like lectures. I love my calculus course because we do problems as we go through class, enabling me to be actively involved with the material I am learning. On the other hand, my lecture chemistry course is less pleasant because there are a million people in a room and the professor is just saying things. Such circumstances do not allow many opportunities for the hands-on style of learning that I prefer.

Rosalyn—human resources manager

In one simple word…yes, I agree with the label "Initiator" for my learning style. My peers, leaders, family members, and friends would all be able to quickly identify me as action-oriented. I tend to be impatient with waiting for decisions and more than likely will jump in with a plan to take action. In my work as a human resources manager this bias for action has served me extremely well. The retail business is constantly changing. Amid that change, some people can be caught spinning with indecisiveness and an inability to act based on the excessive speed in which the business is moving. I, on the other hand, make decisions quickly. A day without action is extremely rare. The ability to identify needs, and act on those needs quickly is essential to my success in the corporate environment. My manager has mentioned how I have an amazing ability to seek out new information and apply it. I think this relates to my curiosity and willingness to take risks.

Alice Y. Kolb and David A. Kolb

Ginny—college student

I am most effective in learning by having the opportunity to "learn by doing." Whether learning a new sport, a new activity, or new information, in order to retain what I have learned, it is important that I apply new learning quickly to real-life situations. For example, when learning how to tie knots for sailing or climbing, I must have the opportunity to repeat the action while watching the instructor do it. Without the immediate application of the action, my retention is painfully low.

In classroom situations, it is challenging for me to learn just from lectures or books. Connecting with my classmates to discuss and debate about a reading or a lecture helps my retention.

Julie—school administrator

I really enjoy and get a lot out of hands-on experiences. Sharing in an experience, working in a team and setting goals together with my colleagues are concrete ways I prefer to learn. Feedback from colleagues and friends would echo these statements. They find me a strong and engaged team member that has good instincts and is a "doer."

I love my job, but also realize that it has helped create an imbalance in my learning style. I realize that I am not a very reflective person. While I always conduct event and program evaluations on *what* I do, I rarely take the time to think about *why* I do what I do. This can also said of my personal life. I react quickly rather than thinking things through. I prefer people to ideas and will be more influenced by an inspirational speech than by a logical theory.

The Experiencing Learning Style

Emphasizes **CE** while balancing **AE** and **RO**. The Experiencing style is distinguished by the ability to find meaning from deep involvement in experience.

Learning Strengths

- Building deep personal relationships
- Strong intuition focused by reflection and action
- Open to new experiences

Learning Challenges

- Understanding theory
- Systematic planning
- Evaluation

If your learning style is **Experiencing**, you learn from your deep involvement in your life experiences and contexts. You rely on your feelings and reactions to people and situations to learn. You are sensitive to other people's feelings and are particularly adept in building meaningful relationships. You are open-minded and accepting, which can lead to difficulty in making independent judgments.

You can be innovative and unconventional in your approach to problem-solving. You approach a problem intuitively rather than logically and later seek validation through reflection and action.

Others may see you as sensitive, empathetic, helpful, and intuitive.

Preferred Learning Space

You prefer learning spaces rich in interactions and ongoing communications with your friends and coworkers. While you may enjoy working in groups, you also need time to work alone to get things done. It is important that you receive constructive feedback on your progress at work and in your personal life. It is important for you to have a personal relationship with your teacher.

Alice Y. Kolb and David A. Kolb

Experiencing—In Their Own Words

Susan—human resources director

Over the years I have often questioned why I so much enjoyed beginning new relationships and felt exhilaration when brainstorming, planning, and implementing projects. Rarely have I found pleasure in working alone and felt stifled in situations when I must do so. Engaging in conversation, learning about and from others is exciting and sometimes I am surprised when people with whom I've had little involvement expose their soul. I have been told I ask questions of people and engage others in such a way as to generate rich discussion and debate in a nonthreatening, thoughtful manner, this may be why they open up so easily.

Camille—college student

Unlike many of my classmates who are more abstract learners, I tend to act and then reflect, instead of the reciprocal, reflecting and then acting. I enjoy working with other students inside and outside of a class setting in order to set goals, to engage in lots of activities and to experiment with different approaches to complete a project. I think I am sensitive and considerate to others, but I also like to influence people and change situations. My career goal is to become an adolescent psychologist because I am good at relating to adolescents with an open-minded approach. I really crave interacting with children; that is why I am working at Children's Museum where I have plenty of opportunity to interact with children.

Marianne—consultant

I learn through experiencing and this is an accurate description of the way I learn best. I typically reflect on real experiences and think of analogies as I hear about new ideas and theories. I ask others for input vs. doing detailed research. Then, I quickly want to actively experiment with a new approach or implementing a new solution. The cycle continues, creating many concrete experiences from which I learn.

The Imagining Learning Style

Combines the learning steps of **CE** and **RO**. The **Imagining** style is distinguished by the ability to create meaning by observing and reflecting on experiences.

Learning Strengths

- Awareness of people's feelings and values
- Listening with an open mind
- Imagining the implications of ambiguous situations

Learning Challenges

- Decision making
- Taking leadership
- Timely action

If your learning style is **Imagining**, you learn by stepping back from experiences to observe and reflect on your feelings about what is going on. You have the ability to see things from different perspectives and from many different points of view. Because of your sensitivity to people's feelings you are able to consider diverse opinions and views and bridge the differences. You are comfortable with ambiguity and tend not to see situations in black and white. Your approach to situations is to observe rather than take action.

You are able to recognize patterns in events, relationships, and group interactions and make sense of what they mean. You probably have broad cultural interests and like to gather information. You are good at imagining the implication of a particular course of action and creating alternative paths and approaches.

Others may see you as caring, accepting, creative, sensitive, and open-minded.

Preferred Learning Space

You like working in groups where there is open and free-flowing conversation where you can gather information, listen with an open mind, and receive personalized feedback. You may enjoy situations that call for generating a wide range of ideas, such as brainstorming sessions. You like teachers who take a facilitating role and are sensitive and creative.

Imagining—In Their Own Words

Annie—consultant

As luck may have it, my LSI indicates a strong reliance upon Imagining. Having no prior knowledge of learning styles when I took the assessment, I did so with an open mind and no preconceived notion of what type of learning style I favored (which turns out to be a strength of an Imagining learner, by the way). In groups I like to sit back and see how the people fit together before taking action, which reflects both observing and understanding people. I am very sensitive to people's feelings and often can tell you more about the tone of a conversation than what was actually discussed. I like brainstorming and use it whenever possible, whether trying to decide on what to eat for dinner with my family or in a meeting at work. I think outside the box (creative) and I like to get to the root of the issue (problem recognition). Every characteristic rings true with how I see myself.

Lorain—nonprofit organization manager

As an imagining learner, I have the ability to take a multiple-perspective "helicopter view," allowing me to see "surfacing" of patterns of emotional energy between individuals, and among and within groups, systems, and events. My ability to see the large picture allows me to notice and anticipate the likelihood of what may happen if a particular decision or action is taken. As a result, I am often able to redirect individual, group, system, or event energy in new directions. The downside of my style is that, because of my extreme imaginative tendency, I tend to be distracted by all the possibilities and views that I see. I often received feedback from people around me that I am a "big picture planner," or "have ability to see things globally."

Robin—consultant/trainer

I can understand why I am an imagining learner. In group situations such as project teams to which I have been assigned, and classes for religious study at my church, I have received feedback that I am someone who watches and listens first, then participates; that when I do participate, people listen and value my input because they know I have thought through the topic or question; that I can represent multiple views of the same situation or topic; and that I have a bias for action and getting things done. As an example, we attended a private golf lesson together and recognized that my husband's approach to improving his golf swing is to analyze the components of an ideal golf swing, to break it down in his mind and then to tape himself to see if his swing is on the same plane as the model swing. I improve my swing by getting the feel of a good swing, learning to tell the difference between the feel of a good swing or a poor swing, and then repeating it over and over until the feel of a good swing is ingrained in my mind and body.

The Reflecting Learning Style

Emphasizes **RO** while balancing **CE** and **AC**. The **Reflecting** style is distinguished by the ability to connect experience and ideas through sustained reflection.

Learning Strengths

- Understanding others' point of view
- Seeing "what's going on" in situations
- Converting intuitions into explicit explanations
- Gathering information

Alice Y. Kolb and David A. Kolb

Learning Challenges

- Initiating action
- Rumination
- Speaking up in groups

If your learning style is **Reflecting**, you use observation and reflection as the primary basis for learning. You have the capacity for deep reflection while balancing the ability to engage both in feeling and thinking. You enjoy situations that call for generating different alternatives and perspectives and identifying problems. Because of your keen sense of observation, you are able to make sense of and recognize the deeper meaning that underlies events, facts, and people's interactions. You value process and talking about your reflections with others to debrief events.

When you organize information or analyze data, you do it in a manner that is meaningful and orderly. When working with teams and organizations, you excel in ability to create processes that produce healthy communication and effective outcomes. You are good in coming up with creative ideas and solutions to problems but prefer to leave the implementation to others. You are sensitive to people's feelings, thoughts, and needs and are able to find common ground by bringing together different ideas and perspectives.

People may see you as quiet, insightful, thorough, sensitive, and deep.

Preferred Learning Space

You thrive in learning spaces rich in dialogue and discussions, but you are also comfortable learning from lectures, independent projects, and from readings. Because of your preference for deep reflection, you may also need time to reflect and make sense of your experience on your own. You value teachers who provide opportunities for individual and group reflection and who are open to exploring ideas.

Reflecting—In Their Own Words

Jerry—human resources manager

The reflecting learning style has been particularly well-suited to the traditional teaching methods I've experienced in my educational career. I have enjoyed classroom lectures and work well independently. I am able to process a wide variety of information, find patterns and themes, and easily understand the underlying theories. As a result, my academic performance has been strong. I am an avid note-taker. My textbooks and professional reading include numerous margin notes about ideas sparked by the reading. These represent the reflecting, brainstorming, and conceptualizing that accompany my learning. This opportunity to reflect and organize information is critical to my ability to retain what I have learned. To move in to Active Experimentation, I am most successful when I can partner with a colleague who demonstrates that strength. Using observation, I am able to learn from role models whose strengths are different from my own.

I have always had many interests, often more intellectual in nature. As I have grown older, my interests have often related to concepts and theories. My health and fitness goals are more motivated by a commitment to the concept of good health than by any external or social factor.

Kirk—organizational development consultant

I can relate very well to the Reflecting style of learning. I see myself as someone who learns best when I can take time to think and reflect on information that I am taking in. I have been told that I "overprocess" situations and events in my life. My husband often takes a deep breath when I say "I would really like to talk more about…" Once I process the information and how I feel about the information or situation, then I can take action with greater ease. When considering a situation in my personal life or my professional life, my first response is usually to get as many different ideas and perspectives from as many people as possible before coming to my own conclusions.

In my professional life, I have frequently been asked to lead brainstorming sessions as it's something that feels very natural to me. I am sensitive to feelings of others and I think this is something I was born with.

Bill—director of operations

As I reflect on my learning style results, it makes sense that I am a reflective learner. I often received feedback from people around me that I had excellent interpersonal skills. In my job role of director of operations, analytical problem-solving skills are valuable in supporting the development of systems, processes, and structures, often involving information management and technology, and strategy, for example. As I reflect, I know that I am excellent at organizing information. For example, some of the most significant contributions I have made include a computer system that serves as a tool for capturing, organizing, tracking, and sharing resident information among counselors.

Here are few examples of feedback I have gotten from various people around me and I think they describe well my learning style:

"You're sensitive to feelings and people."

—Friend.

"You balance well the intuitive, sensitive, emotional
side of things along with the more abstract and
analytical; On the other hand, you could do
some things faster and less thoroughly."

—Coworker.

"You do first apply logic to ideas, but you are
willing to allow persons to pursue them even
if the logic cannot be articulated. You know
that there are other ways of knowing."

—Wife.

The Analyzing Learning Style

Combines learning modes of **RO** and **AC**. The **Analyzing** style is distinguished by the ability to integrate and systematize ideas through reflection.

Learning Strengths

- Organizing information
- Being logical and rational
- Building conceptual models

Learning Challenges

- Risk taking
- Socializing with others
- Dealing with lack of structure

If Analyzing is your learning style, you are best at taking in a wide range of information and putting it into concise, logical form. You probably are less focused on people and more interested in abstract ideas and concepts. Generally, people with this learning style find it more important that a theory has logical soundness than practical value. You like to carefully analyze and assess each step and weigh its relative consequence before taking action. Because you like to plan ahead, you are able to minimize mistakes and anticipate potential problems and pitfalls.

When dealing with people or events, your approach is to rely on your logical and objective understanding of the situation and avoid your feelings to get in the way of your sound judgments.

Others may see you as logical, organized, reliable, careful, and thoughtful.

Preferred Learning Space

You thrive in learning spaces where you can use and develop your analytical and conceptual skills. You may prefer lectures, readings, exploring analytical models, and having time to think things through. You would rather work alone than in groups. You prefer teachers who model their thinking and analysis process in their lectures and interactions with you.

Analyzing—In Their Own Words

Scott—art student

When I came to art school, I decided to major in graphic design. I was always drawn to the conceptual part of the design process. I can see things in abstract ways and that is the fun part of the graphic design. Now I can see why I am an analytical learner. I like to work on my conceptual skills because it is satisfying to me and I am good at it. One time, our teacher gave us a design assignment. I produced a piece I was pretty proud of and I took it to my teacher for him to critique it. He looked at my work and said: "I like your concept and your drawing skills are excellent. But, I don't feel anything from it. It does not communicate to me what you are experiencing." I was surprised by what he said. But I know now, by looking at my LSI kite, what he meant. I do not use my feeling very much when I learn. I rarely go out in the world to experience things. I like to stay in my studio and work on my projects from my head. If I want to become a good artist, I need to become well-rounded by working on my underdeveloped skills.

Jane—higher education administrator

As a strong analytical learner, I excel in "planning systematically." I am touted as an exceptional planner. In fact, I spend a portion of every day planning the day, week, and month ahead. I do this through lists, spreadsheets, calendars, and even Post-It notes, napkins, and e-mails to myself that eventually find their way to another master list. In addition, my current career involves extensive planning of meetings and events. My learning style contributes greatly to my success and positive job performance reviews in this position.

I find that my learning style is an asset in my career and long-term career goals but can at times be a detriment in my personal relationships. By rigorously and constantly making sense of ideas and concepts, I do not allow for much spontaneity or chaos. I occasionally miss out on experiences because they do not fit my agenda. By loosening up and going with the flow more often, I will open the doors to new experiences and opportunities for growth and learning.

Michelle—college student

I understand why I enjoy making sense of things. I am able to gather all kinds of data and information and pull it together to make sense. My classmate pointed out to me that although this may be my strength, this is also where one of my weaknesses becomes evident. She told me, "You oftentimes develop great points in your mind during class, but then you don't openly share them." This is because I am more comfortable discussing an idea with a small group of people or one-on-one and it becomes harder for me to find that same comfort in a large class. I am a very individual thinker. Reflecting and analyzing an idea comes easily to me, but not right away in a classroom. I am better off working alone, outside of a crowded and intimidating atmosphere. Along the same line, I prefer to study alone as opposed to studying in groups because I have always been a strong individual learner. I always enjoyed math, because solving math equations is a purely rational exercise that does not require communication.

The Thinking Learning Style

Emphasizes **AC** while balancing **AE** and **RO**. The **Thinking** style is distinguished by the capacity for disciplined involvement in abstract reasoning, mathematics, and logic.

Learning Strengths

- Logical analysis
- Rational decision making
- Analyzing quantitative data

Learning Challenges

- Working with people
- Keeping an open mind about your ideas
- "Lost in thought"

If Thinking is your learning style, you learn primarily by deep involvement in abstraction. You value thinking things through and like to fit a wide range of data and information into concise ideas and models. You may enjoy working with numbers and engage in mental activities in general that require abstract reasoning and analytical skills. You may prefer working with quantitative over qualitative information. You like to work by yourself and prefer to deal with technical tasks rather than personal issues.

You are good at planning and goal-setting, but you like to concentrate on the quality of your plan rather than achieving the actual goals. You strive for consistency and accuracy in your worldviews and ideas. You tend to be controlled in your emotional expression and like to speak precisely and concisely. When you act, your action tends to be the result of much thought. You work hard to avoid mistakes.

Others may see you as thorough, precise, reliable, consistent, and introspective.

Preferred Learning Space.

You may learn best in well-structured learning spaces with clear directions and learning agendas. You also thrive in environments in which you can design or conduct experiments or manipulate data. You may prefer to work alone and need time to think things through. A teacher's expertise in their field is of primary importance to you.

Thinking—In Their Own Words

Jake—college student

I think my learning style descriptions fit the way I like to learn. I do not like to be lectured and would rather want to be working on a lab doing something with the information instead of just sitting and listening to the professor talk. I think that is why I like math so much because I can think things through and solve problems. I prefer to work on mathematics or physics problems much more than working out problems with a friend or family member.

Marianne—financial analyst

I like to solve problems, make decisions, and I have a slight preference toward the technical tasks vs. personal issues. In a learning setting, I need to see the practical application of the topic or a theory. I need time to absorb information and think through it, planning and organizing information. I absolutely want to know exactly what I have to do to meet and exceed the standard. In fact, when I don't have this information or when others in the group move forward without the information, or don't allow me the time I need to assimilate it, I get frustrated. I need to know what success and failure looks like in the eyes of the person who is judging. I need time alone to process information and rejuvenate. I make "to-do" lists for everything from tasks at work, to the grocery store, or packing for a trip. Doing this helps me to feel organized and focused. I don't like to be responsible for certain types of decisions for fear that I will make the wrong decision. Decisions such as, which direction to take when driving, giving advice, or which gift to purchase. Being so centered in thinking perhaps causes me to struggle between planning and developing options and making decisions.

Brian—editor and newsroom manager

It does not come as surprise to me that learning style assessment shows that I am "thinker." I learn more by thinking, although my preference for acting and watching is also strong. Often, when I set out to learn something new, my first inclination is to find a "how-to" book on the subject. This is especially true if the subject is technical; for example having to do with computer systems, organization development, sailing, or training a puppy. But it's also true in the case of more creative subjects, such as cooking or learning to play the guitar. I'm inclined to want to know the "big picture"—theory, scales, and so on in the case of the guitar—rather than to just sit down and sound out the music.

And while I'm aware of people's feelings and am open to varying opinions on a project or problem, I generally prefer to approach things logically rather than emotionally and tend to short-circuit process and "cut to the chase."

The Deciding Learning Style

Combines learning modes of **AC** and **AE**. The **Deciding** style is distinguished by the ability to use theories and models to decide on problem solutions and courses of action.

Learning Strengths

- Problem solving
- Evaluating ideas and solutions
- Setting goals
- Making decisions

Learning Challenges

- Thinking "out of the box"
- Sensitivity to people's feelings
- Dealing with ambiguity

If **Deciding** is your learning style, you are best at finding practical uses for ideas and theories. You have the ability to solve problems and make decisions based on rational evaluation of solutions to questions or problems. You are good at identifying flaws and mistakes in concepts and ideas by testing them in the real world. You like to set clear goals, evaluate, and then decide on the best path to achieve them. Because you are efficient and focused, you tend not to be distracted by what you consider to be tangential facts or information. This can sometimes lead to missing important information or solving the wrong problem.

Your focus is on technical problem-solving when working with others. When you work with people, you tend to concentrate on helping them to solve their problems efficiently and effectively rather on feelings and interpersonal issues.

People may see you as focused, pragmatic, rational, and decisive.

Preferred Learning Space
You may learn best in learning spaces where you can experiment with new ideas, simulations, laboratory assignments, and practical applications. You prefer teachers who set clear standards and goals and evaluate with problems and questions that have right or wrong answers.

Deciding—In Their Own Words

George—sales manager

My preferred learning style is "deciding" and I believe this to be a good fit in terms of how I see myself. In addition to my regional sales management responsibilities, I also oversee the sales productivity function. My sales productivity team focuses on how to help the organization become more effective and efficient through the practical application of various tools, technology, and training. Given my preference for a "deciding" learning and working style, I tend to enjoy gathering information, from both internal and external sources to the organization. I like to solve problems and make decisions to help the sales team succeed in creating a competitive advantage. As an example of this, I actively experiment with my sales team, taking the new ideas that are generated by my sales productivity team and finding practical applications related to organization structure, incentive compensation, performance recognition, and enabling tools and technology. But as I am an introvert by nature and therefore prefer to deal with technical tasks and problems vs. social and interpersonal issues, I need to understand people better, and be more open-minded. Also, I use little reflection in my work and life in general. In my case I can learn from my wife, who has "imagining" learning style tendencies, and hope to improve our communication knowing now that we approach problems from opposite ends of the spectrum.

Charles—management consultant

As a "deciding" learner, I have a desire to understand things from a conceptual perspective rather than a concrete one. My preference for models and theories validates why I excel at courses that are more conceptual in nature. I have a natural tendency to communicate conceptually instead of concretely. For example, with my wife being more concrete than conceptual, it validates the tendency to "lose her" when I give a conceptual explanation. It also validates my challenge in learning to understand and communicate with my children at a more concrete level. I have a natural desire to apply and act on what I am learning as opposed to reflecting and pondering. I don't feel I fully understand something till I have an opportunity to experiment and test it out. My deciding style explains the tension I feel when I am with those of other learning styles. When I'm with those with an initiating style, I feel a need to push for a clearer conceptual understanding of the situation before moving to action and solutions. When I'm with those with an analyzing style, I feel a need to address the question, "Will this model or theory work?" and "When we will we test it out?" When I'm with those with an imagining style, I feel the need to bring direction and closure after multiple ideas are expressed and generated.

Amanda—management consultant

The Deciding learning style suits me for many different reasons. When I first reflected on this definition, the first thing that stood out was that I *usually converge on the correct solution.* This is definitely how most situations play out for me. I tend to go into situations, either alone or with people, and come out with a clear concise analysis with data and facts that results in a plan for the future. Throughout my life, people have said to me that I can clear away the garbage to find the truth with ease and wisdom beyond my years. People in my life tend to gravitate to me when they need a solution or for my honesty and clear-headed nature. I tend to arrive at an answer to tough decisions more quickly than others might, but this should not be mistaken for rash or impulsive decision-making. Rather, I am sure of my answer once I have analyzed and arrived at that answer, lending a very decisive and definitive air to my interactions. This has done wonders for me in career and my personal world.

The Acting Learning Style

Emphasizes **AE** while balancing **CE** and **AC**. The **Acting** style is distinguished by a strong motivation for goal-directed action that integrates people and tasks.

Learning Strengths

- Combining technical knowledge and personal relationships
- Focused on getting things done
- Leading work teams

Learning Challenges

- Taking time to reflect
- Solving the right problem
- Gathering and analyzing information

If your learning style is **Acting,** you use action as your primary basis for learning. You are goal-oriented and focused on getting things done. You are good at implementing plans or testing ideas by combining your experience of the immediate situation with ideas and concepts for dealing with it. You have the ability to find solutions to questions or problems based on technical analysis while paying attention to the needs of people. You may be equally comfortable in functioning in a practical world that can make use of your feelings and actions as well in a technical world that requires your conceptual abilities. As a result, you excel in identifying and integrating tasks and people's needs.

You are good at improving existing operations and systems and producing results. You can excel in a leadership position that calls for coordinating complex operations and systems. Because of your strong preference for action over reflection, you may tend to commit to an idea without considering its consequences and alternative options or solutions.

Others may see you as dynamic, strategic, personable, and responsible.

Preferred Learning Space

You learn best by on-the-job learning through discussions with colleagues and working in teams. You prefer teachers with practical real-world experience that you can emulate.

Acting—In Teir Own Words

Elizabeth—retail store manager

As an Acting learner, I do find that I move easily to the doing stage, and am more comfortable plunging into get things done. When I have a task ahead, I am eager to get started. Usually I will have a strong gut feeling about the best course of action. My next step will be to look for data to validate my intuition. I do think about what and why my intuition is pointing in a certain direction and like to get my conceptual arms around the topic. I look for a few pieces of information to back up my perception using people and other sources. I don't spend enormous time gathering data although if it is an important decision and I am unsure, I will spend time talking to people I respect. Once ready to act, I do. I am comfortable learning by doing and taking risk. On the positive side, I am able to get lots done, moving from one thing to another, switching gears easily. I don't get overwhelmed that easily by work. On the negative side, sometimes I am surprised by something that I haven't researched thoroughly or that when learning-by-doing the results are not as perfect as I might like.

Nancy—independent consultant

I very much agree that my learning style is Acting. I experience a "need" to act during my learning process. My colleagues, staff, and family all agree that it's my drive for action and the passion in which I move to action, that draws them to me. It's also my Achilles heel, meaning, at times I move to action before I've properly finished gathering all the sources of data, spent time away from the "facts" to consider other options and reflect on other potential ideas. When I'm not careful or when timing is tight and I feel internal pressure to meet deadlines and implement tasks, I will skip over the RO component of learning process completely. I hyper-process information, succumbing to deep analysis that is very quick, but gives little time for the data to digest.

The Balancing Learning Style

Balances **CE, AC, AE, and RO**. The **Balancing** style is distinguished by the ability to adapt flexibly by weighing the pros and cons of acting versus reflecting and experiencing versus thinking.

Learning Strengths

- Flexibility in moving around the learning cycle
- Ability to work with diverse groups of people
- Creative insights

Learning Challenges

- Indecisiveness
- "Jack of all trades, master of none."
- Sustained commitment

If your learning style is **Balancing**, your primary approach to learning is to switch approaches from feeling to thinking and from reflecting to acting. Because of your ability to navigate through the learning cycle you can change your approach to learning based on the situation. You are open to new experiences and equally adept at identifying and solving problems. You are able to see diverse perspectives on issues and bridge differences between people with different styles. In a team environment you are able to adapt to fill in the missing style needed to get the task done and help the team navigate through the learning cycle.

Because of your balanced worldview, you may find it difficult to make decisions about issues or choose between different alternatives. Your tendency to pursue a variety of interests may lead you to change jobs and careers many times over the course of your life.

People may see you as curious, open, flexible, multitalented, and resourceful.

Preferred Learning Space
You tend to be more satisfied in learning environments where you can use all four learning modes: lectures, discussions groups, brainstorming sessions, labs, and on-the-job learning. Because you are able to adapt to the different learning environments, you can learn from teachers with different teaching approaches.

Balancing—In Their Own Words

Cloe—college freshman
It makes a lot of sense why I am a balancing learner. I thought I was different from other people but never understood why and in what ways. For example, when I took the test, it was difficult from me to choose one item over others. They all made sense to me and I said to myself, "Well, I do all these things when I am learning!" When I looked at my classmates' LSI styles, they all had strong preferences one way or the other. I was like, "Here I go again. I don't fit anywhere." I can see what I have to do in each different situation. For example, we had a group activity in class the other day. We had to come up with a solution to a case study that the instructor had assigned to us. I can see that some of my classmates like to brainstorm a lot, and others like just to stand back and think. It came to a point where I knew we need to make a decision about what to do and that was the role I took up on myself. Many times I feel like it sucks to be able to see what is going on when nobody else seems to be able to. Now I have a different perspective and appreciation for who I am. I am a balanced learner and I have a lot of strengths as a result of my learning style.

Mary Lou—art college student

I am not surprised about how I came out in my learning style test. I am a balanced learner for sure. I took a lot of different kind of personality tests in the past and I managed to come out right in the middle in all of them. When people ask me if I am a pro-life or pro-choice, or if I am a liberal or conservative, it is hard for me to take a position because I can see the strengths and weaknesses in both sides of the arguments.

Karen—CEO's chief of staff

"Jack of all trades and master of none." This timeworn phrase is often used to describe journalists, and certainly applied to my two decades in the profession. I covered police, politics, education, and child welfare, to name just a few. My friends from college pursued medicine or graduate school; I just kept learning a little bit about a lot.

Jina—consultant

Because I am comfortable learning in a variety of ways, I am adaptable to different situations and contexts, which makes me a versatile team member. I am generally able to do whatever is needed to get the job done. In addition, I tend to pick up new skills or concepts quickly, which I would attribute to my ability to learn in a variety of ways.

Appendix 3

The experiential learning session designs described below can be used in classes and training programs to explain aspects of ELT and learning styles. The experiences are designed to "teach around the learning cycle" so participants of all styles can sometimes find their home space and practice using other learning styles to develop the capacity for full-cycle learning. Each design activity is coded with the learning styles the activity is designed to activate for participants.

These designs can also be used as a model for curriculum design about other topics. By identifying in advance the learning styles you wish to have learners practice and develop in each activity, a greater focus and intentionality can be achieved. Reviewing the overall design will give a perspective on how well the unit teaches around the whole learning cycle.

Session Design 1: Using the KLSI 4.0 to Understand Individual Learning Styles and Learning Flexibility

Objectives

- To help participants increase their understanding of the way they learn.
- To heighten participants' awareness of their own, and others' learning styles.
- To enable participants to assess their learning strengths and weaknesses, and learning flexibility.
- To set learning goals that promote self-development and growth.

Materials Required

- Participants should be instructed to take the KLSI 4.0 online, print out the interpretative booklet with their scores and bring it to the session.
- The exercise requires a large, open area to afford sufficient room for participants to position themselves on the experiential learning space; a classroom with movable furniture or another large open area is preferable.
- Materials to reproduce the nine-style experiential learning space shown in chapter 2, figure 2.3, in an open area large enough to accommodate the participants (e.g. masking tape to produce the nine-style grid and paper and markers for labels).
- Blank flipcharts: two to three sheets for each small group of four to six members
- Flipchart markers: one per small group

Presentation Issues

To prepare for the session, facilitators should take the instrument themselves and read the KLSI 4.0 Interpretative Report. For answers to questions most likely to be asked about ELT and the KLSI, go to FAQ at www.learningfromexperience.com.

In administering the KLSI, we have noticed that some participants accept it with almost blind faith, treating it as an ultimate measure of their personality traits. We feel the KLSI is used best as an instrument for self-inquiry, and that KLSI scores should be open to cross-validation through other sources of data, checked against how the participants see themselves and how others see them. To reinforce this, this session includes an opportunity for participants to review their scores, in light of what they have learned in the learning styles presentation and their personal experience of their learning strengths and weaknesses.

Time Frames
The total session time and the estimates for each activity step may vary with the size of your group and your facilitating style. Use them as a guide.

Timeline (Total time: 1:30 to 2 hours)

Step 1 0:00–0:20
Styles to Engage: Thinking + Analyzing + Reflecting
Introduce exercises and objectives to participants. Present an overview of the four stages of the Cycle of Learning, the nine Learning Style Types, and the strengths and weaknesses of each style type (see chapter 1 pp. 3–9 and pp. 4–16 of the KLSI 4.0 Interpretative Report.)

Step 2 0:20–0:25
Styles to Engage: Reflecting + Analyzing + Thinking + Deciding
Have participants individually review their learning style kite shape and type description on page 8 of the KLSI 4.0 Interpretative Report and review the other eight styles that follow. They should reflect on whether their learning style type fits for them or if another fits them better. If they wish they can choose another style type for steps 3 and 4.

Step 3 0:25–0:30
Styles to Engage: Acting + Reflecting + Experiencing
Have participants position themselves according to their learning style type
on the Experiential Learning Space. Ask them to observe their position relative to the rest of their group and the overall style emphasis of the group.

Step 4 0:30–0:50
**Styles to Engage: Initiating + Experiencing + Reflecting + Acting +
Analyzing**
Form small groups, three to six members each, whose members share a
similar style. If a style is represented by only one or two people, have them
choose a similar style group to join (e.g. a Deciding style could join with the
Thinking group).

Have each group select a member who will report the results of their
discussion to the large group.

Post the flipchart with the following discussion questions. In the small
groups, have each member in turn respond to the discussion questions. Other
group members may ask questions as each person speaks, but encourage
groups to budget their time so all members can respond to these questions.

Guidelines for Small-Group Discussion

1. Individual Learning Style
   - Do your learning profile scores seem valid to you?
   - How do you describe the way you learn?
   - What is your greatest strength as a learner?
   - What is your greatest weakness as a learner?
2. Personal Learning Goals
   - What do you want to achieve in this session?
   - How do you want to improve your learning skills?
   - What changes would you like to make in your learning style?
3. Preferred Learning Environment
   - What kinds of learning situations are best?

- What makes it difficult for you to learn?
- What can the facilitator or other participants do to help you learn?

Step 5 0:50–1:20
Styles to Engage: Initiating + Experiencing +Reflecting + Analyzing + Thinking
Reassemble the large group and ask each small group in turn to briefly report the results of its discussion. Allow for questions after each report and summarize conclusions at the end of the reports.

Step 6 1:20–1:35
Styles to Engage: **Reflecting + Analyzing + Thinking**

Learning Flexibility
Introduce the concept of learning flexibility. Direct participants to the KLSI 4.0 Interpretative Report and help them understand their learning flexibility index score and profile (showing and explaining your own scores can sometimes help here).

Step 7 1:35–1:45
Styles to Engage: Initiating + Experiencing +Imagining + Reflecting + Analyzing + Thinking + Deciding + Acting + Balancing
Working individually, participants should complete the Personal Learning Goal worksheet following instructions on page 18 of the KLSI 4.0 Interpretative Report.

Step 7 can be given as a homework assignment. If time is limited, proceed to step 8 and 9.

Step 8 1:45–1:55
Styles to Engage: Initiating + Experiencing + Reflecting + Analyzing + Acting
Divide participants into groups of three and instruct them to share their goal plans and give each other their ideas and reactions.

Step 9 1:55–2:05
Styles to Engage: Initiating + Acting + Reflecting + Thinking
Ask the trios to briefly report their conversations and summarize findings.

Session Design 2: The Lemon Exercise: Experiencing and Thinking

Objectives

- To increase understanding of the foundation of the experiential learning cycle—William James's dual-knowledge concept.
- To heighten participants' awareness of their own experiencing and thinking process.
- To enable participants to assess their learning strengths and weaknesses in both modes, and to set learning goals that promote self-development and growth.

Materials Required

- Lemons—one lemon for each student
- Large cardboard box (to hold all lemons)
- Blank flipcharts: three sheets

Preparation
The following articles, available for download at www.learningfromexperience.com, provide useful background information for this session:

Kolb, A. Y., & Kolb, D. A. (2009). The learning way: Metacognitive aspects of experiential learning. *Simulation and Gaming: An Interdisciplinary Journal, 40*(3), 297–327.

Yeganeh, B., & Kolb, D. A. (2009). Mindfulness and experiential learning. *OD Practitioner, 41*(3), 8–14.

Time Frames
The total session time and the estimates for each activity step may vary with the size of your group and your facilitating style. Use them as a guide.

Timeline (Total time: 1 hour, 15 minutes)

Step 1 0:00–0:10
Styles to Engage: Analyzing + Thinking + Deciding
Introduce the exercise and objectives to participants.

Hold up a lemon and ask the group "What is this?" Ask them to describe what they know about lemons. You can provide the first example: lemons are yellow. They may provide more adjectives such as oval, sour, grows on trees, citrus, small, light, and so on. Make a list of all the descriptions on a flipchart, or chalkboard, or something.

Step 2 0:10–0:15
Styles to Engage: **Experiencing + Imagining + Reflecting**

After the list describing lemons is made, give each participant their own personal lemon. Ask them to get to know their personal lemon carefully for about one minute. Make it clear that they will need to remember details about the lemon. Ask them to think of a story about how the lemon came to look like it does. Tell them that they can give their lemon a name.

Step 3 0:15–0:25
Styles to Engage: Reflecting + Analyzing + Deciding
After participants have had time to study their lemon, go around the room with the box and collect all the lemons, and mix them up.

Place the box in the center of the room and tell the participants to pick their lemon out. There may be a small scuffle at the box. If the group is large, pour the lemons on the floor in a large open space to facilitate the process of finding their lemon. It will seem to many that they will not be able to pick out their lemon from a box of twenty to thirty lemons, but we have had groups of fifty people find their lemon with only one or two exceptions.

Step 4 0:25–0:40
Styles to Engage: Experiencing + Reflecting + Initiating + Acting

When everyone has their lemon again, have them return to their seats. Go around the room asking participants how they identified their lemon. They will be eager to explain their personal lemon. Make a list of the characteristics that the students mention, which will vary, but they will be something similar to: large lumps, a big scratch, a patch of green, a very skinny lemon, small or large, and so on.

Step 5 0:40–0:45
Styles to Engage: Reflecting + Analyzing + Thinking
When the list of characteristics is complete, place it next to the first list of general lemon characteristics and ask participants to compare the two lists. Ask "What is the difference between these two lists?" Responses will be like—the first is general and the second is unique; based on prior knowledge versus based on present experience; comes from thinking versus comes from the senses.

Step 6 0:45–1:00
Styles to Engage: Initiating + Analyzing + Thinking

Introduce William James's dual-knowledge theory and its place in the experiential learning cycle—knowing through CE and AC. Emphasize that we all know the world in both ways and that it is by integrating these two ways of knowing through the transformation dimension of action and reflection that we learn and create. Connect the dual-knowledge theory to the two lists. The first list is James's *knowledge about* lemons based on conceptualizing and the second list is *knowledge of acquaintance* based on experiencing.

Step 7 1:00–1:15

Styles to Engage: Balancing + Thinking + Experiencing + Acting + Imagining

Group practice and discussion—ask participants to put themselves in the conceptualizing mode for one minute. Have them share their thoughts.

Now ask them to put themselves in the experiencing mode for one minute. Have them share their experience. Ask:

- Which mode was easier for you to get into?
- What techniques did you use to get into the modes?
- Are you able to "toggle" between modes in your daily life or do you get stuck in one?
- What are the pluses and minuses of each mode for learning? For productivity?
- For creativity? For personal relationships?
- What action steps can you take to integrate both modes in your daily life?

Appendix 4

The Personal Application Assignment (PAA) was developed as a way for participants to consolidate insights gleaned from experiential learning, and for educators to assess participants' learning. It is a holistic evaluation method that gives equal weight to all four modes of the learning cycle. The PAA is a journal or essay assignment in which participants:

1. select an experience, occurring either in or out of the training session, and chronicle the actual events of the experience;
2. review their thoughts and feelings about the experience, making observations about it from a fresh perspective;
3. develop concepts or theories that make sense of the experience;
4. create future action plans based on what they have learned from the experience.

Since each step of the PAA process corresponds to a step in the Cycle of Learning, the PAA guides the learner through all four phases, from actual experience to future planning. The PAA is a useful tool for consolidating learning, for developing new insights about one's experience, and for learning how to learn. It can be used to evaluate participant learning achieved through experiential methods and to help participants consolidate learning derived both from courses, from training sessions, and from first-hand experience.

The PAA can be used as a journal assignment, as an adjunct to training session discussion, or as a follow-up to training games or simulations. The PAA can be used as an adjunct to training discussion as it helps participants to generalize and gain new insights from classroom experiential learning. For young participants or those with overspecialized learning styles, such a guided pass through the learning modes can be a growth-promoting process. In addition, observation, reflection, and conceptualization about experience by participants is critical if the facilitator is to avoid providing merely pleasant or exciting exercises with limited transferable usefulness. Finally, the PAA has been used successfully as a follow-up to day-long simulations and to more limited training sessions. Its flexibility in encouraging expression of subjective feelings and reactions as well as objective concepts and theories seems particularly well-suited to the dynamic atmosphere of the training game or simulation.

Using the PAA

The PAA is most effective when the CE (actual experience) chosen has some personal significance for the participant. For this reason, students sometimes choose a personal experience from outside the learning environment. If the emphasis is solely on personal growth and practice with the learning modes, this is an acceptable choice; however, if the focus is on direct experience that generates theories and insights about a theoretical concept (for example, intergroup dynamics), then a more controlled training exercise might be a better choice. This prevents exploration of experiences that, while personally significant to the participant, might have little relevance to the topic at hand.

We have experienced problems with the PAA as a classroom tool only when participants have not clearly understood its purpose or the guidelines for grading. Since the assignment is probably unlike papers the participants have written in the past, all expectations should be made clear at the outset. The elements of the PAA section summarizes the suggested grading criteria for each section of the PAA. We suggest that this, the sample PAA and the grading criteria summary at the end of this appendix be used as handouts to explain the essay requirements.

Guidelines on Grading, Topic Selection, and Confidentiality

There are five elements to the paper and each normally is weighted equally. A twenty point grading system simplifies the understanding of how each component of the paper is graded and weighted. These include the four elements in the learning style model and a fifth element that takes into account the introduction, integration, synthesis, and general quality of writing in the PAA. The score given in each element depends upon how effectively the student has met all the criteria listed for that section of the paper. For the instructor's part, we believe that instructors need to provide specific feedback as quickly as possible to students on why they were awarded points in each area and, more importantly, what they need to do to improve. To achieve these objectives, the same summary sheet that guides the grading is provided to the student as feedback. This sheet is attached at the end of this handout.

Choosing a good topic is essential. Select an experience that relates to the assigned course topics. It should be an experience that the learner would like to understand better, or that was problematical or significant. When students are excited about learning more about the incident, their papers are lively and interesting. The topic must be meaty enough to take it through the entire learning cycle. The incident does not have to be work-related; an incident in any setting (sports, school, family, church, etc.) that relates to the course topics is acceptable.

The learner should select a recent experience (not something that happened back in high school). The more recent the experience, the more likely it is that one could take actions that could improve one's current interactions with a supervisor, group member, roommate, or others. Two additional issues should be considered in choosing a topic. The first is confidentiality. Students sometimes wish to write on a topic that is of a personal nature. They may be willing for the instructor to read their paper but not want this to be read by other students in the class. This is a reasonable request and confidentiality will be honored. Students who want their paper to be confidential should inform the instructor ahead of time and should write "confidential" at the top of the paper.

Elements of the PAA

1. **Concrete Experience.** In this part of the paper, students briefly describe what happens in the experience. A simple description of the events that occurred is not sufficient. The feelings experienced by the student as well as his or her thoughts and perceptions during the experience are relevant to this discussion. Another way of looking at the concrete experience would be to recognize that it possesses an objective and a subjective component. The objective part presents the facts of the experience, like a newspaper account, without an attempt to analyze the content. The subjective part is the "here-and-now" personal experience of the event. This experience is composed of feelings, perceptions, and thoughts.

   Helpful hints: (1) It often helps students to replay the experience in their mind. After reviewing the experience, students should write a report of what they saw, heard, felt, thought, and heard and saw others doing. (2) Students should avoid presenting the detailed mechanics of the experience unless these are critical to the remainder of the paper. This section of the paper should be no longer than 1.5 pages long. (3) Students should avoid reporting the feelings and thoughts experienced after the experience being described. This retrospection is more appropriate in the reflective observation section.

Example: We all sat at the table together. Not a sound came from any of us. Finally, after what felt like an hour to me, I simply had to say something. "Why are all of you taking this course?" I asked. One person, a small foreign-looking man said, "I needed this course to complete my MBA." Others laughed. Another person, a nicely dressed woman, said, "I'd like to get an easy 'A.'" I thought to myself: What a bummer! I didn't want to be in a group with people who didn't take the subject matter seriously. When the meeting ended, my perceptions of the group had somehow changed. Maybe this was a good group to be in after all. Some of the members had similar interests to mine, and most of them were nice people that I could see getting along with. I felt somehow hopeful that this semester wouldn't be so bad after all.

2. **Reflective Observation.** The student should ask him/herself: What did I observe in the experience and what possible meanings could these observations have? The key task here is to gather as many observations as possible by observing the experience from different points of view. The main skill to work on is perspective-taking or what some people call reframing. Try to look at this experience and describe it from different perspectives. For example, how did other participants view the situation and what did it mean to them? What would a neutral ("objective") observer have seen and heard? If some time has passed since the experience, do you now see the situation differently? Look beneath the surface and try to explain why the people involved behaved the way they did. Reflect on these observations to discover the personal meaning that the situation had for you.

   Helpful hints: (1) If possible, discuss the experience with others who were involved, to gain their views and clarify your perceptions. (2) "Unhook" yourself from the experience and meditate about it in a relaxed atmosphere. Mull over your observations until their personal meaning becomes clear to you. Try to figure out why people, and you in particular, behaved as they did. What can you learn about yourself, looking back on the experience? If you write about a conflict or interaction, be sure to analyze both sides and put yourself in the shoes of the other people involved.

Example: In thinking back on the meeting, I began to see how the group might have taken my comments. My comments were, after all, somewhat aggressive. Some might even call them belligerent. Had I said these things before this class, or at work, I must confess that I would have surprised even myself.

But it seemed there was more going on here than met my eye at the time. Sarah and Bob at first didn't seem to be the kind of people to combine forces on this job, so why was I arguing against them this time? Then it dawned on me: Their departments were about to be combined into the same division! Why hadn't I remembered that during the meeting?

Many thoughts raced through my head. Was the cause of last night's "high" that we won the game? Was it the first time we had worked together as a group? Maybe the fact that member X wasn't there that night helped! But I still had a nagging hunch that my involvement, downplayed as it was from previous meetings, helped.

3. **Abstract Conceptualization.** By relating assigned readings and lectures to what you experienced, you are demonstrating your ability to understand conceptually abstract material through your experiences. This process will help you refine your model of people and organizations. While some assigned readings and lectures will have varying degrees of relevance to your experience, it is important that you make several references and not limit your conceptualizing to just one source. Use at least two *major* concepts or theories from the course readings and cite them correctly.

By reviewing the assigned reading material, you should be able to identify several specific concepts or theories that relate to your experience. First, briefly define the concept or theory as you would for someone who was not familiar with it. What issue or problem does the theory examine? What variables are used to analyze the problem and how does the theory explain the link between causal variables and outcomes. What suggestions does the theory give regarding effective management practices? Second, in a separate paragraph, apply the concept thoroughly to your experience. The tie-in should include the specific details of how the theory relates to and provides insight into your experience. Try to develop diagnostic questions based on the theory that help you to analyze your situation. Does the theory explain what causes certain behaviors or outcomes and were these causes present in your situation? Does the theory distinguish between effective and ineffective practices that help you to understand your situation? Does the experience support or refute parts of the theory? You are encouraged to suggest modifications to a theory to make it fit your particular situation better.

Helpful hints: (1) It is sometimes useful to identify theoretical concepts that interest you first and then search out and elaborate on a personal experience that relates to these concepts. (2) An alternative approach is to select an experience you wish to understand better and then select concepts that apply to your experience.

Example: There are several organizational behavior concepts that help me understand this experience. One is the Thomas-Kilman theory of conflict (Osland, Kolb, Rubin & Turner 2007, pp. 284–285), which is based upon two axes, either the concern for one's own interests or the concern for the interests of the other party. The five styles reflect a low or high position on these two axes and are labeled competition, compromise, avoidance, accommodation, and collaboration.

In the incident I described, my coach began with a collaborative style, high concern for both his own interests and the interests of the other party. He tried to work out a solution that would satisfy both of us but I neither saw nor heard his point of view. I just wanted to get my own way and practice in the same way I had on my previous team. I see now that the conflict style I used was the competitive style, high concern for my own interests and low concern for the interests of the other party. Looking back, this is the style I have used most often throughout my life; I usually got away with it before because I was such a good athlete. However, my experience with the coach supports the textbook's description of the losses that may result from using this style. I lost everything when I was kicked off the team and I certainly alienated the coach and the other players and discouraged them from wanting to work with me.

4. **Active Experimentation.** This section of the paper should begin by summarizing what you have learned as a result of writing the paper. What new personal insights and practical lessons did you learn about how to more effectively deal with these types of experiences. This should be presented in a separate paragraph and not buried within your discussion of an action step. Here's an example of the lessons one student learned:

Effective communication is a difficult skill to master, particularly when communicating with a loved one about an emotional issue. When the situation with Jason happened, I was completely unaware of my communication style and habits. Looking back, I can see that my communication goal was to give and get information by the most efficient means possible. Now that I have taken the time to reflect on the situation from his point of view, the missed opportunities for effective and meaningful conversation are painfully clear. I realize I have to think more carefully about how to communicate and that I need to make some improvements in my communication skills.

Next you should present four action steps that you will take to make you more effective in the future in these situations. (Future actions must be based on the experience reported in the Concrete Experience.) These actions can be stated in the form of guidelines as to how you would act differently or resolutions as to steps you could take to develop or practice particular skills. You should elaborate in detail how you see your action ideas being carried out. A given step might include several related activities to complete it. Sometimes students have a tendency to list an action step and then shift to explaining why they would take the action, without sufficiently explaining the actual behavior they would modify. For example, the statement "I would strive to communicate better because people feel I don't listen very well" does not tell a reader very much about what you would do to communicate better. Saying that "I will strive to communicate better by using active listening techniques where I will paraphrase the other's viewpoint before presenting my own opinion" is a better indication of how you will carry out this action step.

There should be a clear link between your action steps and the concepts presented in the abstract conceptualization section. If the theories you selected provide recommendations for improving management practices, you are encouraged to incorporate these ideas in formulating your action steps. Don't just repeat tips from the text. Try to include at least one action resolution that is based upon new knowledge that you have gained about yourself. If you were to relive your experience, what would you do differently? What would you do to improve the situation?

In past student PAAs, it is often difficult to sort out where one action step ends and another begins. Please provide a separate paragraph for each action step and number or otherwise demarcate the separate action steps. For example, "First, I would...My second action step would be..." This will help the reader differentiate between action steps and will ensure that you provide four distinct action steps as part of your plan. Explain why you would take these action steps. Why would the selected behaviors be likely to improve the situation?

Helpful hints: (1) Project a future experience in which you envision the implementation of your ideas and then elaborate on that experience as a way of demonstrating how your actions will be carried out. (2) Where does this situation exist in your life (home, work, school)? Do you need a support system to make it happen? How will you obtain the cooperation of others to jointly improve the situation? (3) Try to imagine the final results of your experimentation. What will it be like if you accomplish what you want to do?

Example of action steps: How then can I best utilize and improve my achievement motivation? First, I must arrange for some accomplishment feedback. This will be done by designing or perceiving tasks so that I succeed bit-by-bit, gaining a reward each time and thus strengthening my desire to achieve more.

Second, I should look to "models of achievement." If people around me succeed, it will further stimulate me. I will ask them how they go about setting realistic goals for themselves and observe how they get feedback from others regarding their performance.

Third, I should modify my self-image to include my desire for personal challenges and responsibilities and my requirement of continual feedback. (As a first step, I imagine myself as a person who *requires* or *must have* success, responsibility, challenge, and variety.) I will seek out situations that are more likely to provide these challenges in the future.

Fourth, I must learn to control my reveries. Just beyond the borderline of awareness, many of us are constantly talking to ourselves. While it is fun to fantasize, I will try to make sure my aspirations are realistic given my current skills and time available to accomplish my various goals. I will spend time prioritizing my goals to ensure that I don't try to do too much or too little.

Finally, although I would never admit so, I agree that salary is a potential "dissatisfier" for me. Therefore, I must insist on what I perceive as a "fair return" for my performance. I will discuss my salary expectations with my supervisor to ensure I know what is expected and also to ensure that my boss knows my expectations. Wish me luck!

Here is another example of good action steps, written by a student who wanted to stop being a passive follower and become more of a leader.

I am going to take a more active role in team meetings. I will volunteer to be the team facilitator in at least one meeting during this semester. In all other meetings, I am going to make at least two process interventions to help the team function more effectively. To prepare myself, I am going to carefully observe other students who are excellent leaders, and I will read two articles on team leadership. I will also design an evaluation form on my team participation and ask my team to use it to evaluate me after the meeting I facilitate. Based on their feedback, I will continue working on possible weak areas during the rest of this course.

5. **Integration and Writing.** The well-written PAA has a focal issue and a story line with themes that are carried throughout each of the four sections. The idea of synergy applies here: "The whole is

greater than the sum of the parts." If integration is present, then the reader can attend to the content without distraction; if integration is absent, barriers prevent the reader from gaining a full appreciation of the content. Are the major themes that you have identified integrated throughout your paper? Make sure that the reflective observation takes into account the viewpoint of all the key people cited in the concrete experience. Do the concepts cited in abstract conceptualization fit well with these observations? Is there a clear link between the concepts or theories that you cite and the subsequent action steps that you formulate? Citing the theories is not just meant to be an academic exercise—it should help guide the analysis of the situation and the planning of practical steps for improving future situations.

Other barriers that prevent the reader from fully appreciating the paper's content are spelling and grammatical errors, as well as the overall appearance of the final document. Since good writing skills are so important in the business world, there should be no errors in your paper. Use the spell check (and grammar check) on your computer before you hand it in. Sometimes reading a paper aloud will indicate where sections of a paper may need revision to simplify awkward or unclear sentences.

Helpful hints:

(a) Decide what one or two main points you wish to convey in each paragraph. The lead sentence in the paragraph should alert the reader to these points. Start a new paragraph to convey new main points. Paragraphs should be of moderate length. Not a page long!

(b) Keep sentences short. Avoid complex modifying phrases that distract from the main idea.

(c) Label each section: Concrete Experience, Reflective Observation, and so on. Don't place a heading at the bottom of the page with no following text.

(d) Transitions are important (between sentences, paragraphs, and sections) and make the paper flow.

(e) The four sections should be equally well developed and fairly similar in length.

(f) **The paper should not exceed five pages in length.** Please number the pages.

(g) Use 1" margins and double space. Use a font size of 11 or 12.

Sample PAA

Concrete Experience

I worked for one year in the marketing group in the Chicago office of a large public accounting firm. The internal service departments were organized into profit centers and operated like little fiefdoms. We worked very closely with the graphics department. We provided the majority of their work but that did not mean the two departments got along well. In fact, we spent more time battling each other than collaborating. A constant bone of contention for both groups was missed deadlines. Most of the time, a marketing person was the contact with the client, usually a partner in the firm. We set up a production schedule, to which the client would agree, and made every effort to stick to it. But ninety-nine times out of hundred, something would happen on the partner's end that would cause a delay. However, the original deadline was never modified to take these setbacks into account because we were not allowed to tell the partners their requests were unreasonable. This put terrific pressure on *both* departments, but graphics personnel continually accused us of purposely holding onto information or dragging our feet in order to make their jobs more difficult.

It was very frustrating for me to get my projects completed. From the very beginning, I felt they thought I was an incompetent jerk who was just trying to make their job more difficult. It wasn't long before I adopted the perception of the rest of my department—graphics was a bunch of uncooperative whiners. I never expected to get good service from them and I didn't. I dreaded going into their office with changes and kept my communications with them to a minimum. Occasionally, I'd have a confrontation with an artist, which would escalate into an argument with two or three other graphics people. Then I was angry for the rest of the day. I had no idea how to remedy the situation and I was under such pressure to get my work done that I had no time to repair the relationships, even if I had known how to do it.

Reflective Observation
Looking back, I think that if I had not been so caught up in the intergroup fighting, I would have recognized that the graphics personnel were under as much pressure as I was. At the time it always seemed like "once again graphics was being uncooperative." But I never stopped to ask myself why they were being so hostile to me and I never put myself in their shoes. One of the things this taught me was that I can be somewhat self-centered and ignore the problems of others when they are a barrier to getting my work done. When graphics stereotyped me, I let myself be influenced by my coworkers rather than making the effort to develop a positive relationship with graphics and get beyond the stereotypes. I felt like one of the gang when we all shared our horror stories about the latest thing graphics had done.

For their part, graphics was probably struggling to keep up with their work and deadlines. Just when they thought they had things under control, we would appear with new changes and requests. Perhaps a lot of their resentment stemmed from feeling that because of us, they could not control their own workflow. We didn't want to lose the partners' business by asking for extended deadlines since they could have hired an outside firm, but graphics had no investment in our service to the partners. Instead, they were worried about satisfying their own clients. And our last-minute changes got in the way of serving their other clients.

There was another person in a different department who was very positive about the graphics department. At the time I remember thinking, "Oh, he must not deal with them on a regular basis like I do or they wouldn't be so cooperative with him." It never occurred to me that this person was doing something different than I was and, as a result, had a better relationship with the graphics personnel. And it certainly never occurred to me to ask him what he did to have such a great rapport with the group.

Since other people and groups managed to have good relations with graphics, we could hardly be justified in thinking that they were totally in the wrong. But both groups had stereotyped the other and were unwilling to change their opinions. Even though both our managers knew about the problem, they did not intervene, perhaps because the work always got done somehow. These managers were more focused upon tasks than people so they never worried about the personal cost of the conflict, and probably did not know how to resolve the problem.

Abstract Conceptualization

Conflict, defined as "a form of interaction among parties that differ in interests, perceptions, and preferences" ((Osland, Kolb, Rubin & Turner 2007, p. 305) is the concept that best helps me understand my experience. Our two departments had different interests in serving our customers and different perceptions about each other and our work demands.

The situation between marketing and graphics was an example of what happens when too much conflict occurs. The following passage could have been written about us. "The *combination* of negative stereotypes, distrust, internal militance, and aggressive action creates a vicious cycle: 'defensive' aggression by one group validates suspicion and 'defensive' counter aggression by the other, and the conflict escalates unless it is counteracted by external factors" (Osland, Kolb, Rubin & Turner 2007, p. 307). Graphics never believed that we weren't holding back information or dragging our feet on purpose. And we never trusted them to do our work well without giving us a hard time. We both complained bitterly about each other and never lost an opportunity to slander the "enemy" to others in the organization, which is a form of aggression. Brown (reader, p. 306) states that managers must intervene when conflict reaches a dysfunctional level but our managers never did. They probably did not want to "rock the boat" as long as things were getting done. But it makes me wonder how much more effective we could have been, had we been able to work through our differences. Someone should have helped the two groups diagnose the conflict and its underlying causes (competing for the scarce resource of time, struggling with uncontrollable last minute demands and iron deadlines, and allegiance to our department rather than the company as a whole).

Another concept that applies to this incident is perception, the process by which we read meaning into stimuli (textbook, p. 204). Marketing and graphics personnel constructed barriers to communication between each group by using the techniques of selective exposure, selective attention, distrusted source, and erroneous translation. We saw, heard, and paid attention to what we wanted to, not necessarily the behaviors that may have been actually occurring. Our stereotypes were consistently reinforced by the perceptions we chose to respond to.

Active Experimentation

The positive thing about negative experiences is that hopefully I learn from them. I do not have control over other people but if I act appropriately, I will have a much better chance of getting the cooperation I desire. This experience taught me the dangers of going along with the group. My negative actions only made the job and the situation worse. Next time I will behave differently.

If I were in situation like this again, I would first try to do a better job of managing myself. I would remember that it takes two sides to make a conflict. I need to be as objective as possible and not simply go along with the group in criticizing "them" so that I feel more a part of the group. I learned that I could have "sat out" this conflict and simply chosen not to get involved. I should have devoted my energy to work or resolving the conflict rather than fighting. In the future, I will take a step back and analyze whether my emotions rather than my intellect is guiding my behavior.

Second, had I made the effort, I might have been able to establish at least one positive relationship with someone in graphics. I should have asked my positive colleague how he managed to develop such a good relationship with them. I suspect his advice would have been to spend more time with them, treat them with greater respect, refrain from blaming them when things go wrong, and be more empathetic.

Third, I will try harder to see all sides of an issue rather than just my own perspective. I should have made an effort to understand the graphics department's point of view and refrained from stereotyping them. I am going to keep an open mind about others and try to be less judgmental.

Finally, I would talk to my manager about the problem and suggest possible solutions. By making my feelings known and telling her that I wanted to do my part in conflict management maybe she would be more willing to take action. If not, at least I would know that I had tried to be proactive rather than reactive.

Personal Application Assignment Grading Criteria Summary

Concrete Experience—4 points

_____ Does the paper contain a clear, objective description of facts in your personal experience? (Up to 2 points)

_____ Does it contain a subjective description of feelings, perceptions, and thoughts that occurred during (not after) the experience? (Up to 2 points)

_____ Does this section provide enough information so the reader will understand the rest of the paper but not too much irrelevant detail? Remember that **this section should not be longer than 1–1.5 pages**. (Delete 1 point)

Reflective Observation—4 points

_____ Did you look at the experience from the different points of view of all the major actors? (Up to 2 points)

_____ Did you make an attempt to figure out why the people involved, *and you in particular*, behaved as they did? (Up to 1 point)

_____ Did the different perspectives and behavioral analyses add significant meaning to the situation? (Up to 1 point)

Abstract Conceptualization—4 points

_____ Did you briefly define and explain at least two different concepts or theories from the assigned readings that relate to your experience and did you reference them properly? (Up to 2 points)

_____ Did you thoroughly apply the concepts/theories to your experience? (Up to 2 points)

Active Experimentation—4 points

_____ Did you summarize the practical lessons you derived from writing this paper on your experience? (Up to 1 point)

_____ Did you describe thoroughly at least four action steps you will take in the future so you can be more effective? Remember to come up with lessons and/or action steps that respond to all the major themes found in the paper. (Up to 2 points)

_____ Did you identify and include at least one action step that is based upon what you learned about yourself as a result of writing the paper? (Up to 1 point)

Integration, Synthesis, And Writing—4 points

_____ Does the PAA have major themes that are carried throughout each section of the paper and are the sections well-integrated and fairly equally developed? Is the material for each section where it should be? (Up to 1 point)

_____ Is the paper clear and well-written? (Up to 1 point)

_____ Is the paper free of spelling and grammar errors? (Up to 2 points)

Bibliography

Abbey, D. S., Hunt, D. E., & Weiser, J. C. (1985). Variations on a theme by Kolb: A new perspective for understanding counseling and supervision. *The Counseling Psychologist, 13*(3), 477–501.

Ainley, M., Heidi, S., & Berndorff, D. (2002). Interest, learning, and the psychological processes that mediate their relationship. *Journal of Educational Psychology, 94*(3), 545–561

Akrivou, K. (2009). *Differentiation and integration in adult development: The influence of self-complexity and integrative learning on self-integration.* Munich: VDM Verlag.

Alexander, C. N., & Langer, E. (Eds.). (1990). *Higher stages of human development.* New York, NY: Oxford University Press.

Allinson, C. W., & Hayes, J. (1996). The cognitive style index: A measure of intuition-analysis for organizational research. *Journal of Management Studies, 33*(1), 119–135.

Allinson, C. W., Hayes, J., & Davis A. (1994). Matching the cognitive styles of management students and teachers: A preliminary study. *Perceptual and Motor Skills, 79*, 1256–1258.

American Psychological Association Board of Affairs. (1997). *Learner-centered psychological principles: A framework for school redesign and reform.* Retrieved from http://www. apa.org/ed/lcp.html

Angelo, T. A., & Cross, P. (1993). *Classroom assessment techniques.* San Francisco, CA: Jossey-Bass.

Annastasi, A., & Urbina, S. (1997). *Psychological testing.* Upper Saddle River, NJ: Prentice Hall.

Arbaugh, J. B., Dearmond, S., & Rau, B. L. (2013) New uses for existing tools? A call to study online management instruction and instructors. *AMLE, 12*(4), 635–655.

Argote, L., & Miron-Spektor, E. (2011). Organizational learning: From experience to knowledge. *Organization Science, 22*(5): 1123–1137.

Argyris, C. (1957). *Personality and organization: The conflict between system and the individual.* New York, NY: Harper. OCLC 243920.

Argyris, C. (1962). *Interpersonal competence and organizational effectiveness.* Home-Wood, IL: Dorsey.

_____. (1970). On the future of laboratory education. In G. Golembiewski & P. Blumberg (Eds.), *Sensitivity training and the laboratory approach: readings about concepts and applications.* Itasca, IL: Peacock.

_____. (1974). *Theory in practice: Increasing professional effectiveness.* San Francisco, CA: Jossey-Bass.

Argyris, C. (1992). *On organizational learning.* Oxford: Blackwell.

_____, & Schon, D. (1978). *Organizational learning: A theory of action perspective.* Reading, MA: Addison-Wesley.

Aronson, J., Fried, C. B., & Good, C. (2002). Reducing stereotype threat and boosting academic achievement of African-American students: The role of conceptions of intelligence. *Journal of Experimental Social Psychology, 38*, 113–125.

Artzt, A. F., & Armour-Thomas, E. (1998). Mathematics teaching as problem solving: A framework for studying teacher metacognition underlying instructional practice in mathematics. *Instructional Science, 26,* 5–25.

Ashford, S. J. & DeRue, D. S. (2012). Developing as a leader: The power of mindful engagement *Organizational Dynamics 41*(2): 146-154

Atir, S., Rosenzweig, E., & Dunning, D. (2015). When knowledge knows no bounds: Self-perceived expertise predicts claims of impossible knowledge. *Psychological Science, 26*(8), 1295–1303.

Bain, K. (2004). *What the best college teachers do.* Cambridge, MA: Harvard University Press.

Bakan, D. (1966). *The duality of human experience.* Chicago, IL: Rand McNally.

Baker, A. (1995). *Bridging differences and learning through conversation* (Unpublished doctoral dissertation). Case Western Reserve University, Cleveland, OH.

Baker, A. C. (2010). *Catalytic conversations: Organizational communication and innovation.* Armonk, NY: M. E. Sharpe.

Baker, A. C., Jensen, P. J., & Kolb, D. A., & Associates. (2002). *Conversational learning: An experiential approach to knowledge creation.* Westport, CT: Quorum Books.

Baker, C. M., Pesut, D. J., Mcdaniel, A. M., & Fisher, M. L. (2007). Learning skills profiles of master's students in nursing administration: assessing the impact of problem-based learning. *Nursing Education Perspectives, 28*(4), 190–195.

Baker, R. E., Simon, J. R., & Bazeli, F. P. (1987). Selecting instructional design for introductory accounting based on the experiential learning model. *Journal of Accounting Education, 5,* 207–226.

Ballou, R., Bowers, D., Boyatzis, R. E., & Kolb D. A. (1999). Fellowship in lifelong learning: An executive development program for advanced professionals. *Journal of Management Education, 23*(4), 338–354.

Banaga, G. L. (2000). *A calling to work, a labor of love: A phenomenological study of work as calling* (Unpublished doctoral dissertation). Case Western Reserve University, Cleveland, OH.

Bandura, A. (1978). The self system in reciprocal determinism. *American Psychologist, 33,* 344–357.

Bargh, J. A., & Chartrand, T. L. (1999). The unbearable automaticity of being. *American Psychologist, 54*(7), 462–479.

Baron, H. (1996). Strengths and limitations of ipsative measurement. *Journal of Occupational and Organizational Psychology, 69,* 49–56.

Baron, R. A., & Henry, R. A. (2010). How entrepreneurs acquire the capacity to excel: Insights from research on expert performance. *Strategic Entrepreneurship Journal, 4,* 49–65.

Basseches, M. A. (1984). *Dialectical thinking and adult development.* Norwood, NJ: Ablex Publishing Corp.

_____. (2005). The development of dialectical thinking as an approach to integration. *Integral Review, 1,* 47–63.

Bates, W. J. (1982, September–October). The crisis in English studies. *Harvard Magazine.*

Bateson, G. (1972). *Steps to an ecology of mind.* Toronto, ON, Canada: Ballantine Books.

Baumeister, R. F., & Sommer, K. L. (1997). Consciousness, free choice, and automaticity. In R. S. Wyer, Jr. (Ed.), *Advances in social cognition* (vol. X, pp. 75–81). Mahwah, NJ: Erlbaum.

_____, Bratslavsky, E., Muraven, M., & Tice, D. M. (1998). Ego depletion: Is the active self a limited resource. *Journal of Personality and Social Psychology, 74,* 1252–1265.

Baxter-Magolda, M. B. (1992). *Knowing and reasoning in college: Gender-related patterns in students' intellectual development.* San Francisco, CA: Jossey-Bass.

_____. (1999). *Creating contexts for learning and self-authorship.* Nashville, TN: Vanderbilt University Press.

_____. (2001). *Making their own way: Narritives for transforming higher education to promote self-development.* Sterling, VA: Stylus.

_____. (2007). Self-Authorship: The foundation for twenty-first century education. *New Directions for Teaching and Learning, 100,* 69–83.

_____. (2008). Three elements of self-authorship. *Journal of College Student Development, 49*(4), 269–284.

Beilock, S. L., & Carr, T. H. (2001). On the fragility of skilled performance: What governs choking under pressure? *Journal of Experiemntal Psychology: General, 130*(4), 701–725.

Bekoff, M., & Allen, C. (1992). Intentional icons: Towards and evolutionary cognitive ethology. *Ethology, 91,* 1–6.

Bekoff, M., & Byers, J.A. (1981). A critical reanalysis of the ontogeny and phlogeny of mammalian social and locomotor play: an ethological hornest's nest. In Immelman, K., Barlow, G. W., Petrinovitch, L. and Main, M. (Eds.), *Behavioral Development: The Bielefield Interdiciplinary Project.* Cambridge Univesity Press, Cambridge.

Bekoff, M. & Byers, J. A. (1998). *Animal play.* Cambridge, England: Cambridge University Press.

Belenky, M. F., Clinchy, B. M., Goldberger, N. R., & Tarule, J. M. (1986). *Women's ways of knowing: The development of self-voice and mind.* New York, NY: Basic Books.

Bell, A. A. (2005). *The adaptive style inventory: An Assessment of Person-Environment Interactions.* Unpublished manuscript. Department of Educational Leadership, University of Connecticut.

Benne, K. D. (1964). History of the T Group in the laboratory setting. In L. Bradford et al. (Eds.), *T Group theory and laboratory method.* New York, NY: John Wiley.

_____, & Sheats, P. (1948). Functional roles of group members. *Journal of Social Issues, 2,* 41–46.

Bennet, N. (1978). Learning styles of health professionals compared to preference for continuing education program format. (Unpublished Ph.D. dissertation). University of Illinois College of Medicine.

Bennis, W. G. (1980). Interview. *Group and Organization Studies, 5,* 18–34.

_____. (Winter 1981–82). A goal for the eighties: Organizational integrity. *New Jersey Bell Journal, 4*(4), 1–8.

Berdie, R. F. (1945). Range of interests. *Journal of Applied Psychology, 29*(4), 268–281.

Bergsteiner, H. Avery, G. C. & Neumann, R. (2010). Kolb's experiential learning model: Critique from a modeling perspective. *Studies in Continuing Education. 32*(1): 29-46

Berlyne, D. E. (1960). *Conflict, arousal and curiosity*. New York, NY: McGraw-Hill.

Bethell, S., & Morgan, K. (2011). Problem-based and experiential learning: Engaging students in an undergraduate physical education module. *Journal of Hospitality Leisure Sport & Tourism Education, 10*(1), 128–134. doi: 10.3794/johlste.101.365

Biberman, N. J., & Buchanan, J. (1986). Learning style and study skills differences across business and other academic majors. *Journal of Education Business, 61*(7), 303–307.

Bielefeldt, A. R., Dewoolkar, M. M., Caves, K. M., Berdanier, B. W., & Paterson, K. G. (2011). Diverse models for incorporating service projects into engineering capstone design courses. *International Journal of Engineering Education, 27*(6), 1206-1220.

Biggs, J. B. (1987). *Student approaches to learning and studying*. Hawthorn, Australia: Australian Council for Educational Research.

_____. (1992). *Why and how do Hong Kong students learn? Using the learning and study process questionnaires*. Education Paper No. 14. Hong Kong: Faculty of Education, The University of Hong Kong.

Bion, W. R. (1959). *Experience in groups and other papers*. New York, NY: Basic Books.

Blackwell, L. S., Trzesniewski, K. H., & Dweck, C. S. (2007). Implicit theories of intelligence predict achievement across an adolescent transition: A longitudinal study and an intervention. *Child Development, 78*(1), 246–263.

Block, J. (1961). Ego identity, role variability and adjustment. *Journal of Consulting Psychology, 25*(5), 392–397.

Bloom, B. S. (Ed.). (1985). *Developing talent in young people.* New York, NY: Ballantine Books.

_____, & Sosniak, L. A. (November 1981). Talent development versus schooling. *Educational Leadership, 38*, 86–94.

Border, L. L. B. (2007). Understanding learning styles: The key to unlocking deep learning and in depth teaching. *NEA Higher Education Advocate, 24*(5), 5–8.

Boud, D. J., Keogh, R., & Walker, D. (1985). *Reflection: Turning experience into learning.* London, England: Nichols Publishing Company.

_____, & Miller, N. (1996). *Working with experience. Animating learning.* London, England, and New York, NY: Routledge.

_____, & Falchikov, N. (2006). Aligning assessment with long-term learning. *Assessment and Evaluation in Higher Education, 31*(4), 399–413.

_____. (2013). *Enhancing learning through self-assessment.* New York, NY: Routledge.

Boyatzis, R. E. (1994). Stimulating self-directed change: A required MBA course called managerial assessment and development. *Journal of Management Education, 18*(3), 304–323.

_____, Cowen, S. S., & Kolb, D. A. (1995). *Innovation in professional education: Steps on a journey from teaching to learning.* San Francisco, CA: Jossey-Bass.

_____, & Kolb, D. A. (1991). *The learning skills profile.* TRG Hay/McBer, Training Resources Group. 116 Huntington Avenue, Boston, MA 02116.

_____. (1995). From learning styles to learning skills: The executive skills profile. *Journal of Managerial Psychology, 10,* 3–17.

_____. (1997). Assessing individuality in learning: The learning skills profile. *Educational Psychology, 11*(3–4), 279–295.

_____. (1999). Performance, learning, and development as modes of growth and adaptation throughout our lives and careers. In M. Peiperl et al. (Eds.), *Career frontiers: New conceptions of working lives.* London, England: Oxford University Press.

_____, & Mainemelis, B. (2000). *An empirical study of the pluralism of learning and adaptive styles in an MBA program.* Paper presented at the 60th annual meeting of the Academy of Management, Toronto, Ontario, Canada.

_____, Rochford, K., & Jacks, A. I. (2014). Antagonistic neural networks underlying differentiated leadership roles. *Frontiers in HumanNeuroscience, 8,* Article 114.

_____, Stubbs, E. C., & Taylor, S. N. (2002). Learning cognitive and emotional intelligence competencies through graduate management education. *Academy of Management Learning and Education, 1*(2), 150–162.

Boyle, A., & Hutchison, D. (2009). Sophisticated tasks in e-assessment: What are they and what are their benefits? *Assessment & Evaluation in Higher Education, 34*(3), 305–331.

Bransford, J. D., Brown, A. L., & Cocking, R. R. (2000). *How people learn: Brain, mind experience, and school.* Washington, DC: National Academy Press.

Brehmer, B. (1980). In one word: Not from experience. *Acta Psychologicia, 45,* 223–241.

Bridges, K. (1932). Emotional development in early infancy. *Child Development, 3,* 340.

Bronfenbrenner, U. (1977). Toward an experimental ecology of human development. *American Psychologist, 32,* 513–530.

_____. (1979). *The ecology of human development.* Cambridge, MA: Harvard University Press, 1979.

Brookfield, S. D. (1987). *Developing critical thinkers: Challenging adults to explore alternative ways of thinking and acting.* San Francisco, CA: Jossey Bass.

_____. (1995). *Becoming a critically reflective teacher.* San Francisco, CA: Jossey-Bass.

_____. (2009). The concept of critical reflection: Promises and contradictions. *European Journal of Social Work, 12*(4), 293–304.

Brooks Harris, J. E., & Stock-Ward, S. R. (1999). *Workshops: Designing and facilitating experiential learning.* Thousand Oaks, CA: Sage Publications.

Broughton, J. M. (1981). Piaget's structural development psychology III: Function and the problem of knowledge. *Human Development, 24,* 257–285.

Brower, H. H. (2011). Sustainable development through service learning: A pedagogical framework and case example in a third world context. *Academy of Management Learning & Education, 10*(1), 58-76.

Brown, J. S, Collins, A., & Duguid, P. (1989). Situated cognition and the culture of learning. *Educational Researcher, 18*(1), 32–41.

Brown, S. L. (1995). Evolution and play. *ReVision, 17*(4), 2–12.

Brown, K. W., & Ryan, R. M. (2003a). The benefits of being present: Mindfulness and its role in psychological well-being. *Journal of Personality and Social Psychology, 84*, 822–848.

_____. (2003b). Why we don't need self-esteem: On fundamental needs, contingent love, and mindfulness. *Psychological Inquiry, 14*, 27–82.

Bruer, J. T. (1997). Education and the brain: A bridge too far. *Educational Researcher, 26*(8), 4–16.

Bruner, J. S. (1960). *The process of education.* New York, NY: Vintage Books.

_____. (1964). The course of cognitive growth. *American Psychologist, 19*, 1–15.

_____. (1966a). *On knowing: Essays for the left hand.* New York, NY: Atheneum.

_____. (1966b). *Toward a theory of instruction.* New York, NY: W.W. Norton.

_____, Oliver, R., and Greenfield, P. (1966). *Studies in cognitive growth.* New York, NY: John Wiley.

_____. (1971). *The relevance of education*. New York, NY: W.W. Norton.

_____. (1986). *Actual minds, possible worlds*. Cambridge, MA: Harvard University Press.

Buchmann, M., & Schwille, J. (1983). Education: The overcoming of experience. *American Journal of Education, 92*(1), 30–51.

Beutell, N. J., & Kressel, S. S. (1984). An investigation of Kolb's Learning Style Inventory: Social desirability and normative scoring. *Psychological Reports, 55*, 89–90.

Bunker, S. S. (1999). Constructing curriculum: Creating a teaching-learning space. *Nursing Science Quarterly, 12*(4), 297–298.

Button, S. B., Mathieu, J. E., & Zajac, D. M. (1996). Goal orientation in organizational research: A conceptual and empirical foundation. *Organizational Behavior and Human Decision Processes, 67*(1), 26–48.

Caine, R. N. and Caine, G. (1990). Understanding a brain-based approach to learning and teaching. *Educational Leadership*. October 66-70.

Caine, R. N. and Caine, G. (1995). Reinventing schools through brain-based learning. *Educational Leadership*. April 43-47.

Campus News. (2003, February 6) "Edward M. Hundert Inaugural," 1–2.

Callois, R. (2001). *Man, play and games*. Chicago, IL: University of Illinois Press.

Capra, F. (1996). *The web of life*. New York, NY: Anchor Books.

Carlsson, B., Keane, P., & Martin, J. B. (1976). R & D organizations as learning systems. *Sloan Management Review, 17*, 1–15.

Cartwright, D. (Ed.). (1951). *Field theory in social science: Selected theoretical papers by Kurt Lewin.* New York, NY: Harper Torchbooks.

Chapman, L. A. (2006). *An exploration of executive coaching as an experiential learning process within the context of the integrated experiential coaching model* (Unpublished dissertation). Middlesex University, Western Cape, South Africa.

Chen, A., Darst, P. W., & Pangrazi R. P. (2009). What constitutes situational interest? Validating a construct in physical education. *Measurement in Physical Education and Exercise Science, 3*(3), 157–180.

Chen, G., Donahue, L. M., & Klimoski, R. J. (2004). Training undergraduates to work in organizational teams. *Academy of Management Learning and Education, 3*(1), 27–40.

Chen, G., Gully, S. M., & Eden, D. (2001). Validation of a new general self-efficacy scale. *Organizational Research Methods, 4*(1), 62–83.

Clarke, D., Oshiro, S., Wong, C., & Yeung, M. (1977). *A study of the adequacy of the learning environment for business students in Hawaii in the fields of accounting and marketing.* Unpublished paper. University of Hawaii.

Clarke, R. D. (1971). Group-induced shift to risk: A critical appraisal. *Psychological Bulletin, 76*(4), 251–270.

Cohen, S. G., & Bailey, D. E. (1997). What makes teams work: Group effectiveness research from the shop floor to the executive suite. *Journal of Management, 23*(3), 239–290.

Cole, M., et al. (1971). *The cultural context of learning and thinking.* New York, NY: Basic Books.

Cole, M., John-Steiner, V., Scribner, S., & Souberman, E. (Eds.). (1978). *L. S. Vygotsky: Mind in society.* Cambridge, MA: Harvard University Press.

Conway, M. A., Cohen, G., & Stanhope, N. (1991). On the very long-term memory of knowledge acquired through formal education: Twelve years of cognitive psychology. *Journal of Experimental Psychology: General, 120*, 395–409.

_____. (1992). Very long-term memory of knowledge acquired at school and university. *Applied Cognitive Psychology, 6*, 467–482.

Conway, M. A,, Gardiner, J. M., Perfect, T. J., Anderson, S. J., & Cohen, G. M. (1997). Changes in memory awareness during learning: The acquisition of knowledge by psychology undergraduates. *Journal of Experimental Psychology: General, 126*, 393–413.

Cook, T. A. (1914). *The curves of life.* London, England: Constable and Company.

Cook-Greuter, S. R. (1999). *Post-Autonomous ego development: A study of its nature and measurement* (Doctoral dissertation). Cambridge, MA: Harvard Graduate School of Education.

_____. (2000). Mature ego development: A gateway to ego transcendence? *Journal of Adult Development, 7*(4), 227–240.

Corbett, A. (2005). Experiential learning within the process of opportunity identification and exploitation. *Entrepreneurship Theory and Practice, 29*(4), 473–492.

_____. (2007). Learning asymmetries and the discovery of entrepreneurial opportunities. *Journal of Business Venturing, 22*(1), 97–118.

Cornelius-White, J. (2007). Learner-centered teacher-student relationships are effective: A meta-analysis. *Review of Educational Research, 77*(1), 113–143. doi: 10.3102/ 003465430298563

Cornett, C. E. (1983). *What you should know about teaching and learning styles.* Bloomington, IN: Phi Delta Kappa Educational Foundation.

Cornwell, J. M., & Dunlap, W. P. (1994). On the questionable soundness of factoring ipsative data: A response to Saville and Wilson (1991). *Journal of Occupational and Organizational Psychology, 67,* 89–100.

Cowan, N. (1988). Evolving conceptions of memory storage, selective attention, and their mutual constraints within the human information processing system. *Psychological Bulletin, 104,* 163–191.

Coyle, D. (2009). *The talent code.* New York, NY: Bantam Books.

Crary, L. M. (1979). *Assessment of patterns of life structure.* Unpublished manuscript. Department of Organizational Behavior, Case Western Reserve University.

_____. (1981). *Patterns of life structure: Person-Environment designs and their impact on adult lives.* (Unpublished Ph.D. dissertation). Case Western Reserve University.

Dale, E. (1969). *Audio-Visual methods in teaching* (3rd ed.). New York, NY: Holt Rinehart & Winston.

_____. (2010). Reconsidering the trade-off between expertise and flexibility: A cognitive entrenchment perspective. *Academy of Management Review, 35*(4), 579–603.

Darling-Hammond, L., & Snyder, J. (2000). Authentic assessment of teaching in context. *Teaching and Teacher Education, 16*, 523–545.

Darwin, C. (1958). *The autobiography of Charles Darwin: 1809–1882.* London, England: Collins.

_____. (1965). *The expression of the emotions in man and animals.* Chicago, IL: The University of Chicago Press.

_____. (1981). *The descent of man, and selection in relation to sex.* Princeton, NJ: Princeton University Press.

Davidson, N. (Ed.). (1990). *Cooperative learning in mathematics. A handbook for teachers.* Menlo Park, CA: Addison Wesley.

Davis, B., & Sumara, D. J. (1997). Cognition, complexity and teacher education. *Harvard Educational Review, 67*(1), 105–125.

Davis, E. (1995, September). Big mind science. *Shambhala Sun,* pp. 27–33.

de Haan. E., Culpin, V., & Curd, J. (2011). Executive coaching in practice: What determines helpfulness for clients of coaching? *Personnel Review, 40*(1), 24–44.

Deci, E., & Ryan, R. (1985). *Intrinsic motivation and self-determination in human behavior.* New York, NY: Plenum.

De Ciantis, S. M., & Kirton, M. J. (1996). A psychometric reexamination of Kolb's experiential learning cycle construct: A separation of level, style and process. *Educational and Psychological Measurement, 56*(5), 809–820.

Decker, J. H., Lourenco, F. S., Doll, B. B., & Hartley, C. A. (2015). Experiential reward learning outweighs instruction prior to adulthood. *Cognitive, Affective, & Behavioral Neuroscience, 15*, 1–11.

Dennett, D. (1991). *Consciousness explained.* Boston, MA: Little-Brown.

Dewey, J, (1897). My pedagogic creed. *The School Journal, LIV*(3), 77–80.

_____. (1905). The postulate of immediate experience. *Journal of Philosophy, Psychology and Scientific Methods, 2*, 353–357.

_____. (1910). *How we think.* New York, NY: D.C. Heath.

_____. (1913). *Interest and effort in education.* Boston, MA: Houghton Mifflin.

_____. (1916). *Democracy and education.* New York, NY: Macmillan Company.

_____. (1933). *How we think: A restatement of the relation of reflective thinking to the educative process.* New York, NY: D.C. Heath and Company.

_____. (1934). *Art as experience.* New York, NY: Perigee Books.

_____. (1929). *The sources of a science of education.* New York, NY: Horace Liveright.

_____. (1938). *Education and experience.* New York, NY: Simon and Schuster.

_____. (1958). *Experience and nature.* New York, NY: Dover Publications.

_____. (1990). *The school and society and the child and the curriculum.* Chicago, IL: The University of Chicago Press.

Dixon, N. (1999). *The organizational learning cycle: How we can learn collectively.* London, England: McGraw Hill.

Duckworth, E. (1987). *The having of wonderful ideas and other essays on teaching and learning.* New York, NY: Teachers College Press.

Dweck, C. S. (1986). Motivational processes affecting learning. *American Psychologist, 41*(10), 1040–1048.

_____, & Leggett, E. L. (1988). A social-cognitive approach to motivation and personality. *Psychological Review, 95*(2), 256–273.

Dweck, C. S., Hong, Y., & Chiu, C. (1993). Implicit theories: Individual differences in the likelihood and meaning of dispositional inference. *Personality and Social Psychology Bulletin, 19*(5), 644–656.

_____. (2000). *Self-Theories: Their role in motivation, personality, and development.* London, Great Britain: Psychology Press, Taylor & Francis Group.

_____. (2008). The promise and perils of praise. *Educational Leadership, 65,* 34–39.

Easterby-Smith, M. (1997). Disciplines of organizational learning: Contributions and critiques. *Human Relations, 50*(9), 1085–1113.

Edelbring, S. (2012). *Technology in education: Necessary but not sufficient. Understanding learning with virtual patients* (Ph. D. dissertation). Stockholm, Sweden: Karolinska Institute Centre for Medical Education.

Edmondson, A. C. (1999). Psychological safety and learning behavior in work teams. *Administrative Science Quarterly, 44,* 350–383.

_____. (2008). The competitive imperative of learning. *Harvard Business Review,* July–August 60–67.

_____. (2009). Psychological safety and learning behavior in work teams. *Administrative Science Quarterly, 44,* 350–383.

_____, Bohmer, R. M., & Pisano, G. P. (2001). Disrupted routines: Team learning and new technology implementation in hospitals. *Administrative Science Quarterly, 46,* 685–716.

Edmondson, A. C., & Lei, Z. (2014). Psychological safety: The history renaissance and future of an interpersonal construct. *Annual review of Organizational Psychology and Organization Behavior, 1,* 23–43.

Edwards, D., & Mercer, N. (1987). *Common knowledge: The development of understanding in the classroom.* London, England: Methuen

Eickmann, P., Kolb, A. Y., & Kolb, D. A. (2004). Designing learning. In F. Collopy & R. Boland (Eds.), *Managing as designing: Creating a new vocabulary for management education and research.* Stanford, CA: Stanford University Press.

Eisenstein, E. M., & Hutchinson, J. W. (2006, May). Action-based learning: Goals and attention in the acquisition of market knowledge. *Journal of Marketing Research, XLIII*, 244–258.

Elkind, D. (1970). *Children and adolescence: Interpretative essays on Jean Piaget*. New York, NY: Oxford University Press.

_____. (1988). *The hurried child*. Cambridge, MA: Perseus Books.

_____. (2007). *The power of play*. Cambridge, MA: Da Capo Lifelong Books.

Ellis, M. J. (1973). *Why people play*. Englewood Cliffs, NJ: Prentice Hall.

Entwistle, N. (1981). *Styles of learning and teaching: An integrated outline of educational psychology for students, teachers, and lecturers*. New York, NY: Wiley.

Ericsson, K. A., Krampe, R. T., & Tesch-Römer, C. (1993). The role of deliberate practice in the acquisition of expert performance. *Psychological Review, 100*, 363–406.

Ericsson, K. A., & Charness, L. (1994). Expert performance: Its structure and acquisition. *American Psychologist, 49*(8), 725–747.

_____. (2006). The influence of experience and deliberate practice on the development of superior expert performance. In K. A. Ericsson, N. Charness, R. Hoffman, & J. Feltovich (Eds.), *The Cambridge handbook of expertise and expert performance* (pp. 683–703). New York, NY: Cambridge University Press.

Erikson, E. (1958). *Young man Luther*. New York, NY: W. W. Norton.

_____. (1959). Identity and the life cycle. *Psychological Issues, 1*, 1–171.

_____. (1961). The roots of virtue. In J. Huxley (Ed.), *The humanist frame*. New York, NY: Harper & Row.

_____. (1950). *Childhood and society*. New York, NY: W. W. Norton & Company.

Evans, J. St. B. T. (2008). Dual-Processing accounts of reasoning, judgment, and social cognition. *Annual Review of Psychology, 59*, 255–278.

Fagen, R. (1981). *Animal play behavior*. New York, NY: Oxford University Press.

_____. (1984). Play and behavioral flexibility. In P. K. Smith (Ed.), *Play in animals and humans* (pp. 159–173). New York, NY: Basil Blackwell.

_____. (1994). Applause for aurora: Sociobiological considerations on exploration and play. In H. Keller, K. Schneider, & B. Henderson (Eds.), *Curiosity and exploration* (pp. 333–339). New York, NY: Springer.

Fambrough, M. (2000). *Forming and reforming gender identity: The experience of discovering and following one's calling* (Unpublished Doctoral Dissertation). Case Western Reserve University.

Fazey, J. A., & Martin, F. (2002). Understanding the space of experiential variation. *Active Learning in Higher Education, 3*, 234–250.

Feldman, D. (1980). *Beyond universals in cognitive development*. Norwood, NJ: Ablex Publishing.

Feldman, K., & Newcomb, T. (1969). *The impact of college on students*, Vols. I and II. San Francisco, CA: Jossey-Bass.

Feldman, S. (1974). *Escape from the doll's house*. New York, NY: McGraw-Hill.

Fenwick, T. J. (2000). Expanding conceptions of experiential learning: A review of five contemporary perspectives on cognition. *Adult Education Quarterly, 50*(4), 243–272.

_____. (2003). Reclaiming and re-embodying experiential learning through complexity science. *Studies in the Education of Adults, 35*(2), 123–141.

Fernandez, C. L. (1986). *Role elaboration: The influence of personal and situational factors* (Unpublished qualifying paper). Case Western Reserve University, Cleveland, OH.

_____. (1988). *Role shaping in a high-tech organization using experiential learning theory* (Unpublished doctoral dissertation). Case Western Reserve University, Cleveland, OH.

Festinger, L., Reiken, H. W., & Schachter, S. (1956). *When prophecy fails*. Minneapolis: University of Minnesota Press.

Finkel, D. L. (2000). *Teaching with your mouth shut*. Portsmouth, NH: Heinemann.

Flavell, J. (1963). *The developmental psychology of Jean Piaget*. New York, NY: Van Nostrand Reinhold Co.

_____. (1971). Stage related properties of cognitive development. *Cognitive Psychology, 2,* 421–453.

_____. (1979). Meta-cognition and cognitive monitoring. *American Psychologist, 34*(10), 906–911.

Fletcher, J. K., & Ragins, B. R. (2007). Stone center relational cultural theory: A window on relational mentoring. In B. R. Ragins & K. E. Kram (Eds.), *The handbook of mentoring at work: Theory, research, and practice* (pp. 373–399). Thousand Oaks, CA: Sage.

Follett, M. P. (1918). *The new state – Group organization, the solution for popular government.* New York, NY: Longman, Green and Co.

_____. (1924). *Creative experience.* New York, NY: Longmans Green & Co.

Foy, N. (1977, September–October). Action learning comes to industry. *Harvard Business Review,* 158–168.

Freedman, R. D., & Stumpf, S. A. (1978). What can one learn from the learning style inventory? *Academy of Management Journal, 21*(2), 275–282.

Freire, P. (1992). *Pedagogy of the oppressed.* New York, NY: Continuum.

_____. (1973). *Education for critical consciousness.* New York, NY: Continuum.

Freud, S. (1965). *The interpretation of dreams.* New York, NY: Avon Books.

Fry, R. E. (1978). *Diagnosing professional learning environments: An observational framework for assessing situational complexity* (Unpublished Ph.D. thesis), Massachusetts Institute of Technology.

Fuller, I. C. (2012). Taking students outdoors to learn in high places. *Area, 44*(1), 7-13. Doi: 10.1111/j.1475-4762.2010.00990.

Furnham, A., Jackson, C. J., & Miller, T. (1999). Personality, learning style and work performance. *Personality and Individual Differences, 27*(6), 1113-1122.

Gadamer, H.-G. (1989). *Truth and method* (2nd ed.). New York, NY: Crossroad.

Gallimore, R., & Tharp, W. (2004). What a coach can teach a teacher, 1975–2004: Reflections and reanalysis of John Wooden's teaching practices. *The Sport Psychologist, 18*, 119–137.

Gardner, B. S., & Korth, S. J. (1997). Classroom strategies that facilitate transfer of learning to the workplace. *Innovative Higher Education, 22*(1), 45–60.

_____. (1999). A framework for learning to work in teams. *Journal of Education for Business, 74*(1), 28–33.

Garner, I. (2000). Problems and inconsistencies with Kolb's learning styles. *Educational Psychology, 20*(3), 341–349.

Gawande, A. (2011). Top athletes and singers have coaches. Should you? Retrieved from http://www.newyorker.com/magazine/2011/10/03/personal-best

Geiger, M. A., & Boyle, E. J. (1993). An examination of ipsative and normative versions of Kolb's revised learning style. *Educational and Psychological Measurement, 53,* 717–726.

_____, & Pinto, J. K. (1992). A factor analysis of Kolb's revised learning style inventory. *Educational and Psychological Measurement, 52*(3), 753–759.

Gemmell, R. M. (2012). *Socio-cognitive foundations of entrepreneurial venturing* (Unpublished Ph.D dissertation). Weatherhead School of Management, Case Western Reserve University.

_____. (2017). Learning styles of entrepreneurs in knowledge-intensive industries. *International Journal of Entrepreneurial Behavior &Research.*

_____, Boland, R. J., & Kolb, D. A. (2011). The socio-cognitive dynamics of entrepreneurial ideation. *Entrepreneurship Theory and Practice, 36*(5), 1053–1073.

Gendlin, E. T. (1961). Experiencing: A variable in the process of therapeutic change. *American Journal of Psychotherapy, 15,* 233–245.

_____. (1962). *Experiencing and the creation of meaning.* Glencoe, IL: Free Press.

_____. (1964). A theory of personality change. In P. Worschel & D. Byrne (Eds.), *Personality change* (pp. 100–148). New York, NY: John Wiley.

_____. (1978). *Focusing.* New York, NY: Bantam Books.

Gilligan, C. (1982). *In a different voice: Psychological theory and women's development.* Cambridge, MA: Harvard University Press.

Ginsburg, H. & Opper, S. (1969). *Piaget's theory of intellectual development.* Englewood Cliffs, NJ: Prentice Hall

Godden, D. M. (2012). Rethinking the debriefing paradigm: The rationality of belief perserverance. *Logos & Episteme, III*(1), 51–74.

Good, C., Aronson, J., & Inzlicht, M. (2003). Improving adolescents' standardized test performance: An intervention to reduce the effects of stereotype threat. *Journal of Applied Developmental Psychology, 24,* 645–662.

Goodall, J. (1995). Chimpanzee and others at play. *ReVision, 7*(4), 14–20.

Gould, S. J. (1977). *Ontogeny and phylogeny.* Cambridge, MA: Harvard University Press.

Grasha, A. F. (1994). A matter of style: The teacher as expert, formal authority, personal model, facilitator, and delegator. *College Teaching, 42*(4), 142–149.

Green, E. (2014). *Building a better teacher.* New York, NY: W. W. Norton & Company.

Groos, K. (1898). *The play of animals.* New York, NY: D. Appleton.

Guilford, J. P. (1988). Some changes in the structure of intellect model. *Educational and Psychological Measurement, 48,*1-4.

Guisinger, S., & Blatt, S. J. (1994). Individuality and relatedness: Evolution of a fundamental dialectic. *American Psychologist, 49*(2),104–111.

Gurpinar, E., Bati, H., & Tetik, C. (2011). Learning styles of medical students change in relation to time. Advances in Physiology Education, 35(3), 307-311. Doi: 10.1152/advan.00047.2011

Guzzo, R. A., & Shea, G. P. (1992). Group performance and inter-group relations in organizations. In M. D. Dunnette & L. M. Hough (Eds.), *Handbook of industrial and organizational psychology* (2nd ed., Vol. 3, pp. 261–313). Palo Alto, CA: Consulting Psychologists Press.

Gypen, J. (1980). *Learning style adaptation in professional careers: The case of engineers and social workers* (Unpublished doctoral dissertation). Case Western Reserve University.

Habermas, J. (1984, 1987). *The theory of communicative action.* Volume 1 (1984) & 2 (1987). Boston, MA: Beacon Press.

Hackman, J. R. (2002). *Leading teams.* Cambridge, MA: Harvard Business School Press.

Hall, J. (1996). Training in teamwork for students of library and information studies. *Education for Information, 14*(1), 19–30.

Halstead, A., & Martin, L. (2002). Learning styles: A tool for selecting students for group work. *International Journal of Electrical Engineering Education, 39*(3), 245–252.

Hannaford, C. (1995). *Smart moves: Why learning is not all in your head.* Arlington, VA: Great Ocean Publishers.

Hans, J. (1989). *The question of value: Thinking through Nietzsche, Heidegger and Freud.* Carbondale and Edwardsville: Southern Illinois University Press.

Harland, L. K. (2002). *Forced-Choice personality tests in management development contexts: An experimental study of test-taker reactions.* Paper presented at Midwest Academy of Management Meetings—HR and Careers Division.

Harrelson, G. L., & Leaver-Dunn, D. (2002). Using experiential learning cycle in clinical instruction. *Human Kinetics, 7*(5), 23–27.

Hartel, R. W. (1995). Teaching and learning styles in food science. *Food Technology, 49*(4), 96–109.

Harvey, J. (2001). The Abilene paradox: The management of agreement. *Organizational Dynamics, 17,* 16–34.

Hayes, J., & Allinson, C. W. (1998). Cognitive style and the theory and practice of individual and collective learning in organizations. *Human Relations, 51*(7), 847–871.

Hazelwood, D. (1999). *The utilization of expertise: Conversational analysis of software systems analysts and clients working together* (Unpublished doctoral dissertation). Case Western Reserve University, Cleveland, OH.

Healey, J. M. (1990). *Endangered minds.* New York, NY: Simon and Schuster.

Height, W. L., & Black, J. E. (2000). A comparative approach to play: Cross-species and cross-cultural perspectives of play in development. *Human Development, 44,* 228–234.

Hendricks, M. H. (2001). Research basis of focusing oriented experiential psychotherapy. In D. Cain & J. Seeman (Eds.), *Humanistic psychotherapy: Handbook of research and practice.* Washington, DC: American Psychological Association.

Herbert, D. M. B., & Burt, J. S. (2001). Memory awareness and schematisation: learning in the university context. *Applied Cognitive Psychology, 15,* 617–637.

_____. (2004). The effects of different review opportunities on schematisation of knowledge. *Learning and Instruction, 13,* 73–92.

Heuman, L. (2011, Fall). Focusing: Interview with Eugene Gendlin. *Tricycle,* pp. 40–109.

Hickcox, L. K. (1990). *An historical review of Kolb's formulation of experiential learning theory* (Unpublished doctoral dissertation). University of Oregon, Corvallis.

_____. (2002). Personalizing teaching through experiential learning. *College Teaching, 50*(4), 123–127.

Hicks, L. E. (1970). Some properties of ipsative, normative and forced-choice normative measures. *Psychological Bulletin, 74,* 167–184.

Hidi, S., & Renninger, K. A. (2006). The four-phase model of interest development. *Educational Psychologist, 41*(2), 111–127.

Hinds, P. J. (1999). The curse of expertise: The effects of expertise and de-biasing methods on predictions of novice performance. *Journal of Experimental Psychology: Applied, 5,* 205–221.

_____, Patterson, M., & Pfeffer, J. (2001). Bothered by abstraction: The effect of expertise on knowledge transfer and subsequent novice performance. *Journal of Applied Psychology, 86,* 1232–1243.

Hole, G. H., & Einon, D. F. (1984). Play in rodents. In P. K. Smith (Ed.), *Play in animals and humans* (pp. 95–118). New York, NY: Basil Blackwell.

Holman, D., Pavlica, K., & Thorpe, R. (1997). Rethinking Kolb's theory of experiential learning in management education: The contribution of social constructionism and activity theory. *Management Learning, 28*(2), 197–215.

Hoover, J. D., Giambatista, R. C., & Belkin, L. Y. (2012). Eyes on, hands on: Vicarious observational learning as an enhancement of direct experience. *Academy of Management Learning & Education, 11*(4), 591–608.

Hopkins, R. (1993). David Kolb's experiential learning-machine. *Journal of Phenomenological Psychology, 24*(1), 46–62.

Huba, M., & Freed, J. E. (2000). *Learner-centered assessment on college campuses.* Boston, MA: Allyn and Bacon.

Huczynski, A., & Boddy, D. (1979). The learning organization: An approach to management education and development. *Studies in Higher Education, 4*(2), 211–222.

Huizinga, J. (1950). *Homo Ludens.* Boston, MA: The Beacon Press.

Humphrey, C. (2009). By the light of the Tao. *European Journal of Social Work, 12*(3), 377–390.

Hunt, D. E. (1974). *Matching models in education.* Toronto, ON, Canada: Ontario Institute for Studies in Education.

_____. (1987). *Beginning with ourselves in practice, theory and human affairs.* Cambridge, MA: Brookline Books.

_____. (1991). *The renewal of personal energy.* Toronto, ON, Canada: Ontario Institute for Studies in Education.

Hutchins, R. M. (1953). *The University of Utopia*. Chicago, IL: University of Chicago Press.

Hutt, C. (1981). Toward a taxonomy and conceptual model of play. In H. Day (Ed.), *Advances in motivation and aesthetics* (pp. 251–297). New York, NY: Plenum Press.

Hutt, G. K., aka Samuel DeVries. (2007). *Experiential learning spaces: Hermetic transformational leadership for psychological safety, consciousness development and math anxiety related inferiority complex depotentiation* (PhD dissertation). Department of Organizational Behavior, Case Western Reserve University.

Hyland, D. (1984). *The question of play*. Lanham, MD: University Press of America.

Iliff, C. H. (1994). *Kolb's learning style inventory: A meta-analysis* (Unpublished doctoral dissertation). Boston University, Boston, MA.

Immordino-Yang M. H. (2008). All smoke and mirror neurons: Goals as sociocultural and emotional organizers of perception and action in learning. *Mind, Brain and Education, 2*(2), 67–73.

Isaacs, W. N. (1993). Taking flight: Dialogue, collective thinking and organizational learning. *Organizational Dynamics, 22*, 24–39.

Jackson, C. J. (2002). Predicting team performance from a learning process model. *Journal of Managerial Psychology, 17*(1), 6–13.

Jackson, P. W. (1998). *John Dewey and the lessons of art*. New Haven, CT: Yale University Press.

James, W. (1890). *The principles of psychology* (Vols. I and II). New York, NY: Holt, Rinehart and Winston.

_____. (1904). Does "consciousness" exist? *Journal of Philosophy, Psychology, and Scientific Method, 1*, 477–491.

_____. (1907). *Pragmatism: A new name for some old ways of thinking.* New York, NY: Longmans, Green and Company.

_____. (1912/2010). *Essays in radical empiricism.* New York, NY, and London, England: Longmans, Green and Co.

_____. (1977). Percept and concept: The import of concepts. In J. McDermott (Ed.), *The writings of William James.* Chicago, IL: University of Chicago Press.

Jamieson, G. E. (2010). *Investigating the Kolb Learning Style Inventory's ipsative scores using semantic differential and likert scaling* (Unpublished MA thesis in Education). Northern Michigan University.

Janis, I. L. (1972). *Victims of groupthink.* Boston, MA: Houghton Mifflin.

Jarrett, C. (2013). A calm look at the most hyped concept in neuroscience—Mirror neurons. *Wired/Science.* Retrieved April 2, 2015, from http://www.wired.com/2013/12/a-calm-look-at-the-most-hyped-concept-in-neuroscience-mirror-neurons/

Jarvis, P. (1987). *Adult learning in the social context.* London, England: Croom Helm.

_____. (1995). *Adult and continuing education. Theory and practice* (2nd ed.). London, England: Routledge.

Jaworski, A. (1993). *The power of silence*. Newbury Park, CA: Sage Publications.

Jensen, P. J. (1995). *Streams of meaning making in conversation* (Unpublished doctoral dissertation). Case Western Reserve University, Cleveland, OH.

_____, & Kolb, D. A. (1994). Learning and development. In M. Keeton (Ed.), *Perspectives on experiential learning* (pp. 79–84). Chicago, IL: CAEL.

_____. (2002). Conversation as communion: Spiritual, feminist, moral and natural perspectives. Chapter 2 in A. C. Baker, P. J. Jensen, & D. A. Kolb and Associates (Eds.), *Conversational learning: An experiential approach to knowledge creation* (pp. 16–29). Westport, CT: Quorum Books.

Jervis, P. (1983). Analyzing decision behavior: Learning models and learning styles as diagnostic aids. *Personnel Review, 12*, 26–38.

Johnson, C. E., Wood, R., & Blinkhorn, S. F. (1988). Spuriousier and spuriouser: The use of ipsative personality tests. *Journal of Occupational Psychology, 61*, 153–162.

Johnson, D. W., & Johnson, F. P. (1994). *Joining together: Group theory and group skills*. Boston: Allyn& Bacon.

Johnson, J. A., Howey, R. M., Reedy, Y. B., Gibble, H. A. & Ortiz, J. M. (1989). Extending the Construct Validity of the Organicim-Mechanism Paradigm Inventory. Poster presented at the First Annual Convention of the American Psychological Society, June 11, 1989, Alexandria, VA.

Jones, C., Mokhtari, K., & Reicherd, C. (2003). Are students' learning styles discipline specific?" *Community College Journal of Research and Practice, 27*(5), 363–375.

Joy, S., & Kolb, D. A. (2009). Are there cultural differences in learning style? *International Journal of Intercultural Relations, 33*(1), 69–85.

Jules, C. (2007). *Diversity of member composition and team learning in organizations* (Unpublished Ph.D. dissertation). Case Western Reserve University.

Jung, C. (1912). On the psychology of the unconscious. In CW 7: *Two essays on analytical psychology collected works.* New York, NY: Pantheon (Bollingen Series, Vols 1–20), 1957–1979.

_____. (1931). Foreword and Commentary. (R. Wilhelm, Trans.). *The Secret of the Golden Flower.* New York, NY: Harcourt, Brace & World.

_____. (1930). *The structure and dynamics of the psyche. CW 8 Collected Works.* New York, NY: Pantheon (Bollingen Series, Vols 1–20), 1957–1979.

_____. (1973). *Letters.* Princeton, NJ: Princeton University Press.

_____. (1977). *Psychological types* (R. F. C. Hull, Trans.) (pp. 12–13, 28, 68). Collected Works of C. G. Jung, Vol. 6. Bollingen Series XX. Princeton, NJ: Princeton University Press.

_____. (1977). The symbolic life. In H. Read, M. Fordham, G. Adler, & W. McGuire (Eds.) (R. F. C. Hull, Trans.), *Collected works of Carl Jung* (Vol. 18). Princeton, NJ: Bollingen Series XX, Princeton University Press.

_____. (2009). *The red book: Liber Novus.* New York, NY: W. W. Norton & Company.

Kabat-Zinn, J. (1994). *Wherever you go there you are.* New York, NY: Hyperion.

_____. (2003). Mindfulness-based interventions in context: past, present and future. *Clinical Psychology: Science and Practice, 10*, 144–156.

Kahn, M. (1981). The seminar: An experiment in humanistic education. *Journal of Humanistic Psychology, 21*(2), 61–67.

Kahneman, D., & Riis, J. (2005). Living and thinking about it: Two perspectives on life. In F. A. Huppert, B. Kaverne, & N. Baylis (Eds.), *The science of well-being*. London, England: Oxford University Press.

_____. (2011). *Thinking, fast and slow*. New York, NY: Farrar, Straus and Giroux.

Karpatschof, B., & Elkjaer, H. K. (2000). *Yet the bumblebee flies: The reliability of ipsative scores examined by empirical data and a simulation study*. Copenhagen, Denmark: Department of Psychology, University of Copenhagen: Research Report no. 1.

Karpov, Y. V., & Haywood, H. C. (1998). Two ways to elaborate Vygotsky's concept of mediation. *American Psychologist, 53*(1), 27–36.

Kaskowitz, G. (1995). Factor analysis of the model constructs suggested by Kolb's learning skills profile. *Perceptual and Motor Skills, 80*(2), 479–486.

Kay, R., & Bawden, R. (1996). Learning to be systematic: some reflections from a learning organization. *The Learning Organization, 3*(5), 18–25.

Kayes, D.C. , Kayes, A. B. , & Yamazaki, Y. 2005. Essential competencies for cross-cultural knowledge absorption. *Journal of Managerial Psychology, 20*, 7, 578-589.

Kayes, A. B. , Kayes, D. C. , & Yamazaki, Y. 2006. Transferring knowledge across cultures: A learning competencies approach. *Performance Improvement Quarterly, 18*, 4, 87-100.

Kayes, D. C. (2001). *Experiential learning in teams: A study in learning style, group process and integrative complexity in ad hoc groups* (Unpublished doctoral dissertation). Case Western Reserve University, Cleveland, OH.

_____. (2004). The 1996 Mt. Everest climbing disaster: The breakdown of learning in teams. *Human Relations, 57*(10), 1236–1284.

_____. (2006). *Destructive goal pursuit: The Mount Everest climbing disaster.* New York, NY: Palgrave Macmillan.

_____. (2002). Experiential learning and its critics: Preserving the role of experience in management learning and education. *Academy of Management Learning and Education, 1*(2), 137–149.

_____. (2015). *Organizational resilience: How learning sustains organizations in crisis, disaster, and breakdown.* New York, NY: Oxford University Press.

Kayes, A. B., & Kayes D. C. (2011). *The learning advantage: Six practices of learning-directed leadership.* New York, NY: Palgrave Macmillan.

Kayes, A. A., Kayes, D. C., Kolb, A. Y., & Kolb, D. A. (2004). *The Kolb team learning experience: Improving team effectiveness through structured learning experiences.* Boston, MA: Hay Resources Direct.

Kayes, A. B., Kayes D. C., & Kolb, D. A. (2005a). Experiential learning in teams. *Simulation and Gaming, 36*(3), 330–354.

_____. (2005b). Developing teams using the Kolb team learning experience. *Simulation and Gaming, 36*(3), 355–363.

Kearney, S., & Perkins, T. (2014). Engaging students through assessment: The success and limitations of the ASPAL (Authentic Self and Peer Assessment for Learning) Model. *Journal of University and Teaching Practice, 11*(3), 1–14.

Keeton, M., & Tate, P. (Eds.). (1978). *Learning by experience—What, why, how.* San Francisco, CA: Jossey-Bass.

Keeton, M., Sheckley, B. G., & Griggs, J. K. (2002). *Efficiency and effectiveness in higher education.* Dubuque, IA: Kendall/Hunt Publishing Company.

Kegan, R. (1982). *The evolving self: Problem and process in human development.* Cambridge, MA: Harvard University Press.

_____. (1994). *In over our heads: The demands of modern life.* Cambridge, MA: Harvard University Press.

_____, & Lahey, L. L. (2009). *Immunity to change.* Boston, MA: Harvard Business Press.

Kember, D., & Gow, L. (1994). Orientations to teaching and their effect on the quality of student learning. *Journal of Higher Education, 65*, 58–73.

Keys, L. (1994). Action learning: Executive development of choice for the 1990s. *Journal of Management Development, 13*(8), 50–56.

Kim, D. H. (1993). The link between individual and organizational learning. *Sloan Management Review, Fall*, 37–50.

King, P. M. (2003). Student learning in higher education. In S. R. Komives, D. B. Woodward Jr., & Associates (Eds.), *Student services: A handbook for the profession* (pp. 234–268). San Francisco, CA: Jossey Bass.

King, P., & Kitchner, K. (1994). *Developing reflective judgment.* San Francisco, CA: Jossey-Bass.

Kirshner, P., Sweller, J., & Clark, R. (2006). Why minimal guidance during instruction does not work: An analysis of the failure of constructivist, discovery, problem-based, experiential, and inquiry-based teaching. *Educational Psychologist, 41*(2), 75–86.

Kisfalvi, V., & Oliver, D. (2015). Creating and maintaining a safe space in experiential learning. *Journal of Management Education, 39*(6), 713–740.

Knight, K. H., Elfenbein, M. H. & Messina, J. A. (1995). A preliminary scale to measure connected and separate Knowing: The Knowing Style Inventory. *Sex Roles. 33*: 499-513

Knight, K. H., Elfenbein, M. H. & Martin, M. B. (1997). Relationship of connected and separate knowing to the learning styles of Kolb, formal reasoning and intelligence. *Sex Roles. 37*: 401-414

Koh, K., Tan, C., & Ng, P. T. (2012). Creating thinking schools through authentic assessment: The case in Singapore. *Educational Assessment, Evaluation and Accountability, 24*(2), 135–149.

Koh, K., & Luke, A. (2009). Authentic and conventional assessment in Singapore schools: an empirical study of teacher assignments and student work. *Assessment in Education: Principles, Policy and Practice, 16*(3), 291–318.

Kohlberg, L., & Ryncarz, R. A. (1990). Beyond justice reasoning: Moral development and the consideration of a seventh stage. In C. N. Alexander & E. Langer (Eds.), *Higher stages of human development.* New York, NY: Oxford University Press.

Kolb, A. Y. (2000). *Play: An interdisciplinary integration of research* (Unpublished doctoral dissertation). Case Western Reserve University, Cleveland, OH.

_____, Murphy, V., Yamazaki, & Puerta, M. (2003). *SAGES Report.* Unpublished document. Case Western Reserve University.

Kolb, A. Y., Godwin, L., Murphy, V., Joy, S., Ghazal, L., & Coombe, D. (2005). *Leading a SAGES seminar: An instructor's guide.* Cleveland, OH: Case Western Reserve University.

Kolb, A. Y. and Kolb D. A. (2003). ORBH 570: Learning and Development. Weatherhead School of Management Department of Organizational Behavior Case Western Reserve University

_____Kolb, D. A. (2005a). Learning styles and learning spaces: Enhancing experiential learning in higher education. *Academy of Management Learning and Education, 4*(2), 193–212.

_____. (2005b). *The Kolb Learning Style Inventory 3.1: Technical specifications.* Boston, MA: Hay Resources Direct.

_____. (2006). Learning styles and learning spaces: A review of the multidisciplinary application of experiential learning in higher education. In R. Sims & S. Sims (Eds.), *Learning styles and learning: A key to meeting the accountability demands in education* (pp. 45–91). New York, NY: Nova Publishers.

_____. (2009). The learning way: Meta-cognitive aspects of experiential learning. *Simulation and Gaming: An Interdisciplinary Journal, 40*(3), 297–327.

_____. (2010). Learning to play, playing to learn: A case study of a *ludic* learning space. *Journal of Organizational Change Management, 23*(1), 26–50.

_____. (2011). *Learning style inventory version 4.0.* Boston, MA: Hay Resources Direct.

_____. (2013a) *The Kolb learning style inventory 4.0: A comprehensive guide to the theory, psychometrics, research on validity and educational applications.* Boston, MA: Hay Resources Direct, www.haygroup.com/leadershipandtalentondemand

_____. (2013b). *Learning style inventory version 3.2.* Boston, MA: Hay Resources Direct.

_____. (2017). *Experiential learning theory bibliography: Volume 1–5 1971–2017.* Cleveland, OH: Experience Based Learning Systems, Inc. Retrieved from www.learningfromexperience.com

Kolb, A. Y., Kolb, D. A., Passarelli, A., & Sharma, G. (2014). On becoming an experiential educator: The educator role profile. *Simulation and Gaming, 45*(2), 204–234. doi: 10.1177/1046878114534383.

Kolb, D. A. (1971). *Individual learning styles and the learning process.*(Working Paper #535–571). Sloan School of Management, Massachusetts Institute of Technology, 1971.

Kolb, D. A. (1976a). *Learning style inventory*. Boston, MA: McBer & Company.

_____. (1976b). *Learning style inventory: Technical manual*. Boston, MA: McBer & Company.

_____. (1976c). On management and the learning process. *California Management Review, 18*(3), 21–31.

_____. (1978). *Applications of experiential learning theory to the information sciences*. Paper delivered at the National Science Foundation Conference on contributions of the behavioral sciences to research in information science, December 1978.

_____. (1981a) Experiential learning theory and the learning style inventory: A reply to Freedman and Stumpf. *The Academy of Management Review, 6*, 289–296.

_____. (1981b). Learning styles and disciplinary differences. In A. Chickering (Ed.), *The modern American college*. San Francisco, CA: Jossey Bass.

_____. (1983). Problem management: Learning from experience. In S. Srivastva & Associates (Eds.), *The executive mind*. San Francisco, CA: Jossey-Bass.

_____. (1984). *Experiential learning: Experience as the source of learning and development*. Upper Saddle River, NJ: Prentice-Hall.

_____. (1985a). *Learning style inventory, Revised Edition*. Boston, MA: McBer & Company.

_____. (1985b). *Learning style inventory: Technical manual*. Boston, MA: McBer & Company.

_____. (1993). *Learning style inventory, version 2a*. Boston, MA: Hay Resources Direct,

_____. (1998). Experiential learning: From discourse model to conversation. *Lifelong Learning in Europe, 3*, 148–153.

_____. (1999a). *Learning style inventory, version 3*. Boston, MA: Hay Resources Direct, trg_mcber@haygroup.com.

_____. (1999b). *Learning style inventory, version 3: Technical specifications*. Boston, MA: Hay Resources Direct, trg_mcber@haygroup.com

_____, Boyatzis, R., & Mainemelis, C. (2001). Experiential learning theory: Previous research and new directions. In R. Sternberg & L. Zhang (Eds.), *Perspectives on cognitive learning, and thinking styles*. Mahwah, NJ: Lawrence Erlbaum Associates.

_____. (2005). *Learning style inventory version 3.1*. Boston, MA: Hay Resources Direct.

_____, Rubin, I. M., & McIntyre, J. (Eds.) (1971). *Organizational psychology: An experiential approach*. Englewood Cliffs, NJ: Prentice Hall.

Kolb, D. A., Rubin, I., & Schein, E. (1972). *The TECH Freshman Integration Research Project: A summary report*. Unpublished report, M.I.T.

Kolb, D. A., & Goldman, M. (1973). *Toward a typology of learning styles and learning environments: An investigation of the impact of learning styles and discipline demands on the academic performance, social adaptation and career choices of M.I.T. seniors.* M.I.T. Sloan School Working Paper No. 688–73, 1973.

Kolb, D. A., & Fry, R. E. (1975). Toward an applied theory of experiential learning. In C. Cooper (Ed.), *Theories of group processes.* London, England: Wiley.

Kolb, D. A., & Wolfe, D. (1981). *Professional education and career development: A cross-sectional study of adaptive competencies in experiential learning.* Final report NIE grant no. NIE-G-77-0053, ERIC no. ED 209 493 CE 030 519.

Kolb, D. A., Lublin, S., Spoth, J., & Baker, R. (1986). Strategic management development: Using experiential learning theory to assess and develop managerial competence. *The Journal of Management Development, 5*(3), 13–24.

_____. (1988). Integrity, advanced professional development, and learning. In S. Srivastava (Ed.), *Executive integrity: The search for high human values in organizational life* (pp. 68–88). San Francisco, CA: Jossey-Bass.

_____. (1991). The challenges of advanced professional development. In L. Landon (Ed.), *Roads to the learning society.* Chicago, IL: Council for Adult & Experiential Learning.

_____, & Rainey M. A. (2013). Leading in a learning way: A 21st century perspective on leadership using experiential learning theory," *The NTL Handbook of Organization Development and Change: Principles, Practices, and Perspectives.* Arlington, VA: NTL Institute.

_____, & Peterson, K. (2013). Tailor your coaching to people's learning styles. In *HBR guide to coaching your employees*. Cambridge, MA: Harvard Business Publishing.

_____. (2015). *Experiential learning: Experience as the source of learning and development* (2nd ed.). Upper Saddle River, NJ: Pearson Education.

_____, & Yeganeh, B. (2016). Deliberate experiential learning: Mastering the art of learning from experience. In K. Elsbach, D. Christopher Kayes, & A. Kayes (Eds.), *Contemporary organizational behavior in action* (1st ed.). Upper Saddle River, NJ: Pearson Education.

Konak, A., Clark, T. K., & Nasereddin, M. (2014). Using Kolb's experiential learning cycle to improve student learning in virtual computer laboratories. *Computers & Education, 72*, 11–22.

Kosower, E., & Berman, N. (1996). Comparison of pediatric resident and faculty learning styles: Implications for medical education. *The American Journal of the Medical Sciences, 312*(5), 214–218.

Lahey, L. L., & Kegan, R. (2009). *Immunity to change*. Boston, MA: Harvard Business Press.

Lahteenmaki, S., Toivonen, J., & Mattila, M. (2001). Critical aspects of organizational learning research and proposals for its measurement. *British Journal of Management, 12*(2), 113–129.

Lakoff, G., & Johnson, M. (1980). *Metaphors we live by*. Chicago, IL: University of Chicago Press.

Lambert, N. M., & McCombs, B. (Eds.). (1998). *How students learn: Reforming schools through learner-centered education*. Washington, DC: American Psychological Association.

Langer, E. J. (1989). *Mindfulness*. Cambridge, MA: DeCapo Press.

_____. (1997). *The power of mindful learning*. Cambridge, MA: Persesus Publishing.

Latané, B., Williams, K., & Harkins. S. (1979). Many hands make light the work: The causes and consequences of social loafing. *Journal of Personality and Social Psychology, 37*, 823–832.

Lave, J. (1988). *Cognition in practice: Mind, mathematics and culture in everyday life*. Cambridge, England: Cambridge University Press.

_____, & Wenger, E. (1991). *Situated learning: Legitimate peripheral participation*. Cambridge, England: Cambridge University Press.

Lawler, E. E., III, Mohrman, S. A., & Ledford, G. E. (1992). *Employee involvement and total quality management: Practices and results in Fortune 1000 companies*. San Francisco, CA: Jossey-Bass.

_____. (1995). *Creating high-performance organizations: Practices and results of employee involvement and quality management in Fortune 1000 companies*. San Francisco, CA: Jossey-Bass.

Lawrence, P., & Lorsch, J. (1967). *Organization and Environment*. Boston, MA: Division of Research, Harvard Business School.

Leary, D. E. (1992). William James and the art of human understanding. *American Psychologist, 47*(2), 152–169.

LeDoux, J. (1997). *The emotional brain*. New York, NY: Putnam.

Lehman, H. C. (1953). *Age and achievement*. Princeton, NJ: Princeton University Press.

Leistyna, P. (2004). *Presence of mind: Education and the politics of deception.* Boulder, CO: Westview.

Leonard, G. (1991). *Mastery: The keys to long-term success and fulfillment.* New York, NY: Dutton.

Leroy, F., & Ramanantsoa, B. (1997). The cognitive and behavioral dimensions of organizational learning in a merger: An empirical study. *Journal of Management Studies, 34*(6), 871–894.

Levy, S. R., Plaks, J. E., Hong, Y., Chiu, C., & Dweck, C. S. (2001). Static versus dynamic theories and the perception of groups: Different routes to different destinations. *Personality and Social Psychology Review, 5*(2), 156–168.

Lewin, K. (1951). *Field theory in social sciences.* New York, NY: Harper & Row.

Light, R. J. (2001). *Making the most of college: Students speak their minds.* Cambridge, MA: Harvard University Press.

Lindblom-Ylanne, S., Trigwell, K., Nevgi, A., & Ashwin, P. (2006). How approaches to teaching are affected by discipline and teaching context. *Studies in Higher Education, 31*(3), 285–298.

Lingham, T. (2004). *Developing a measure of conversational learning spaces in teams* (Unpublished doctoral dissertation). Department of Organizational Behavior, Case Western Reserve University, Cleveland, OH.

Lippitt, R. (1949). *Training in community relations.* New York, NY: Harper & Row.

Lipshitz, R. (1983). Knowing and practicing: Teaching behavioral sciences at the Israel Defense Forces Command and General Staff College. *Journal of Management Studies, 20*(1), 121–141.

Litchfield, B., & Dempsey, J. V. (2015). Authentic assessment of knowledge, skills and attitudes. *New Directions for Teaching and Learning, 142,* 65–80.

Litman, J. A., & Spielberger, C. D. (2003). Measuring epistemic curiosity and its diversive and specific components. *Journal of Personality Assessment, 80*(1), 75–86.

Loevinger, J. (1966). The meaning and measurement of ego development. *American Psychologist,* 21, 195–206.

_____. (1976). *Ego development.* San Francisco, CA: Jossey-Bass.

_____, & Wessler, R. (1978). *Measuring ego development* (Vol. 1). San Francisco, CA: Jossey-Bass.

_____. (1993). Measurement of personality: True or false. *Psychological Inquiry, 4,* 1–16.

_____. (1993). Completing a life sentence. In P. M. Westenberg, A. Blasi, & L. D. Cohn (Eds.), *Personality development: Theoretical, empirical and clinical investigations of loevinger's conception of ego development* (pp. 347–354). Mahwah, NJ: Lawrence Erlbaum Associates.

Loo, R. (2002a). A meta-analytic examination of Kolb's learning style preferences among business majors. *Journal of Education for Business, 77*(5), 25–50.

_____. (2002b). The distribution of learning styles and types for hard and soft business majors. *Educational Psychology, 22*(3), 349–360.

Lorenz, K. (1971). *Studies in human and animal behavior.* Cambridge, MA: Harvard University Press.

_____. (1994). *Man meets dog.* New York, NY: Kodansha International.

MacKenzie, A. A., & White, R. T. (1982). Fieldwork in geography and long-term memory. *American Educational Research Journal, 19*, 623–632.

Maddi, S., & Kobasa, S. (1984). *The hardy executive under stress.* Homewood, IL: Dow-Jones Irwin.

Mager, R. F. (1962). *Preparing instructional objectives.* Palo Alto, CA: Fearon Publishers.

Mainemelis, C. (2001). *When the muse takes it all: A conceptual and empirical investigation of timelessness and its effects on creativity in organizations* (Unpublished doctoral dissertation). Case Western Reserve University, Cleveland, OH.

_____, Boyatzis, R., & Kolb, D. A. (2002). Learning styles and adaptive flexibility: Testing experiential learning theory. *Management Learning, 33*(1), 5–33.

Mainemelis, C., & Ronson, S. (2006). Ideas are born in fields of play: Towards a theory of play and creativity in organizational settings. *Research on Organizational Behavior, 27*, 81–131.

Malinen, A. (2000). *Toward the essence of adult experiential learning.* SoPhi: Univrsity of Jyvaskyla, Finland.

Malkki, K., & Lindblom-Ylanne, S. (2012). From reflection to action? Barriers and bridges between higher education teachers' thought and actions. *Studies in Higher Education, 37*(1), 33–50.

March, J. G. (2010). *The ambiguities of experience.* Ithaca, NY: Cornell University Press.

Marrow, A. J. (1969). *The practical theorist: The life and work of Kurt Lewin.* New York, NY: Basic Books.

Marshall, J. C., & Merritt, S. L. (1986). Reliability and construct validity of the learning style questionnaire. *Educational and Psychological Measurement, 46,* 257–262.

Marton, F., & Saljo, R. (1976). On qualitative differences in learning. Outcome and process. *British Journal of Educational Psychology, 46,* 4–11.

Maslow, A. H. (1968). *Toward a psychology of being* (2nd ed.). New York, NY: Van Nostrand Reinhold.

Matsuo, M. (2014). Instructional skills for on-the-job training and experiential learning: An empirical study of Japanese firms. *International Journal of Training and Development, 18*(4), 225–240.

Matthews, G., & Oddy, K. (1997). Ipsative and normative scales in adjectival measurement of personality: Problems of bias and discrepancy. *International Journal of Selection and Assessment, 5*(3), 169–182.

Maturana, H. (1970). The biology of cognition. In H. Maturana and F. Varela (Eds.), *Autopoeisis and Cognition.* Dordrecht, Holland: D. Reidel.

_____, & Varela, F. (1980). *Autopoeisis and cognition.* Dordrecht, Holland: D. Reidel.

_____.& Varela, F. (1987). *The tree of knowledge: Biological roots of human understanding.* Boston, MA: Shambala.

McCloskey, H., & Schaar, J. (1963). Psychological dimensions of anomie. *American Psychological Review, 30*(1), 14–40.

Mcgoldrick, K., Battle, A., & Gallagher, S. (2000). Service-Learning and the economics course: Theory and practice. *The American Economist, 44*(1), 43–52.

McCarthy, B. (1996). *About learning* Excel, Inc.

McCarthy, B. (2000). *About teaching.* Excel, Inc.

McCrae, R. R., Costa, J., & Martin, T. A. (2005). The NEO–PI–3: A more readable revised NEO personality inventory. *Journal of Personality Assessment, 84*(3), 261–270.

McCrae, R. R., & Costa, P. T. (1987). Validation of the five-factor model of personality across instruments and observers. *Journal of Personality and Social Psychology, 52*(1), 81–90.

McGregor, D. (2006). *The human side of enterprise.* New York, NY: McGraw Hill.

McMurray, D. (1998). Learning styles and organizational behavior in Japanese EFL classrooms. *Journal of Fukui Prefectural University, 13,* 29–45.

McNemar, W. (1957). *Psychological statistics.* New York, NY: John Wiley.

Merritt, S. L., & Marshall, J. C. (1984). Reliability and construct validity of ipsative and normative forms of the learning style inventory. *Educational and Psychological Measurement, 44,* 463–472.

Mead, G. (1934). *Mind, self and society, from the standpoint of a social behaviorist.* Chicago, IL: University of Chicago Press.

Mentkowski, M., & Much, N. (1982). *Careering after college: Perspectives on lifelong learning and career development.* Milwaukee, WI: Alverno Productions.

Mentkowski, M., & Strait, M. J. (1983). *A longitudinal study of student change in cognitive development and generic abilities in an outcome-centered liberal arts curriculum.* Paper presented at the annual meeting of the American Educational Research Association, Montreal, Canada, April, 1983.

Mentkowski, M., & Associates. (2000). *Learning that lasts: Integrating learning, development and performance in college and beyond.* San Francisco, CA: Jossey Bass.

Mezirow, J. (1990). *Transformative dimensions of adult learning.* San Francisco, CA: Jossey Bass.

_____. (1996). Contemporary paradigms of learning. *Adult Education Quarterly, 46*(3), 158–173.

Michelson, E. (1997). Multicultural approaches to portfolio development. *New Directions for Adult and Continuing Education, 75*, 41–53.

_____. (1998). Re-Membering: The return of the body to experiential learning. *Studies in Continuing Education, 20*(2), 217–233.

_____. (1999). Carnival, paranoia and experiential learning. *Studies in the Education of Adults, 31*(2), 140–154.

Michaelsen, L., Bauman Knight, A., & Fink, L. D. (Eds.). (2004). *Team-based learning: A transformative use of small groups in college teaching.* Sterling, VA: Stylus Publishing.

Miettinen, R. (2000). The concept of experiential learning and John Dewey's theory of reflective thought and action. *International Journal of Lifelong Education, 19*(1), 54–72.

Miller, S. N. (1974). The playful, the crazy, and the nature of pretense. *Rice University Studies, 60*(3), 31–51.

Miller, J. B., & Stiver, I. (1997). *The healing connection.* Boston, MA: Beacon Press.

Mills, T. (1967). *Sociology of small groups.* Englewood Cliffs, NJ: Prentice-Hall.

Milne, D., James, I., Keegan, D., & Dudley, M. (2002). Teacher's PETS: A new observational measure of experiential training interactions. *Clinical Psychology and Psychotherapy, 9*, 187–199.

Mintzberg, H. (1973). *The nature of managerial work.* New York, NY: Harper & Row.

Mischel, W. (1984). Convergences and challenges in the search for consistency. *American Psychologist, 39*, 351–364.

Moon, B. A. (2008). *Learning style influence on relationship sales success.* Unpublished EDM Quantitative Research Report. Weatherhead School of Management, Case Western Reserve University.

Molden, D. C., & C. S. Dweck. (2006). Finding "meaning" in psychology: A lay theories approach to self-regulation, social perception and social development. *American Psychologist, 61*(3), 192–203.

Montagu, A. (1984). *Growing young.* Granby, MA: Bergin & Garvey.

Mother T. (1993). *Total surrender.* New York, NY: Walker and Company.

Moustakas, C. (1997). *Relationship play therapy.* Northvale, NJ: Jason Aronson.

Mumford, A. (1991). Individual and organizational learning: Balance in the pursuit of change. *Studies in Continuing Education, 13*(2), 115–125.

Myers-Briggs, I. (1962). *The Myers-Briggs type indicator manual.* Princeton, NJ: Educational Testing Service.

Nachmanovitch, S. (1990). *Free play.* New York: Putnam Publishing.

Nater, S., & Gallimore, R. (2010). *You haven't taught until they have learned.* Morgantown, WV: Fitness Information Technology.

Nelson, E. A., & Grinder, R. E. (1985). Toward an ex cathedra doctrine of learning. *Contemporary Psychology, 30*(8), 622–623.

Nelson, T. O. (1996). Consciousness and meta-cognition. *American Psychologist, 51*(2), 102–116.

Neugarten and Associates. (1964). *Personality in middle and late life.* New York, NY: Atherton Press.

New Zealand Ministry of Education. (2004). *Making meaning: Making a difference.* New Zealand: Learning Media Limited. Online Version. Retrieved from www.tki.org.nz/r/health/cia/make_meaning/index_e. php

Nisbett, R. E., Peng, K., Choi, I., & Norenzayan, A. (2001). Culture and systems of thought: Holistic versus analytic cognition. *Psychological Review, 108*(2), 291–310.

Nishida, K. (1911/1990). *An inquiry into the good* (Maso Abe and Christopher Ives, Trans.). New Haven, CT: Yale University Press.

Noam, G. G. (1993). Ego development: True or false?" *Psychological Inquiry, 4,* 43–48.

Nonaka, I., & Takeuchi, H. (1995). *The knowledge-creating company.* Ney York, NY: Oxford University Press.

Nonaka, I., & Konno, N. (1998). The concept of 'Ba': Building a foundation for knowledge creation. *California Management Review, 40*(3), 40–54.

Nonaka, I., Toyama, R., & Konno, N. (2000). SECI, *Ba* and leadership: A unified model of dynamic knowledge creation. *Long Range Planning, 33,* 5–34.

Nouwen, H. (1975). *Reaching out.* New York, NY: Doubleday.

Novin, A. M., Arjomand, L. H., & Jourdan, L. (2003). An investigation into the preferred learning styles of accounting, management, marketing and general business majors. *Teaching and Learning, 18*(1), 24–31.

Nyirenda, J. E. (1996). The relevance of Paulo Freire's contributions to education and development in present day Africa. *Africa Media Review, 10*(1), 1–20.

OECD. (2012). *Education at a glance 2012: OECD indicators.* Paris: OECD Publishing.

O'Laughlin, M. (1992). Rethinking science education: Beyond Piagetian constructivism toward a sociocultural model of teaching and learning. *Journal of Research in Science Teaching, 29*(8), 791–820.

Olsen, M. (1969). Political alienation scale. In J. Robinson & P. Shauer (Eds.), *Measures of social psychological attitudes* (pp. 181–183). Ann Arbor: Institute for Social Research, University of Michigan.

Onwuegbuzie, A. J., & Daley C. E. (1998). Similarity of learning styles of students and a teacher in achievement in a research methods course. *Psychological Reports, 82*, 163–168.

Oreg, S. (2003). Resistance to change: Developing an individual differences measure. *Journal of Applied Psychology, 88*(4), 680–693.

Ornstein, R. E. (1972). *The psychology of consciousness.* New York, NY: W. H. Freeman & Company.

_____. (1977). *The psychology of consciousness.* New York, NY: Harcourt Brace, Jovanovich.

Orwell, G. (1968). Politics and the English language. In S. Orwell & I. Angus (Eds.), *In front of your nose* (Vol. 4). The Collected Essays of George Orwell. New York, NY: Harcourt Brace & World.

Osgood-Campbell, E. (2015). Investigating the educational implications of embodied cognition: A model interdisciplinary inquiry in mind, brain, and education curricula. *Mind, Brain and Education, 9*(1), 3–9.

Osipow, S. H. (1973). *Theories of career development* (2nd ed.). New York, NY: Appleton-Century-Crofts.

Osland, J. S., Kolb, D. A., Rubin I. M., & Turner M. E. (2007). *Organizational behavior: An experiential approach* (8th ed.). Upper Saddle River, NJ: Prentice Hall.

Ottati, V., Price, E. D., Wilson, C., & Sumaktoyo, N. (2015). When self-perceptions of expertise increase closed-minded cognition: The earned dogmatism effect. *Journal of Experimental Social Psychology, 61*, 131–138.

Ou, A. Y., Tsui, A. S., Kinicki, A. J., Waldman, D. A., Xiao, Z., & Song, L. J. (2014). Humble chief executive officers' connections to top management team integration and middle managers' responses. *Administrative Science Quarterly, 59*(1), 34–72.

Owings, R., Peterson, G., Bransford, J., Morris, C., and Stein, B. (1980). Spontaneous monitoring and regulation of learning: A comparison of successful and less successful fifth graders. *Journal of Educational Psychology, 72*, 250–256.

Palmer, P. (1983). *To know as we are known: Education as a spiritual journey.* San Francisco, CA: Harper and Row.

_____. (1990). *The active life: A spirituality of work, creativity and caring.* San Francisco, CA: Harper and Row.

_____. (1998). *The courage to teach: Exploring the inner landscape of a teacher's life.* San Francisco, CA: Jossey-Bass.

Pappano, L. (2012). The year of the MOOC. *The New York Times, 2*(12).

Park, C. (1996). *Our place in nature: Naturalism, human mind and professional practice* (Unpublished doctoral dissertation). Case Western Reserve University, Cleveland, OH.

Park, W., & Bang, H. (2002, March 26–27). *Team role balance and team performance.* Paper presented at the Belbin Biennial Conference, "Changing Role of Management in the 21st Century," Clare College, Cambridge.

Parker, R. (1984). Small group cooperative learning in the classroom. *OSCC Bulletin, 27*(7).

Pashler, H., Mcdaniel, M., Rohrer, D., & Bjork, R. (2008). Learning styles: Concepts and evidence. *Psychological Science in the Public Interest, 9*(3), 105–119.

Passarelli, A. M. (2014). Harnessing the power of a massive open online course (MOOC): Inspiring leadership through emotional intelligence. *Academy of Management Learning and Education, June,* 298–300.

_____, & Kolb D. A. (2011). The learning way—Learning from experience as the path to lifelong learning and development. Chapter 6. In M. London (Ed.), *Handbook of lifelong learning* (pp. 70–90). New York, NY: Oxford University Press.

_____. (2012). Using experiential learning theory to promote student learning and development in programs of education abroad. In M. V. Berg, M. Page, & K. Lou (Eds.), *Student Learning Abroad* Sterling, VA: Stylus.

Pathi, V., Manning, M., & Kolb, D. A. (1989). *Forced choice measures: Some issues in the use of pair comparison and rank ordering formats.* Unpublished Working paper. Department of Organizational Behavior, CWRU.

Pauchant, T. (1995). *In search of meaning.* San Francisco, CA: Jossey-Bass.

Pauleen, D. J., Marshall, S., & Egort, I. (2004). ICT-supported team-based experiential learning: Classroom perspectives. *Education + Training, 46*(2), 90–99.

Peirce, C. S. (1877). The Fixation of Belief. *Popular Science Monthly, 12,* 1–15.

Perlmutter, S. (1990). *Cognitive complexity and time perspective in hybrid organizations* (Unpublished doctoral dissertation). Case Western Reserve University.

Perkins, M. (1971). Matter, sensation and understanding. *American Philosophical Quarterly, 8,* 1–12.

Perry, W. (1970). *Forms of intellectual and ethical development in the college years: A scheme.* New York, NY: Holt, Rinehart & Winston.

Peterson, K., Decato, L., & Kolb, D. A. (2015). Moving and learning: Expanding style and increasing flexibility. *Journal of Experiential Education, 38,* 228–244.

Piaget, J. (1952). *The origins of intelligence in children.* New York, NY: International University Press.

_____. (1962). *Play, dreams and imitation in childhood.* New York, NY: W. W. Norton.

_____. (1968). *Structuralism.* New York, NY: Harper Torchbooks.

_____. (1970a). *Genetic epistemology*. New York, NY: Columbia University Press.

_____. (1970b). *The place of the sciences of man in the system of sciences*. New York, NY: Harper Torchbooks.

_____. (1971). *Psychology and epistemology*. Middlesex, England: Penguin Books.

_____. (1978, July). What is psychology? *American Psychologist, July 1978*, 648–652.

Pickworth, G. E., & Schoeman, W. J. (2000). The psychometric properties of the learning style inventory and the learning style questionnaire: Two normative measures of learning styles. *South African Journal of Psychology, 30*(2), 44–53.

Piers, M. W. (Ed.). (1972). *Play and development: A symposium with contributions by Jean Piaget, Peter H. Wolf, Rene A. Spitz, Konrad Lorenz, Lois Barclay Murphy, Erik Erikson*. New York, NY: W.W. Norton & Company.

Plowden Report. (1967). *Children and their primary schools*. London, England: Central Advisory Council for Education.

Poncelet A., & Hirsh, D. (2014). Longitudinal Integrated Clerkships (LIC) Chapter 10. In B. Z. Morgenstern (Ed.), *Alliance for clinical education: Guidebook for clerkship directors*. North Syracuse, NY: Gegensatz Press.

Popper, M., & Lipshitz, R. (2000). Organizational learning—Mechanisms, culture, and feasibility. *Management Learning, 31*(2), 181–196.

Power, M. J. (2007). The multistory self: Why the self is more than the sum of its autoparts. *Journal of Clinical Psychology, 63*(2), 187–198.

Prince, M. J. & Felder R. M. (2006). Inductive teaching and learning methods: Definitions, comparisons and research bases. *Journal of Engineering Education.95* (2): 123-138

Rainey, M.A., Hekelman, F.P., Galazka, S.S., & Kolb, D.A. (1993, February). The Executive Skills Profile: A method for assessing development needs among family medicine faculty. *Family Medicine. 24:*100-103.

Ramnarayan, S., & Reddy, N. M. (1989). Institutional learning: The essence of strategic management. *Vikalpa, 14*(1), 21–33.

Ramsden, P (1992). *Learning to teach in higher education.* London, England: Routledge.

Raschick, M., Maypole, D. E., & Day, P. (1998). Improving field education through Kolb learning theory. *Journal of Social Work Education, 34*(1), 31–43.

Read, H., Fordham, M., & Adler, G. (Eds.). (1961–67). *The collected works of C. G. Jung.* Bollingen, Switzerland: Bollingen Foundation.

Reese, J. (1998). *Enhancing law student performance: Learning styles interventions* Unpublished report. Saratoga Springs, NY: National Center on Adult Learning, Empire State College.

Renninger, K. A. (2000). Individual interest and its implications for understanding intrinsic motivation. In C. Sansone & J. M. Harackiewicz

(Eds.), *Intrinsic and extrinsic motivation: The search for optimal motivation and performance* (pp. 375–407). New York, NY: Academic.

Revans, R. W. (1971). *Developing effective managers: A new approach to management education.* London, England: Blond and Briggs.

_____. (1980). *Action learning: A new approach for managers.* London, England: Blond and Briggs.

Reynolds, M. (1997). Learning styles: A critique. *Management Learning, 28*(2), 115–134.

_____. (1998). Reflection and critical reflection in management learning. *Management Learning, 29*(2), 183–200.

Rilke, R. M. (2012). *Letters to a young poet.* Snowball Publishing.

Ripley, A. (2013). *The smartest kids in the world.* New York, NY: Simon & Schuster.

Robertson, D. L. (1988). *Self-directed growth.* Muncie, IN: Accelerated Development, Inc.

Rogers, C. (1951). *Client-Centered therapy: Its current practice, implications and theory.* London, England: Constable.

_____. (1959). A theory of therapy, personality, and interpersonal relationships, as developed in the client-centered framework. In S. Koch (Ed.), *Psychology: A study of a science, vol. 3 formulations of the person and the social context* (pp. 184–256). New York, NY: McGraw Hill.

_____. (1961). *On becoming a person.* Boston, MA: Houghton Mifflin.

_____. (1964). Toward a modern approach to values: The valuing process in the mature person. *Journal of Abnormal and Social Psychology, 63*(2), 160–167.

_____. (1969). *Freedom to learn.* Columbus, OH: Charles E. Merrill Publishing Company.

Rogoff, B. (2003). *The cultural nature of human development.* London, England: Oxford University Press.

Romero, J. E., Tepper, B. J., & Tertrault, L. A. (1992). Development and validation of new scales to measure Kolb's (1985) learning style dimensions. *Educational and Psychological Measurement, 52,* 171–180.

Romme, G. L., & van Witteloostruijn, A. (1999). Circular organizing and triple loop learning. *Journal of Organizational Change Management, 12*(5), 439–453.

Rose, N., &d Abi-Rached, J. M. (2013). *Neuro: The new brain sciences and the management of the mind.* Princeton, NJ: Princeton University Press.

Rowe, F. A., & Waters, M. L. (1992). Can personality-type instruments profile majors in management programs? *Journal of Education for Business, 68*(1), 10–15.

Rowe, M. B. (1974). Pausing phenomena: Influence on the quality of instruction. *Journal of Psycholinguistic Research, 3*(3), 203–224.

Rowling, J. K. (2008, July–August). A stripping away of the inessential. *Harvard Magazine,* 55–56.

Rubin, Z. (1981). Does personality really change after 20?, *Psychology Today*, May 1981, 18–27.

Russ, S. W. (2004). *Play in child development and psychotherapy*. Mahwah, NJ: Erlbaum.

Ryan, R. M., & Deci, E. L. (2000). Self-determination theory and the facilitation of intrinsic motivation, social development, and well-being. *American Psychologist, 55*(1), 68–78.

_____. (2004). Autonomy is no illusion: Self-determination theory and the empirical study of authenticity, awareness and will. Chapter 28. In J. Greenberg, S. L. Koole, & T. Pyscznski (Eds.), *Handbook of experimental existential psychology* (pp. 449–479). New York, NY: Guilford Press.

Sagan, C. (1977). *The dragons of Eden*. New York, NY: Random House.

Sahlberg, P. (2010). *Finnish lessons*. New York, NY: Teachers College Press.

Samples, B. (1976). *The metaphoric mind*. Reading, MA: Addison-Wesley.

Samuelson, J. (1982). *Career development and cognitive styles*. Unpublished paper, Ohio State University.

Sandmire, D. A., & Boyce, P. F. (2004). Pairing of opposite learning styles among allied health students: Effects on collaborative performance. *Journal of Allied Health, 33*(2), 156–163.

Sandmire, D. A., Vroman, K. G., & Sanders, R. (2000). The influence of learning styles on collaborative performances of allied health students in a clinical exercise. *Journal of Allied Health, 29*(3), 143–149.

Sanford, N. (1962). *The American college*. New York, NY: Wiley.

_____. (1966). *Self and society: Social change and individual development.* New York, NY: Atherton Press.

_____. (1981). Notes toward a theory of personality development at 80 or any old age. In J Starde (Ed.), *Wisdom and old age.* Berkeley, CA: Ross Books.

Sanner, B., & Bunderson, J. S. (2015). When feeling safe isn't enough: Contextualizing models of safety and learning in teams. *Organizational Psychology Review*, doi: 0.1177/2041386614565145

Santos, P., Cook, J., & Hernández-Leo, D. (2015). M-AssIST: Interaction and scaffolding matters in authentic assessment. *Educational Technology & Society, 18*(2), 33–45.

Saville, P., & Wilson, E. (1991). The reliability and validity of normative and ipsative approaches in the measurement of personality. *Journal of Occupational Psychology, 64*, 219–238.

Schaefer, J. J., Vanderbilt, A. A., Cason, C. L., Bauman, E. B., Glavin, R. J., Lee, F. W., & Navedo, D. D. (2011). Literature review, instructional design and pedagogy science in healthcare simulation. *Simulation in Healthcare, 6*, S30-S41. doi: 10.1097/SIH.0b013e31822237b4

Schein, E., & Bennis, W. (1965). *Personal and organizational change through group methods.* New York, NY: John Wiley.

Schemp, P. G., McCullick, B., & Mason, I. S. (2006). The development of expert coaching. In R. Jones (Ed.), *The sports coach as educator: Re-conceptualising sports coaching* (pp. 145–161). London, England: Routledge.

Schmidmaier, R., Eiber, S., Ebersbach, R., Schiller, M., Hege, I., Holzer, M., et al. (2013). Learning the facts in medical school is not enough: Which factors predict successful application of procedural knowledge in a laboratory setting? *BMC Medical Education, 13*, 28.

Schon, D. A. (1983). *The reflective practitioner.* New York, NY: Basic Books.

Schroder, H. M., Driver, M. J., & Streufert, S. (1967). *Human information processing.* New York, NY: Holt, Rinehart & Winston.

Schweickart, P. P. (1996). Speech is silver, silence is gold. Chapter 10. In N. R. Goldberger et al. (Eds.), *Knowledge, difference, and power* (pp. 305–334). New York, NY: Basic Books.

Schwitzgabel, R., & Kolb, D. A. (1974) *Changing human behavior: Principles of planned intervention.* New York, NY: McGraw-Hill.

Scott, W. A. (1966). Flexibility, rigidity, and adaptation: Toward clarification of concepts. In O. J. Harvey (Ed.), *Experience, structure and adaptability* (pp. 369–400). New York, NY: Springer.

Selltiz, C., Jahoda, M., Deutsch, M., & Cook, S. (1960). *Research methods in social relations.* New York, NY: Henry Holt and Company.

Seaman, J. (2008). Experience, reflect, critique: The end of the "learning cycles" era. *Journal of Experiential Learning, 31*(1), 3–18.

Semb. G. B., & Ellis, J. A. (1994). Knowledge taught in school: What is remembered? *Review of Educational Research, 64*(2), 253–286.

Senge, P. M. (1990a). *The fifth discipline.* New York, NY: Doubleday.

_____. (1990b). The leader's new work: Building learning organizations. *Sloan Management Review, 32,* 7–23.

Sharma, G., & Kolb, D. A. (2010). The learning flexibility index: Assessing contextual flexibility in learning style. Chapter 5. In S. Rayner & E. Cools (Eds.), *Style differences in cognition, learning and management: Theory, research and practice* (pp. 60–77). New York, NY: Routledge Publishers.

Sharp, J. E. (2001, October 10–13). *Teaching teamwork communication with Kolb learning style theory [session F2C1].* Presented at the 31st ASEE/IEEE Frontiers in Education Conference, Reno, NV.

Shepard, H. A. (1984). On the realization of human potential: A path with heart. In M. B. Arthur, L. Barilyn, D. J. Levinson, & H. A. Shephard (Eds.), *Working with careers.* Columbia University School of Business.

Shermer, M. (2011). *The believing brain: From ghosts and gods to politics and conspiracies—How we construct beliefs and reinforce them as truths* (p. 135). Neo York, NY:Macmillan. Kindle Edition.

Shields, S. A., Zawadzki, M. J., & Johnson, R. N. (2011). The impact of the workshop activity for gender equity simulation in the academy (WAGES-Academic) in demonstrating cumulative effects of gender bias. *Journal of Diversity in Higher Education, 4*(2), 120-129. doi: 10.1037/a0022953

Shirey, L. L., & Reynolds, R. E. (1988). Effect of interest on attention and learning. *Journal of Educational Psychology, 80*(2), 159–166.

Shotter, J. (1989). Vygotsky's psychology: Joint activity in a developmental zone. *New Ideas in Psychology, 7*(2), 185–204.

Silvia, P. J. (2001). Interest and interests: The psychology of constructive capriciousness. *Review of General Psychology, 5*(3), 270–290.

Simonin, B. L. (1997). The importance of collaborative know-how: An empirical test of the learning organization. *Academy of Management Journal, 40*(5), 1150–1174.

Sims, R. R. (1980). *Preparation for professional careers and changing job roles: An assessment of professional education.* Qualifying paper, Department of Organizational Behavior, Case Western Reserve University.

_____. (1981). *Assessing competencies in experiential learning theory: A person-job congruence model of effectiveness in professional careers* (Unpublished Ph.D. dissertation). Case Western Reserve University.

_____. (1983). Kolb's experiential learning theory: A framework for assessing person-job interaction. *Academy of Management Review, 8*(2), 501–508.

Singer, D. G., Golinkoff, R. M., & Hirsh-Pasek, K. (2006). *Play = learning: How play motivates and enhances children's cognitive and social-emotional growth.* New York, NY: Oxford University Press.

Sisson, E. D. (1948). Forced choice: The new Army rating. *Personnel Psychology, 8,* 297–299.

Slavich, G. M. & Zimbardo, P. G. (2012). Transformational teaching: Theoretical underpinnings, basic principles, and core methods. *Educ Psychol Rev*

DOI 10.1007/s10648-012-9199-6

Smith, D. (1990). *Physician managerial skills: Assessing the critical competencies of the physician executive* (Unpublished doctoral dissertation). Department of Organizational Behavior, Case Western Reserve University.

Smith, P. K. (1982). Does play matter? Functional and evolutionary aspects of animal in human play. *Behavioral and Brain Sciences, 5,* 139–184.

_____. (1984). Evolutionary origins of play. In P. K. Smith (Ed.), *Play in animals and humans* (pp. 1–4). New York, NY: Basil Blackwell.

Smith, M. K. (2012). Mary Parker Follett and informal education. *The Encyclopedia of Informal Education.* Retrieved from http://www.infed.org/thinkers/et-foll.htm. Last update: May 29, 2012.

_____, & Kolb, D.A. (2010). On experiential learning. *The Encyclopedia of Informal Education,* 2010. Retrieved March 11, 2015, from http://www.infed.org/b-explrn.htm.

Sosniak, L. A. (1987). From tyro to virtuoso: A long-term commitment to learning. In Wilson, F. R. & Roehmann, F. L. (Eds.), *The biology of music making: Music and child development* (pp. 272–289). Proceeding of the 1987 Denver Conference.

Spariosu, M. (1989). *Dionysus reborn.* New York, NY: Cornell University Press.

Specht, L. B., & Sandlin, P. K. (1991). The differential effects of experiential learning activities and traditional lecture classes. *Simulation & Gaming, 22*(2), 196–210.

Staude, J. (1981). *The adult development of C. G. Jung.* Boston, MA: Routledge & Kegan Paul.

Staw, B. M. (1982). The escalation of commitment to a course of action. *Academy of Management Review, 6,* 577–587.

Stein, J. (Ed.). (1966). *The Random House Dictionary of the English language: The unabridged edition.* New York, NY: Random House.

Steingard, D. (1997). *Values integration in socially responsible business: From separation thesis to spiritual relationality* (Unpublished doctoral dissertation). Case Western Reserve University, Cleveland, OH.

Stephens, M. (1994). The theologian of talk. *Los Angeles Times Magazine,* October 23, 1994.

Stevens, M. A., & Campion, M. J. (1994). The knowledge, skill and ability requirements for teamwork: Implications for human resource management. *Journal of Management, 20,* 503–530.

Strange, C. C., & Banning, J. H. *Educating by design: Creating campus learning environments that work.* San Francisco, CA: Jossey Bass.

Sturges, P. T., Ellis, J. A., & Wulfeck, W. H. (1981). *Effects of performance-oriented text upon long-term retention of factual material.* Tech. Rep. NPRDC TR-81-22. San Diego, CA: Navy Personnel Research and Development Center.

Su, Y. (2011). Lifelong learning as being: The Heideggerian perspective. *Adult Education Quarterly, 61*(1), 57–72.

Subramaniam, P. R. (2009) Motivational effects of interest on student engagement and learning in physical education: A review. *International Journal of Physical Education, 46*(2), 1–19.

Sullivan, H. G. (1997). *Creating common ground for collaborative learning: A Gestalt perspective for experiential learning* (Unpublished doctoral dissertation). Case Western Reserve University, Cleveland, OH.

Summers, L. H. (2003, July–August). On undergraduate education. *Harvard Magazine*, 63–65.

Sutton-Smith, B. (1997). *The ambiguity of play*. Cambridge, MA: Harvard University Press.

Swartz, D. L. (2002). The sociology of habit: The perspective of Pierre Bourdieu. *The Occupational Therapy Journal of Research, 22*, 61S–69S.

Tangney, J. P. (2000). Humility: Theoretical perspectives, empirical findings and directions for future research. *Journal of Social and Clinical Psychology, 19*, 70–82.

_____. (2002). Humility. In C. R. Snyder (Ed.), *Handbook of positive psychology* (pp. 411–419). New York, NY: Oxford University Press.

Taylor, A. A., Backlund, P. & Niklasson, L. (2012). The coaching cycle: A coaching-by-gaming approach in serious games. *Simulation and Gaming 43*(5): 648-672.

Taylor, E. I., & Wozniak, R. H. (1996). *Pure experience: The response to William James*. Bristol, England: Thoemmes Press.

Taylor, F. C. (1973). *Relationship between student personality and performance in an experiential theoretical group dynamics course* (Faculty Working Paper #132). Kent State University.

Templeton, J. M. (1997). *Worldwide laws of life*. Philadelphia, PA: Templeton Foundation Press.

Terman, L., & Oden, M. (1947). *The gifted child grows up*. Stanford, CA: Stanford University Press.

Tharpe, R. G., & Gallimore, R. (1988). *Rousing minds to life: Teaching, learning and schooling in social context*. Cambridge, England: Cambridge University Press.

Thatcher, D. C. (1990). Promoting learning through games and simulations. *Simulation & Gaming 21*(3) 262-273

Thomas, G. F. (2002). Individual and organizational learning: A developmental perspective on Gilsdorf, Rymer and ABC. *The Journal of Business Communication, 39*(3), 379–387.

Thompson, L. M. (1999). *Love of learning as the driver for self-directed learning in the workplace* (Unpublished doctoral dissertation). Case Western Reserve University.

Timken, G. L., & McNamee, J. (2012). New perspectives for teaching physical education: Preservice teachers' reflections on outdoor and adventure education. *Journal of Teaching in Physical Education, 31*(1), 21-38.

Tong, J. J., Yao, X., Lu, Z. X., & Wang, L. (2013). Impact pattern of dialectical thinking on perceived leadership training outcomes. *Journal of Applied Social Psychology, 43*(6), 1248-1258. doi: 10.1111/jasp.12087

Torbert, W. (1972). *Learning from experience: Toward consciousness*. New York, NY: Columbia University Press.

_____. (1980). Organizing experiential learning. In D. E. Wolfe & E. Byrne (Eds.), *Developing experiential learning in professional education, no. 8*. San Francisco, CA: Jossey-Bass.

Torrealba, D. (1972). *Convergent and divergent learning styles.* Master's thesis, Massachusetts Institute of Technology, Sloan School of Management.

Tough, A. (1977). *Major learning efforts: Recent research and future directions.* Toronto, ON, Canada: Ontario Institute for Studies in Education.

Trigwell, K., & Prosser, M. (1996). Changing approaches to teaching: a relational perspective. *Studies in Higher Education, 21,* 275–284.

Trinh, M. P., & Kolb, D. A. (2011). Eastern experiential learning: Eastern principles for learning wholeness. *Journal of Career Planning and Adult Development,* Special Issue "Recovering Craft: Holistic Work and Empowerment," William Charland, (guest editor) *27*(4), 29–36.

_____. (2016). *Overcoming the shadow of expertise: How humility, learning goal orientation and learning identity help experts become more flexible* (Unpublished doctoral dissertation). Department of Organizational Behavior, Case Western Reserve University.

Tulving, E. (1983). *Elements of episodic memory.* New York, NY: Oxford University Press.

_____. (1985a). How many memory systems are there? *American Psychologist, 40,* 385–398.

_____. (1985b). Memory and consciousness. *Canadian Psychology, 26,* 1–12.

_____. (2005). Episodic memory and autonoesis: Uniquely human? In H. S. Terrace & J. Metcalfe (Eds.), *The missing link in cognition: Origins of self-reflective consciousness.* London, England: Oxford University Press.

Turesky, E. F., & Gallagher, D. (2011). Know thyself: Coaching for leadership using Kolb's experiential learning theory. *The Coaching Psychologist, 7*(1), 5–14.

Turner, T. (1973). Piaget's structuralism. *American Anthropologist, 76,* 351–373.

Turner, V. (1974). Liminal to liminoid, in play, flow, and ritual: An essay in comparative symbology. *Rice University Studies, 60*(3), 52–92.

Twain, M. (1988). *The family Mark Twain.* New York, NY: Dorset Press.

Vail, P. B. (1996). *Learning as a way of being: Strategies for survival in a world of permanent white water.* San Francisco, CA: Jossey Bass.

Vandenberg, B. (1991). Is epistemology enough: An existential consideration of development. *American Psychologist, 46*(12), 1278–1286.

Vanhear, J. (2013). The use of concept mapping and vee heuristics in higher education to promote critical reflection and meaningful learning. *Journal for Educators, Teachers and Trainers, 4*(4), 180–194.

Varela, F. J., Thompson, E., & Rosch, E. (1991). *The embodied mind: Cognitive science and human experience.* Cambridge, MA: MIT Press.

Varlas, L. (2010). Responding to the research: Harvey Silver and Matthew Perini address learning styles. *Education Update, 52*(5), 6–7.

Veres, J. G., III, Sims, R. R., & Locklear. T. S. (1991). Improving the reliability of Kolb's revised learning style inventory. *Educational and Psychological Measurement, 51,* 143–150.

Vince, R. (1997). Behind and beyond Kolb's learning cycle. *Journal of Management Education, 22*(3), 304–319.

Vygotsky, L. S. (1962). *Thought and language.* New York, NY: John Wiley and MIT Press.

_____. (1966). Play and its role in the mental development of the child. *Voprosy Psikhologii, 12,* 62–76.

_____. (1978). *Mind in society: The development of higher psychological processes.* Cambridge, MA: Harvard University Press.

Waitzkin, J. (2007). *The art of learning: A journey in the pursuit of excellence.* New York, NY: Free Press.

Wallach, M. A., Kogan, N., & Bem, D. J. (1964). Diffusion of responsibility and level of risk taking in groups. *Journal of Abnormal and Social Psychology, 68,* 263–274.

Weirstra, R. F. A., & DeJong, J. A. (2002). A scaling theoretical evaluation of Kolb's learning style inventory-2. In M. Valcke & D Gombeir (Eds.), *Learning styles: Reliability and validity* (pp. 431–440). Proceedings of the 7th annual European learning styles information network, 26–28 June, Ghent. Ghent: University of Ghent.

Werner, H. (1948). *Comparative psychology of mental development.* New York, NY: International University Press.

_____. (1957). The concept of development from a comparative and organismic point of view. In D. B. Harris (Ed.), *The Concept of Development: An issue in the study of human behavior* (pp. 125–148). Minneapolis: University of Minnesota Press.

West, M. (1974). Social play in the domestic cat. *American Zoologist, 14,* 427–436.

Wheeler, M. A., Stuss, D. T., & Tulving, E. (1997). Toward a theory of episodic memory: The frontal lobes and autonoetic consciousness. *Psychological Bulletin, 121,* 331–354.

Whillans, A. V., Weidman, A. C., & Dunn, E. W. (2016). Valuing time over money is associated with greater happiness. *Psychological and Personality Science.* Published online. doi*:* 10.1177/1948550615623842

White, J. (1993). *The role of individual characteristics and structures of social knowledge on ethical reasoning using an experiential learning model* (Unpublished doctoral dissertation). Case Western Reserve University, Cleveland, OH.

Whitehead, A. N. (1978). *Process and reality.* New York, NY: The Free Press.

Wiggins, G. (1989). A true test: Toward more authentic and equitable assessment. *Phi Delta Kappan, 70*(9), 703–713.

Wilber, K. (1995). *Sex, ecology, and spirituality.* Boston, MA: Shambala.

Wilkins, P. (2000). Unconditional positive regard reconsidered. *British Journal of Guidance and Counselling, 28*(1), 23–36.

Willingham, D. T. (2005). Do visual, auditory and kinesthetic learners need visual, auditory and kinesthetic instruction? *American Educator, 29*(2), 31–35.

_____. (2009). *Why don't students like school: A cognitive scientist answers questions about how the mind works and what it means for the classroom.* San Francisco, CA: Jossey Bass.

Willingham, W., Valley, J., & Keeton, M. (1977). *Assessing experiential learning: A summary report of the CAEL Project.* Columbia, MD: CAEL.

Wilson, A. L., & Hayes, E. R. (2002). From the editors: The problem of (learning in-from-to) experience. *Adult Education Quarterly, 52*(3), 173–175.

Wilson, L. W. (2013). *The second Principle/Brain based learning.* Retrieved from http://thesecondprinciple.com/4/26/15

Winnicott, D. W. (1965). *The maturational process and the facilitating environment.* New York, NY: International University Press.

_____. (1971). *Playing and reality.* New York, NY: Routledge.

Witkin, H. (1976). Cognitive styles in academic performance and in teacher-student relations. In S. Messick (Ed.), *Individuality in learning.* San Francisco, CA: Jossey-Bass.

Wolf, D. P. (1984). Repertoire, style and format: Notions worth borrowing form children's play. In P. K. Smith (Ed.), *Play in animals and humans* (pp. 175–193). New York, NY: Basil Blackwell.

Wolfe, J. (1977). *Learning styles rewarded in a complex simulation with implications for business policy and organizational behavior research.* Paper presented at the Academy of Management, University of Illinois.

Wolfe, D., & Kolb, D. (1980). Beyond specialization: The quest for integration in midcareer. In B. Derr (Ed.), *Work, family and the career: New frontiers in theory and research.* New York, NY: Praeger Publishers.

_____. (1982). *Learning processes in adult development: A study of cognitive and social factors in mid-life transition. Final Report to the Spencer* Foundation.

Wood, D., Bruner, J., & Ross, G. (1978). The role of tutoring in problem solving. *Journal of Child Psychology and Psychiatry, 17,* 89–100.

Wyss-Flamm, E. D. (2002). *Conversational learning and psychological safety in multicultural teams* (Unpublished Ph.D. dissertation). Case Western Reserve University.

Yamazaki, Y., & Kayes, D. C. (2004). An experiential approach to cross-cultural learning: A review and integration of competencies of successful expatriate adaptation. *Academy of Management Learning and Education, 3*(4), 362–379.

_____, & Kayes, D. C. (2007). Expatriate learning: Exploring how Japanese managers adapt in the United States. *International Journal of Human Resource Management, 18*(8), 1373–1395.

Yang, J. (2008, July 7). My latest product launch was a failure. How do I move on?" *Fortune*, p. 28.

Yeganeh, B. (2006). *Mindful experiential learning* (Unpublished dissertation). Case Western Reserve University.

_____, & Kolb, D. A. (2009). Mindfulness and experiential learning. *OD Practitioner, 41*(3), 8–14.

Zhang, M., Macpherson, A., & Jones, O. (2006). Conceptualizing the learning process in SME's: Improving innovation through external orientation. *International Small Business Journal, 24*(3), 299–323.

Zull, J. (2002). *The art of changing the brain*. Sterling, VA: Stylus.

_____. (2011). *From brain to mind: Using neuroscience to guide change in education*. Sterling, VA: Stylus.

_____. (2012). The brain, learning and study abroad. In M. V. Berg, M. Page, & K. Lou (Eds.), *Student learning abroad*. Sterling, VA: Stylus.

About the Authors

Alice Y. Kolb

Alice Kolb is the president of Experience Based Learning Systems (EBLS), a research and development organization devoted to research and application of experiential learning in organizations worldwide. EBLS has developed many experiential exercises and self-assessment instruments including the latest KLSI 4.0. The EBLS program of research on ELT continues in collaboration with an international network of researchers, practitioners, and learning partners.

As president of EBLS she facilitates research and practice initiatives of the international network. She was a codeveloper of the Kolb Learning Style Inventory 4.0 and led the team that developed the Kolb Educator Role Profile, an inventory designed to help educators apply experiential learning principles in their work.

She was born and raised in Brazil and went to Japan where she received her BA in Japanese Studies from Tokyo University of Foreign Studies, and completed her MA and doctoral program in Human Resources Management at Hitotsubashi University. She received a MS in Human Resource Management from Cleveland State University and PhD in Organizational Behavior from Case Western Reserve University where she was an adjunct professor in the Weatherhead School of Management. She is fluent in Portuguese, Spanish, Japanese, and English.

Her research focus on creating learning spaces conducive to deep learning led to her paper "Learning styles and learning spaces: Enhancing experiential learning in higher education" published in *Academy of Management*

Learning and Education and "Learning to play, playing to learn: A case study of a ludic learning space," published in the *Journal of Organizational Change Management*. She received the 2008 "Educational Pioneers of the Year Award" from the National Society for Experiential Education (with David Kolb).

David A. Kolb

David Kolb is the chairman of Experience Based Learning Systems (EBLS), an organization that he founded in 1980 to advance research and practice on experiential learning. He received his BA in psychology, philosophy, and religion at Knox College and PhD in Social Psychology from Harvard University. He was a professor of Organizational Behavior and Management at the MIT Sloan School of Management and at the Weatherhead School of Management, Case Western Reserve University, where he is currently emeritus professor of Organizational Behavior.

He is best known for his research on experiential learning and learning styles described in the 2015 Second Edition of *Experiential Learning: Experience as the Source of Learning and Development*. Other books include—*How you learn is how you live: Using nine ways of learning to transform your life; Conversational Learning: An Experiential Approach to Knowledge Creation; Innovation in Professional Education: Steps on a Journey from Teaching to Learning;* and *Organizational Behavior: An Experiential Approach*. In addition, he has authored many journal articles and book chapters on experiential learning. David has received several research awards and four honorary degrees recognizing his contributions to experiential learning in higher education.

Made in the USA
Las Vegas, NV
21 January 2024

84727826R00350